Microsoft Exchange Server 2013: Configuration & Clients

Pocket Consultant

William Stanek
Author and Series Editor

PUBLISHED BY
Microsoft Press
A Division of Microsoft Corporation
One Microsoft Way
Redmond, Washington 98052-6399

Library of Congress Control Number: 2013946283
ISBN: 978-0-7356-8168-2

Printed and bound in the United States of America.

Second Printing: July 2014

Microsoft Press books are available through booksellers and distributors worldwide. If
you need support related to this book, email Microsoft Press Book Support at mspinput@
microsoft.com. Please tell us what you think of this book at http://www.microsoft.com/
learning/booksurvey.

Acquisitions Editor: Anne Hamilton
Developmental Editor: Karen Szall
Project Editor: Karen Szall
Editorial Production: Megan Smith-Creed
Technical Reviewer: Todd Meister; Technical Review services provided by Content Master,
a member of CM Group, Ltd.
Copyeditor: Megan Smith-Creed
Indexer: Perri Weinberg Schenker
Cover: Best & Company Design

To my readers—Microsoft Exchange Server 2013 Pocket Consultant: Configuration & Clients *is my 41st book for Microsoft Press. Thank you for being there with me through many books and many years.*

To my wife—*For many years, through many books, many millions of words, and many thousands of pages, she's been there, providing support and encouragement and making every place we've lived a home.*

To my kids—*For helping me see the world in new ways, for having exceptional patience and boundless love, and for making every day an adventure.*

To Anne, Karen, Martin, Lucinda, Juliana, and many others who've helped out in ways both large and small.

—WILLIAM R. STANEK

Contents at a Glance

Contents

What do you think of this book? We want to hear from you!

Microsoft is interested in hearing your feedback so we can continually improve our
books and learning resources for you. To participate in a brief online survey, please visit:

microsoft.com/learning/booksurvey

Chapter 8 **Working with distribution groups and
address lists** **251**

What do you think of this book? We want to hear from you!

Microsoft is interested in hearing your feedback so we can continually improve our
books and learning resources for you. To participate in a brief online survey, please visit:

microsoft.com/learning/booksurvey

Introduction

Microsoft Exchange Server 2013 Pocket Consultant: Configuration & Clients is designed to be a concise and compulsively usable resource for Microsoft Exchange Server 2013 administrators. This is the readable resource guide that you'll want on your desk at all times. The book covers everything you need to perform the core administrative tasks for configuring Exchange Server 2013 and setting up Exchange clients, whether your servers are running on Windows Server 2012 or Windows Server 2008 R2. Because the focus of this book is on giving you maximum value in a pocket-size guide, you don't have to wade through hundreds of pages of extraneous information to find what you're looking for. Instead, you'll find exactly what you need to get the job done.

In short, this book is designed to be the one resource you turn to whenever you have questions about configuring Exchange Server 2013 and setting up Exchange clients. To this end, the book zeroes in on daily administrative procedures, frequently performed tasks, documented examples, and options that are representative although not necessarily exhaustive. One of the goals is to keep the content so concise that the book remains compact and easy to navigate while at the same time ensuring that it is packed with as much information as possible. Thus, instead of a hefty 1,000-page tome or a lightweight 100-page quick reference, you get a valuable resource guide that can help you quickly and easily perform common tasks and solve problems.

Although you might not install Exchange Server 2013 on touch-enabled computers, you can use these devices to manage your installation. If you do manage the software this way, understanding the touch UI as well as the revised interface options will be crucial to your success. For this reason, I reference both the touch UI and the traditional mouse and keyboard techniques throughout this book.

Touch-enabled computers allow you to manipulate onscreen elements in ways that weren't possible previously. In addition to entering text by using an onscreen keyboard, you can also use the following actions to interact with the UI:

- **Tap** Tap an item by touching it with your finger. A tap or double-tap of elements on the screen generally is the equivalent of a mouse click or double-click.
- **Press and hold** Press your finger on the screen and leave it there for a few seconds. Pressing and holding elements on the screen generally is the equivalent of a right-click.
- **Swipe to select** Slide an item a short distance in the opposite direction compared to how the page scrolls. This selects the item and also reveals any related commands. If pressing and holding doesn't display commands and options for an item, try using swipe to select instead.
- **Swipe from edge (slide in from edge)** Starting from the edge of the screen, swipe or slide in. Sliding in from the right edge opens the charms panel. Sliding in from the left edge shows open apps and allows you to easily

switch between them. Sliding in from the top or bottom edge shows commands for the active element.

- **Pinch** Touch an item with two or more fingers and then move the fingers toward each other. Pinching zooms in or shows less information.
- **Stretch** Touch an item with two or more fingers and then move the fingers away from each other. Stretching zooms out or shows more information.

As you've probably noticed, a great deal of information about Exchange Server 2013 is available on the web and in other printed books. You can find tutorials, reference sites, discussion groups, and more to make using Exchange Server 2013 easier. However, the advantage of reading this book is that much of the information you need to learn about Exchange Server 2013 is organized in one place and presented in a straightforward and orderly fashion. This book has everything you need to master Exchange Server 2013 configurations and clients.

In this book, I teach you how features work, why they work the way they do, and how to customize them to meet your needs. I also offer specific examples of how certain features can meet your needs and how you can use other features to troubleshoot and resolve issues you might have. In addition, this book provides tips, best practices, and examples of how to optimize Exchange Server 2013. This book won't just teach you how to configure Exchange Server 2013; it will teach you how to squeeze every last bit of power out of it and make the most from the features and options it includes.

Unlike many other books about administering Exchange Server 2013, this book doesn't focus on a specific user level. This isn't a lightweight beginner book. Regardless of whether you are a beginning administrator or a seasoned professional, many of the concepts in this book will be valuable to you, and you can apply them to your Exchange Server 2013 installations.

Who is this book for?

Microsoft Exchange Server 2013 Pocket Consultant: Configuration & Clients covers the Standard and Enterprise editions of Exchange Server 2013. The book is designed for the following readers:

- Current Exchange Server 2013 administrators
- Current Windows administrators who want to learn Exchange Server 2013
- Administrators upgrading to Exchange Server 2013 from Exchange 2007 or Exchange 2010
- Administrators transitioning to Exchange Server 2013 from Exchange 2003
- Administrators transferring from other messaging servers
- Managers and supervisors who have been delegated authority to manage mailboxes or other aspects of Exchange Server 2013

To pack in as much information as possible, I had to assume that you have basic networking skills and a basic understanding of email and messaging servers. With this in mind, I don't devote entire chapters to explaining why email systems are needed or how they work. I don't devote entire chapters to installing Exchange

Server 2013 either. I do, however, provide complete details on the components of Exchange organizations and how you can use these components. You will also find complete details on essential Exchange configuration tasks.

I also assume that you are fairly familiar with Windows Server. If you need help learning Windows Server, I highly recommend that you buy *Windows Server 2012 Pocket Consultant* (Microsoft Press, 2012) or *Windows Server 2012 Inside Out* (Microsoft Press, 2013).

How is this book organized?

Rome wasn't built in a day, and this book wasn't intended to be read in a day, in a week, or even in a month. Ideally, you'll read this book at your own pace, a little each day as you work your way through. This book is organized into nine chapters. The chapters are arranged in a logical order, taking you from planning and deployment tasks to configuration tasks.

Ease of reference is an essential part of this hands-on guide. This book has an expanded table of contents and an extensive index for finding answers to problems quickly. Many other quick-reference features have been added to the book as well, including quick step-by-step procedures, lists, tables with fast facts, and extensive cross references.

As with all titles in the Pocket Consultant series, *Microsoft Exchange Server 2013 Pocket Consultant: Configuration & Clients* is designed to be a concise and easy-to-use resource. This is the readable resource guide that you'll want on your desktop at all times. The book covers everything you need to perform the core configuration tasks for Exchange servers and Exchange clients. Specifically, this book focuses on:

- Deploying Exchange Server 2013
- Exchange administration essentials
- Managing Exchange clients
- Administration of users, contacts, and mailboxes
- Configuring distribution groups and address lists
- Implementing Exchange Server security and permissions

Although designed and written to stand on its own, this book also can be used with *Microsoft Exchange Server 2013 Pocket Consultant: Databases, Services & Management*, which focuses on:

- Managing availability groups and Exchange databases
- Managing mail flow and transport services
- Working with Client Access servers
- Managing mobile messaging users
- Maintaining and monitoring Exchange servers
- Backing up and restoring Exchange servers

Because the focus is on giving you maximum value in a pocket-size guide, you don't have to wade through hundreds of pages of extraneous information to find what you're looking for. Instead, you'll find exactly what you need to get the job done, and you'll find it quickly.

In short, the book is designed to be the one resource you turn to whenever you have questions regarding core configuration tasks for Exchange servers and Exchange clients. To this end, the book zeroes in on daily administration procedures, frequently performed tasks, documented examples, and options that are representative while not necessarily inclusive. One of my goals is to keep the content so concise that the book remains compact and easy to navigate while at the same time ensuring that it is packed with as much information as possible.

Conventions used in this book

I've used a variety of elements to help keep the text clear and easy to follow. You'll find code terms and listings in monospace type, except when I tell you to actually type a command. In that case, the command appears in bold type. When I introduce and define a new term, I put it in italics.

Other conventions include:

- **Caution** To warn you of potential problems you should look out for.
- **Important** To highlight important concepts and issues
- **More Info** To provide more information on the subject.
- **Note** To provide details on a point that needs emphasis.
- **Real World** To provide real-world advice when discussing advanced topics.
- **Tip** To offer helpful hints or additional information.

I truly hope you find that *Microsoft Exchange Server 2013 Pocket Consultant: Configuration & Clients* provides everything you need to perform essential administrative tasks as quickly and efficiently as possible. You are welcome to send your thoughts to me at *williamstanek@aol.com*. Follow me on Twitter at WilliamStanek and on Facebook at *www.facebook.com/William.Stanek.Author*.

Other resources

No single resource for learning everything you'll ever need to know about Exchange Server 2013 exists. While some books are offered as all-in-one guides, there's simply no way one book can do it all. With this in mind, I hope you use this book as it is intended to be used—as a concise and easy-to-use resource. It covers everything you need to perform core configuration tasks for Exchange servers and Exchange clients, but it is by no means exhaustive.

Your current knowledge will largely determine your success with this or any other Exchange resource or book. As you encounter new topics, take the time to practice what you've learned and read about. Seek out further information as necessary to get the practical hands-on knowledge and experience you need.

For topics this book doesn't cover, you may want to look to *Microsoft Exchange Server 2013 Pocket Consultant: Databases, Services & Management*. I also recommend that you regularly visit the Microsoft website for Exchange Server (*microsoft.com/exchangeserver/*) and *support.microsoft.com* to stay current with the latest changes. To help you get the most out of this book, you can visit my corresponding website at *pocket-consultant.com*. This site contains information about Exchange Server 2013 and updates to the book.

Errata & book support

We've made every effort to ensure the accuracy of this book and its companion content. Any errors that have been reported since this book was published are listed on our Microsoft Press site:

> *http://aka.ms/ExPC2013CC/errata*

If you find an error that is not already listed, you can report it to us through the same page.

If you need additional support, email Microsoft Press Book Support at *mspinput@microsoft.com*.

Please note that product support for Microsoft software is not offered through the addresses above.

We want to hear from you

At Microsoft Press, your satisfaction is our top priority, and your feedback our most valuable asset. Please tell us what you think of this book at:

> *http://www.microsoft.com/learning/booksurvey*

The survey is short, and we read every one of your comments and ideas. Thanks in advance for your input!

Stay in touch

Let's keep the conversation going! We're on Twitter: *http://twitter.com/MicrosoftPress*.

CHAPTER 1

Exchange Server 2013 administration overview

Microsoft Exchange Server 2013 was a difficult product to work with as originally delivered, especially with regard to interoperability and update scenarios. Fortunately, a few things have happened that should markedly change your experience with Exchange Server 2013. First, Exchange Server 2013 has been updated significantly since its original release, and that's fantastic news for anyone wanting to deploy this powerful messaging system. Second, I've been working with the product since the summer of 2012, and I've learned to zig and zag through the rough patches. In this chapter and the next, I'll help you chart a course through the special challenges presented by Exchange Server 2013 and, in particular, the interoperability and update issues. Before we get to that, however, let's begin at the beginning.

Although I discuss the impact of extensive architectural and administrative changes of Exchange 2013 throughout this and other chapters of this book, you need to know some of this information up front because it radically changes the way you implement and manage your Exchange organization. Why? With these changes, your Exchange 2013 organization will look very different than Microsoft Exchange Server 2010 or earlier organizations.

As you get started with Exchange Server 2013, you should concentrate on the following areas:

- How Exchange Server 2013 architecture has changed
- How Exchange Server 2013 works with your hardware
- What versions and editions of Exchange Server 2013 are available and how they meet your needs
- How Exchange Server 2013 works with Windows–based operating systems
- How Exchange Server 2013 works with Active Directory
- What administration tools are available

Getting started with Exchange 2013 and Exchange Online

You can implement Exchange services in several ways, including:

- **On-premises** With an on-premises implementation, you deploy Exchange server hardware on your network and manage all aspects of the implementation, including server configuration, organization configuration, and recipient configuration.
- **Online** With an online (or cloud-only) implementation, you rely on hardware and services provided by Microsoft. All aspects of the server configuration are managed by Microsoft. You manage the service-level settings, organization configuration, and recipient configuration.
- **Hybrid** With a hybrid implementation, you integrate on-premises and online implementations. The on-premises and Exchange Online organizations use a shared domain namespace, so mail is securely routed between them, and you can easily share data between the implementations.

When you use an online implementation, Microsoft manages the hardware configuration and ensures availability. Otherwise, you are responsible for any on-premises hardware.

Exchange Server 2013 builds on the radical changes in Exchange Server 2010 but is vastly different from Exchange Server 2010. Like Exchange Server 2010, Exchange Server 2013 does away with the concepts of storage groups, Local Continuous Replication (LCR), Single Copy Clusters (SCC), and clustered mailbox servers. This means that:

- Databases are no longer associated with storage groups.
- Database availability groups are used to group databases for high availability.
- Databases are managed at the organization level instead of at the server level.

Exchange Server 2013 integrates high availability into the core architecture by enhancing aspects of Cluster Continuous Replication (CCR) and Standby Continuous Replication (SCR) and combining them into a single, high-availability solution for both on-site and off-site data replication. Exchange Server 2013 also provides for automatic failover and recovery without requiring clusters when you deploy multiple mailbox servers. Because of these changes, building a high-availability mailbox server solution doesn't require cluster hardware or advanced cluster configuration.

Instead, database availability groups provide the base component for high availability. Failover is automatic for mailbox databases that are part of the same database availability group.

The basic rules for database availability groups have not changed since implementation in Exchange Server 2010. Each mailbox server can have multiple databases, and each database can have as many as 16 copies. A single database availability group can have up to 16 mailbox servers that provide automatic database-level recovery. Any server in a database availability group can host a copy of a mailbox database from any other server in the database availability group.

This seamless high-availability functionality is possible because mailbox databases are disconnected from servers and the same globally unique identifier (GUID) is assigned to every copy of a mailbox database. Because there are no storage groups, continuous replication occurs at the database level. Transaction logs are replicated to each member of a database availability group that has a copy of a mailbox database and are replayed into the copy of the mailbox database. Failover can occur at either the database level or the server level.

Exchange Server 2013 has a significantly different architecture than its predecessors. While Exchange 2007 and Exchange 2010 components were split into different server roles for scaling out Exchange organizations, Exchange 2013 streamlines the server roles and architecture while still allowing you to fully scale Exchange organizations to meet the needs of enterprises of all sizes. Specifically, Exchange 2013 does not have separate server roles for Hub Transport servers or Unified Messaging servers. The related components are now part of the Mailbox Server role. This results in significant changes to mail flow and is one of many reasons the Information Store processes were rewritten in Exchange 2013. The new Information Store (Microsoft.Exchange.Store.Service.exe) is written in C# and is fully integrated with the Microsoft Exchange Replication service (MSExchangeRepl.exe) and the Microsoft Exchange DAG Management service (MSExchangeDagMgmt.exe). Additionally, each database now runs under its own process, which helps to isolate any issues with the Managed Store to a particular database.

Other than the Mailbox Sever role, the only other installable role for Exchange 2013 is the Client Access server role, which also can be installed on a Mailbox server. Every Exchange 2013 organization needs at least one Mailbox server and at least one Client Access server. While you can install both roles on a single server, you cannot later uninstall one role without uninstalling the other role. Further, Exchange 2013 as originally released doesn't include an Edge Transport role or functionality (though this may be released in a future update to Exchange 2013). You can, however, use and deploy legacy Edge Transport servers, and I'll discuss this in more detail in Chapter 2, "Deploying Exchange Server 2013."

Although you can continue to use separate Client Access servers, the related architecture has changed considerably as well. The Mailbox server role includes the client access protocols and handles all activity for mailboxes. Client Access servers, on the other hand, are thin and stateless. They don't queue any data. They don't process or render data. They serve only to provide authentication, limited redirection, and proxy services.

These architecture changes mean that Exchange 2013 server roles are now loosely coupled rather than tightly coupled, which eliminates any previous session affinity requirements. The Mailbox server that stores the active database copy for a mailbox performs all the data processing, data rendering, and data transformation required. The Client Access server connects the client to the Mailbox server and performs authentication, redirection, and proxying only as needed. Because there is no required session affinity between the Mailbox server and the Client Access server, connections proxied by a Client Access server can be balanced using basic load-balancing technologies such as round robin Domain Name System (DNS) and least connection. Supported protocols for client connections include HTTP, POP, IMAP, RPC over HTTP, and SMTP. As RPC is no longer supported as a direct access protocol, all Outlook client connections must take place using RPC over HTTP.

It's important to point out that Exchange 2013 is designed to work with Outlook 2007 and more recent versions and also continues to support Outlook Web App for mobile access. Rather than connecting to servers using Fully Qualified Domain Names as was done in the past, Outlook 2007 and more recent versions use Autodiscover to create connection points based on the domain portion of the user's primary SMTP address and each mailbox's Globally Unique Identifier (GUID).

The simplified architecture reduces the namespace requirements for Exchange site designs. If you're coexisting with Exchange 2010 or you're installing a new Exchange 2013 organization, you need only one namespace for client protocols and one namespace for Autodiscover. To continue to support SMTP, you also need an SMTP namespace.

For Exchange 2013, you'll ideally want to deploy Mailbox servers on hardware that easily scales up while building Client Access servers with scaling out in mind.

Exchange Server 2013 and your hardware

Before you deploy Exchange Server 2013, you should carefully plan the messaging architecture. As part of your implementation planning, you need to look closely at preinstallation requirements and the hardware you will use. Exchange Server is a complex messaging platform with many components that work together to provide a comprehensive solution for routing, delivering, and accessing email messages, voice-mail messages, faxes, contacts, and calendar information.

Successful Exchange Server administration depends on three things:

- Knowledgeable Exchange administrators
- Strong architecture
- Appropriate hardware

The first two ingredients are covered: you're the administrator, you're smart enough to buy this book to help you through the rough spots, and you've enlisted Exchange Online, Exchange Server 2013, or both to provide your high-performance messaging needs. This brings us to the issue of hardware. If you're using Exchange Online, Microsoft provides the hardware. Otherwise, for on-premises implementations, Exchange Server 2013 should run on a system with adequate memory, processing speed, and disk space. You also need an appropriate data-protection and system-protection plan at the hardware level.

Exchange Server 2013 requires two different types of server hardware. You want to select hardware for Mailbox servers with scaling up in mind while selecting hardware for Client Access servers with scaling out in mind. Scaling up typically means adding additional or faster, better CPUs and memory to existing servers to meet capacity needs. Scaling out typically means adding additional servers to meet capacity needs.

Key guidelines for choosing hardware for Exchange Server are as follows:

- **Memory** The minimum random access memory (RAM) is 8 gigabytes (GB) for servers with both the Mailbox Server and Client Access Server roles, 8 GB for Mailbox servers, and 4 GB for Client Access servers. In most cases, you'll want to have at least twice the recommended minimum amount of memory. The primary reason for this is performance. Most of the Mailbox server installations I run use 16 GB of RAM as a starting point, even in small installations. In multiple Exchange server installations, the Mailbox server should have at least 2 GB of RAM plus 5 megabytes (MB) of RAM per mailbox (with a minimum of 8 GB regardless). For all Exchange server configurations, the paging file should be at least equal to the amount of RAM in the server plus 10 MB.

- **CPU** Exchange Server 2013 runs on the x64 family of processors from AMD and Intel, including AMD64 and Intel 64. You can achieve significant performance improvements with a high level of processor cache. Look closely at the L1, L2, and L3 cache options available—a higher cache can yield much better performance overall. Look also at the speed of the front-side bus. The faster the bus speed, the faster the CPU can access memory.

  Exchange Server 2013 runs only on 64-bit hardware. The primary advantages of 64-bit processors over 32-bit processors are related to memory limitations and data access. Because 64-bit processors can address more than 4 GB of memory at a time without physical address extension, they can store greater amounts of data in main memory, providing direct access to and faster processing of data. In addition, 64-bit processors can process data and execute instruction sets that are twice as large as 32-bit processors. Accessing 64 bits of data (versus 32 bits) offers a significant advantage when processing complex calculations that require a high level of precision.

- **SMP** Exchange Server 2013 supports symmetric multiprocessors, and you'll see significant performance improvements if you use multiple CPUs—not just multiple cores in a single CPU. Although the clock speed of the CPU is important, so are the number of logical processor cores and the number of threads that can be simultaneously processed. That said, if Exchange Server is supporting a small organization with a single domain, one CPU with multiple cores may be enough. If the server supports a medium or large organization or handles mail for multiple domains, you will want to consider adding processors. When it comes to processor cores, I prefer two multicore processors to a single processor with the same number of cores, given current price and performance tradeoffs. An alternative is to distribute the workload across different servers based on where you locate resources.

- **Disk drives**   The data storage capacity you need depends entirely on the number and size of the data that will pass through, be journaled on, or stored on the Exchange server. You need enough disk space to store all data and logs, plus workspace, system files, and virtual memory. Input/output (I/O) throughput is just as important as drive capacity. Rather than use one large drive, you should use several drives, which allows you to configure fault tolerance with RAID. As part of your hardware planning, it's important to point out that Exchange 2013 supports multiple databases on the same volume, allowing you to have a mix of active and passive copies on a single volume. Keep in mind, however, the input/output per second (IOPS) capabilities for the underlying physical disks. Also note that even if you've been assigned multiple logical unit numbers (LUNs) for use from storage these different LUNs may be spread over the same physical disks.

- **Data protection**   You can add protection against unexpected drive failures by using redundant storage. For the boot and system disks, use RAID 1 on internal drives. However, because of the new high-availability features, you might not want to use software RAID for Exchange data and logs. You also might not want to use expensive disk storage systems either. Instead, deploy multiple Exchange servers with the required server roles.

  If you decide to use software-based redundant storage, you can use disk striping without parity or disk striping with parity for data volumes. Disk striping without parity offers good read/write performance, but a failed drive means that Exchange Server can't continue operation on an affected database until the drive is replaced and data is restored from backup. Disk mirroring creates duplicate copies of data on separate drives; you can rebuild a mirrored unit to restore full operations and can continue operations if one of the drives fails. Disk striping with parity offers good protection against single drive failure, but it has poor write performance. For best performance and fault tolerance, RAID 10 (also referred to as RAID 0 + 1), which consists of disk mirroring and disk striping without parity, is also an option.

- **Uninterruptible power supply**   Exchange Server 2013 is designed to maintain database integrity at all times and can recover information using transaction logs. This doesn't protect the server hardware, however, from sudden power loss or power spikes, both of which can seriously damage hardware. To prevent this, connect your server to an uninterruptible power supply (UPS). A UPS gives you time to shut down the server or servers properly in the event of a power outage. Proper shutdown is especially important on servers using write-back caching controllers. These controllers temporarily store data in cache. Without proper shutdown, this data can be lost before it is written to disk. To prevent data loss, write-back caching controllers typically have batteries that help ensure that changes can be written to disk after the system comes back online.

If you follow these hardware guidelines and modify them for specific messaging roles, as discussed in the next section, you'll be well on your way to success with Exchange Server 2013.

REAL WORLD Mirroring can be implemented with software RAID 1 on Windows Server. As software-based RAID is implemented using dynamic disks, it's important to note that beginning with Windows Server 2012 dynamic disks are being phased out in favor of Storage Spaces. However, for mirroring boot and system volumes on internal disks, Microsoft recommends continuing to use dynamic disks and RAID 1.

If you decide to use software-based redundant storage, remember that storage arrays typically already have an underlying redundant storage configuration and you might have to use a storage array–specific tool to help you distinguish between LUNs and the underlying physical disks. Herein, I focus on software-based redundancy implemented with RAID or Storage Spaces rather than the underlying hardware redundancy implemented in storage arrays.

Windows Server is transitioning to standards-based storage beginning with Windows Server 2012. This transition means several popular tools and favored features are being phased out. Officially, a tool or feature that is being phased out is referred to as *deprecated*. When Microsoft deprecates a tool or feature, it might not be in future releases of the operating system (while continuing to be available in current releases). Rather than not cover popular tools and features, I've chosen to discuss what is actually available in the current operating system, including both favored standbys and new options. One of these new options is Storage Spaces. With Storage Spaces:

- Simple volumes can stretch across multiple disks, similar to disk striping with parity (RAID 0).

- Mirrored volumes are mirrored across multiple disks. Although this is similar to disk mirroring (RAID 1), it is more sophisticated in that data is mirrored onto two or three disks at a time. If a storage space has two or three disks, you are fully protected against a single disk failure, and if a storage space has five or more disks, you are fully protected against two simultaneous disk failures.

- Parity volumes use disk striping with parity. Although this is similar to RAID 5, it is more sophisticated in that there are more protections and efficiencies.

Exchange Server 2013 editions

Several editions of Exchange Server 2013 are available, including Exchange Server 2013 Standard and Exchange Server 2013 Enterprise. The various server editions support the same core features and administration tools, which means you can use the techniques discussed throughout this book regardless of which Exchange Server 2013 edition you are using. For reference, the specific feature differences between Standard Edition and Enterprise Edition are as follows:

- **Exchange Server 2013 Standard** Designed to provide essential messaging services for small to medium organizations and branch office locations. This server edition supports up to five databases.

- **Exchange Server 2013 Enterprise** Designed to provide essential messaging services for organizations with increased availability, reliability, and manageability needs. When you are running Cumulative Update 2 or later, this server edition supports up to 100 databases (including all active databases and copies of databases) on a particular server.

NOTE Throughout this book, I refer to Exchange Server 2013 in different ways, and each has a different meaning. Typically, I refer to the software product as *Exchange 2013* or as *Exchange Server*, which you can take to mean *Microsoft Exchange Server 2013*. When necessary, I use *Exchange Server 2013* to draw attention to the fact that I am discussing a feature that's new or has changed in the most recent version of the product. Each of these terms means essentially the same thing. If I refer to a previous version of Exchange Server, I always do so specifically, such as Exchange 2007 or Exchange 2010. Finally, I often use the term *Exchange server* (note the lowercase *s* in server) to refer to an actual server computer, as in "There are eight Exchange servers in this database availability group."

REAL WORLD Microsoft provides a single binary for x64 systems, and the same binary file is used for both the Standard and Enterprise editions. The license key provided during installation is what determines which edition is established.

You can use a valid product key to upgrade from a trial edition to the Standard edition or the Enterprise edition of Exchange Server 2013 without having to reinstall. Using a valid product key, you can also upgrade from the Standard to the Enterprise edition. You can also relicense an Exchange server by entering a new product key for the installed edition, which is useful if you accidentally used the same product key on multiple servers and want to correct the mistake.

There are several caveats. When you change the product key on a Mailbox server, you must restart the Microsoft Exchange Information Store service to apply the change. Additionally, you cannot use product keys to downgrade editions. To downgrade editions, you must uninstall Exchange Server and then reinstall it.

You can install Exchange Server 2013 on servers running full-server installations of Windows Server 2008 R2 as well as on a full-server installation of Windows Server 2012 RTM or R2. You cannot install Exchange 2013 on servers running server core or minimal server interface. With Windows Server 2008 R2, you must reinstall the server using the full installation option. With Windows Server 2012 RTM or R2, you must convert the server core or minimal server interface installation to a full installation by running the following command from an elevated PowerShell prompt:

```
Install-WindowsFeature Server-Gui-Mgmt-Infra, Server-Gui-Shell -Restart
```

The specific editions supported are as follows:

- Windows Server 2012 RTM or R2 Standard or Datacenter
- Windows Server 2008 R2 Standard with Service Pack 1 (SP1)
- Windows Server 2008 R2 Enterprise with Service Pack 1 (SP1)
- Windows Server 2008 R2 Datacenter RTM or later

A client accessing an Exchange server requires a Client Access License (CAL). With either Exchange Server edition, the client can use a Standard CAL, an Enterprise CAL, or both. The Standard CAL allows for the use of email, shared calendaring, contacts, task management, Microsoft Outlook Web App, and Exchange ActiveSync. The Enterprise CAL allows for the use of unified messaging, advanced mobile management, data loss prevention, and custom retention policies. An Enterprise CAL is sold as an add-on to the Standard CAL. A client must have one Standard CAL and one Enterprise CAL add-on to make full use of all Exchange Server features.

MORE INFO At the time of this writing, specific details on what's included with each CAL are available at *http://office.microsoft.com/en-us/exchange/microsoft-exchange-server-licensing-licensing-overview-FX103746915.aspx.*

Beyond the editions and CALs, Exchange Server 2013 has several variants. Microsoft offers on-premises and online implementations of Exchange Server. An on-premises Exchange Server is one that you install in your organization. An online Exchange Server is delivered as a subscription service from Microsoft. In Exchange Server 2013, you can manage both on-premises and online implementations of Exchange Server using the same management tools. These implementations can be separate from each other or you can configure a hybrid installation that allows single sign-on and easy movement of mailboxes and database between on-premises and online implementations.

As a prerequisite for installing any server running any on-premises version of Exchange Server 2013, Active Directory must be at Windows Server 2003 forest functionality mode or higher. Additionally, the schema master for the Active Directory forest along with at least one global catalog server in each Active Directory site and at least one domain controller in each Active Directory site must be running one of the following operating systems:

- Windows Server 2012 RTM or R2 Standard or Datacenter
- Windows Server 2008 R2 Standard or Enterprise
- Windows Server 2008 R2 Datacenter RTM or later
- Windows Server 2008 Standard or Enterprise (32-bit or 64-bit)
- Windows Server 2008 Datacenter RTM or later
- Windows Server 2003 Standard Edition with Service Pack 2 (SP2) or later (32-bit or 64-bit)
- Windows Server 2003 Enterprise Edition with SP2 or later (32-bit or 64-bit)

NOTE Using Active Directory with Exchange Server 2013 is covered in more detail in the "Exchange Server and Active Directory" section of this chapter and the "Integrating Exchange Server roles with Active Directory" section of Chapter 2.

Additionally, Exchange Server 2013 supports IPv6 only when IPv4 is also installed. When you deploy IPv6, Exchange servers can send data to and receive data from devices, clients, and servers that use IPv6 addresses. Although you can disable IPv4 so that only IPv6 is enabled, Exchange still requires that IPv4 be installed. Further, the domain should be configured to use multiple-label DNS names, such as cpandl.com or adatum.local, rather than single-label DNS names, such as cpandl or adatum. However, single label names can be used.

You install Exchange 2013 using Exchange Setup. Exchange 2013 requires Microsoft .NET Framework version 4.5 and Windows Management Framework 3.0, which are included with Windows Server 2012 RTM or R2 (but not included with Windows Server 2008 R2). If needed, these components should be installed before you start Exchange Setup and are available at *http://go.microsoft.com/fwlink /p/?LinkId=257868* and *http://go.microsoft.com/fwlink/?LinkId=272757* respectively.

Other requirements depend on whether you are installing a Mailbox server or a Client Access server:

- Mailbox servers require Microsoft Unified Communications Managed API 4.0, Core Runtime 64-bit (*http://go.microsoft.com/fwlink/p/?linkId=258269*), Microsoft Office 2010 Filter Pack 64-bit (*http://go.microsoft.com/fwlink /p/?linkID=191548*), and Microsoft Office 2010 Filter Pack SP1 64-bit (*http:// go.microsoft.com/fwlink/p/?LinkId=254043*), which must be installed in the order shown.

- Client Access servers require Microsoft Unified Communications Managed API 4.0, Core Runtime 64-bit (*http://go.microsoft.com/fwlink/p/?linkId=258269*).

If you don't install these additional components prior to running Exchange Setup, the Readiness Checks will fail and links to these resources will be provided. If this happens, you can use the links provided to obtain and install the components and then simply tap or click Retry to have Setup perform the readiness checks again. Once these checks pass, you'll be able to continue with the installation.

Exchange 2013 has a new set of management tools, including Exchange Admin Center, Exchange Management Shell, and Exchange Toolbox. When you install a Mailbox server or a Client Access server, the management tools are installed automatically. You can use Exchange Setup to install the management tools on domain-joined computers running 64-bit editions of Windows 7 SP1 and Windows 8 or later as well.

Although there are no prerequisites for Windows 8 or later, there are several prerequisites for Windows 7. Windows 7 computers must have Microsoft .NET Framework version 4.5 and Windows Management Framework 3.0 installed. You also must enable IIS 6 management compatibility by adding the IIS 6 Management Console, which is a feature that can be enabled using Control Panel. In Control Panel, select Program and then select Turn Windows Features On Or Off. In the Windows Features dialog box, under Internet Information Services, Web Management Tools, IIS 6 Management Compatibility, select IIS 6 Management Console, and then tap or click OK.

Exchange Server 2013 uses the Windows Installer (the Installer) and has a fully integrated installation process. This means you can configure Exchange Server 2013 much like you can any other application you install on the operating system. The installation can be performed from a command prompt as well.

Chapter 2 provides detailed instructions for installing Exchange Server 2013. You install Exchange 2013 only on domain-joined computers. Whether you use the Standard or Enterprise edition, you have similar options. You can install an internal messaging server by selecting the individual server roles to install and combining the Mailbox role and Client Access role as required for your environment. Generally, you will not want an internal Exchange server to also be configured as a domain controller with a global catalog.

When you start an installation, Setup checks the system configuration to determine the local time zone, the operating system, the logged-on user, and the status of the registry keys related to Exchange Server 2013. Installation will fail if you are trying to run Setup on an operating system that isn't supported or if a required service pack is missing. You'll also run into problems if you start Setup without using elevated administrator privileges.

After checking the system configuration, Setup allows you to check for updates to the installation process, provided the server has a connection to the Internet. Setup then checks available space on the %SystemDrive% to ensure a temporary folder under %SystemDrive%\Windows\Temp\ExchangeSetup can be used during the installation process. About 1.3 GB of space is needed for the working files.

When done copying its work files to the temporary folder, Setup tries to connect to a domain controller and validate the state of Active Directory. If Setup cannot find a domain controller or encounters other errors when validating Active Directory, the installation process will fail and you'll see related errors during the readiness checks.

IMPORTANT By default, Setup chooses a domain controller in the local domain and site. In order to determine the domain information and contact a domain controller, the computer on which you are installing Exchange 2013 must be domain joined and have properly configured TCP/IP settings, and DNS name resolution must be properly configured in your organization. Because Active Directory site configuration also is important for installing Exchange 2013 and setting up an Exchange organization, ensure Active Directory sites and subnets are properly configured prior to installing Exchange 2013.

Once connected to a domain controller, Setup selects a global catalog server to work with and then looks for an Exchange Configuration container within Active Directory. Setup next determines the organization-level operations that need to be performed, which can include initializing Active Directory, updating Active Directory schema, establishing or updating the Exchange organization configuration, and updating the domain configuration.

As you continue through Setup, you'll be able to select the server roles to install, the install location, and more. With the exception of the working files, which are copied to the temporary folder, no changes are made until the server passes the readiness checks. Normally, even when problems are encountered, Setup will continue all the way to the readiness checks. As part of the readiness checks, Setup checks for required components, such as those listed previously.

Other required components include Windows Features that Setup will install automatically if they aren't already installed. These features include Desktop Experience, many components of IIS, Windows Identity Foundation, and the administrative tools for clustering. Although you can manually install these features, it's a long list, and Setup will do the work for you if you let it.

Exchange 2013 includes the following anti-spam capabilities:

- **Sender filtering**   Allows administrators to maintain a list of senders who are blocked from sending messages to the organization. Administrators can block individual senders by email address. Administrators also can block all senders from domains and subdomains.

- **Recipient filtering**   Allows administrators to block message delivery to nonexistent recipients, distribution lists for internal users only, and mailboxes for internal use only. Exchange performs recipient lookups on incoming messages and block messages, which prevents certain types of attacks and malicious attempts at information discovery.

- **Sender ID verification**   Verifies that incoming email messages are from the Internet domain from which they claim to come. Exchange verifies the sender ID by examining the sender's IP address and comparing it to the related security record on the sender's public DNS server.

- **Content filtering**   Uses intelligent message filtering to scan message content and identify spam. Spam can be automatically deleted, quarantined, or filed as junk email.

> **TIP**   Using the Exchange Server management tools, administrators can manage messages sent to the quarantine mailbox and take appropriate actions, such as deleting messages, flagging them as false positives, or allowing them to be delivered as junk email. Messages delivered as junk email are converted to plain text to strip out any potential viruses they might contain.

- **Sender reputation scoring**   Helps to determine the relative trustworthiness of unknown senders through sender ID verification and by examining message content and sender behavior history. A sender can then be added temporarily to the Blocked Senders list.

The way you use these features will depend on the configuration of your Exchange organization. If you've deployed legacy Edge Transport servers, you enable and configure these features on your Edge Transport servers. Otherwise, you enable and configure these features on your Mailbox servers.

Exchange 2013 also has anti-malware capabilities, which are enabled by default. Malware scanning is performed on all messages at the server level, as messages are sent or received. When users open and read messages in their mailboxes, the messages they see have already been scanned. Exchange Server checks for updates to malware definitions every hour. Exchange downloads the malware engines and definitions using a TCP connection over port 80 from the Internet.

> **TIP**   Normally, you'll manually perform the first download of the anti-malware engine and definition updates prior to placing a server into production so you can verify that the initial process was successful and then configure default anti-malware policy prior to users having access to a server.

Although these anti-spam and anti-malware features are extensive, they are not comprehensive. For comprehensive protection, you can pair these features with a cloud-based service, such as Microsoft Exchange Online Protection. By combining the built-in anti-spam and anti-malware features with a cloud-based protection service you can set up substantial, layered protection. Additionally, if you use a third-party anti-malware solution for Exchange 2013, you can disable the built-in anti-malware filtering.

Exchange Server and Windows

When you install Exchange Server on a server operating system, Exchange Server makes extensive modifications to the environment. These modifications include new system services, integrated authentication, and new security groups.

Services for Exchange Server

When you install Exchange Server and Forefront Protection for Exchange Server on Windows, multiple services are installed and configured on the server. Table 1-1 provides a summary of key services, how they are used, and which server components they are associated with.

TABLE 1-1 Summary of key services used by Exchange 2013

SERVICE NAME	DESCRIPTION
IIS Admin	Enables the server to administer the IIS metabase. The IIS metabase stores configuration information for web applications used by Exchange. All roles need IIS for WinRM and remote Powershell. CAS needs IIS for Outlook Web App and Web services.
Microsoft Exchange Active Directory Topology	Provides Active Directory topology information to Exchange services. If this service is stopped, most Exchange services will not be able to start.
Microsoft Exchange Anti-Spam Update	Maintains the anti-spam data for Forefront Protection on an Exchange server.
Microsoft Exchange DAG Management	Provides monitoring services for Database Availability Groups, including monitoring of storage management and database layout management. (Only applies to Exchange 2013 with CU2 or later.)
Microsoft Exchange EdgeSync	Provides EdgeSync services between Mailbox and Edge servers.
Microsoft Exchange Frontend Transport	Proxies inbound and outbound SMTP connections.
Microsoft Exchange IMAP4	Provides IMAP4 services to clients.
Microsoft Exchange IMAP4 Backend	Provides IMAP4 services to mailboxes.

SERVICE NAME	DESCRIPTION
Microsoft Exchange Information Store	Manages the Microsoft Exchange Information Store. This includes mailbox stores.
Microsoft Exchange Mailbox Assistants	Manages assistants responsible for calendar updates, booking resources, and other mailbox processing.
Microsoft Exchange Mailbox Replication	Enables online mailbox moves by processing mailbox move requests.
Microsoft Exchange Mailbox Transport Delivery	Receives mail items from the Transport service and ensures they are processed and then delivered into mailbox.
Microsoft Exchange Mailbox Transport Submission	Receives mail items being sent and ensures they are converted from MAPI to MIME and then submitted to the Transport service.
Microsoft Exchange POP3	Provides Post Office Protocol version 3 (POP3) services to clients.
Microsoft Exchange POP3 Backend	Provides Post Office Protocol version 3 (POP3) services to mailboxes.
Microsoft Exchange Protected Service Host	Provides a secure host for Exchange Server services.
Microsoft Exchange Replication Service	Provides replication functionality used for continuous replication.
Microsoft Exchange RPC Client Access	Manages client remote procedure call (RPC) connections for Exchange Server.
Microsoft Exchange Search	Handles queries and controls indexing of mailboxes to improve search performance.
Microsoft Exchange Server Extension for Windows Server Backup	Provides extensions for Windows Server Backup that allow you to back up and recover Exchange application data using Windows Server Backup.
Microsoft Exchange Service Host	Provides a host for essential Exchange services.
Microsoft Exchange Throttling	Provides throttling functions to limit the rate of user operations.
Microsoft Exchange Transport	Provides mail transport for Exchange Server.

SERVICE NAME	DESCRIPTION
Microsoft Exchange Transport Log Search	Provides search capability for Exchange transport log files.
Microsoft Exchange Unified Messaging	Enables voice and fax messages to be stored in Exchange and gives users telephone access to email, voice mail, the calendar, contacts, or an automated attendant.
Microsoft Exchange Unified Messaging Call Router	Provides capabilities necessary for routing calls.
Secure Socket Tunneling Protocol Service	Provides support for Secure Socket Tunneling Protocol (SSTP) for securely connecting to remote computers.
Web Management Service	Enables remote and delegated management for the web server, sites, and applications.
Windows Remote Management Service	Implements the WS-Management protocol. Required for remote management using the Exchange console and Windows PowerShell.
World Wide Web Publishing Services	Provides web connectivity and administration features for IIS.

Exchange Server authentication and security

In Exchange Server 2013, email addresses, distribution groups, and other directory resources are stored in the directory database provided by Active Directory. Active Directory is a directory service running on Windows domain controllers. When there are multiple domain controllers, the controllers automatically replicate directory data with each other using a multimaster replication model. This model allows any domain controller to process directory changes and then replicate those changes to other domain controllers.

The first time you install Exchange Server 2013 in a Windows domain, the installation process updates and extends Active Directory to include objects and attributes used by Exchange Server 2013. Unlike earlier releases of Exchange Server, you do not use Active Directory Users And Computers to manage mailboxes, messaging features, messaging options, or email addresses associated with user accounts. You perform these tasks using the Exchange management tools.

Exchange Server 2013 fully supports the Windows Server security model and by default relies on this security mechanism to control access to directory resources. This means you can control access to mailboxes and membership in distribution groups and you can perform other Exchange security administration tasks through the standard Windows Server permissions set. For example, to add a user to a distribution group, you simply make the user a member of the distribution group in Active Directory Users And Computers.

Because Exchange Server uses Windows Server security, you can't create a mailbox without first creating a user account that will use the mailbox. Every Exchange mailbox must be associated with a domain account—even those used by Exchange for general messaging tasks. In Exchange Admin Center, you can create a new user account as part of the process of creating a new mailbox.

You use Exchange Admin Center to manage Exchange servers according to their roles and the type of information you want to manage. You'll learn more about this in Chapter 3, "Exchange Server 2013 administration essentials."

Exchange Server security groups

Exchange Server 2013 uses predefined universal security groups to separate administration of Exchange permissions from administration of other permissions. When you add an administrator to one of these security groups, the administrator inherits the permissions permitted by that role.

The predefined security groups have permissions to manage the following types of Exchange data in Active Directory:

- **Organization configuration data**   This type of data is not associated with a specific server and is used to manage databases, policies, address lists, and other types of organizational configuration details.
- **Server configuration data**   This type of data is associated with a specific server and is used to manage the server's messaging configuration.
- **Recipient configuration data**   This type of data is associated with mailboxes, mail-enabled contacts, and distribution groups.

The predefined groups are as follows:

- **Compliance Management**   Members of this group have permission to configure compliance settings.
- **Delegated Setup**   Members of this group have permission to install and uninstall Exchange on provisioned servers.
- **Discovery Management**   Members of this group can perform mailbox searches for data that meets specific criteria.
- **Exchange Servers**   Members of this group are Exchange servers in the organization. This group allows Exchange servers to work together.
- **Exchange Trusted Subsystem**   Members of this group are Exchange servers that run Exchange cmdlets using WinRM. Members of this group have permission to read and modify all Exchange configuration settings as well as user accounts and groups.
- **Exchange Windows Permissions**   Members of this group are Exchange servers that run Exchange cmdlets using WinRM. Members of this group have permission to read and modify user accounts and groups.
- **Help Desk**   Members of this group can view any property or object within the Exchange organization and have limited management permissions, including the right to change and reset passwords.
- **Hygiene Management**   Members of this group can manage the anti-spam and antivirus features of Exchange.

- **Managed Availability Servers**   Every Exchange 2013 server is a member of this group. Managed availability is new for Exchange 2013. It's an internal process that provides native health monitoring and recovery for protocol processes to ensure availability of Exchange services. For more information, see Chapter 3.

- **Organization Management**   Members of this group have full access to all Exchange properties and objects in the Exchange organization.

- **Public Folder Management**   Members of this group can manage public folders and perform most public folder management operations.

- **Recipient Management**   Members of this group have permissions to modify Exchange user attributes in Active Directory and perform most mailbox operations.

- **Records Management**   Members of this group can manage compliance features, including retention policies, message classifications, and transport rules.

- **Server Management**   Members of this group can manage all Exchange servers in the organization but do not have permission to perform global operations.

- **UM Management**   Members of this group can manage all aspects of unified messaging, including Unified Messaging server configuration and unified messaging recipient configuration.

- **View-Only Organization Management**   Members of this group have read-only access to the entire Exchange organization tree in the Active Directory configuration container and read-only access to all the Windows domain containers that have Exchange recipients.

Exchange Server and Active Directory

Exchange Server 2013 is tightly integrated with Active Directory. Not only does Exchange Server 2013 store information in Active Directory, but it also uses the Active Directory routing topology to determine how to route messages within the organization. Routing to and from the organization is handled using transport servers.

Understanding how Exchange stores information

Exchange stores four types of data in Active Directory: schema data (stored in the Schema partition), configuration data (stored in the Configuration partition), domain data (stored in the Domain partition), and application data (stored in application-specific partitions). In Active Directory, schema rules determine what types of objects are available and what attributes those objects have. When you install the first Exchange server in the forest, the Active Directory preparation process adds many Exchange-specific object classes and attributes to the Schema partition in Active Directory. This allows Exchange-specific objects, such as agents and connectors, to be created. It also allows you to extend existing objects, such as users and groups, with new attributes, such as attributes that allow user objects to be used for sending and receiving email. Every domain controller and global catalog server in the organization has a complete copy of the Schema partition.

During the installation of the first Exchange server in the forest, Exchange configuration information is generated and stored in Active Directory. Exchange configuration information, like other configuration information, is also stored in the Configuration partition. For Active Directory, the configuration information describes the structure of the directory, and the Configuration container includes all of the domains, trees, and forests, as well as the locations of domain controllers and global catalogs. For Exchange, the configuration information is used to describe the structure of the Exchange organization. The Configuration container includes lists of templates, policies, and other global organization–level details. Every domain controller and global catalog server in the organization has a complete copy of the Configuration partition.

In Active Directory, the Domain partition stores domain-specific objects, such as users and groups, and the stored values of attributes associated with those objects. As you create, modify, or delete objects, Exchange stores the details about those objects in the Domain partition. During the installation of the first Exchange server in the forest, Exchange objects are created in the current domain. Whenever you create new recipients or modify Exchange details, the related changes are reflected in the Domain partition as well. Every domain controller has a complete copy of the Domain partition for the domain for which it is authoritative. Every global catalog server in the forest maintains information about a subset of every Domain partition in the forest.

Understanding how Exchange routes messages

Within the organization, the Transport service on Mailbox servers uses the information about sites stored in Active Directory to determine how to route messages, and these servers can also route messages across site links. They do this by querying Active Directory about its site membership and the site membership of other servers, and then using the information they discover to route messages appropriately. Because of this, when you are deploying an Exchange Server 2013 organization, no additional configuration is required to establish routing in the Active Directory forest.

For mail delivery within the organization, additional routing configuration is necessary only in these specific scenarios:

- If you deploy an Exchange Server 2013 organization with multiple forests, you must install Exchange Server 2013 in each forest and then connect the forests using appropriate cross-forest trusts. The trust allows users to see address and availability data across the forests.

- In an Exchange Server 2013 organization, if you want direct mail flow between Exchange servers in different forests, you must configure SMTP send connectors and SMTP receive connectors on the Mailbox servers that should communicate directly with each other.

You can use two types of Mail Transport servers: Mailbox servers and legacy Edge Transport servers. You deploy Mailbox servers within the organization. The Transport service on Mailbox servers handles mail delivery and receipt of mail. Two new services are used to deliver mail items to and receive mail items from other servers:

- **Microsoft Exchange Mailbox Transport Delivery service**   Handles inbound mail items. After receiving mail items for delivery to a mailbox on the current server, the service submits the mail items for processing and then delivers them into the appropriate mailbox database on the server.

- **Microsoft Exchange Mailbox Transport Submission service**   Handles outbound mail items. After receiving mail items for submission, the service ensures messages are converted from MAPI to MIME and then passes them along to the Transport service. The Transport service then routes the mail items for delivery.

With Mailbox servers as your transports, no other special configuration is needed for message routing to external destinations. You must configure only the standard mail setup, which includes identifying DNS servers to use for lookups. With legacy Edge Transport servers, you can optimize mail routing and delivery by configuring one-way synchronization from the internal Mailbox servers to the perimeter network's Edge Transport servers. Beyond this, no other special configuration is required for mail routing and delivery.

You deploy legacy Edge Transport servers in the organization's perimeter network for added security. Typically a perimeter network is a secure network set up outside the organization's private network. When you have Edge Transport servers, mail items from outside the organization are received first by the Edge transport servers, which can perform anti-malware and anti-spam checks before passing along mail items to internal Mailbox servers for delivery. Mail items for submission outside the organization are passed from internal Mailbox servers to Edge Transport servers which then submit the mail items for delivery outside the organization.

Exchange Online and Office 365

Exchange Online is a cloud-based service from Microsoft that allows you to implement an online or hybrid implementation of Exchange. Although Exchange Online can be your only solution for all your enterprise messaging needs, a hybrid implementation gives you an integrated online and on-premises solution.

You can get Exchange Online as a standalone service or as part of an Office 365 plan. Currently, Microsoft offers several Exchange Online plans, including a basic plan and an advanced plan. The key differences between the basic and advanced plans are the inclusion of in-place hold and data loss prevention options that may be needed to meet compliance and regulatory requirements. Both plans support Active Directory integration for single sign-on, synchronization with your on-premises Active Directory infrastructure, and creation of hybrid Exchange organizations.

Microsoft offers a variety of Office 365 plans. Some of these plans include access to Office Web Apps, the full desktop versions of Office, or both, as well as access to

Exchange Online. You'll likely want to use an Office 365 midsize business or enterprise plan. These plans include Active Directory integration, which is required if you want to create a hybrid Exchange organization.

Using the graphical administration tools

Exchange Server 2013 includes several types of tools for administration. You'll use the graphical tools most frequently. They include Exchange Admin Center, Office Admin Center, and Exchange Toolbox.

Exchange Admin Center, shown in Figure 1-1, replaces Exchange Management Console. Although previous Exchange management tools were implemented using Microsoft Management Console (MMC), Exchange Admin Center is web based and works similar to Exchange Control Panel (ECP). However, Exchange Admin Center is much more advanced, and you'll use this console for managing on-premises, online, and hybrid deployments of Exchange 2013.

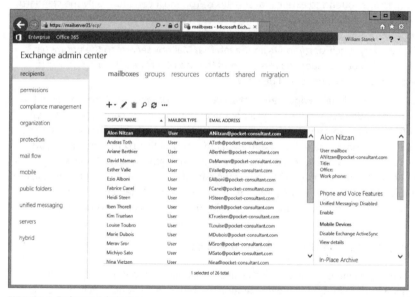

FIGURE 1-1 Exchange Admin Center.

Exchange Admin Center is a web application running on a Client Access server providing services for the Exchange organization. This application is installed automatically when you install a Client Access server. To manage Exchange installations from just about anywhere, you simply need to enter the Uniform Resource Locator (URL) path for the application in your browser's Address field. You can then access Exchange Admin Center. For on-premises installations, the default internal URL for Exchange Admin Center is *https://ClientAccessServerName/ecp* and the external URL is *https://yourserver.yourdomain.com/ecp*. For example, if your Client Access server is named CASserver12, you'd enter **https://casserver12/ecp** as the URL for internal access.

When you are accessing an on-premises installation from within your organization (and behind your organization's firewall), you use the internal URL. When you are accessing an on-premises installation outside your organization, you use the external URL. As discussed in Chapter 3, there are many ways to configure access to this app. You can change the default URL, restrict access to the internal URL only, and more.

> **REAL WORLD** If you deploy Exchange 2013 and Exchange 2010 in the same organization and your personal mailbox is on an Exchange 2010 Mailbox server, you'll see the Exchange 2010 Exchange Control Panel by default. To access Exchange Admin Center, you must add the Exchange version to the URL.
>
> You do this by appending **?ExchClientVer=15** to the internal or external URL. For example, if your external URL is *https://mail.pocket-consultant.com*, you'd enter **https://mail.pocket-consultant.com/ecp?ExchClientVer=15** as the URL.
>
> If your personal mailbox is on Exchange 2013 and you want to access the Exchange 2010 Exchange Control Panel, you can do this as well. In this case, you enter the client version as 14 rather than 15, as shown in this example: **https://mail.pocket-consultant.com /ecp?ExchClientVer=14**.

You manage Exchange Online using the cross-premises management options in Exchange Admin Center. With an online or hybrid installation, you'll also be provided an access URL for Office Admin Center, such as *https://portal.microsoftonline.com /admin/default.aspx*. After you log in, you'll see the Office Admin Center dashboard, shown in Figure 1-2.

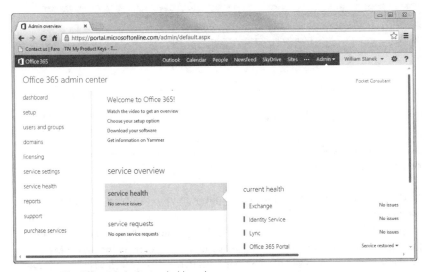

FIGURE 1-2 The Office Admin Center dashboard.

From the Office Admin Center dashboard, you have full access to Exchange Online and Office 365 and can manage the related service-level settings. You'll have options for configuring the Office tenant domain, managing subscriptions and licensing, viewing service health, getting Exchange usage reports, and more.

On any computer where you've installed the Exchange management tools, you'll be able to access the Exchange Toolbox from Start. With Windows Server 2008 R2, select Start, choose All Programs, and then use the Microsoft Exchange Server 2013 menu. With Windows Server 2012 RTM or R2, you'll find an Exchange Toolbox tile on the Start screen. Whether you are working with the Start menu or the Start screen, you can pin the Exchange Toolbox to the desktop taskbar by pressing and holding or right-clicking the related icon and then selecting Pin To Taskbar.

As Figure 1-3 shows, Exchange Toolbox has been streamlined considerably for Exchange 2013. The Toolbox provides access to a suite of related tools, including the following:

- **Details Templates Editor**   Helps administrators customize client-side GUI presentation of object properties accessed through address lists. You can use this tool to customize the presentation of contacts, users, groups, public folders, and more in the client interface.

- **Remote Connectivity Analyzer**   Allows administrators to perform connectivity tests for inbound email, ActiveSync, Exchange Web Services, Outlook Anywhere, and Outlook RPC over HTTP.

- **Queue Viewer**   Allows administrators to track message queues and mail flow. Also allows administrators to manage message queuing and remove messages.

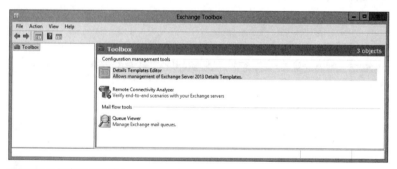

FIGURE 1-3 Exchange Toolbox.

Other administration tools that you might want to use with Exchange Server are summarized in Table 1-2.

You access most of the tools listed in Table 1-2 from the Tools menu in Server Manager. Server Manager can be started by tapping or clicking the Server Manager icon in the taskbar. With Windows Server 2012 RTM or R2, you also can start Server Manager by typing **Server Manager** in the Apps Search box.

TABLE 1-2 Quick Reference Administration Tools to Use with Exchange Server 2013

ADMINISTRATIVE TOOL	PURPOSE
DNS	Manages the DNS service.
Event Viewer	Manages events and logs.
Failover Cluster Management	The Failover Cluster Management tools and the related command-line interface must be installed on your Exchange 2013 servers. This allows you to use scripts for managing availability groups.
IIS Manager	Manages Web servers used by Exchange as well as the management service configuration.
Server Manager	Provides setup and configuration options for the local server as well as options for managing roles, features, and related settings on remote servers.

Using Exchange Management Shell

The graphical tools provide just about everything you need to work with Exchange organizations. Still, there are many times when you might want to work from the command line, especially if you want to automate installation, administration, or maintenance with scripts. To help with all your command-line needs, Exchange Server includes Exchange Management Shell.

Exchange Management Shell is an extension shell for Windows PowerShell that includes a wide array of built-in commands for working with Exchange Server. Windows PowerShell commands are referred to as cmdlets (pronounced *command-lets*) to differentiate these commands from less powerful commands built into the command prompt and from more full-featured utility programs that can be invoked at the command prompt.

> **NOTE** For ease of reading and reference, I'll usually refer to command prompt commands, command shell cmdlets, and command-line invoked utilities simply as commands.

On any computer where you've installed the Exchange management tools, you'll be able to access Exchange Management Shell from Start. With Windows Server 2008 R2, select Start, choose All Programs, and then use the Microsoft Exchange Server 2013 menu. With Windows Server 2012 RTM or R2, you'll find an Exchange Management Shell tile on the Start screen. Whether you are working with the Start menu or the Start screen, you can pin Exchange Management Shell to the desktop taskbar by pressing and holding or right-clicking the related icon and then selecting Pin To Taskbar. Exchange Management Shell is shown in Figure 1-4.

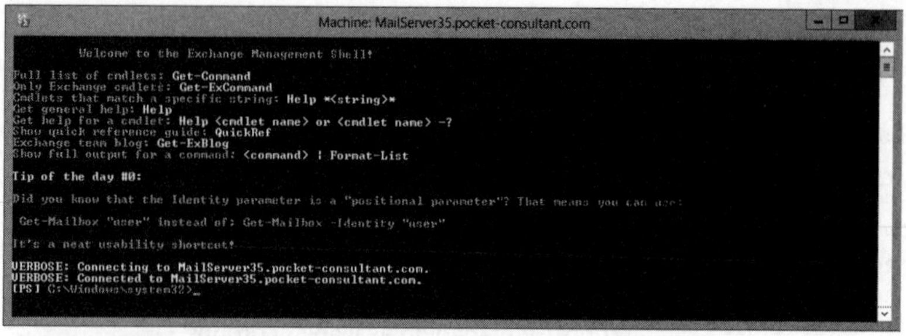

FIGURE 1-4 Exchange Management Shell.

REAL WORLD Exchange Admin Center is a web-based management console that runs as an application on your Client Access servers. When you install the Client Access server role for Exchange 2013, the server is configured automatically with a Windows PowerShell gateway that acts as a proxy service. This proxy service allows you to run remote commands in web browsers and in remote sessions. Whenever you work with Exchange Admin Center or Exchange Management Shell, the commands are executed via this proxy—even if you log on locally. Thus, every time you work with Exchange Server, you are using a remote session.

When you log in to Exchange Admin Center, you are using the Default Web Site running on Internet Information Services (IIS) which processes your actions. Every command you perform in Exchange Admin Center is remotely executed via the Windows PowerShell gateway, as is any command you perform in Exchange Management Shell. Any task you can perform in Exchange Admin Center can be performed in Exchange Management Shell.

The basics of working with Exchange Management Shell are straightforward:

- Type **get-command** to get a full list of all available cmdlets on the server.
- Type **get-excommand** to get a full list of all Exchange-specific cmdlets available.
- Type **help** *cmdletName* to get help information, where *cmdletName* is the name of the command you are looking up.
- Type **Update-ExchangeHelp** to update the help files for Exchange-specific cmdlets (CU2 or later only).

IMPORTANT When you are working with Exchange Management Shell, the default recipient scope is set the same as your logon domain. If you are in a multi-domain environment and want to work with recipients throughout the Active Directory forest, make sure the Shell session has ViewEntireForest enabled. Enter **Get-ADServerSettings** to view the current Active Directory Server settings. Enter **Set-ADServerSettings -ViewEntireForest $true** to set the recipient scope to the entire forest.

You'll find a comprehensive discussion of Exchange Management Shell and Windows PowerShell in Chapter 4, "Using Exchange Management Shell," as well as examples of using cmdlets for Exchange Server management throughout the book. Although you can manage Exchange Online with PowerShell, you'll need use special remoting techniques, which also are discussed in Chapter 4.

Whenever you remotely manage Exchange services using Powershell, you are relying on the Windows PowerShell remoting features. These features are supported by the WS-Management protocol and the Windows Remote Management (WinRM) service that implements WS-Management in Windows.

Windows Management Framework includes Windows PowerShell and WinRM. Computers running Windows 8 and later, as well as Windows Server 2012 and later, include Windows Management Framework 3.0 or later. You must install Windows Management Framework on computers running Windows 7 SP1 or later, as well as computers running Windows Server 2008 R2 SP1 or later. You can download the framework from *http://go.microsoft.com/fwlink/p/?LinkId=272757*.

With Windows Server 2012 RTM or R2, you can verify the availability of WinRM services and configure Windows PowerShell for remoting by following these steps:

1. Type **PowerShell** in the Apps Search box. To start Windows PowerShell as an administrator press and hold or right-click the Windows PowerShell shortcut and select Run As Administrator.

2. The WinRM service is configured for manual startup by default. You must change the startup type to Automatic and start the service on each computer you want to work with. At the PowerShell prompt, you can verify that the WinRM service is running by using the following command:

```
get-service winrm
```

As shown in the following example, the value of the Status property in the output should be Running:

```
Status    Name            DisplayName
------    ----            -----------
Running   WinRM           Windows Remote Management
```

If the service is stopped, enter the following command to start the service and configure it to start automatically in the future:

```
set-service -name winrm -startuptype automatic -status running
```

3. To configure Windows PowerShell for remoting, type the following command:

```
Enable-PSRemoting -force
```

Exchange 2013 is designed to be remotely managed from domain-joined computers. If your computer is connected to a public network, you need to disconnect from the public network, connect to a domain, and then repeat this step. If one or more of your computer's connections has the Public connection type, but you are actually connected to a domain network, you need to change the network connection type in Network And Sharing Center and then repeat this step.

In many cases, you will be able to work with remote computers in other domains. However, if the remote computer is not in a trusted domain, the remote computer might not be able to authenticate your credentials. To enable authentication, you need to add the remote computer to the list of trusted hosts for the local computer in WinRM. To do so, type the following:

```
winrm s winrm/config/client '@{TrustedHosts="RemoteComputer"}'
```

where *RemoteComputer* is the name of the remote computer, such as:

```
winrm s winrm/config/client '@{TrustedHosts="MailServer12"}'
```

If you cannot connect to a remote host, verify that the service on the remote host is running and is accepting requests by running the following command on the remote host:

```
winrm quickconfig
```

This command analyzes and configures the WinRM service. If the WinRM service is set up correctly, you'll see output similar to the following:

```
WinRM already is set up to receive requests on this machine.
WinRM already is set up for remote management on this machine
```

If the WinRM service is not set up correctly, you'll see errors and need to respond affirmatively to several prompts that allow you to automatically configure remote management. When this process completes, WinRM should be set up correctly.

Whenever you use Windows PowerShell remoting features, you must start Windows PowerShell as an administrator by pressing and holding or right-clicking the Windows PowerShell shortcut and selecting Run As Administrator. When starting Windows PowerShell from another program, such as the command prompt (cmd.exe), you must start that program as an administrator.

CHAPTER 2

Deploying Exchange Server 2013

You can implement Exchange services in several ways:

- **On-premises** An implementation where you deploy Exchange server hardware on your network and manage all aspects of the implementation, including server configuration, organization configuration, and recipient configuration. Administrators manage Exchange using Exchange Admin Center and Exchange Management Shell. Users access Exchange using Outlook Web App and a URL provided by your organization or with Microsoft Office Outlook.

- **Online** An implementation where you rely on hardware and services provided by Microsoft. Here, you subscribe to Exchange Online, manage service-level settings using Office 365 Admin Center, and manage the organization and recipient configuration using Exchange Admin Center. Users access Exchange using Outlook Web App and a URL provided by Microsoft or with Microsoft Outlook.

- **Hybrid** An implementation where you have integrated on-premises and online components. Here, the on-premises and Exchange Online organizations have a shared domain namespace, and mail is securely routed between them. These organizations share a unified global address list, free/busy data, and calendar data. Administrators manage Exchange using a combination of the on-premises and online tools. Users can access Exchange using Outlook Web App and the same URL whether their mailbox is stored on premises or online. Users also can access Exchange using Microsoft Outlook.

When you use an online implementation, Microsoft manages the hardware configuration and ensures availability. Otherwise, you are responsible for any on-premises hardware. Before you deploy an on-premises or hybrid implementation of Exchange 2013, you should carefully plan the messaging architecture. Every Exchange implementation has three layers in its architecture:

- **Network layer**   The network layer provides the foundation for computer-to-computer communications and essential name resolution features. The network layer has both physical and logical components. The physical components include the IP addresses, the IP subnets, local area network (LAN) or wide area network (WAN) links used by messaging systems as well as the routers that connect these links, and firewalls that protect the infrastructure. The logical components are the Domain Name System (DNS) zones that define the naming boundaries and contain the essential resource records required for name resolution.

- **Directory layer**   The directory layer provides the foundation necessary for authentication, authorization, and replication. The directory layer is built on the Active Directory directory service and has both physical and logical components. The physical components include the domain controllers, Global Catalog servers, and site links used for authentication, authorization, and replication. The logical components include the Active Directory forests, sites, domains, and organizational units that are used to group objects for resource sharing, centralized management, and replication control. The logical components also include the users and groups that are part of the Active Directory infrastructure.

- **Messaging layer**   The messaging layer provides the foundation for messaging and collaboration. The messaging layer has both physical and logical components. The physical components include individual Exchange servers that determine how messages are delivered and mail connectors that determine how messages are routed outside an Exchange server's routing boundaries. The logical components specify the organizational boundaries for messaging, mailboxes used for storing messages, public folders used for storing data, and distribution lists used for distributing messages to multiple recipients.

Whether you are deploying Exchange Server for the first time in your organization or upgrading to Exchange Server 2013 from an earlier release of Exchange Server, you need to closely review each layer of this architecture and plan for required changes. As part of your implementation planning, you also need to look closely at the roles your Exchange servers will perform and modify the hardware accordingly to meet the requirements of these roles on a per-server basis. Exchange Server is a complex messaging platform with many components that work together to provide a comprehensive solution for routing, delivering, and accessing email messages, voice-mail messages, faxes, contacts, and calendar information.

Exchange Server messaging roles

With Exchange Server Setup, you can deploy servers with specific roles throughout the enterprise. Prior to setup and configuration, you need to decide how you will use Exchange Server 2013, what roles you will deploy, and where you will locate those roles. Afterward, you can plan for your deployment and then roll out Exchange Server 2013.

As part of your planning and testing, you'll want to use the Exchange Server 2013 Deployment Assistant and the Exchange Remote Connectivity Analyzer. Both are web-based tools that provide step-by-step guidance. The Deployment Assistant, which can help you plan online, on-premises, and hybrid deployments, is available at *http://go.microsoft.com/fwlink/p/?LinkId=277105*, and the Connectivity Analyzer, which can help you diagnose connectivity issues, is available at *https://testexchangeconnectivity.com*.

Understanding Exchange Server messaging roles

On-premises implementations of Exchange Server have three layers in their architecture: a network layer, directory layer, and messaging layer. The messaging layer is where you define and deploy the Exchange Server roles. The Exchange servers at the core of the messaging layer can operate in the following roles:

- **Mailbox Server** A back-end server that hosts mailboxes, public folders, and related messaging data, such as address lists, resource scheduling, and meeting items.

- **Client Access Server** A middle-tier server that accepts connections to Exchange Server from a variety of clients. This server hosts the protocols used by all clients when checking messages. On the local network, Outlook MAPI clients are connected directly to the Client Access server to check mail using SMTP. Remote users can check their mail over the Internet by using Outlook Anywhere, Outlook Web App, Exchange ActiveSync, POP3, or IMAP4.

- **Legacy Edge Transport Server** An additional mail routing server that routes mail into and out of the Exchange organization. This server is designed to be deployed in an organization's perimeter network and is used to establish a secure boundary between the organization and the Internet. This server accepts mail coming into the organization from the Internet and from trusted servers in external organizations, processes the mail to protect against some types of spam messages and viruses, and routes all accepted messages to a Mailbox server inside the organization.

At the time of this writing, Exchange 2013 supports the Mailbox Server and Client Access Server roles. If you want to use Edge Transports, you must deploy these transports on servers running either Exchange 2007 or Exchange 2010. Two other server roles available for Exchange 2010, Unified Messaging and Hub Transport, are now implemented as services running on Exchange 2013 Mailbox servers:

- **Unified Messaging service** A middle-tier service that integrates a private branch exchange (PBX) system with Exchange Server 2013, allowing voice messages and faxes to be stored with email in a user's mailbox. Unified messaging supports call answering with automated greetings and message recording, fax receiving, and dial-in access. With dial-in access, users can use Outlook Voice Access to check voice mail, email, and calendar information; to review or dial contacts; and to configure preferences and personal options. To receive faxes, you need an integrated solution from a Microsoft partner.

- **Transport service**   A mail routing service that handles mail flow, routing, and delivery within the Exchange organization. This service processes all mail that is sent inside the organization before it is delivered to a mailbox in the organization or routed to users outside the organization. Processing ensures that senders and recipients are resolved and filtered as appropriate, content is filtered and has its format converted if necessary, and attachments are screened. To meet any regulatory or organizational compliance requirements, the Mailbox server can also record, or journal, messages and add disclaimers to them.

The Mailbox and Client Access roles are the building blocks of on-premises Exchange organizations. Table 2-1 provides an overview of the basic processor configurations I recommend for these roles. Processors can have multiple cores. Following the configurations shown in the table, I recommend that you build Client Access servers for scaling out and Mailbox servers for scaling up. If you deploy legacy Edge Transport servers, they should be built for scaling out as well.

TABLE 2-1 Recommended configurations for Exchange Server roles

SERVER ROLE	MINIMUM PROCESSORS	RECOMMENDED PROCESSORS	BUILD FOR
Legacy Edge Transport	1	4	Scale out
Client Access	1–2	2–4	Scale out
Mailbox	1–2	4–8	Scale up
Multiple server roles	2	4–8	Scale up

Because you can combine the Mailbox and Client Access roles on a single server, one of the most basic Exchange organizations you can create is one that includes a single Exchange server that provides the Mailbox Server and Client Access Server roles. These roles are the minimum required for routing and delivering messages to both local and remote messaging clients. For added security and protection, you can deploy the legacy Edge Transport server role in a perimeter network on one or more separate servers. As part of site planning, keep in mind every Active Directory site that has a Mailbox server must also have a Client Access server.

Although a basic implementation of Exchange Server might include only one server, you'll likely find investing in multiple servers is more effective in terms of time, money, and resources. Why? High availability is integrated into the core architecture of Exchange Server 2013 and can be easily enabled.

With the Mailbox Server role, you can configure automatic failover by making the Mailbox servers members of the same database availability group. Each Mailbox server in the group can then have a copy of the mailbox databases from the other Mailbox servers in the group. Each mailbox database can have up to 16 copies, and this means you can have up to 16 Mailbox servers in a database availability group as well.

Client Access servers in Exchange 2013 are lightweight, stateless proxy servers. They provide the proxy and redirection logic for client protocols. For load balancing and failover redundancy, you previously needed to configure Client Access arrays and there typically was a specific affinity between the client and the Client Access server. Because of the client-server affinity, Microsoft recommended using application layer–based load balancing solutions, which ensured that requests from a connected client went through the same Client Access server endpoint.

With Exchange 2013, no configuration of Client Access arrays is needed. Client Access servers that are in the same Active Directory site are automatically added to an array for that site. Further, no specific affinity is required between the client and the Client Access server. This allows any available Client Access server to proxy a client's request. If a server proxying a connection fails, the client connection is simply proxied by the next available Client Access server. This is possible because proxy and redirection logic for client protocols is built in.

Client Access servers running on Exchange 2013 also support layer 4 load balancing which distributes requests at the transport layer. In this case, the client connects to Exchange using a single virtual IP address, and a load balancer selects a server to receive the request. Because there is no affinity required, the load balancer doesn't have to ensure that all requests from a client go to the same server. Not only does this simplify the load balancer's job and greatly reduce the processing overhead, it allows administrators to add or remove servers at any time. It also means very basic load balancing techniques, such as round robin and least connection, can be used. Although load balancing round robin can be configured in DNS, you also can configure this and other load balancing options using Windows Network Load Balancing. However, because servers in database availability groups are already using clustering technology, they can't also use Windows Network Load Balancing. Thus, when you deploy Mailbox servers in availability groups and want to use Windows Network Load Balancing to load balance client access, the Mailbox Server and Client Access Server roles must be running on separate servers.

For site resilience, you can deploy two Active Directory sites in separate geographic locations and then synchronize data between the two sites. With Exchange 2010, you had to perform a switchover from one site to the other if you lost all of your Client Access servers, the virtual IP for the array, or multiple servers in a database availability group. This is not required for Exchange 2013. If you lose a Client Access server array in one site, failover to the other site can happen at the client level automatically. Clients can be automatically redirected to a second site that has operating Client Access servers, and those servers act as proxies to the user's Mailbox server in the original site.

Deploying Mailbox servers: The essentials

The underlying functionality of a Mailbox server is similar to that of a database server. Every mailbox-enabled recipient defined in the organization has a mailbox that is used to store messaging data. Groups of related mailboxes are organized using databases, and each database can have one or more database copies associated with it.

With Exchange Server 2007, you needed dedicated hardware for clustered Mailbox servers, those servers could not run other roles, and failover occurred at the server level. Microsoft re-engineered Exchange 2010 and Exchange 2013 to provide continuous availability while eliminating these restrictions. For Exchange 2013 specifically, this means:

- You do not need dedicated clustering hardware for highly available Mailbox servers. Key components of Windows clustering are managed automatically by Exchange Server.

- You do not need to use Local Continuous Replication (LCR), Cluster Continuous Replication (CCR), or Standby Continuous Replication (SCR). LCR has been discontinued. Key features of CCR and SCR have been combined, enhanced, and made available through database availability groups.

- You can combine Exchange roles on highly available Mailbox servers, provided you don't plan to use Windows Network Load Balancing. This means you could create a fully redundant Exchange organization using only two Exchange servers. In this case, each server would have the Mailbox and Client Access roles. You would also need a witness server for the database availability group, which doesn't have to be an Exchange server.

The underlying technology built into database availability groups is the key ingredient that makes high availability possible. The related framework ensures failover clustering occurs in the background and doesn't normally require administrator intervention. As a result, Exchange Server 2013 doesn't need or use a cluster resource dynamic-link library (DLL) and uses only a small portion of the Windows clustering components, including heartbeat capabilities and the cluster database.

Database availability groups use continuous replication to achieve high availability. With continuous replication, Exchange Server 2013 uses its built-in asynchronous replication technology to create copies of mailbox databases and then keeps the copies up to date using transaction log shipping and replay. Lagged copies can automatically play down log files to automatically recovery from certain types of issues. For example, if Exchange detects that a low disk space threshold has been reached, Exchange automatically replays the logs into the lagged copy to play down the log files. If Exchange detects that page patching is required, Exchange automatically replays the logs into the lagged copy to perform page patching. If Exchange detects that there are fewer than three available healthy copies (whether active or passive) for more than 24 hours, Exchange automatically replays the logs into the lagged copy to play down the log files.

Any server in a group can host a copy of a mailbox database from any other server in the group. When a server is added to a group, it works with other servers in the group to provide automatic recovery from failures that affect mailbox data-bases, including server failure, database corruption, disk failure, and network con-nectivity failure. Although Exchange 2010 used a scheduled script to alert you that only a single copy of a database was available, this functionality is now integrated into Exchange along with other managed availability features for internal monitor-ing and recovery.

When you create a database availability group, Exchange adds an object to Active Directory representing the group. This object stores information about the group, including details about servers that are members of the group. When you add the first server to the group, a failover cluster is created automatically and the heartbeat is initiated. As you add member servers to the group, the heartbeat com-ponents and the cluster database are used to track and manage information about the group and its member servers, including server status, database mount status, replication status, and mount location.

Because Exchange Server 2013 databases are represented at the organization level, they are effectively disconnected from the servers on which they are stored, which makes it easier to move databases from one server to another. However, it also means you can work with databases in many different ways and that there are also several requirements when working with databases. Keep the following in mind when working with databases in Exchange Server 2013:

- Database names must be unique throughout your Exchange organization. This means you cannot name two databases identically even if they are on two different Mailbox servers.

- Every mailbox database, except copies, have a different globally unique iden-tifier (GUID). Copies of a database have the same GUID.

- Mailbox servers that are part of the same database availability group do not require cluster-managed shared storage. However, the full paths for all data-base copies must be identical on host Mailbox servers.

- Exchange 2013 no longer has public folder databases. Instead, special mailboxes are now used to store the public folder hierarchy and content. Like traditional mailboxes, special mailboxes for public folders are stored in mailbox databases and are replicated as part of any database availability group you configure.

For a successful deployment of a Mailbox server, the storage subsystem must meet the storage capacity requirements and must be able to perform the expected number of input/output (I/O) operations per second. Storage capacity requirements are determined by the number of mailboxes hosted on a server and the total stor-age size allowed per mailbox. For example, if a server hosts 2,500 mailboxes that you allow to store up to 2 gigabytes (GB) each, you need to ensure there are at least 5 terabytes of storage capacity above and beyond the storage needs of the operat-ing system and Exchange itself.

I/O performance of the storage subsystem is measured in relation to the latency (delay) for each read/write operation to be performed. The more mailboxes you store on a specific drive or drive array, the more read/write operations there are performed and the greater the potential delay. To improve performance, you can use multiple mailbox databases on separate disks. You might also want to store databases with their transaction log files on separate disk drives, such that database A and related logs are on disk 1, database B and related logs are on disk 2, and so on. In some scenarios, you might want the databases and logs to be on separate disks.

I/O performance in Exchange Server 2013 running on 64-bit architecture is improved substantially over 32-bit architecture. On Mailbox servers, a 64-bit architecture enables a database cache size of up to approximately 90 percent of total random access memory (RAM). A larger cache increases the probability that data requested by a client will be serviced out of memory instead of by the storage subsystem.

Unlike Exchange 2010 which required separate volumes for each database copy whether passive or active, Exchange 2013 allows a server to host multiple databases on the same volume. This allows you to have a mix of active and passive copies on the same volume. As part of your planning, look closely at the input/output per second (IOPS) capabilities of your storage architecture and place database copies appropriately. Because active copies will use more IOPS than passive copies, you'll typically want no more than one active database copy on a volume while allowing multiple passive copies. For example, if you're configuring a four-server database availability group, you might want to configure storage so that each server has a large volume with its active database copy and passive copies of the databases on the other servers.

Like Exchange 2010, Exchange 2013 is optimized so that servers can use large disks with 2 to 8 terabytes of storage efficiently. However, as part of your planning, you need to understand how Exchange 2013 uses automatic reseed to recover from disk failure, database corruption events, and other issues that require a reseed of a database copy. With automatic reseed, Exchange can automatically restore database redundancy using spare disks that have been pre-provisioned.

The larger the database, the longer it takes Exchange to reseed it. If a database is too large, it can't be reseeded in a reasonable amount of time. With a typical reseed rate of 20 MB per second, it would take Exchange:

- About 28 hours to reseed a 2-terabyte database.
- About 42 hours to reseed a 3-terabyte database.
- About 56 hours to reseed a 4-terabyte database.

Because of this, the total reseed time may be the most important limiting factor for sizing databases.

Deploying Client Access servers: The essentials

With Exchange 2010, the underlying functionality of a Client Access server was similar to that of an application server that made extensive use of Web services. These servers needed to be built to handle increased I/O operations, which meant processors, memory, network, and disk I/O were all potential sources of bottlenecks. Because they also performed content conversion, you could improve performance by optimizing disk storage.

As part of the major architecture changes for Exchange 2013, Client Access servers no longer handle all of the client-related messaging tasks in an Exchange implementation, nor do they perform content conversion. Instead, all processing and content conversion is performed on Mailbox servers, and Client Access servers are used only for authentication, proxy services, and limited redirection.

Client Access servers provide access through the Outlook MAPI, Internet Message Access Protocol version 4 revision 1 (IMAP4), Post Office Protocol version 3 (POP3), and Hypertext Transfer Protocol (HTTP) Internet protocols. By default, when you install a Client Access server, these services are available to both internal and external clients. You can modify the default configuration at any time and specify whether the Client Access server will be accessible to clients outside the organization. You also can configure the external URLs for each Client Access Server-related service.

Exchange Server 2013 allows access using Microsoft Outlook with Simple Mail Transfer Protocol (SMTP), Outlook Anywhere (RPC over HTTP), Outlook Web App, and Exchange ActiveSync. Internet Message Access Protocol 4 (IMAP4) and Post Office Protocol 3 (POP3) are available as alternatives to standard protocols. IMAP4 is a protocol for reading mail and accessing public and private folders on remote servers. POP3 is a protocol for retrieving mail from remote servers. Client Access servers provide access to free/busy data by using the Availability service, and they enable clients to download automatic configuration settings from the Autodiscover service.

Exchange 2013 uses the Active Directory infrastructure to determine its site membership and the site membership of other servers. The Microsoft Exchange Active Directory Topology service running on an Exchange server is responsible for updating the site attribute of an Exchange server in the directory.

Once a server determines its site membership, the server identifies which domain controllers and global catalogs to use for processing Active Directory queries. Because this information is available in the directory, Exchange servers don't need to use DNS to resolve a server address to a subnet associated with an Active Directory site.

Exchange 2013 Mailbox servers interact directly with Outlook clients, Client Access servers, and Active Directory. Mailbox servers use Lightweight Directory Access Protocol (LDAP) to obtain recipient, server, and organization configuration information from Active Directory. Client Access servers accept connections to Mailbox servers over the local network and over the Internet. Client Access servers send requests from clients to the appropriate Mailbox server and return data from Mailbox servers to clients, including online address book files, free/busy data, calendar schedules, and client profile settings.

Some clients use POP3 or IMAP4 connections to communicate with the Exchange server. Other clients use SMTP, POP3, or IMAP4 to communicate with the Exchange server. Client Access servers proxy POP3, IMAP4, and SMTP communications between clients and Mailbox servers using POP3, IMAP4, and SMTP redirection respectively.

Outlook Web App, Exchange Active Sync, Exchange Admin Center, and Power-Shell communications are handled in much the same way as communications for standard Outlook clients.

Outlook clients on the corporate network access the Client Access server to send and retrieve messages using either SMTP or Outlook Anywhere (RPC over HTTP), as do clients outside the corporate network. Regardless of whether they are on or outside the corporate network, Outlook clients access public folder data using Outlook Anywhere. To retrieve a user's Active Directory information, Client Access servers use LDAP or Name Service Provider Interface (NSPI). By default, communications between Client Access servers and Mailbox servers is encrypted, as are communications with domain controllers and global catalogs.

NOTE In Exchange 2013, RPC connections are made directly to the MAPI RPC connection point on the Client Access server and the NSPI endpoint on the Client Access server. HTTP connections are still made to the RPC Proxy component on the Client Access server. The Client Access server then communicates with the appropriate Mailbox server. For directory information, Outlook communicates with an NSPI endpoint located on the Client Access server. NSPI communicates with the Active Directory driver, which then communicates with Active Directory.

Each Active Directory site with Mailbox servers should have at least one Client Access server. When there are multiple Client Access servers in a site, these servers are automatically configured in an array. Client Access arrays provide load balancing and failover support for all client access features. Each array has an external domain name, and client requests are directed to this external domain name, allowing for transparent load balancing as well as failover and failback. When a load-balanced resource fails on one server, the remaining servers in the array take over the workload of the failed server. When the failed server comes back online, the server can automatically rejoin the array, and the load-balancing feature starts to distribute the load to the server automatically. Failover takes only a few seconds in most cases.

The external URLs for CAS-related services should point to the array rather than to individual servers, and the internal URLs should point to individual servers. Because of this, you should set the external URLs for Exchange ActiveSync, Outlook Web applications, Exchange Admin Center, and the Offline Address Book relative to the external domain name for the array. For example, Exchange ActiveSync runs as a web application named Microsoft-Server-ActiveSync. When setting up Exchange ActiveSync URLs on each individual Mailbox server, you should configure the internal URL to point to a specific CAS server, such as *https://casserver48.pocket-consultant.com /Microsoft-Server-ActiveSync*, and the external URL to point to a location relative to the array, such as *https://array1.pocket-consultant.com/Microsoft-Server-ActiveSync*.

In Exchange 2010, Exchange Management Shell had several cmdlets you used to register and manage arrays in Active Directory. Because arrays are now created automatically, Exchange 2013 has only the Get-ClientAccessArray cmdlet for working with arrays. This cmdlet lists information about available or specified Client Access arrays. Its basic syntax is as follows:

```
Get-ClientAccessArray [-Identity ArrayIdentity]
[-DomainController FullyQualifiedName] [-Site SiteId]
```

Load balancing can be implemented using hardware or software. Windows Server includes the Windows Network Load Balancing service. Network Load Balancing doesn't use shared resources or clustered storage devices. Instead, each server has a copy of the Client Access services and features that are being load balanced, and local storage typically is used. Generally, users usually don't know that they're accessing a group of servers rather than a single server. The reason for this is that the array appears to be a single server. Clients connect to the array using the array's external domain name, and this virtual address is mapped automatically to a specific server based on availability. It is important to note that you cannot use Windows Network Load Balancing for establishing a Client Access array if the Client Access servers are co-located on a Mailbox server in a database availability group.

Deploying Transport services: The essentials

The Transport service on Mailbox servers and the Edge Transport role perform similar tasks. You use both for messaging routing, and both have a similar set of filters to protect an organization from spam and viruses. The key difference is in where you place servers with these roles. You place a Mailbox server in the internal network and configure it as a member of the organizational domain. If you use a server with the legacy Edge Transport role, you place it in the organization's perimeter network, and you do not configure it as a member of the organizational domain.

For computers with the Mailbox server or legacy Edge Transport role, the server cannot have the SMTP or Network News Transfer Protocol (NNTP) service installed separately. Although you install legacy Edge Transport servers outside the Active Directory forest, you must have a DNS suffix configured, and you must be able to perform name resolution from the legacy Edge Transport server to any Mailbox servers.

> **TIP** Transports store all incoming mail in a database file called mail.que until the transport verifies that all of the next hops for that message have been completed. This database has an associated transaction log in which changes are first committed. If you are using an Exchange server's internal drive(s) for storage in a high-volume environment in which one million or more messages are persisted, you should consider placing the database and the transaction log on separate disks for optimal performance and fault tolerance. With Storage Area Networks (SANs), it might not be immediately apparent whether disks are physically separate. This is because the volumes you see are logical references to a portion of the storage subsystem. In this case, you might be able to use the Storage Manager For SANs console or a similar tool to help you select logical unit numbers (LUNs) that are on physically separate disks.

> **MORE INFO** Transports have many different queues for messages. These queues are all stored in a single Extensible Storage Engine (ESE) database called mail.que. By default, this database is located in %ExchangeInstallPath%\TransportRoles\data\Queue. Thanks to shadow redundancy, the deletion of a message in the database is delayed until the transport verifies that all of the next hops for that message have completed delivery. If any of the next hops fail before reporting back successful delivery, the message is resubmitted for delivery to that next hop.

Both Mailbox servers and legacy Edge Transport servers can perform protocol logging and message tracking. Only Mailbox servers perform content conversion to format messages for recipients. Protocol logging allows you to verify whether a protocol is performing as expected and whether any issues need attention. Because this feature is designed for troubleshooting, it is disabled by default. Message tracking creates logs that track messages sent and received. Incoming mail from the Internet is converted to Summary Transport Neutral Encoding Format (STNEF) prior to being delivered. STNEF messages are always MIME-encoded and always have a Content-Transfer-Encoding value of Binary. Because content conversion is performed in the temp folder, you can improve performance by ensuring that the temp folder is not on the same physical disk as the paging file and operating system.

The transport pipeline used by Exchange 2013 is different from the transport pipeline for Exchange 2010 and has the following key components:

- Front End Transport service
- Transport service
- Mailbox Transport Submission service
- Mailbox Transport Delivery service

The Front End Transport service running on Client Access servers proxies all inbound and outbound SMTP traffic for Exchange 2013. Although the Transport service running on Mailbox servers performs nearly the same tasks as the Hub Transport role, it's important to point out the differences. As with Exchange 2010, the Transport service handles all SMTP mail flow. The service also performs message categorization and message content inspection. Unlike Exchange 2010, however, the Transport service doesn't communicate directly with mailbox databases. Instead, the Mailbox Transport Submission and Mailbox Transport Delivery services are used to provide separate mail submission and delivery processes.

The basic submission process works like this:

1. The Mailbox Transport Submission service receives SMTP messages from the Transport service on the local Mailbox server or on other Mailbox servers.
2. The Mailbox Transport Submission service connects to the local mailbox database.
3. The Mailbox Transport Submission service uses RPC to deliver the message.

The basic delivery process works like this:

1. The Mailbox Transport Delivery service connects to the local mailbox database using RPC to retrieve messages.
2. The Mailbox Transport Delivery service submits messages over SMTP to the Transport service on the local Mailbox server or on other Mailbox servers.
3. The Transport service routes messages using SMTP.

Messages from inside the organization enter the transport pipeline through a Receive connector, from the Mailbox Transport Delivery service, from the Pickup or Replay directories, or from agent submission. Messages from outside the organization enter the transport pipeline through a Receive connector in the Front End Transport service on a Client Access server and are then routed to the Transport service on a Mailbox server.

Deploying unified messaging: The essentials

Unified messaging allows you to integrate voice mail, fax, and email functionality so that the related data can be stored in a user's Exchange mailbox. To implement unified messaging, your organization must have a PBX that is connected to the LAN, and you must deploy Mailbox servers running Exchange Server 2013. After it is deployed, the Unified Messaging service running on a Mailbox server has the job of providing call answering, fax receiving, subscriber access, and auto-attendant features that allow access to content over the telephone and storage of content received from the PBX. However, it is the job of the Unified Messaging Call Router service running on Client Access servers to provide call routing and proxy services that allow calls to be connected.

Although some current PBXs, referred to as *IP-PBXs*, are Internet Protocol–capable, all other PBXs require a separate Internet Protocol/Voice over Internet Protocol (IP/VoIP) gateway to connect to the LAN. After you connect a PBX to the LAN, you can link it to Exchange by deploying and appropriately configuring the Unified Messaging service. The Desktop Experience feature, which is required to install Exchange server, provides the Microsoft Speech service, Microsoft Windows Media Encoder, and Microsoft Windows Media Audio Voice Code components used by the Unified Messaging service.

The Unified Messaging service doesn't perform a great deal of I/O operations, and the primary potential bottlenecks for this service are the processors, memory, and network. Disk I/O operations for this service are primarily limited to accessing routing details and dial plans, which include auto-attendant and mail policy settings.

If you are planning to use Unified Messaging in a hybrid Exchange implementation, you'll also need to configure session board controllers (SBCs). SBCs have two IP interfaces: one for your network and another that connects over the Internet. Your VoIP, IP-PBX, and SBC components must be configured to communicate with your Mailbox and Client Access servers. You also must create and configure a Unified Messaging IP gateway to represent each deployed device.

Integrating Exchange server roles with Active Directory

Exchange Server 2013 makes extensive use of Active Directory. Each Exchange server must access Active Directory to retrieve information about recipients and other Exchange server roles. Various Exchange server roles and services use Active Directory in other ways as well, as discussed in the sections that follow.

> **NOTE** Exchange 2013 works only with read-writeable domain controllers.

Using Mailbox servers with Active Directory

Mailbox servers are service locations for email messages, voice-mail messages, and faxes. For outgoing mail, Mailbox servers can access Active Directory to retrieve information about the location of Mailbox servers in their site. Then they can use this information to forward messages for routing.

The Transport service running on Mailbox servers contacts Active Directory for message categorization. The Categorizer queries Active Directory to perform recipient lookup, retrieves the information needed to locate a recipient's mailbox (according to the mailbox store in which it is created), and determines any restrictions or permissions that might apply to the recipient. The Categorizer also queries Active Directory to expand the membership of distribution lists and to perform the LDAP query processing when mail is sent to a dynamic distribution list.

After the Categorizer determines the location of a mailbox, the Transport service uses Active Directory site configuration information to determine the routing topology and locate the site of the mailbox. If the mailbox is in the same Active Directory site as the Mailbox server, the Transport service delivers the message directly to the user's mailbox. If the mailbox is in a different Active Directory site than the Mailbox server, the Transport service delivers the message to a Mailbox server in the remote Active Directory site.

Mailbox servers store all configuration information in Active Directory. This configuration information includes the details of any transport or journaling rules and connectors. When this information is needed, a Mailbox server accesses it in Active Directory.

Mailbox servers also store configuration information about mailbox users, mailbox stores, agents, address lists, and policies in Active Directory. Mailbox servers retrieve this information to enforce recipient policies, mailbox policies, system policies, and global settings.

Using Client Access servers with Active Directory

Client Access servers receive connections from local and remote clients. At a high level, when a user connection is received, the Client Access server contacts Active Directory to authenticate the user and to determine the location of the user's mailbox. If the user's mailbox is in the same Active Directory site as the Client Access server, the user is connected to the mailbox. If the user's mailbox is in an Active Directory site other than the one the Client Access server is located in, the connection is redirected to a Client Access server in the same Active Directory site as the user's mailbox.

When you use load balancing on your Client Access servers, Exchange 2013 creates arrays in Active Directory and associates each array with a specific Active Directory site. Each CAS array can be associated with only one Active Directory site. As with stand-alone CAS servers, the site information determines how connections are directed. If the user's mailbox is in the same Active Directory site as the array, the user is connected to a CAS server and via the CAS server to the mailbox. If the user's mailbox is in an Active Directory site other than the one in which the Client Access array is located, the connection is redirected.

You must have one Client Access server in each Active Directory site that contains a Mailbox server. At least one of your Client Access servers must be designated as Internet-facing. The Internet-facing CAS server proxies requests from Outlook Web App, Exchange ActiveSync, and Exchange Web Services to the Client Access server closest to the user's mailbox.

With Exchange 2010, proxying was not used for POP3 or IMAP4, and you needed to manually configure cross-site connectivity so clients connecting on one site could access their mailboxes at another site. Exchange 2013 automatically proxies from a Client Access server in one site to the correct server in another site.

Using Unified Messaging with Active Directory

The Unified Messaging service accesses Active Directory to retrieve global configuration information, such as dial plans and IP gateway details. When a message is received by the Unified Messaging service, the service searches for Active Directory recipients to match the telephone number to a recipient address. When the service has resolved this information, it can determine the location of the recipient's mailbox and then submit the message to the appropriate Mailbox server for submission to the mailbox.

Using Edge Transport servers with Active Directory

You deploy legacy Edge Transport servers in perimeter networks to isolate them from the internal network. As such, they are not members of the internal domain and do not have direct access to the organization's internal Active Directory servers for the purposes of recipient lookup or categorization. Thus, unlike the Transport service on Mailbox servers, legacy Edge Transport servers cannot contact an Active Directory server to help route messages.

To route messages into the organization, an administrator can configure a subscription from the legacy Edge Transport server to the Active Directory site that allows it to store recipient and configuration information about the Exchange organization in its AD LDS data store. After a legacy Edge Transport server is subscribed to an Active Directory site, it is associated with the Mailbox servers in that site for the purpose of message routing. Thereafter, Mailbox servers in the organization route messages being delivered to the Internet to the site associated with the legacy Edge Transport server, and Mailbox servers in this site relay the messages to the legacy Edge Transport server. The legacy Edge Transport server, in turn, routes the messages to the Internet.

The EdgeSync service running on Mailbox servers is a one-way synchronization process that pushes information from Active Directory to the legacy Edge Transport server. Periodically, the EdgeSync service synchronizes the data to keep the Edge Transport server's data store up to date. The EdgeSync service also establishes the connectors needed to send and receive information that is being moved between the organization and the Edge Transport server and between the Edge Transport server and the Internet. The key data pushed to the Edge Transport server includes:

- Accepted and remote domains
- Valid recipients
- Safe senders
- Send connectors
- Available Mailbox servers
- Available SMTP servers

- Message classifications
- TLS Send and Receive Domain Secure lists

After the initial replication is performed, the EdgeSync service synchronizes the data periodically. Configuration information is synced once every hour, and it can take up to one hour for configuration changes to be replicated. Recipient information is synced once every four hours, and it can take up to four hours for changes to be replicated. If necessary, administrators can initiate an immediate synchronization using the Start-EdgeSynchronization cmdlet in Exchange Management Shell.

NOTE During synchronization, objects can be added to, deleted from, or modified in the Edge Transport server's AD LDS data store. To protect the integrity and security of the organization, no information is ever pushed from the Edge Transport server's AD LDS data store to Active Directory.

Integrating Exchange Server 2013 into existing Exchange organizations

Existing Exchange Server 2007 and Exchange Server 2010 installations can coexist with Exchange Server 2013 installations. Generally, you do this by integrating Exchange Server 2013 into your existing Exchange Server 2007 or Exchange Server 2010 organization. Integration requires the following:

- Preparing Active Directory and the domain for the extensive Active Directory changes that will occur when you install Exchange Server 2013.

- Configuring Exchange Server 2013 so that it can communicate with servers running Exchange Server 2007 and Exchange Server 2010.

If you need a legacy server, you need to keep or add it to the Exchange organization before adding the new Exchange 2013 servers. Then, you have a coexistence implementation. You cannot upgrade existing Exchange Server 2007 or Exchange Server 2010 servers to Exchange Server 2013. You must install Exchange Server 2013 on new hardware, and then move the mailboxes from your existing installations to the new installation. See the "Moving to Exchange Server 2013" section later in this chapter for more details.

As an alternative to coexistence, you can deploy a new Exchange 2013 organization. After you deploy a new Exchange 2013 organization, you can't add servers that are running earlier versions of Exchange to the organization. Adding earlier versions of Exchange to an Exchange 2013 organization is not supported.

Coexistence and Active Directory

For coexistence with legacy Exchange Server versions, Exchange Server 2013 Cumulative Update 1 (CU1) is the minimum version. Exchange Server 2013 (Release to Manufacturer) RTM doesn't support legacy Exchange organizations. Keep the following in mind:

- Exchange 2003 and earlier versions are not supported for coexistence.

- Exchange 2007 is supported for coexistence only when all Exchange 2007 servers are running Rollup 10 for Exchange 2007 SP3 or later.
- Exchange 2010 is supported for coexistence only when all Exchange 2010 servers are running SP3 or later.

Before you install any build of Exchange Server 2013 in a legacy Exchange Server organization, ensure that Exchange Server 2010 is fully deployed. The reason for this is that you can install additional Exchange Server 2010 servers running a particular server role only if you've deployed a server with one of these roles prior to installing Exchange Server 2013. Therefore, if you haven't previously deployed all four Exchange Server 2010 server roles in your legacy Exchange Server organization, you may want to do so prior to installing any build of Exchange Server 2013.

Exchange Server 2013 contains extensive Active Directory schema changes and other Active Directory updates, so you might want to prepare Active Directory and the domain for these changes prior to installing Exchange Server 2013 for the first time, especially in a large enterprise.

To do this, follow these steps:

1. Prepare the schema by running the following command prior to executing the Exchange Server 2013 Setup:

   ```
   setup.exe /PrepareSchema /IAcceptExchangeServerLicenseTerms
   ```

   This command connects to the schema master and imports the LDAP data interchange format files that are used to update the schema with Exchange 2013 specific attributes. Optionally, use the /DomainController parameter to specify the name of the schema master. You must run this command on a 64-bit computer in the same domain and site as the schema master. If schema needs to be updated and you haven't previously prepared schema, you must ensure the account you use is delegated membership in the Schema Admins group. Wait for the changes to replicate before continuing.

2. Prepare Active Directory for Exchange 2013 by running the following command prior to executing the Exchange Server 2013 Setup:

   ```
   setup.exe /PrepareAD /IAcceptExchangeServerLicenseTerms
   ```

   You must run this command in the same domain and site as the schema master. This computer must be able to connect to all domains in the forest on TCP port 389. To run this command, you must be a member of the Domain Admins groups for the local domain or the Enterprise Admins group. Wait for the changes to replicate before continuing.

   The PrepareAD option performs a number of tasks:

   - Creates the Microsoft Exchange container and the Exchange organization container in the directory if they don't exist, such as when you are installing a new Exchange organization. Here, you must set a name for the organization using the /OrganizationName parameter.
   - Verifies that the schema has been updated for Exchange 2013. It does this by checking the objectVersion property for the Exchange configuration container and ensuring the value is 15449 or higher. The command

also sets the Exchange product ID of the Exchange organization to that of the version you are installing. The base value for Exchange 2013 RTM is 15.00.0516.032. This value is incremented when you deploy Cumulative Updates to Exchange.

- Creates any containers that are required in Active Directory for Exchange 2013, creates the default Accepted Domains entry if a default was not previously set, and imports the Rights.ldf file to add the extended rights required for Exchange to the directory.

- Creates the Microsoft Exchange Security Groups organizational unit in the root domain of the forest and then creates the following management role groups used by Exchange to this organizational unit if these haven't been previously created: Compliance Management, Delegated Setup, Discovery Management, Help Desk, Hygiene Management, Organization Management, Public Folder Management, Recipient Management, Records Management, Server Management, UM Management, and View-Only Organization Management. As necessary, also adds these groups to the otherWellKnownObjects attribute on the Exchange Services Configuration container.

- Creates the Unified Messaging Voice Originator contact in the Microsoft Exchange System Objects container of the root domain and then prepares the local domain for Exchange 2013.

3. The domain in which you ran **setup.exe /PrepareAD** is already prepared. For all other domains that will have mail-enabled users or in which you will install Exchange 2013, you must log in and run:

```
setup.exe /PrepareDomain /IAcceptExchangeServerLicenseTerms.
```

You also can specify the name of the domain in which you want to run the command, such as:

```
setup.exe/PrepareDomain:Tech.Pocket-Consultant.com
/IAcceptExchangeServerLicenseTerms
```

Alternatively, you can run:

```
setup.exe /PrepareAllDomains /IAcceptExchangeServerLicenseTerms
```

to prepare all domains in the forest. To run this command, you normally must be a member of the Domain Admins groups for the local domain or the Enterprise Admins group. However, if the domain was created after running /PrepareAD, the account you use must be a member of the Exchange 2013 Organization Management role group and the Domain Admins groups in the domain.

For new organizations, this command creates the Microsoft Exchange System Objects container and sets its permissions. For all organizations, this command:

- Sets the objectVersion property in the Microsoft Exchange System Objects container so that it references the version of domain preparation for Exchange 2013, which is 13236 or higher.

- Creates a domain global group in the current domain called Exchange Install Domain Servers and adds this group in the Microsoft Exchange System Objects container as well as the Exchange Servers group in the root domain.

- Assigns permissions in the domain for the Exchange Servers group and the Organization Management group.

Although Exchange Server 2013 Setup can perform these processes for you during the upgrade, the changes can take some time to replicate throughout a large organization. By performing these tasks manually, you can streamline the upgrade process. You also can ensure the tasks are run with accounts that have appropriate permissions.

As a prerequisite for installing Exchange Server 2013, Active Directory must be at Windows Server 2003 forest functionality mode or higher. Additionally, the schema master for the Active Directory forest along with at least one global catalog server and at least one domain controller in each Active Directory site must be running one of the following operating systems:

- Windows Server 2012 RTM or R2 Standard or Datacenter
- Windows Server 2008 R2 Standard or Enterprise
- Windows Server 2008 R2 Datacenter RTM or later
- Windows Server 2008 Standard or Enterprise (32-bit or 64-bit)
- Windows Server 2008 Datacenter RTM or later
- Windows Server 2003 Standard Edition with Service Pack 2 (SP2) or later (32-bit or 64-bit)
- Windows Server 2003 Enterprise Edition with SP2 or later (32-bit or 64-bit)

When you deploy IPv6, Exchange 2013 servers can send data to and receive data from devices, servers, and clients that use IPv6 addresses. However, Exchange 2013 supports IPv6 only when IPv4 is also installed. Further, although you can disable IPv4 so that only IPv6 is enabled, Exchange still requires that IPv4 be installed.

Configuring Exchange Server 2013 for use with existing Exchange organizations

When managing Exchange servers, you should use the administrative tools for that Exchange Server version. Exchange Admin Center and Exchange Management Shell are the primary management tools for Exchange Server 2013. Mailboxes located on Exchange Server 2007 and Exchange Server 2010 servers are also displayed in Exchange Admin Center.

You can manage the Exchange 2007 or 2010 mailbox properties using Exchange Admin Center or Exchange Management Shell. You can use either tool to move mailbox recipients from Exchange 2007 or Exchange 2010 to Exchange 2013.

When deploying Exchange 2013 in an Exchange 2007 or Exchange 2010 organization, keep the following in mind:

- If you want to use the Exchange Server 2013 Client Access server role, you must deploy the Client Access server role in each Active Directory site that contains the Mailbox Server role. Clients will see the Outlook Web App or Exchange ActiveSync version that is on their mailbox store. With Client Access arrays, the Client Access servers must all be members of the same Active Directory site.

- Exchange 2007 mailboxes can be enabled with unified messaging, but they will need an Exchange 2007 Unified Messaging server. Similarly, Exchange 2010 mailboxes can be enabled with unified messaging, but they will need an Exchange 2010 Unified Messaging server.

- If you want to use the legacy Edge Transport server role, you must deploy this server before installing Exchange 2013. You will then need to configure SMTP connectors to accept mail from and send mail to the Internet. Other modifications are required to mail Exchange and smart host records. Further, you can synchronize the Edge Transport server's AD LDS data with Active Directory only if the Exchange Server 2013 Active Directory preparation process has been performed.

- For management, you must deploy at least one Mailbox server and one Client Access server running Exchange 2013.

Setting the default Offline Address Book

A new Offline Address Book (OAB) will be created when you deploy the first Exchange 2013 Mailbox server in an existing Exchange organization. All existing clients that use OAB will see this new OAB by default the next time they perform an OAB update, and they also will perform a full OAB download. If you don't want this to happen, you must configure existing mailbox databases to explicitly point to the current default OAB before you deploy the first Exchange 2013 server.

You can do this by following these steps:

1. In Exchange Management Console, navigate to Organization Configuration, Mailbox, Database Management, and then open the Mailbox Database Properties dialog box for the mailbox database you want to work with.

2. On the Client Settings tab of the Mailbox Database Properties dialog box, you'll see an entry for the Offline Address Book and a related Browse button. Use this option to explicitly set the default OAB.

3. Repeat this process for each mailbox database that you want to update.

You also can use Exchange Management Shell to view all mailbox databases without a default OAB explicitly set on them and then explicitly set a default OAB. Start by entering the following command:

```
Get-MailboxDatabase | Where {$_.OfflineAddressBook -eq $Null} |
FT Name,OfflineAddressBook -AutoSize
```

If no values are returned, a default OAB is already explicitly set throughout the organization. If values are returned, you need to configure some databases with an explicitly defined default OAB. The following commands locate all mailbox databases in an Exchange 2007 or Exchange 2010 environment with no default OAB defined at the database level and then set these mailbox databases to the current default OAB in the organization:

```
Get-MailboxDatabase | Where {$_.OfflineAddressBook -eq $Null} |
Set-MailboxDatabase -OfflineAddressBook (Get-OfflineAddressBook |
Where {$_.IsDefault -eq $True})
```

If you have both Exchange 2007 and Exchange 2010 deployed on premises, you must run the command twice (using the respective Exchange Management Shell for each version).

Finally, you can confirm that all mailbox databases now have an explicitly defined default OAB, by re-running the first command. The command should return no values.

Moving to Exchange Server 2013

Most organizations have existing Exchange installations. When moving Exchange 2007 or Exchange 2010 installations to Exchange Server 2013, you cannot perform an in-place upgrade. Instead, you must install new Exchange Server 2013 servers into the existing organization and then migrate to Exchange Server 2013.

Migration from Exchange 2007 or Exchange 2010 to Exchange 2013 involves installing Exchange Server 2013 on new servers and then moving the mailboxes and public folders from your existing installations to the new installation. In a migration, only mailbox and public folder data is moved, and any Exchange configuration data is not maintained.

The steps you perform to migrate from Exchange 2007 or Exchange 2010 to Exchange 2013 are as follows:

1. Plan to migrate all Exchange servers in a particular site to Exchange 2013 at the same time. You should start with Internet-accessible Active Directory sites and then migrate internal Active Directory sites. For each Exchange 2013 Client Access server, you can configure only one Outlook Web App URL for redirection.

2. If you plan to have a legacy Edge Transport server in your Exchange 2013 organization, install it prior to installing Exchange 2013 on any server in your organization.

3. Install Exchange Server 2013 on new hardware and make it a member of the appropriate domain in the forest. You should install the Mailbox Server role first and then the Client Access Server role. You can install these roles on a single server or on multiple servers. You must deploy a Client Access server in each Active Directory site that has a Mailbox server.

4. Move Internet mail flow from Exchange 2007 or Exchange 2010 to Exchange 2013.

5. Move mailboxes and public folders from the existing Exchange 2007 or Exchange 2010 installations to the new Exchange Server 2013 Mailbox server or servers. If you move a mailbox that is part of an email address policy, the email address for the mailbox is automatically updated based on the settings in the email address policy. In this case, the new email address becomes the primary address, and the old email address becomes the secondary address.

   During a migration, the version of a CAS feature that a user sees, such as Outlook Web App, depends on where the user's mailbox is located. If the mailbox is on an Exchange 2007 server, the user sees Exchange 2007 versions of CAS features. When you move the mailbox to Exchange 2013, the user will see Exchange 2013 versions of CAS features.

REAL WORLD   You move mailboxes from Exchange 2007 or Exchange 2010 to Exchange 2013 by using an online move. Perform the move from the Exchange 2013 server by using move mailbox requests, either with Exchange Management Shell or Exchange Admin Center. You can't use the Exchange Management tools for Exchange 2007 or Exchange 2010 to move the mailboxes.

6.   Once you've complete the move and have validated the configuration, you can remove unneeded Exchange 2007 or Exchange 2010 servers from the organization.

CAUTION   Before removing the last Exchange 2007 or Exchange 2010 server with a particular role, you must be sure that you will never need to introduce an Exchange 2007 server with the role again. Once you remove the last Exchange 2007 or Exchange 2010 server with a particular role, you can never add another one with that role.

Running and modifying Exchange Server 2013 Setup

Exchange 2013 Setup is the program you use to perform installation tasks for Exchange 2013. You use Exchange 2013 Setup to install Exchange Server roles and the Exchange management tools. You can install Exchange 2013 from media or from a download. The same media or download is used for both Exchange Server 2013 Enterprise and Exchange Server 2013 Standard.

Downloads are packaged, self-extracting, executable files. When you access the download page, tap or click Download to start the download process. Next, copy the download to your computer for installation at a later time by tapping or clicking Save. After you copy the download to the computer on which you plan to install Exchange, you can double-tap or double-click the executable file to extract the Exchange 2013 Setup components to a folder. When prompted, be sure to specify an exact folder to put all the setup components in one place. Within this folder, you'll find a program called Setup.exe. This is the Exchange Server 2013 Setup program.

You use Setup to install Exchange Server 2013 and to add roles to a server. If you want to uninstall a server, you use Programs And Features in Control Panel. Because Exchange 2013 requires that you uninstall all installed roles at the same time, you cannot uninstall only the Mailbox role or only the Client Access role from a server.

Installing new Exchange servers

For servers deployed within the organization, you can install the Mailbox and Client Access roles on a single computer. As the size and needs of the organization increase, however, it becomes more and more beneficial to host these roles on separate servers. Keep the following in mind:

- You can achieve increased security by isolating the Internet-facing Client Access role and deploying it on a server other than one that also hosts the Mailbox role.

- You can achieve high availability for the Mailbox role simply by installing two or more Mailbox servers, creating a database availability group, adding mailbox databases to this group, and then adding database copies.
- You can achieve high availability for message transport simply by installing multiple Mailbox servers. Thanks to the shadow redundancy feature, a message that is submitted to a Mailbox server is stored in the transport database until the transport server verifies that all of the next hops for that message have completed delivery. If the next hop doesn't report successful delivery, the message is resubmitted for delivery. In addition, when messages are in the transport dumpster, they aren't removed until they are replicated to all the appropriate mailbox databases.
- You can achieve high availability for the Client Access role by installing the role on multiple servers and, optionally, configuring network or hardware load balancing. Using load balancing requires planning.

When you use multiple Exchange servers, you should deploy the roles in this order:

1. Mailbox server
2. Client Access server

For client access to work correctly, install at least one Client Access server in each Active Directory site that has a Mailbox server. For message transport, install at least one Mailbox server for each group of Active Directory sites that are well connected on a common LAN. For example, if the organization consists of sites A and B, which are well connected on a common LAN, and sites C and D, which are well connected on a common LAN, with wide area network (WAN) links connecting sites A and B to sites C and D, a minimal implementation would be to have Mailbox servers only in site A and site C. However, Microsoft recommends that you have the Client Access and Mailbox Server roles in each Active Directory site with mail-enabled clients.

Because you install legacy Edge Transport servers outside the Active Directory forest, you can deploy additional Edge Transports at any time. By configuring multiple Edge Transport servers, you can ensure that if one server fails, Edge Transport services continue. If you also configure your Edge Transport servers with round-robin DNS, you can load balance between them.

REAL WORLD If you are installing Exchange Server on a new network, such as one for a new company or a development environment, be sure that you've properly configured Active Directory and DNS before installing Exchange Server. You need to create a domain. Typically, you do this by installing a server and establishing the server as a domain controller in a new forest.

When you set up DNS, be sure you configure the appropriate reverse lookup zones. You should have one reverse lookup zone for each subnet. If you forget to set up the reverse zones and do this after installing your servers, be sure that the appropriate PTR records have been created for your domain controllers and Exchange servers. In Active Directory Sites And Services, check that the sites and subnets are configured appropriately. You need to create a subnet in Active Directory to represent each of the subnets on your network. If DNS reverse zones and Active Directory subnets are not configured properly, you will likely experience long startup times on your servers, and Exchange services will likely not start properly.

Installing Exchange Server

Before you run Exchange Server 2013 Setup make sure that the server meets the system requirements and prerequisites as discussed in the Chapter 1, "Exchange Server 2013 administration overview" section "Exchange Server 2013 editions." You can run Exchange Server 2013 only on full installations of Windows Server 2008 R2 and Windows Server 2012. You cannot install Exchange Server 2013 on a server running in Windows Server Core mode. Instead, you must convert the Core mode to a full installation. The supported editions are as follows:

- Windows Server 2012 RTM or R2 Standard or Datacenter
- Windows Server 2008 R2 Standard with Service Pack 1 (SP1)
- Windows Server 2008 R2 Enterprise with Service Pack 1 (SP1)
- Windows Server 2008 R2 Datacenter RTM or later

NOTE You can use Setup to install the Exchange Server 2013 management tools on 64-bit editions of Windows 7 SP1 and Windows 8 or later.

You can run Exchange Server 2013 Setup in one of several modes, including:

- **Install**   Used when you're installing a new server role or adding a server role to an existing installation.
- **Upgrade**   Used when you have an existing installation of Exchange and you're installing a service pack or cumulative update.
- **Uninstall**   Used when you're removing the Exchange installation.

IMPORTANT Exchange Server 2013 doesn't support in-place upgrades from any previous version of Exchange. Further, after you install Exchange Server 2013, you won't be able to rename the server.

Generally, you should install Exchange Server 2013 on member servers rather than on domain controllers. This will ensure Exchange operates with strictest security allowed and has optimal performance. If you do install Exchange Server 2013 on a domain controller, you won't be able to demote the server. Once Exchange 2013 is installed, changing a server's role from a member server to a directory server, or vice versa, isn't supported.

If something goes wrong with the installation and re-running Setup and following the prompts doesn't help you resolve the problem, you have several options. You can restore the server from backup or you can run Exchange Server 2013 Setup in recovery mode by running **setup /m:RecoverServer** at a command prompt. If you are recovering to a different server, the server must use the same fully qualified domain name (FQDN) as the failed server.

When you recover a server, you don't specify the roles to restore. Setup detects the Exchange Server object in Active Directory and installs the corresponding files and configuration automatically. After you recover the server, you can restore databases and reconfigure any additional settings.

When you are ready to run Setup, you can begin the installation and install server roles by completing the following steps:

1. Log on to the server using an administrator account. When you install the Mailbox and Client Access roles, you must use a domain account that is a member of the Enterprise Administrators group. If you've already prepared Active Directory, this account must also be a member of the Exchange Organization Administrators group.

   IMPORTANT Before beginning setup, you should close any open Windows PowerShell or Microsoft Management Console (MMC) windows. Otherwise you will see a warning during the readiness checks that you need to close these windows. The installation process makes updates to Windows PowerShell and MMC and requires exclusive access.

   REAL WORLD Ensure the server's TCP/IP settings are properly configured before beginning setup. Also, ensure that the server is a member of the domain in which you want the Exchange organization to be configured. During setup, the server will try to identify the Active Directory site in which it is located. The server will try to connect with a domain controller and global catalog sever in this site.

2. Do one of the following:

   - If you are using an installation disc, insert the Exchange Server 2013 DVD into the DVD-ROM drive. If Autorun is enabled, Exchange Server 2013 Setup should start automatically. Otherwise, double-tap or double-click Setup.exe on the root folder of the DVD.

   - If you are using a download, access the folder where you extracted the Exchange setup files and then start Exchange 2013 Setup by double-tapping or double-clicking Setup.exe.

   IMPORTANT If you've enabled User Access Control (UAC), you must press and hold or right-click Setup.exe and select Run As Administrator.

3. On the Check For Updates page, shown in Figure 2-1, you can specify whether to check for updates to the setup process. If you don't want to check for updates, select Don't Check For Updates before you tap or click Next to continue. Setup will then copy files and initialize resources. The server also tries to validate the state of Active Directory.

   If the server is unable to validate the state of Active Directory and choose a domain controller to work with, Setup will log errors and may also report that a domain controller could not be located. If errors are reported, do not continue with the installation. Instead, exit Setup and resolve the communication problem.

Check for Updates?

You can have Setup download Exchange Server 2013 updates from the Internet before you install Exchange. If updates are available, they'll be downloaded and used by Setup. By downloading updates now, you'll have the latest security and product updates. If you don't want to check for updates right now, or if you don't have access to the Internet, skip this step. If you skip this step, be sure to download and install any available updates after you've completed Setup.

Select one of the following options:

⦿ Connect to the Internet and check for updates

◯ Don't check for updates right now

E▊ Exchange   next

FIGURE 2-1 Exchange Server Setup allows you to check for updates to the setup process.

4. The Introduction page begins the installation process. Tap or click Next to continue.

5. On the License Agreement page, review the software license terms. If you agree to the terms, select I Accept The Terms In The License Agreement, and then tap or click Next.

6. On the Recommended Settings page, shown in Figure 2-2, select whether you want to use the recommended settings. If you select Use Recommended Settings, Exchange will automatically send error reports and information about your computer hardware and how you use Exchange to Microsoft. If you select Don't Use Recommended Settings, error and usage reporting are disabled, but you can enable them at any time after Setup completes. Tap or click Next to continue.

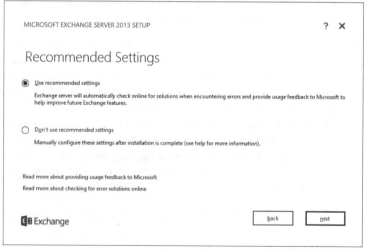

Recommended Settings

⦿ Use recommended settings

Exchange server will automatically check online for solutions when encountering errors and provide usage feedback to Microsoft to help improve future Exchange features.

◯ Don't use recommended settings

Manually configure these settings after installation is complete (see help for more information).

Read more about providing usage feedback to Microsoft
Read more about checking for error solutions online

E▊ Exchange   back   next

FIGURE 2-2 Using the Recommended Settings to automatically send error reports and information about your computer hardware to Microsoft.

7. On the Server Role Selection page, shown in Figure 2-3, choose whether you want to install the Mailbox role, the Client Access role, both roles, or just the management tools on this computer. You can add additional server roles later if you choose not to install them during this installation. An organization must have at least one Mailbox role and at least one Client Access server role installed. Both roles can be installed on the same computer. However, unlike previous releases, you cannot uninstall only one role from a server—both roles must be uninstalled together. The management tools are installed automatically if you install any server role.

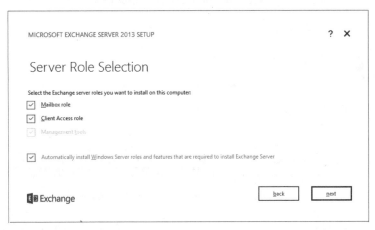

FIGURE 2-3 Selecting the server roles to install.

8. Select Automatically Install Windows Server Roles And Features That Are Required To Install Exchange Server to have Setup install any required Windows prerequisites. You may need to reboot the computer to complete the installation of some Windows features. If you don't select this option, you must install the required Windows features manually. Tap or click Next to continue.

9. On the Installation Space And Location page, note the space required for the installation. Tap or click Browse to choose a location for the installation. Ensure you have enough disk space available on the related drive. Tap or click Next to continue.

10. If this is the first Exchange server in your organization, on the Exchange Organization page, shown in Figure 2-4, type a name for your Exchange organization or accept the default value of First Organization. The Exchange organization name must be 64 characters or less and can contain only the characters A through Z, a through z, 0 through 9, space (as long as the space is not leading or trailing), and hyphen or dash. You can't leave the organization name blank. Tap or click Next to continue.

REAL WORLD Exchange 2013 supports shared permissions and split permissions. Split permissions allow organizations to separate Exchange management and Active Directory management. Role Based Access Control (RBAC) is the recommended split permissions model used with Exchange. If you want to use shared permissions or split permissions that use RBAC, do not select the Apply Active Directory Split Permissions check box. If your organization has strict requirements for separate management of Active Directory and Exchange Server and RBAC will not meet your needs, select the Apply Active Directory Split Permissions check box. However, you will then be unable to create users, groups, contacts, and other Active Directory objects using the Exchange management tools.

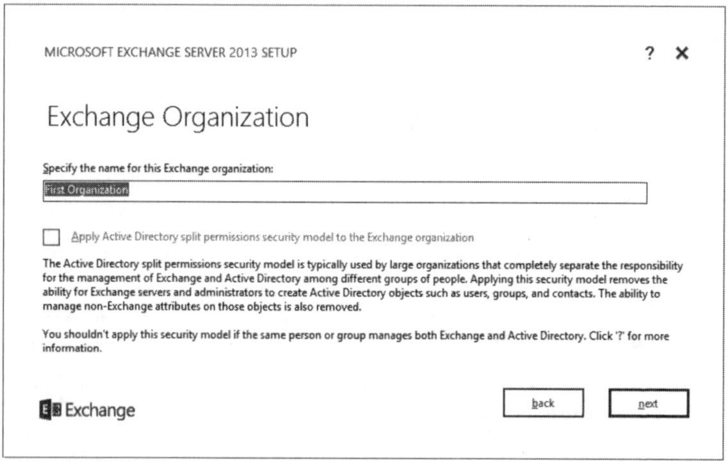

MICROSOFT EXCHANGE SERVER 2013 SETUP   ?   ✗

Exchange Organization

Specify the name for this Exchange organization:

First Organization

☐   Apply Active Directory split permissions security model to the Exchange organization

The Active Directory split permissions security model is typically used by large organizations that completely separate the responsibility for the management of Exchange and Active Directory among different groups of people. Applying this security model removes the ability for Exchange servers and administrators to create Active Directory objects such as users, groups, and contacts. The ability to manage non-Exchange attributes on those objects is also removed.

You shouldn't apply this security model if the same person or group manages both Exchange and Active Directory. Click '?' for more information.

E█ Exchange   back   next

FIGURE 2-4 Setting the name of the Exchange organization.

11. If you're installing the Mailbox role, on the Malware Protection Settings page, choose whether you want to enable or disable malware scanning. If you disable malware scanning, it can be enabled later. Tap or click Next to continue.

12. On the Readiness Checks page, shown in Figure 2-5, ensure the prerequisite checks completed successfully. Note any warnings. Note any errors as well. You must resolve any reported errors before you can install Exchange Server 2013. For most errors, you don't need to exit Setup. After resolving a reported error, tap or click Retry to run the prerequisite checks again.

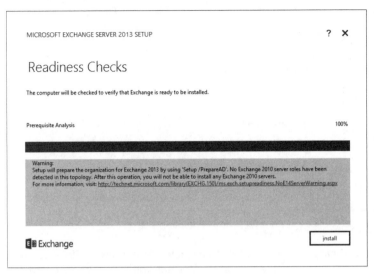

FIGURE 2-5 Reviewing any warnings on the Readiness Checks page.

13. When all readiness checks have completed successfully, tap or click Install to install Exchange 2013. The installation process should take about 60 minutes.

The Setup Progress page, shown in Figure 2-6, tracks the progress of the installation. The installation is performed in a series of steps, with the progress for the current step tracked with a progress bar and as a percentage of completion. The number of steps varies, depending on the tasks Setup must perform to prepare the environment as well as the options you selected. Typically, the steps you see will include:

a. Organization preparation

b. Preparing setup

c. Stopping services

d. Exchange Files... Language Files

e. Restoring services

f. Languages

g. Management tools

h. Mailbox role: Transport service

i. Mailbox role: Client Access service

j. Mailbox role: Unified Messaging service

k. Mailbox role: Mailbox service

l. Client Access role: Front End Transport service

m. Client Access role: Front End service

n. Finalizing setup

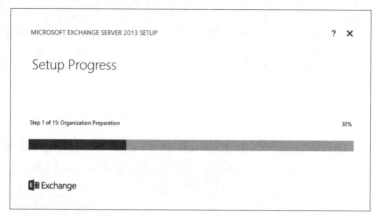

FIGURE 2-6 Tracking the progress of the installation.

14. Finally, you'll see the Setup Completed page, shown in Figure 2-7, when Setup completes the installation. Although you must restart the server to finalize the installation, you may want to select the Launch Exchange Administration Center check box before selecting Finish and then set the product key.

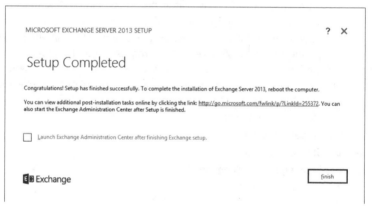

FIGURE 2-7 The setup is complete.

NOTE Alternatively, you can manually start Exchange Admin Center by opening Internet Explorer and entering the Exchange Admin Center URL. By default, this URL is *https://ServerName/ecp/* where *ServerName* is the name of the server, such as: *https://mailserver35/ecp/*.

By default, Exchange 2013 runs in trial mode. To get out of trial mode, you must validate the installation. In the left pane of Exchange Admin Center, tap or click Servers. As shown in Figure 2-8, a link is provided for entering a product key. Tapping or clicking this link opens the properties dialog box for the mail server with the general page displayed. Enter a valid product key in the boxes provided and then tap or click Save.

FIGURE 2-8 Opening Exchange Admin Center.

You can change the product key at any time on the general page. Select Change Product Key, enter a valid product key, and then tap or click Save.

You can upgrade a Standard edition to an Enterprise edition using the options on the general page as well. Select Change Product Key, enter a valid product key for Enterprise edition, and then tap or click Save.

Verifying and completing the installation

You can verify that Exchange Server 2013 installed successfully by running the Get-ExchangeServer cmdlet in Exchange Management Shell. This command displays a list of all Exchange 2013 server roles that are installed on a specified server.

During installation, Exchange Setup logs events in the Application log of Event Viewer. You can review the Application log to make sure there are no warning or error messages related to Exchange setup. Typically, these events have event IDs 1003 and 1004, with the source as MSExchangeSetup.

You also can learn more about the installation by reviewing the setup log file created during the setup process. This log file is stored in the *%SystemDrive%*\ ExchangeSetupLogs folder with the name ExchangeSetup.log. The *%SystemDrive%* variable represents the root directory of the drive where the operating system is installed. Because these logs contain standard text, you can perform a search using the keyword *error* to find any setup errors that occurred.

As discussed previously, Setup must be able to contact Active Directory. If Setup is unable do this, errors will be logged and the Exchange organization will not be prepared properly. In the following example, Setup couldn't validate the state of Active Directory and couldn't locate a domain controller:

```
[06/02/2013 20:18:31.0253] [0] Setup is choosing the domain controller
to use
[06/02/2013 20:18:42.0630] [0] Setup is choosing a local domain
controller...
```

```
[06/02/2013 20:18:45.0033] [0] [ERROR] Setup encountered a problem while
validating the state of Active Directory: Could not find any Domain
Controller in domain pocket-consultant.com.
[06/02/2013 20:18:45.0158] [0] [ERROR] Could not find any Domain Controller
in domain pocket-consultant.com.
[06/02/2013 20:18:45.0205] [0] [ERROR] Domain controller not found in the
domain "pocket-consultant.com".
[06/02/2013 20:18:45.0205] [0] Setup will use the domain controller ''.
[06/02/2013 20:18:45.0205] [0] Setup will use the global catalog ''.
[06/02/2013 20:18:45.0955] [0] No Exchange configuration container was
found for the organization. Message: 'Could not find any Domain Controller
in domain pocket-consultant.com.'.
```

Because of this problem, Setup didn't fully prepare the organization and had problems configuring the Mailbox role: Transport service and the other services as well. With Exchange 2013 RTM, the scripts for setup waited for up to 40 minutes during the Mailbox role: Transport service configuration, while continuously checking and eventually timing out. Setup took much longer than usual, but did continue all the way to completion. Although this long wait was an indicator of a problem, later updates to Setup for Cumulative Update 1 and beyond removed the waits, so there are no longer long lags that may indicate a problem.

When Setup is able to validate the state of Active Directory, the log records a very different set of events as shown in the following example:

```
[06/02/2013 20:40:07.0115] [0] Setup is choosing the domain controller
to use
[06/02/2013 20:40:14.0135] [0] Setup is choosing a local domain
controller...
[06/02/2013 20:40:24.0729] [0] Setup has chosen the local domain controller
CorpServer24.pocket-consultant.com for initial queries
[06/02/2013 20:40:24.0885] [0] PrepareAD has either not been run or has not
replicated to the domain controller used by Setup. Setup will attempt to
use the Schema Master domain controller CorpServer24.pocket-consultant.com
[06/02/2013 20:40:24.0885] [0] The schema master domain controller is
available
[06/02/2013 20:40:24.0901] [0] The schema master domain controller is in
the local domain; setup will use CorpServer24.pocket-consultant.com
[06/02/2013 20:40:24.0901] [0] Setup is choosing a global catalog...
[06/02/2013 20:40:24.0917] [0] Setup has chosen the global catalog server
CorpServer24.pocket-consultant.com.
[06/02/2013 20:40:24.0932] [0] Setup will use the domain controller
'CorpServer24.pocket-consultant.com'.
[06/02/2013 20:40:24.0932] [0] Setup will use the global catalog
'CorpServer24.pocket-consultant.com'.
[06/02/2013 20:40:24.0948] [0] No Exchange configuration container was
found for the organization. Message: 'Could not find the Exchange
Configuration Container'.
```

Here, Setup was able to select a domain controller to work with, locate the schema master, and choose a global catalog server. Note that Setup reports that PrepareAD was not run or replicated and that no Exchange configuration container was found. This is normal for a new installation of Exchange 2013. Shortly after validating the state of Active Directory, Setup will determine the organization-level operations to perform. For a new installation of Exchange 2013, related entries should look similar to the following:

```
[06/02/2013 20:40:26.0339] [0] Setup is determining what organization-level
operations to perform.
[06/02/2013 20:40:26.0339] [0] Setup has detected a missing value. Setup is
adding the value PrepareSchema.
[06/02/2013 20:40:26.0339] [0] Setup has detected a missing value. Setup is
adding the value PrepareOrganization.
[06/02/2013 20:40:26.0339] [0] Setup has detected a missing value. Setup is
adding the value PrepareDomain.
```

Here, Setup reports that it will prepare the Active Directory schema, the Exchange organization, and the domain. You can confirm each by looking for the elements that should have been created or configured as discussed in the section titled "Coexistence and Active Directory" earlier in the chapter.

To complete the installation for an initial deployment of Exchange into an organization, you need to perform the following tasks:

- For Client Access servers:
  - If you plan to use ActiveSync for mobile messaging clients, configure direct push, authentication, and mobile devices.
  - Configure internal and external URLs for the Outlook web applications, Exchange ActiveSync, Exchange Admin Center, and Offline Address Book.
  - Configure authentication and display options, as appropriate.
  - Enable the server for POP3 and IMAP4, as appropriate.
  - A self-signed digital certificate is created by default but won't be automatically trusted by clients. You can either establish trust or obtain a certificate from a third party that the client trusts.

- For Mailbox servers:
  - Configure domains for which you will accept email. You need an accepted domain entry for each SMTP domain for which you will accept email.
  - Configure Send connectors as appropriate. If you are unsure about the Send connectors that are needed, create an Internet Send connector at a minimum. Use the address space of "*" to route all outbound mail to the Internet.
  - If you also deployed the Edge Transport server role, you need to subscribe to the Edge Transport server so that the EdgeSync service can establish one-way replication of recipient and configuration information from Active Directory to the AD LDS store on the Edge Transport server.
  - Configure DNS MX resource records for each accepted domain.
  - Configure OAB distribution for Outlook 2007 and later clients.
  - Configure database availability groups and mailbox database copies, as appropriate.

- For Unified Messaging service:
  - Configure a unified messaging dial plan, and add the server to it.

- Configure unified messaging hunt groups.
- Enable users for unified messaging, as appropriate.
- Configure your IP/VoIP gateways or IP-PBXs to work with Exchange Server.
- Configure a Unified Messaging IP gateway in Exchange Server.
- As desired, create auto-attendant and mailbox policies and configure additional dial plans, gateways, and hunt groups.

Adding, modifying, or uninstalling server roles

The Exchange Server 2013 installation process uses Windows Installer. Using Windows Installer helps to streamline and stabilize the installation process, and it makes modification of installation components fairly easy. Thanks to Windows Installer, you can install additional roles by re-running Setup from media or the download folder and resume a failed installation or modification simply by re-running Exchange Setup.

Although Exchange Setup doesn't allow you to remove individual roles from a server, you can use the options on the Programs And Features page under Control Panel, Programs to uninstall Exchange Server. To do this, follow these steps:

1. In Control Panel, tap or click the Uninstall A Program link under Programs. In Programs And Features, select the Microsoft Exchange Server 2013 entry to display the Uninstall button.

2. If you want to remove all roles and uninstall Exchange Server, tap or click Uninstall. Clear the check boxes for roles you want to remove. Tap or click Next, and then follow the prompts.

Before you can remove the Mailbox role from a server, you must move or delete all mailboxes hosted in mailbox databases on the server and all offline address books hosted in public folders.

Understanding cumulative updates and service packs

Microsoft has been using cumulative updates and service packs with Exchange Server for some time. Starting with Exchange Server 2007, Microsoft began releasing customer rollup updates instead of individual hotfixes. Here, each rollup contained one or more routine product updates, one or more security updates, or both that were delivered and applied in a single package. The goal was to simplify delivery of updates and make maintaining Exchange Server easier. However, because security updates were delivered with hotfixes in a single package, you couldn't install security updates separately from hotfixes. Additionally, service packs for Exchange Server 2007 were delivered as full product updates and installed as an upgrade.

Working with cumulative updates and service packs

With Exchange Server 2013, Microsoft decided to deliver routine product updates and security updates separately. Under this servicing model, routine product updates are delivered periodically as a single, cumulative update, and security updates are delivered separately. While this allows you to install security updates as they are released without having to install a cumulative update, cumulative updates themselves will contain security updates. As with earlier releases of service packs in Exchange Server, cumulative updates are delivered as full product updates and installed as upgrades.

To better align on-premises Exchange and Exchange Online, Microsoft tries to release cumulative updates on a fixed schedule and applies cumulative updates to their hosted Exchange servers prior to official release. Thus, when an update is released you know it has been applied to all Exchange Online servers and all of the mailboxes stored in the cloud.

> **IMPORTANT**   Microsoft is releasing cumulative updates for other products, including Lync and SharePoint, on separate fixed schedules as well. Ideally, this will be a quarterly release schedule with four cumulative updates released each year during the product's lifecycle.

Cumulative updates more closely resemble service packs than rollup updates. Not only may cumulative updates contain hotfixes and security updates, they may also contain new features, product enhancements, and other changes that affect the way the product works. While language modifications were previously limited to Service Pack releases, cumulative updates may contain updates to language resources. A cumulative update also may contain Active Directory schema updates. If so, the schema changes will be additive and backward compatible with previous release and product versions.

> **IMPORTANT**   Cumulative updates do not replace service packs. Microsoft will continue to release service packs for Exchange Server 2013.

Every cumulative update and service pack is a full release of the product. This means, you install cumulative updates and service packs as product upgrades and that each update package will be larger than the previous product or update package. Because you install cumulative updates and service packs as upgrades, any customizations you've made to Exchange Server (using web.config files on Client Access servers, EdgeTransport.exe.config files on Mailbox servers, registry changes, or other custom configuration options on servers) are not preserved. This means you will lose any customizations. To prevent this, you must save your customizations and then re-apply them after applying a cumulative update or service pack.

> **REAL WORLD**   Don't forget that it is possible the upgrade process will fail. If this happens, you can recover from the failed upgrade like you would recover from a failed service pack installation, which may include running Exchange Server 2013 Setup with a special recovery option. To do this, you enter the command SETUP /m:RecoverServer.

In the unlikely event that the upgrade fails and is unrecoverable, you will need to re-install Exchange Server. This re-installation process will create a new server object and should not result in the loss of mailbox or queue data. However, you will need to re-seed or re-attach existing databases after the re-installation process.

Applying cumulative updates and service packs

You apply cumulative updates and service packs using Exchange Server Setup. Because each cumulative update and service pack is a new build of Exchange Server 2013, you don't need to apply cumulative updates or service packs in sequence. You can apply the latest cumulative update or service pack at any time. For example, if you deployed Exchange Server 2013 RTM but didn't upgrade to Exchange Server Cumulative Update 1, you could upgrade the original installation directly to Exchange Server Cumulative Update 2.

> **IMPORTANT** When you are deploying Exchange servers, you don't need to deploy Exchange Server 2013 RTM and then upgrade to a cumulative update or service pack later. Because each cumulative update or service pack is a complete build, you can fully deploy the Exchange server using only the current cumulative update or service pack.

In a Database Availability Group configuration, all servers should be running the same cumulative update or service pack of Exchange Server 2013—except during an upgrade. During an upgrade, individual servers within a Database Availability Group can have different cumulative update or service pack versions. This mixed state is expected to be only temporary. Database Availability Group should not operate in a mixed state for long periods of time.

Similarly, all servers in a Client Access array should be running the same cumulative update or service pack of Exchange Server 2013—except during an upgrade. During an upgrade, individual servers within a Client Access array can have different cumulative update or service pack versions. Again, this mixed state is expected to be temporary.

Cumulative updates and service packs are published at the Microsoft Download Center. Because staying current with cumulative updates and service packs may present a special challenge for some Exchange installations, it is important to note that cumulative updates are supported only for three months after the release of the subsequent cumulative update. With Microsoft's goal of delivering cumulative updates quarterly, this typically means that a prior cumulative update is supported for about six months.

Tracking Exchange Server version numbers

Versioning with Exchange Server 2013 gets a little tricky. This is because Exchange Server can have both service packs and cumulative updates for those service packs. To differentiate between versions, Microsoft references both the Exchange Server version and the cumulative update.

The official release of Exchange Server 2013 is referred to as Exchange Server 2013 RTM. Cumulative updates for this release are referred to using the full release name plus the cumulative update number. Thus, Exchange Server 2013 RTM with Cumulative Update 1 is referred to as Exchange Server 2013 RTM CU1.

As Microsoft releases service packs for Exchange Server 2013, those service packs will be full product rollups that include prior cumulative updates of the product. Cumulative updates for Exchange Server 2013 with specific service packs will be released as well. In this instance, cumulative updates are referred to using the full release name, the service pack name, and the cumulative update number. Thus, Exchange Server 2013 SP1 with Cumulative Update 1 is referred to as Exchange Server 2013 SP1 CU1.

Keep in mind the version of Exchange Server is updated when you install a cumulative update, a service pack, or both. This means that one way to determine what cumulative update, service pack, or both is applied is to check the version number of an Exchange server. The build number for Exchange 2013 RTM is 516.32; the build number for Exchange 2013 RTM Cumulative Update 1 is 620.29; the build number for Exchange 2013 RTM Cumulative Update 2 is 712.22, and so on.

REAL WORLD The Exchange 2013 management tools make it easy to determine version numbers. In Exchange Admin Center, simply select Servers in the feature pane and then select Servers to see a list of Exchange servers by name, install roles, and version. In Exchange Management Shell, you can display a similar list by entering the following command:

```
Get-ExchangeServer | select name, serverrole, admin*
```

Using security updates with cumulative updates and service packs

The servicing model changes the way security updates are released as well. For Exchange Server 2013, security updates are designated for a specific cumulative update and contain all of the fixes available at the time of release in a single update package. Thus, to ensure a server has the most recent security fixes, you need to apply only the most recently released security update for a specific cumulative update. For example, if you are using Exchange Server 2013 with CU2, you ensure a server has the most recent security fixes by applying the most recent security update for CU2.

As cumulative updates themselves contain security updates, you need to apply only security updates that have been released after a specified cumulative update. Thus, if for some reason you didn't apply security updates for Exchange Server 2013 CU1 and have now upgraded to Exchange Server 2013 CU2, you don't need to apply any of the security updates that are specific to Exchange Server 2013 CU1 (or Exchange Server 2013 RTM).

Security updates for Exchange Server 2013 are available via Microsoft Update and are published at the Microsoft Download Center. Finally, it is important to point out that security updates released for a particular cumulative update will not need to be uninstalled before moving to the next cumulative update.

New service packs for Exchange 2013 will include all the prior cumulative updates and security updates. Thus, when you install Exchange 2013 Service Pack 1, you don't also need to install any prior cumulative updates and security updates.

Installing cumulative updates and service packs

Cumulative updates and service packs are full builds of Exchange Server 2013. You install a cumulative update or service pack as an upgrade, and there is no rollback process should installation fail. Because of this, you should ensure you have a full recovery plan in place prior to applying a cumulative update. Typically, this means having server backups and other backup plans in place prior to installing an update.

You'll find cumulative updates and service packs for Exchange Server 2013 at the Microsoft Download Center. A single download is provided for both Exchange Server 2013 Enterprise and Exchange Server 2013 Standard. For example, Exchange Server 2013 CU2 is available at *http://www.microsoft.com/en-us/download /details.aspx?id=39609*. A current list of cumulative updates can be found at *http://technet.microsoft.com/en-us/library/jj907309(v=exchg.150).aspx*.

When you access the download page, tap or click Download to start the download process. Next, copy the download to your computer for installation at a later time by tapping or clicking Save. Copy the download to your server if necessary.

When you run the executable, Windows verifies the file, and you'll then be able to extract the download to a folder. Be sure to specify an exact folder so that all the setup components are put in one place. Within this folder, you'll find a program called Setup.exe. This is the Exchange Server 2013 Setup program.

Preparing to install a cumulative update or service pack

Before you run Exchange Setup make sure you read the release notes for the cumulative update or service pack. Also make sure that any server on which you plan to install the cumulative update or service pack meets the system requirements and prerequisites for Exchange Server 2013.

You can run Exchange Server 2013 only on full installations of Windows Server 2008 R2 and Windows Server 2012 RTM or R2. Exchange Server 2013 doesn't support in-place upgrades from any previous version of Exchange. After you install a cumulative update or service pack, you cannot uninstall the cumulative update or service pack to revert to an earlier version of Exchange Server 2013. If you uninstall a cumulative update or service pack, Exchange Server 2013 is removed from the server.

As cumulative updates and service packs may contain Active Directory schema changes and other Active Directory updates, you may want to update Active Directory prior to deploying a cumulative update or service pack on any server in your organization, especially in a large enterprise. Here, keep the following in mind:

- If the update contains schema changes, run the following command prior to executing the Exchange Server 2013 Setup.exe:

```
setup.exe /PrepareSchema /IAcceptExchangeServerLicenseTerms
```

- If the update contains enterprise Active Directory changes (such as role-based Access Control updates), run the following command prior to executing the Exchange Server 2013 Setup.exe:

```
setup.exe /PrepareAD /IAcceptExchangeServerLicenseTerms
```

- If the update contains changes to the permissions within the Active Directory domain partition, run the following command in each domain containing Exchange servers or mailboxes:

```
setup.exe /PrepareDomain /IAcceptExchangeServerLicenseTerms
```

- If required, ensure that you run these commands using the Setup program provided in the cumulative update you are working with.

Although Exchange Server 2013 Setup can perform these processes for you during the upgrade, the changes can take some time to replicate throughout a large organization. By performing these tasks manually, you can streamline the upgrade process. You also can ensure the tasks are run with accounts that have appropriate permissions. Keep the following in mind:

- If schema needs to be updated and you haven't previously prepared schema, you must ensure the account you use is delegated membership in the Schema Admins group.
- If you're installing the first Exchange 2013 server in the organization, the account you use must have membership in the Enterprise Admins group.
- If you've already prepared the schema and aren't installing the first Exchange 2013 server in the organization, the account you use must be a member of the Exchange 2013 Organization Management role group.

NOTE Administrators who are members of the Delegated Setup group can deploy Exchange 2013 servers that have been previously provisioned by a member of the Organization Management group.

You must apply a cumulative update or service pack by upgrading your Exchange 2013 servers in the required order. First, you upgrade Mailbox servers and then you upgrade Client Access servers. After you install a cumulative update or service pack, you must restart the server so that changes can be made to the registry and operating system.

If something goes wrong with the installation and re-running Setup and following the prompts doesn't help you resolve the problem, you have several options. You can restore the server from backup or you can run Exchange Server 2013 Setup in recovery mode by running **setup /m:RecoverServer** at a command prompt. If you are recovering to a different server, the server must use the same FQDN as the failed server.

When you recover a server, you don't specify the roles to restore. Setup detects the Exchange Server object in Active Directory and installs the corresponding files and configuration automatically. After you recover the server, you can restore databases and reconfigure any additional settings.

Installing a cumulative update or service pack

As discussed previously, a current list of cumulative updates and service packs for Exchange Server 2013 can be found at *http://technet.microsoft.com/en-us/library /jj907309(v=exchg.150).aspx*.

When you are ready to run Setup and install an update, you can begin the installation. If you are installing a new server using a current cumulative update or service pack, follow the procedure as discussed previously under "Installing Exchange Server." Otherwise, to update an existing installation of Exchange 2013, complete the following steps:

1. Log on to the server using an administrator account. When you install the Mailbox and Client Access roles, you must use a domain account that is a member of the Enterprise Administrators group. If you've already prepared Active Directory, this account must also be a member of the Exchange Organization Administrators group.

    IMPORTANT Before beginning setup, you should ensure that the server's Windows PowerShell Script Execution Policy is set to unrestricted. Check the current setting by entering Get-ExecutionPolicy at a PowerShell prompt. Set the execution policy to unrestricted by entering Set-ExecutionPolicy Unrestricted. If you don't modify the execution policy, Exchange Server may not be upgraded properly. Afterward, close any open Windows PowerShell or MMC windows. Otherwise you will see a warning during the readiness checks that you need to close these windows. The installation process makes updates to Windows PowerShell and MMC and requires exclusive access.

    CAUTION If you are applying a cumulative update or service pack to an existing Exchange 2013 server, any customized per-server settings you made in Exchange configuration files will be overwritten. To prevent this, save your customized settings before you run Setup. This will help you easily reconfigure your server after the update.

2. Access the folder where you extracted the Exchange setup files, and then start Exchange 2013 Setup by double-tapping or double-clicking Setup.exe. If you've enabled User Access Control (UAC), you must press and hold or right-click Setup.exe and select Run As Administrator.

3. On the Check For Updates page, you can specify whether to check for updates to the setup process. If you don't want to check for updates, select Don't Check For Updates before you tap or click Next to continue. Setup will then copy files and initialize resources, as shown in Figure 2-9 and Figure 2-10.

    The server also tries to validate the state of Active Directory. If the server is unable to validate the state of Active Directory and choose a domain controller to work with, Setup will log errors and may also report that a domain controller could not be located. If errors are reported, do not continue with the installation. Instead, exit Setup and resolve the communication problem.

FIGURE 2-9 Exchange Server Setup copies files needed for installation to a temporary folder.

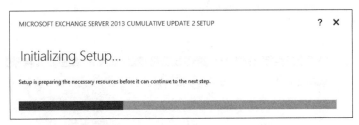

FIGURE 2-10 Exchange Server Setup prepares resources.

4. If you are installing a new server, you'll see the Introduction page. If you are updating an existing server, you'll see the Upgrade page, shown in Figure 2-11. Tap or click Next to continue.

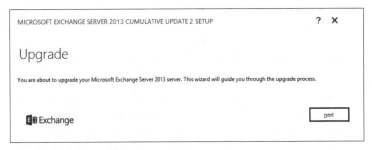

FIGURE 2-11 The Upgrade page.

IMPORTANT Seeing the Upgrade page is a confirmation that Setup identified the existing Exchange 2013 installation on the server. There is a problem if you are applying an update or service pack to a server already running Exchange 2013 and don't see the Upgrade page at this point. You may need to restart the server or resume Exchange services that have been stopped and then re-run Setup.

5. On the License Agreement page, review the software license terms. If you agree to the terms, select I Accept The Terms In The License Agreement, and then tap or click Next.

6. On the Readiness Checks page, shown in Figure 2-12, ensure the prerequisite checks completed successfully. If they haven't, you must resolve any reported errors before you can update Exchange Server 2013. For most errors, you don't need to exit Setup. After resolving a reported error, tap or click Retry to run the prerequisite checks again.

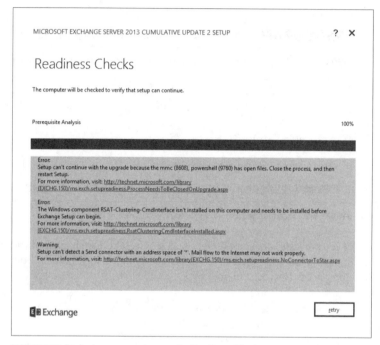

MICROSOFT EXCHANGE SERVER 2013 CUMULATIVE UPDATE 2 SETUP   ? ✕

Readiness Checks

The computer will be checked to verify that setup can continue.

Prerequisite Analysis   100%

Error:
Setup can't continue with the upgrade because the mmc (8608), powershell (9760) has open files. Close the process, and then restart Setup.
For more information, visit: http://technet.microsoft.com/library (EXCHG.150)/ms.exch.setupreadiness.ProcessNeedsToBeClosedOnUpgrade.aspx

Error:
The Windows component RSAT-Clustering-CmdInterface isn't installed on this computer and needs to be installed before Exchange Setup can begin.
For more information, visit: http://technet.microsoft.com/library (EXCHG.150)/ms.exch.setupreadiness.RsatClusteringCmdInterfaceInstalled.aspx

Warning:
Setup can't detect a Send connector with an address space of "*". Mail flow to the Internet may not work properly.
For more information, visit: http://technet.microsoft.com/library(EXCHG.150)/ms.exch.setupreadiness.NoConnectorToStar.aspx

Exchange   retry

FIGURE 2-12 Reviewing any warnings on the Readiness Checks page.

NOTE A cumulative update or service pack may require additional Windows components. For example, Cumulative Update 1 required the Failover Cluster Command Line Interface component be installed. This is a Remote Server Administration Tool component that could be selected on the feature page of the Add Roles And Features Wizard. The component was listed under Remote Server Administration Tools, Feature Administration Tools, Failover Clustering Tools.

7. When all readiness checks have completed successfully, tap or click Install to update Exchange 2013. The installation process should take about 60 minutes.

The Setup Progress page, shown in Figure 2-13, tracks the progress of the installation. The installation is performed in a series of steps, with the progress for the current step tracked with a progress bar and as a percentage of completion. The number of steps varies, depending on the tasks Setup must perform to prepare the environment, as well as the options you selected.

As part of the update, Setup removes existing Exchange files from the installation and then copies new files into the appropriate directories. Finally, you'll see the Setup Completed page, shown in Figure 2-14, when Setup completes the installation.

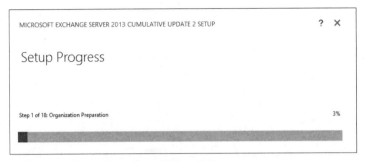

MICROSOFT EXCHANGE SERVER 2013 CUMULATIVE UPDATE 2 SETUP   ?   X

Setup Progress

Step 1 of 18: Organization Preparation   3%

FIGURE 2-13 Tracking the progress of the installation.

MICROSOFT EXCHANGE SERVER 2013 CUMULATIVE UPDATE 2 SETUP   ?   X

Setup Completed

Congratulations! Setup has finished successfully. To complete the installation of Exchange Server 2013, reboot the computer. You can also start the Exchange Administration Center after Setup is finished.

☐   Launch Exchange Administration Center after finishing Exchange setup.

Exchange   finish

FIGURE 2-14 The setup is complete.

You must restart the server to finalize the installation. After you restart the server, you can verify the update using the techniques discussed previously under "Verifying and completing the installation." Because any customized per-server settings in Exchange configuration files are overwritten, you'll need to restore the related files or re-create the customized settings.

Exchange administration essentials

Whether you're using Microsoft Exchange Server 2013 and Exchange Online for the first time or honing your skills, you'll need to master many key concepts to work effectively. You'll need to know the following:

- How to access and work with Exchange Admin Center
- How connections are authenticated and proxied
- How Exchange uses virtual directories
- Why Exchange requires SSL certificates
- Which Windows processes are used with Exchange Server

You also need to know how to bypass Exchange Admin Center and Exchange Management Shell so that you can work directly with Exchange Server. These topics are all covered in this chapter.

Accessing and using Exchange Admin Center

Exchange Admin Center is a browser-based application designed for managing on-premises, online, and hybrid Exchange organizations. You access Exchange Admin Center through the Client Access servers deployed in your Exchange organization. Although the application can be configured with an internal access URL and an external access URL, only an internal access URL is configured by default. This means that by default you can access Exchange Admin Center only when you are on the corporate network.

Accessing Exchange Admin Center

Exchange Admin Center is designed to be used with many operating systems and browsers. However, to ensure all features are available you should use Exchange Admin Center only with the following browser and operating system combinations:

- For Windows 7 and Windows Server 2008 R2 use Internet Explorer 9 or later, Firefox 17 or later, or Chrome 24 or later.
- For Windows 8 or later and Windows Server 2012 RTM or R2 use Internet Explorer 10 or later, Firefox 17 or later, or Chrome 24 or later.
- For Mac OS X 10.5 or later use Firefox 17 or later, Safari 6 or later, or Chrome 24 or later.
- For Linux use Firefox 17 or later, or Chrome 24 or later.

Although Exchange Admin Center replaces Exchange Management Console and Exchange Control Panel (ECP), ECP continues to be the name for the related virtual directory. You access Exchange Admin Center by following these steps:

1. Open your web browser and enter the secure URL for Exchange Admin Center. If you are outside the corporate network, enter the external URL, such as *https://mail.cpandl.com/ecp*. If you are inside the corporate network, enter the internal URL, such as *https://mailserver48/ecp*.

   The version of Exchange Admin Center you see depends on the version of Exchange running on the Mailbox server hosting your personal mailbox. Exchange 2010 runs version 14, and you can specify this version explicitly by appending **?ExchClientVer=14** to the internal or external URL.

   Exchange 2013 runs version 15, and you can specify this version explicitly by appending **?ExchClientVer=15** to the internal or external URL. For example, if your external URL is *https://mail.pocket-consultant.com*, you could enter **https://mail.pocket-consultant.com/ecp?ExchClientVer=15** as the URL.

   NOTE By default, you must use HTTPS to connect. If you don't, you'll see an error stating "Access is denied." Using HTTPS ensures data transmitted between the client browser and the server is encrypted and secured.

2. If your browser displays a security alert stating there's a problem with the site's security certificate or that the connection is untrusted, proceed anyway. This alert is displayed because the browser does not trust the self-signed certificate that was automatically created when the Exchange server was installed.

   - With Internet Explorer, the error states "There's a problem with this website's security certificate." Proceed by selecting the Continue To This Web Site (Not Recommended) link.
   - With Google Chrome, the error states "The site's security certificate is not trusted." Continue by clicking Proceed Anyway.
   - With Mozilla Firefox, the error states "This connection is untrusted." Proceed by selecting I Understand The Risks and then selecting Add Exception. Finally, in the Add Security Exception dialog box, select Confirm Security Exception.

3. You'll see the logon page for Exchange Admin Center. Enter your user name and password, and then tap or click Sign In.

   Be sure to specify your user name in DOMAIN\username format. The domain can either be the DNS domain, such as pocket-consultant.com, or the Net-BIOS domain name, such as pocket-consulta. For example, the user AnneW could specify her logon name as pocket-consultant.com\annew or pocket-consulta\annew.

4. If you are logging on for the first time, select your preferred display language and time zone, and then tap or click Save.

After you log on to Exchange Admin Center, you'll see the list view with manageable features listed in the feature pane (see Figure 3-1). When you select a feature in the feature pane, you'll then see the related topics or "tabs" for that feature. The manageable items for a selected topic or tab are displayed in the main area of the browser window. For example, when you select Recipients in the feature pane, the topics or tabs that you can work with are: Mailboxes, Groups, Resources, Contacts, Shared, and Migration.

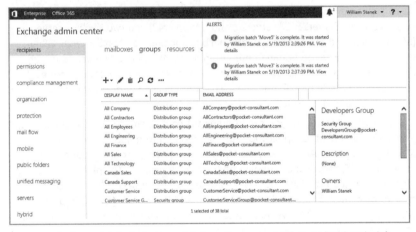

FIGURE 3-1 Exchange Admin Center uses a list view with manageable features listed on the left.

The navigation bar at the top of the window has several important options. You use the Enterprise and Office 365 options for cross-premises navigation. If there are notifications, tapping or clicking the Notification icon displays the notifications as shown in Figure 3-1. The User button shows the currently logged on user. Tapping or clicking the User button allows you to log out or sign in as another user.

Although ECP for Exchange 2010 would return only 500 recipients at a time, Exchange Admin Center doesn't have this limitation since results are paged so that you can go through results one page at a time. Up to 20,000 recipients can be returned in the result set. When working with recipients, you can tap or click More to display options to:

- Add or remove columns
- Export data for the listed recipients to a .csv file
- Perform advanced searches

If you customize the view by adding or removing columns, the settings are saved for the computer that you are using to access Exchange Admin Center. However, because the settings are saved as browser cookies, clearing the browser history will remove the custom settings.

When working with recipients, you typically can select multiple items and perform bulk editing as long as you select like items, such as mailbox users or mail-enabled contacts. Select multiple items using the Shift or Ctrl key and then use bulk editing options in the details pane to bulk edit the selected items.

Authenticating and proxying connections

When you access Exchange Admin Center in a browser, a lot is happening in the background that you don't see. Although you access the application using a specific Client Access server in your organization, Client Access servers themselves only act as front-end proxies. They authenticate and proxy connections for Mailbox servers, and the Mailbox servers perform the actual back-end processing. To understand this process better, consider the following scenario:

You're an administrator for Pocket-consultant.com, which has three Client Access servers (CAServer11, CAServer23, and CAServer42) and two Mailbox servers (MailServer18 and MailServer26). Your mailbox is located on MailServer26. When you log on to Exchange Admin Center using *https://casserver23.pocket-consultant.com/ecp* as the access URL, CAServer23 authenticates your request and proxies the connection to MailServer26. Any administration tasks you perform are processed on MailServer26 and the results are passed back to you via CAServer23.

As shown in Figure 3-2, you can examine the configuration settings for Exchange Admin Center and other applications using Internet Information Services (IIS) Manager. The Client Access server to which you connect processes your remote actions via the ECP application running on the default website. The physical directory for this application is %ExchangeInstallPath%\ClientAccess\Ecp. This application runs in the context of an application pool named MSExchangeECPAppPool. In the %ExchangeInstallPath%\ClientAccess\Ecp directory on your server, you'll find a web.config file that defines the settings for the ECP application.

The Mailbox server where your mailbox resides performs its tasks and processing via the ECP application running on the Exchange Back End website. The physical directory for this application is %ExchangeInstallPath%\ClientAccess\Ecp. This application runs in the context of an application pool named MSExchangeECPAppPool. In the %ExchangeInstallPath%\ClientAccess\Ecp directory on your server, you'll find a web.config file that defines the settings for the ECP application.

Because the Client Access role and the Mailbox role can be installed on the same server, the Client Access server to which you connect and the Mailbox server where your mailbox resides can actually be the same physical server. In this case, the proxying between front-end and back-end services uses the same technique but involves only a single server.

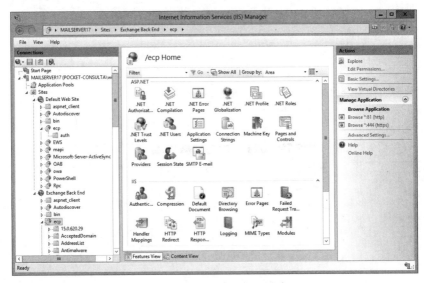

FIGURE 3-2 Viewing the applications that handle Exchange processing.

Working with Exchange Server certificates

When you install an Exchange server, the setup process creates several self-signed security certificates that are used for authentication. The default certificates available depend on whether the server has the Mailbox Server role, the Client Access Server role, or both installed and can include:

- **Microsoft Exchange** A self-signed certificate used by IMAP, POP, IIS, and SMTP. If Autodiscover is configured, this certificate is also used for Autodiscover. This is the primary certificate used by Exchange.

- **Microsoft Server Auth Certificate** A self-signed certificate for authenticating SMTP connections.

- **Exchange Delegation Federation** A self-signed certificate used when federated sharing is configured in the Exchange organization.

- **WMSVC** A self-signed certificate used by the Windows Management service.

As Figure 3-3 shows, you can view these certificates in Exchange Admin Center by selecting Servers in the feature pane and then selecting Certificates. Because the default certificates are not issued by a trusted authority, you see a related error message whenever you use HTTPS to access services hosted by your Client Access servers, including Exchange Admin Center, the PowerShell application, and Microsoft Outlook Web App.

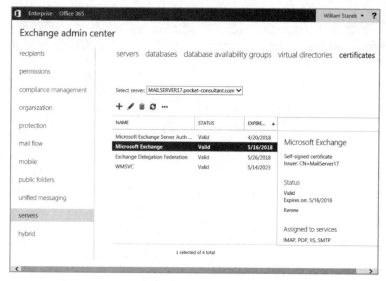

FIGURE 3-3 Viewing the SSL certificates installed on Exchange servers.

The best way to eliminate this error message is to install a certificate from a trusted authority on your Client Access servers. Web browsers should already be configured to trust certificates issued by your organization's certification authority (CA) or by a trusted third-party authority. Typically, browsers need additional configuration only when you use your own CA with non-domain-joined machines.

The services a certificate can be used with include Internet Message Access Protocol (IMAP), Post Office Protocol (POP), SMTP, Internet Information Services (IIS), and Unified Messaging (UM). The default self-signed certificates are assigned services automatically during setup based on the roles installed on the Exchange server.

When you work with certificates, it's critical that you ensure the certificate is used for the right subject name and alternative names. As an example, the Microsoft Exchange certificate created by default has the Subject set as cn=*ServerName*, where *ServerName* is the name of the server, such as cn=MailServer21, and the Subject Alternative Names is set as DNS Name=*ServerName*, DNS NAME=*FullyQualifiedServerName*, and DNS Name=*DomainName*. If Autodiscover is configured, there's also a Subject Alternative Name entry for DNS Name=Autodiscover.*DomainName*. For example, MailServer21 in the Pocket-consultant.com domain means the subject name is set as:

```
cn=MailServer21
```

and the Subject Alternative Name entries typically are:

```
DNS Name = MailServer21
DNS Name = MailServer21.pocket-consultant.com
DNS Name = pocket-consultant.com
DNS Name = Autodiscover.pocket-consultant.com
```

REAL WORLD I caution against using Exchange Admin Center and Exchange Management Shell to work with Exchange certificates. You may prefer instead to access Exchange directly using the technique discussed in "Bypassing Exchange Admin Center and troubleshooting" later in this chapter. Anyone who has experienced problems after remotely managing Exchange certificates may agree—and I also have experienced related issues firsthand on multiple occasions. Specifically, if you modify certificates using either tool, you might find that Outlook Web App (OWA) and Exchange Admin Center are inaccessible as a result of a required SSL certificate becoming corrupted or being invalidated. If this happens, you will need to access Exchange directly and re-create the required certificate or certificates.

One way to safeguard yourself against this problem is to create copies of the original certificates using the Certificates snap-in. When you add this snap-in to a Microsoft Management Console, specify that you want to manage certificates for a computer account. You'll then find the certificates under the Personal node. Export each certificate in turn using the Certificate Export Wizard. To start this wizard, press and hold or right-click a certificate, select All Tasks, and then select Export.

If your organization has a CA, have your security administrator issue a certificate. Generate the certificate by completing the following steps.

1. In a web browser, open Certificate Services by entering the appropriate URL, such as **https://CertServer03/certsrv**.

2. Specify that you want to create a new request and then choose the advanced creation option.

3. Submit a certificate request by using a base 64 encoded PKS #7 or PKS #12 file.

4. Once the certificate request file is generated, open the file in a text editor.

5. While you are working with Certificate Services in your browser, access the request. Copy the contents of the certificate request file and paste them into the request.

6. Select web server as the server type, and leave all other attributes blank.

7. Save the certificate.

After you create the certificate, you must make it available on the designated Exchange server. To do this, access the Exchange server and then import the certificate using Import-ExchangeCertificate. Next, use Enable-ExchangeCertificate to enable the certificate for specific Exchange services.

If you can purchase a certificate from a trusted third-party authority, you also must make the certificate available on the designated Exchange server. To do this, access the Exchange server and then import the certificate using Import-Exchange-Certificate. Next, use Enable-ExchangeCertificate to enable the certificate for specific Exchange services. Finally, ensure that the new certificate is in use and test web services by using Test-OutlookWebServices as shown in the following example:

```
test-outlookwebservices | fl
```

By default Test-OutlookWebServices verifies the Availability service, Autodiscover, Offline Address Book, and Exchange Web Services. You can test Outlook client connectivity and Outlook Anywhere using Test-OutlookConnectivity. You can test connectivity to the Outlook Web App and ECP virtual directories using Test-OwaConnectivity and Test-EcpConnectivity, respectively. However, before you can use any of the Test cmdlets, you must create a test account by running the Scripts\New-TestCasConnectivityUser.ps1 script. You'll find this script in the %ExchangeInstallPath%, which by default is C:\Program Files\Microsoft\Exchange Server\V15\. The password you set for the test account is temporary and will be automatically changed every seven days.

Once you've imported and enabled the certificate, you can then view the certificate in Exchange Admin Center or by using Get-ExchangeCertificate to confirm it is configured as expected. You'll want to ensure the status is valid, the expiration date is appropriate, the subject name is correct, the subject alternative names are correct, and that the assigned services are appropriate.

Configuring Exchange Admin Center

You can configure Exchange Admin Center for single-server and multiserver environments. In a single-server environment, you use one Client Access server for all of your remote management needs. In a multiple-server environment, you can instruct administrators to use different URLs to access different Client Access servers, or you can use Client Access arrays with multiple, load-balanced servers and give all administrators the same access URL.

> **REAL WORLD** If you have multiple Client Access servers in the same Active Directory site, you put them all in the same single CAS array, and then you point to the CAS array. Note that the load balancing performed by the array is automatically for RPC Client Access only. You need to use some other means to load balance the HTTPS requests against the array.

> **NOTE** You can use Exchange Admin Center with firewalls. You configure your network to use a perimeter network with firewalls in front of the designated Client Access servers and then open port 443 to the IP addresses of your Client Access servers. If Secure Sockets Layer (SSL) is enabled and you want to use SSL exclusively, you only need port 443, and you don't need to open port 80.

You can manage the Exchange Admin Center application using Internet Information Services (IIS) Manager or Exchange Management Shell. The related commands for Exchange Management Shell are as follows:

- **Get-ECPVirtualDirectory** Displays information about the ECP application running on the Web server providing services for Exchange. By default only front-end virtual directories are listed. Add -ShowMailboxVirtualDirectories to also display the back-end virtual directories.

  ```
  Get-ECPVirtualDirectory [-Identity AppName]
  [-ADPropertiesOnly <$true | $false>]
  [-ShowMailboxVirtualDirectories <$true | $false>]
  ```

```
[-DomainController DomainControllerName]

Get-ECPVirtualDirectory -Server ExchangeServerName
[-ADPropertiesOnly <$true | $false>]
[-ShowMailboxVirtualDirectories <$true | $false>]
[-DomainController DomainControllerName]
```

- **New-ECPVirtualDirectory** Creates a new ECP application running on the Web server providing services for Exchange. You should use this command only for troubleshooting scenarios where you are required to remove and re-create the ECP virtual directory.

```
New-ECPVirtualDirectory [-AppPoolId AppPoolName]
[-DomainController DomainControllerName] [-ExternalUrl URL]
[-InternalUrl URL] [-WebSiteName SiteName]
```

- **Remove-ECPVirtualDirectory** Use the Remove-ECPVirtualDirectory cmdlet to remove a specified ECP application providing services for Exchange.

```
Remove-ECPVirtualDirectory -Identity AppName
[-DomainController DomainControllerName]
```

- **Set-ECPVirtualDirectory** Modifies the configuration settings for a specified ECP application providing services for Exchange. Set -AdminEnabled to $false to turn off Internet access to the Exchange Admin Center.

```
Set-ECPVirtualDirectory -Identity AppName
[-AdminEnabled <$true | $false>]
[-BasicAuthentication <$true | $false>] [-DomainController
DomainControllerName] [-ExternalAuthenticationMethods Methods]
[-DigestAuthentication <$true | $false>]
[-FormsAuthentication <$true | $false>]
[-ExternalUrl URL] [-GzipLevel <Off | Low | High | Error>]
[-InternalUrl URL] [-LiveIdAuthentication <$true | $false>]
[-WindowsAuthentication <$true | $false>]
```

- **Test-ECPConnectivity** Displays information about the ECP application running on the Web server providing services for Exchange.

```
Test-ECPConnectivity [-ClientAccessServer ServerName]
[-MailboxServer ServerName] [-DomainController DomainControllerName]
[-RTSEndPoint EndPointID] [-TestType <Internal | External>]
[-MonitoringContext <$true | $false>]
[-ResetTestAccountCredentials <$true | $false>]
[-Timeout NumSeconds] [-TrustAnySSLCertificate <$true | $false>]
[-VirtualDirectoryName DirectoryName]
```

At the Exchange Management Shell prompt, you can confirm the location of the Exchange Admin Center application by typing **get-ecpvirtualdirectory**.

Get-ECPVirtualDirectory lists the name of the application, the associated website, and the server on which the application is running, as shown in the following example:

```
Name                           Server
-------                        -------
ecp (Default Web Site)         MailServer18
```

In this example, a standard configuration is being used, on which the application named ECP is running on the Default Web Site on MailServer18. You can use Set-ECPVirtualDirectory to specify the internal and external URL to use as well as the permitted authentication types. Authentication types you can enable or disable include basic authentication, Windows authentication, and Live ID basic authentication. You can use New-ECPVirtualDirectory to create or re-create an ECP application on a Web server providing services for Exchange and Remove-ECPVirtualDirectory to remove an ECP application. You can verify that Exchange Admin Center is working properly using Test-ECPConnectivity.

The PowerShell application has a similar set of commands. In Exchange Management Shell, the related commands are New-PowerShellVirtualDirectory, Get-PowerShellVirtualDirectory, Set-PowerShellVirtualDirectory, and Test-PowerShellConnectivity. If you enter **Get-PowerShellVirtualDirectory | Format-List**, you'll get configuration details for each Client Access server in the Exchange organization. You can use SetPowerShellVirtualDirectory to enable or disable authentication mechanisms, including basic authentication, certificate authentication, Live ID basic authentication, Live ID NTLM negotiate authentication, and Windows authentication. You can also specify the internal and external URLs for the PowerShell virtual directory on a per-server basis. By default, servers have only internal URLs for PowerShell. For troubleshooting issues related to the PowerShell virtual directory, enter **Test-PowerShellConnectivity** followed by the URL to test, such as *https://mailer1.cpandl.com/powershell*.

You'll also find commands for working with virtual directories related to:

- Outlook Web Access, including New-OwaVirtualDirectory, Get-OwaVirtualDirectory, Set-OwaVirtualDirectory, and Remove-OwaVirtualDirectory
- Offline Address Books, including New-OabVirtualDirectory, Get-OabVirtualDirectory, Set-OabVirtualDirectory, and Remove-OabVirtualDirectory
- Autodiscover, including New-AutodiscoverVirtualDirectory, Get-AutodiscoverVirtualDirectory, Set-AutodiscoverVirtualDirectory, and Remove-AutodiscoverVirtualDirectory

Keep in mind that there are separate but interconnected virtual directories on both Client Access servers and Mailbox servers. Typically, front-end virtual directories are used for authentication and proxying while back-end virtual directories are used for actual processing. Although the front-end and back-end virtual directories have different components and configurations, the Exchange cmdlets for creating these virtual directories are designed to configure the appropriate settings and components for either front-end or back-end use as appropriate.

When an Exchange server has both the Client Access server and the Mailbox server role, you should specify explicitly whether you want to work with the front-end or back-end components. You do this by specifying the related website name. The Default Web Site is used by the front-end components and the Exchange Back End website is used by back-end components.

Bypassing Exchange Admin Center and troubleshooting

Exchange makes extensive use of IIS. Client Access servers use IIS for front-end services, such as authentication and proxying, while Mailbox servers use IIS for back-end processing. On Client Access servers, front-end apps for Outlook Web App, ECP, PowerShell, OAB, and Autodiscover apps are configured on the Default Web Site. On Mailbox servers, back-end apps for Outlook Web App, ECP, PowerShell, OAB, and Autodiscover are configured on the Exchange Back End website.

Understanding remote execution in Exchange Admin Center

When you access Outlook Web App in a web browser, you are performing remote operations via the PowerShell application running on the Web server providing Exchange services whether you are logged on locally to an Exchange server or working remotely. The same is true for ECP, but the process is a little more complex, as shown in the following high-level view of the login and workflow process:

1. Generally, Outlook Web App handles the initial login for ECP. Thus, when you access ECP using a URL such as *https://mailserver17/ecp*, the browser actually is redirected to Outlook Web App with a URL such as *https://mailserver17 /owa/auth/logon.aspx?replaceCurrent=1&url=https%3a%2f%2fmailserver17% 2fecp%2f.*

2. Once you log on to Exchange, you are connected to the designated Client Access server using the ECP app running on the Default Web Site.

3. ECP performs authentication checks that validate your access to the Exchange 2013 server and determine the Exchange role groups and roles your account is a member of. You must be a member of at least one management role.

4. ECP creates a remote session with the Exchange 2013 server. A remote session is a runspace that establishes a common working environment for executing commands on remote computers.

5. The ECP app on the Client Access server acts as proxy for the ECP app on the Mailbox server. By default, you are connected to the Mailbox server on which your user mailbox resides.

6. As you perform tasks, these tasks are executed via the PowerShell app, which also has front-end and back-end components.

IMPORTANT Every step of the login and workflow process relies on properly configured SSL certificates. HTTPS uses SSL certificates to establish and encrypt connections. SSL certificates are also used to initialize and validate remote sessions. Although you could disable the requirement for HTTPS and allow HTTP to be used for connections, the remote sessions themselves would still rely on properly configured SSL certificates.

Thus, many interconnected components must be functioning correctly for you to connect to and work with Exchange Server.

Bypassing Exchange Admin Center and Exchange Management Shell

As discussed in Chapter 4, "Using Exchange Management Shell," the Exchange Management Shell uses remote sessions that run via the PowerShell application running on IIS. Because of this, you often need a way to work directly with Exchange Server, especially when you are trying to diagnose and resolve problems. Intuitively, you might think that you should do this in the same way you establish a remote session with Exchange Online. For example, if you want to connect to MailServer18, you might want to use the following code:

```
$Session = New-PSSession -ConfigurationName Microsoft.Exchange
-ConnectionUri https://mailserver18/powershell/ -Authentication Basic
-Credential wrstanek@pocket-consultant.com -AllowRedirection

Import-PSSession $Session
```

However, if there are any configuration problems, including issues with SSL certificates, you won't be able to connect to or work with Exchange Server in this way. Instead, you'll have to bypass the web-based management interfaces and connect directly to an Exchange server using the following technique:

1. Log on to the Client Access server or Mailbox server you want to work with—either at the console or using a remote desktop connection.

2. Open an administrative PowerShell window by pressing and holding or right-clicking Windows PowerShell and then tapping or clicking Run As Administrator.

3. Import all Exchange-related snapins for Windows PowerShell by entering **Add-PSSnapin *exchange***. You'll then be able to work directly with Exchange and any related cmdlets.

Because Exchange has a two-tier architecture, you'll often need to perform troubleshooting tasks on both the front-end Client Access servers and back-end Mailbox servers. Rather than log on locally to each server, you may want to work remotely. You can invoke commands, establish direct remote sessions, or execute commands remotely using the -ComputerName parameter available with certain cmdlets. (For more information, see Chapter 4, "Using Sessions, Jobs, and Remoting" in *Windows PowerShell 2.0 Administrator's Pocket Consultant [Microsoft Press, 2009]*).

To invoke commands on remote servers or establish a direct remote session, use the following technique:

1. Log on to any workstation or server where you've installed the Exchange management tools. (Doing so ensures the Exchange related snap-ins are available.)

2. Open an administrative PowerShell window by pressing and holding or right-clicking Windows PowerShell, and then tapping or clicking Run As Administrator.

3. Import all Exchange-related snapins for Windows PowerShell by entering **Add-PSSnapin *exchange***.

4. Either invoke commands on the remote Exchange server or establish a remote session with the remote Exchange server. In your remote sessions, be sure to connect directly, as shown in the following example:

```
$Session = New-PSSession -computername mailserver18
-Credential pocket-consulta\williams

Import-PSSession $Session
```

IMPORTANT When you work with Exchange in this way, you establish connections via the Windows Remote Management (WinRM) service. On an Exchange server, WinRM and related services are set up automatically. On your management computer, you need to install the required components and configure WinRM as discussed previously in "Using Exchange Management Shell" in Chapter 1, "Exchange Server 2013 administration overview." See also "Customizing remote management services" later in this chapter.

Troubleshooting Outlook Web App, ECP, PowerShell, and More

Sometimes users and administrators see a blank page or an error when they try to log on to Outlook Web App or ECP. This problem and other connection issues, such as those related to OAB, Autodiscover, and PowerShell, can occur because of a wide variety of configuration issues, including:

- Invalid or missing TCP/IP settings
- Corrupted or improperly configured virtual directories
- Missing, expired, invalid, or improperly configured SSL certificates

However, before you look at specific issues, ensure required services are running as discussed in "Checking required services" later in this chapter. Be sure to examine the running services on both the front-end and back-end servers.

Typically, the next logical step is to validate the TCP/IP settings of the front-end and back-end servers. Not only do front-end and back-end servers need to communicate with each other, they also need to communicate with domain controllers.

If Exchange Server can't communicate properly with a domain controller, you may see an error similar to the following when you open Exchange Admin Center or Exchange Management Shell:

```
The LDAP server is unavailable.
Description: An unhandled exception occurred during the execution of the
current web request. Please review the stack trace for more information
about the error and where it originated in the code.

Exception Details: System.DirectoryServices.Protocols.LdapException: The
LDAP server is unavailable.

Source Error:
```

An unhandled exception was generated during the execution of the current web request. Information regarding the origin and location of the exception can be identified using the exception stack trace below.

Stack Trace:

```
[LdapException: The LDAP server is unavailable.]
   System.DirectoryServices.Protocols.LdapConnection.Connect() +160015
   System.DirectoryServices.Protocols.LdapConnection.BindHelper
(NetworkCredential newCredential, Boolean needSetCredential) +264
   Microsoft.Exchange.Data.Directory.PooledLdapConnection.BindWithRetry
(Int32 maxRetries) +702
```

Resolve the problem by doing the following:

- Ensure the server has the proper TCP/IP settings and is connected to the network.
- Ensure a domain controller is available for the server to communicate with.

Users or administrators may see a blank page when they try to log on to Outlook Web App or ECP as a result of a configuration or certificate problem. If you've determined that required services are running and that the TCP/IP settings are correct, next try to isolate and identify the specific issue.

Try to log on to Outlook Web App or ECP in a browser. Sometimes when you log on to Outlook Web App or ECP, you'll see a runtime error that indicates an improperly configured virtual directory or an application error due to misconfiguration in IIS (see Figure 3-4). Other times, the browser window may simply be empty or blank as mentioned previously.

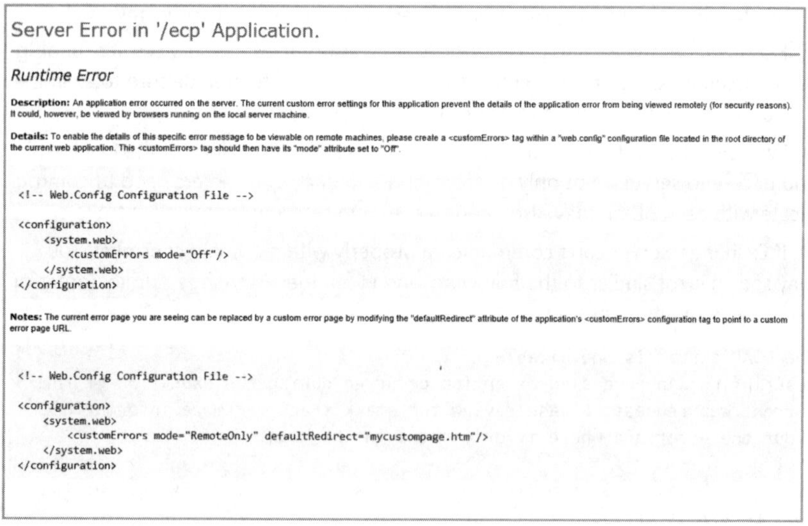

Server Error in '/ecp' Application.

Runtime Error

Description: An application error occurred on the server. The current custom error settings for this application prevent the details of the application error from being viewed remotely (for security reasons). It could, however, be viewed by browsers running on the local server machine.

Details: To enable the details of this specific error message to be viewable on remote machines, please create a <customErrors> tag within a "web.config" configuration file located in the root directory of the current web application. This <customErrors> tag should then have its "mode" attribute set to "Off".

```
<!-- Web.Config Configuration File -->

<configuration>
    <system.web>
        <customErrors mode="Off"/>
    </system.web>
</configuration>
```

Notes: The current error page you are seeing can be replaced by a custom error page by modifying the "defaultRedirect" attribute of the application's <customErrors> configuration tag to point to a custom error page URL.

```
<!-- Web.Config Configuration File -->

<configuration>
    <system.web>
        <customErrors mode="RemoteOnly" defaultRedirect="mycustompage.htm"/>
    </system.web>
</configuration>
```

FIGURE 3-4 A runtime or application error can indicate an improperly configured virtual directory or a misconfiguration in IIS.

For deeper troubleshooting, log on to the Client Access server where the problem is occurring and open Exchange Management Shell. Next, try to log on to the Mailbox server hosting the mailbox for the users or administrators experiencing the problem and open Exchange Management Shell. If there's a problem with SSL certificates rather than virtual directory configuration, you'll see an error similar to the following:

```
New-PSSession : [mailserver17] Connecting to remote server mailserver17
failed with the following error message : The server certificate on the
destination computer (mailserver17:443) has the following errors:
The SSL certificate is signed by an unknown certificate authority. For more
information, see the about_Remote_Troubleshooting Help topic.
At line:1 char:12
+ $Session = New-PSSession -ConfigurationName Microsoft.Exchange
-ConnectionUri ht ...
+ ~~~~~~~~~~~~~~~~~~~~~~~~~~~~~~~~~~~~~~~~~~~~~~~~~~~~~~~~~~~~~~~~~~~~~~
~~~~~~~~~~~~~~~~
    + CategoryInfo          : OpenError
 (System.Manageme....RemoteRunspace:RemoteRunspace) [New-PSSession],
PSRemotingTransportException
    + FullyQualifiedErrorId : 12175,PSSessionOpenFailed
```

If there's a problem with virtual directory configuration, you may see another type of error, such as:

```
New-PSSession : [mailserver17.pocket-consultant.com] Processing data from
remote server mailserver17.pocket-consultant.com failed with the following
error message: The WinRM Shell client cannot process the request. The shell
handle passed to the WSMan Shell function is not valid. The shell handle is
valid only when WSManCreateShell function completes successfully. Change
 the request including a valid shell handle and try again. For more
information, see the about_Remote_Troubleshooting Help topic.
At line:1 char:1
+ New-PSSession -ConnectionURI "$connectionUri" -ConfigurationName
Microsoft.Excha ... + ~~~~~~~~~~~~~~~~~~~~~~~~~~~~~~~~~~~~~~~~~~~~~~~~~~~~~~
~~~~~~~~~~~~~~~~~~~~~~~~~~~~~~
    + CategoryInfo          : OpenError:
 (System.Manageme....RemoteRunspace:RemoteRunspace) [New-PSSession],
PSRemotingTransportException
 + FullyQualifiedErrorId : -2144108212,PSSessionOpenFailed
```

To help diagnose the problem, you can test services using Test-OutlookWebServices. By default, Test-OutlookWebServices verifies the Availability service, Outlook Anywhere, Offline Address Book, and Unified Messaging. You can test Outlook Web App, ECP, and PowerShell using Test-OwaConnectivity, Test-EcpConnectivity, and Test-PowerShellConnectivity respectively.

Resolving SSL certificate issues

To resolve a certificate issue, you'll need to restore or re-create the primary SSL certificate on the Client Access server, the Mailbox server, or both. By default, the self-signed certificate named Microsoft Exchange is the certificate used for authentication and encrypting communications whenever you use Outlook Web App, ECP, or the management tools to work with Exchange. If you backed up the certificates on the server or exported the certificates as discussed previously in this chapter in "Working with Exchange Server certificates," you can restore the original certificate to restore services.

If you don't have a backup or an export of the primary SSL certificate, you'll need to re-create the certificate. You can create a new self-signed certificate using New-ExchangeCertificate. The following example shows how to configure services, the subject name, and subject alternative names for MailServer21 in the Pocket-Consultant.com domain:

```
New-ExchangeCertificate -SubjectName "cn=MailServer21"
-DomainName pocket-consultant.com -IncludeServerFQDN
-Services IIS, IMAP, POP, SMTP
```

> **IMPORTANT**   If there's a problem preventing you from using Exchange Admin Center and Exchange Management Shell, you'll need to bypass the web-based management interfaces and connect directly to Exchange Server using the technique discussed earlier in the chapter.

With certificates issued by a local CA or a third-party CA, you can use the original certificate file. Import the certificate using Import-ExchangeCertificate and then use Enable-ExchangeCertificate to enable the certificate for IIS, IMAP, POP, and SMTP services. You can ensure that the certificate is in use and test services as discussed previously.

Resolving Outlook Web App, ECP, or other virtual directory issues

To resolve a virtual directory issue, you can remove and then re-create the virtual directory. You won't always know whether the problem exists in the front-end configuration, the back-end configuration, or both, so you may need to remove and re-create the virtual directory on the related Client Access server and the related Mailbox server. I recommend removing and re-creating the front-end virtual directory first and then checking to see if this resolves the problem before removing and re-creating the back-end virtual directory.

As an example, if you've determined the Outlook Web App virtual directory is misconfigured, you can remove it using Remove-OwaVirtualDirectory and then re-create it using New-OwaVirtualDirectory. For example, the following commands remove and then re-create the Outlook Web App virtual directory from the Default Web Site on MailServer17:

```
remove-owavirtualdirectory -identity "mailserver17\owa (Default Web Site)"

new-owavirtualdirectory -server mailserver17
-websitename "Default Web Site"
```

IMPORTANT Keep in mind that if there's a problem preventing you from using Exchange Admin Center and Exchange Management Shell, you'll need to bypass the web-based management interfaces and connect directly to Exchange Server using the technique discussed earlier in the chapter. You'll then be able to remove the virtual directory and then re-create it. When you are logged on to the server you are configuring, you don't need to use the -Server parameter with New-OwaVirtualDirectory.

By default, the New-OwaVirtualDirectory and New-EcpVirtualDirectory commands enable basic authentication and forms authentication but do not enable Windows authentication. Because Windows authentication is required for Outlook Web App and ECP, you must use the commands Set-OwaVirtualDirectory and Set-EcpVirtualDirectory to modify the default authentication settings. The following example enables Windows authentication and disables basic and forms authentication:

```
set-owavirtualdirectory -identity "mailserver17\owa (Default Web Site)"
-WindowsAuthentication $True -Basicauthentication $false
-Formsauthentication $false
```

After you re-create a virtual directory you should restart IIS services. You can do this in IIS Manager or by entering the following command at an elevated command prompt or shell:

```
iisreset
```

You can then test the service using Test-OwaConnectivity, or you can try to log on to Outlook Web App. If this doesn't resolve the problem, you can remove, re-create, and configure the Outlook Web App virtual directory on the back-end server, as shown in this example:

```
remove-owavirtualdirectory -identity "mailserver21\owa (Exchange Back End)"

new-owavirtualdirectory -server mailserver21
-websitename "Exchange Back End"

set-owavirtualdirectory -identity "mailserver21\owa (Exchange Back End)"
-WindowsAuthentication $True -Basicauthentication $false
-Formsauthentication $false
```

Complete the process by restarting IIS services and then check to ensure the problem is resolved. If the problem isn't resolved, look to related services. For example, remote PowerShell must be properly configured for Outlook Web App and ECP to work. If you suspect the PowerShell virtual directory is misconfigured, you can remove and re-create it as well.

Validating Exchange Server licensing

With Exchange Server 2013, you do not enter a product key during initial setup. Instead, you provide the product key after installation using Exchange Admin Center. Until you enter a product key, Exchange Server 2013 runs in trial mode.

The product key you provide determines which edition is established on an Exchange server. You can use a valid product key to go from a trial edition to Standard Edition or Enterprise Edition of Exchange Server 2013 without having to reinstall the program.

To determine the established edition and licensing for an Exchange server complete the following steps:

1. In Exchange Admin Center, select Servers in the feature pane.
2. In the main pane, select the server you want to work with.
3. Look in the details pane to see the server roles, version, established edition, and license details.

To enter a product key complete the following steps:

1. In Exchange Admin Center, select Servers in the feature pane.
2. In the main pane, select the server you want to work with.
3. In the details pane, select Enter Product Key. This opens the Exchange Server dialog box.
4. Enter the product key for the Exchange Server 2013 edition you want to establish, either Standard or Enterprise, and then tap or click Save.

> **NOTE** The product key is a 25-character alphanumeric string, grouped in sets of five characters separated by hyphens. You can find the product key on the Exchange Server 2013 media or license.

5. You should see a dialog box stating the product key has been validated and the product ID has been created. If there's a problem with the product key, you'll see an invalid key warning. Tap or click OK. Re-enter or correct the product key and then tap or click Save again. Keep the following in mind:

   - Whenever you set or change the product key on a Mailbox server, you must restart the Microsoft Exchange Information Store service to apply the change.
   - While you can upgrade from Standard to Enterprise edition simply by entering a key for Enterprise edition, you cannot use product keys to downgrade editions. To downgrade editions, you must uninstall Exchange Server and then reinstall the older version.

Using Exchange Management Shell, you can enter a server's product key using the Set-ExchangeServer cmdlet. Sample 3-1 shows the syntax and usage. For the identity parameter, use the server's name, such as MailServer25.

SAMPLE 3-1 Setting the Exchange product key syntax and usage

Syntax

```
Set-ExchangeServer -Identity 'ServerName'
-ProductKey 'ProductKey'
```

Usage

```
Set-ExchangeServer -Identity 'MailServer25'
-ProductKey 'AAAAA-BBBBB-CCCCC-DDDDD-EEEEE'
```

TIP By using a valid product key, you can change from the Standard to the Enterprise edition. You also can relicense an Exchange server by entering a new product key for the installed edition, which is useful if you accidentally used the same product key on multiple servers and want to correct the mistake. The best way to do this is to enter the product key using the Set-ExchangeServer cmdlet.

Using and managing Exchange services

Each Exchange server in the organization relies on a set of services for routing messages, processing transactions, replicating data, and much more. Table 1-1 in Chapter 1, "Exchange Server 2013 administration overview" lists these services.

TIP Of all the Exchange services, the one service that relies on having a network connection at startup is the Microsoft Exchange Information Store service. If you start an Exchange server and the server doesn't have a network connection, the Microsoft Exchange Information Store service might fail to start. As a result, you might have to manually start the service. Sometimes, you'll find the service has a Stopping state. In this case, you have to wait until the server completely stops the service before you restart it.

Working with Exchange services

To manage Exchange services, use the Services node in the Computer Management console, which you start by completing the following steps:

1. Type **compmgmt** in the Apps Search box, and then select Computer Management. Or, on the Tools menu in Server Manager, select Computer Management.

2. To connect to a remote Exchange server, press and hold or right-click the Computer Management entry in the console tree, and then select Connect To Another Computer from the shortcut menu. You can now choose the Exchange server for which you want to manage services.

3. Expand the Services And Applications node, and then select Services.

Figure 3-5 shows the Services view in the Computer Management console. The key fields of this window are as follows:

- **Name** The name of the service.
- **Description** A short description of the service and its purpose.
- **Status** The status of the service as started, paused, or stopped. (Stopped is indicated by a blank entry.)
- **Startup Type** The startup setting for the service.

NOTE Automatic services are started when the computer is started. Manual services are started by users or other services. Disabled services are turned off and can't be started. To start a disabled service, you must first enable it and then start it.

- **Log On As** The account the service logs on as. The default, in most cases, is the local system account.

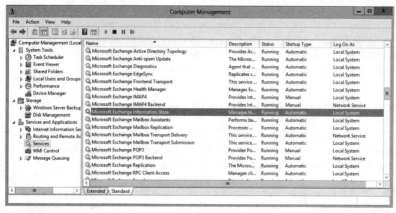

FIGURE 3-5 Using the Services node of the Computer Management console to manage Exchange Server services.

Checking required services

You can use Test-ServiceHealth to determine whether all Windows services that Exchange requires are running. As shown in the following example and sample output, the command output lists required services that are running as well as required services that aren't running for each configured Exchange role:

```
test-servicehealth
```

```
Role                     : Mailbox Server Role
RequiredServicesRunning  : True
ServicesRunning          : {IISAdmin, MSExchangeADTopology,
MSExchangeDelivery, MSExchangeIS, MSExchangeMailboxAssistants,
MSExchangeRepl, MSExchangeRPC, MSExchangeServiceHost,
MSExchangeSubmission, MSExchangeThrottling, MSExchangeTransportLogSearch,
W3Svc, WinRM}
ServicesNotRunning       : {}


Role                     : Client Access Server Role
RequiredServicesRunning  : True
ServicesRunning          : {IISAdmin, MSExchangeADTopology, MSExchangeIMAP4,
MSExchangeMailboxReplication, MSExchangePOP3, MSExchangeRPC,
MSExchangeServiceHost, W3Svc, WinRM}
ServicesNotRunning       : {}


Role                     : Unified Messaging Server Role
RequiredServicesRunning  : True
ServicesRunning          : {IISAdmin, MSExchangeADTopology,
MSExchangeServiceHost, MSExchangeUM, W3Svc, WinRM}
ServicesNotRunning       : {}
```

```
Role                    : Hub Transport Server Role
RequiredServicesRunning : True
ServicesRunning         : {IISAdmin, MSExchangeADTopology,
MSExchangeEdgeSync, MSExchangeServiceHost,
MSExchangeTransport, MSExchangeTransportLogSearch, W3Svc, WinRM}
ServicesNotRunning      : {}
```

NOTE If there's a problem preventing you from using Exchange Admin Center and Exchange Management Shell, you'll need to bypass the web-based management interfaces and connect directly to Exchange Server using the technique discussed earlier in the chapter.

Starting, stopping, and pausing Exchange Server services

As an administrator, you'll often have to start, stop, or pause Exchange services. You manage Exchange services through the Computer Management console or through the Services console.

To start, stop, or pause services in the Computer Management console, follow these steps:

1. If necessary, connect to the remote Exchange server for which you want to manage services, as discussed earlier in this section.

2. Expand the Services And Applications node, and then select Services.

3. Press and hold or right-click the service you want to manipulate, and then select Start, Stop, or Pause, as appropriate. You can also choose Restart to have Windows stop and then start the service after a brief pause. Also, if you pause a service, use the Resume option to resume normal operation.

TIP When services that are set to start automatically fail, the status is listed as blank, and you usually receive notification in a pop-up window. Service failures can also be logged to the system's event logs. You can configure recovery actions to handle service failure automatically. For example, you can have Windows attempt to restart the service for you. See the section of this chapter titled "Configuring service recovery" for details.

Configuring service startup

Essential Exchange services are configured to start automatically and normally shouldn't be configured with another startup option. That said, if you're troubleshooting a problem, you might want a service to start manually or you might want to temporarily disable a service.

Configure service startup by completing the following steps:

1. In the Computer Management console, connect to the Exchange server for which you want to manage services.

2. Expand the Services And Applications node, and then select Services.

3. Press and hold or right-click the service you want to configure, and then select Properties.

4. On the General tab, use the Startup Type drop-down list to choose a startup option. Select Automatic to start a service when the computer starts. Select Manual to allow services to be started manually. Select Disabled to disable the service. Tap or click OK.

> **NOTE** The Disabled option doesn't stop the service if it's currently running. It just prevents the service from starting the next time you start the server. To stop the service, you must tap or click Stop.

Configuring service recovery

You can configure Windows services to take specific actions when a service fails. For example, you can attempt to restart the service or reboot the server. To configure recovery options for a service, follow these steps:

1. In the Computer Management console, connect to the computer for which you want to manage services.

2. Expand the Services And Applications node, and then select Services.

3. Press and hold or right-click the service you want to configure, and then select Properties.

4. On the Recovery tab, you can configure recovery options for the first, second, and subsequent recovery attempts. The available options are as follows:

    - Take No Action
    - Restart The Service
    - Run A Program
    - Restart The Computer

5. Configure other options based on your previously selected recovery options. If you elected to restart the service, you need to specify the restart delay. After stopping the service, Windows Server waits for the specified delay period before trying to start the service. In most cases, a delay of one to two minutes should be sufficient. Tap or click OK.

When you configure recovery options for critical services, you might try to restart the service on the first and second attempts and then reboot the server on the third attempt. If you notice that a service keeps failing, do some troubleshooting to diagnose and resolve the underlying issue causing the failure.

Customizing Remote Management services

The Exchange management tools use the Microsoft .NET Framework, Windows Remote Management (WinRM), and Windows PowerShell for remote management. WinRM is implemented in the Windows Remote Management service, which is also referred to as the WS-Management Service or simply the Management Service. To remotely manage Exchange, your management computer must run this service and be configured to use the transports, ports, and authentication methods that your Exchange servers use. The Exchange server you want to connect to must also run this service. If this service isn't running on your management computer and on the server, remote connections will fail. For remote management, you normally connect to the PowerShell virtual directory configured in IIS on a Client Access server.

By default, the Management Service connects to and listens on TCP port 80 for HTTP connections and on TCP port 443 for secure HTTP connections. Because firewalls and proxy servers might affect your ability to connect to remote locations over these ports, talk with your company's network or security administrator to determine what steps need to be taken to allow administration over these ports. Typically, the network/security administrator will have to open these TCP ports to allow remote communication between your computer or network and the remote server or network.

The Management Service is preconfigured to share ports with IIS when it runs on the same computer, but it does not depend on IIS. To support remote management, you need to install basic authentication and Windows authentication for IIS on your Exchange servers. These authentication techniques are used when you work remotely.

When you are working with an elevated, administrator command prompt, you can use the WinRM command-line utility to view and manage the remote management configuration. Type **winrm get winrm/config** to display detailed information about the remote management configuration. As Listing 3-1 shows, this lists the configuration details for every aspect of WinRM.

LISTING 3-1 Sample configuration for WinRM

```
Config
    MaxEnvelopeSizekb = 150
    MaxTimeoutms = 60000
    MaxBatchItems = 32000
    MaxProviderRequests = 4294967295
    Client
        NetworkDelayms = 5000
        URLPrefix = wsman
        AllowUnencrypted = false
        Auth
            Basic = true
            Digest = true
            Kerberos = true
            Negotiate = true
            Certificate = true
            CredSSP = false
        DefaultPorts
            HTTP = 80
            HTTPS = 443
        TrustedHosts = CorpServer65
    Service
        RootSDDL = O:NSG:BAD:P(A;;GA;;;BA)S:P(AU;FA;GA;;;WD)(AU;SA;GWGX)
        MaxConcurrentOperations = 4294967295
        EnumerationTimeoutms = 60000
        MaxConnections = 25
        MaxPacketRetrievalTimeSeconds = 120
        AllowUnencrypted = false
```

```
Auth
    Basic = false
    Kerberos = true
    Negotiate = true
    Certificate = false
    CredSSP = false
    CbtHardeningLevel = Relaxed
DefaultPorts
    HTTP = 80
    HTTPS = 443
IPv4Filter = *
IPv6Filter = *
CertificateThumbprint
Winrs
    AllowRemoteShellAccess = true
    IdleTimeout = 180000
    MaxConcurrentUsers = 5
    MaxShellRunTime = 2147483647
    MaxProcessesPerShell = 15
    MaxMemoryPerShellMB = 150
    MaxShellsPerUser = 5
```

If you examine the listing, you'll notice there is a hierarchy of information. The base of this hierarchy, the Config level, is referenced with the path winrm/config. Then there are sublevels for client, service, and WinRS, referenced as winrm/config/client, winrm/config/service, and winrm/config/winrs, respectively. You can change the value of most configuration parameters by using the following command:

```
winrm set ConfigPath @{ParameterName="Value"}
```

where *ConfigPath* is the configuration path, *ParameterName* is the name of the parameter you want to work with, and *Value* sets the value for the parameter, such as:

```
winrm set winrm/config/winrs @{MaxShellsPerUser="4"}
```

In this example, the MaxShellsPerUser parameter is set under WinRM/Config/WinRS. Keep in mind that some parameters are read-only and cannot be set in this way.

WinRM requires at least one listener to indicate the transports and IP addresses on which management requests can be accepted. The transport must be HTTP, HTTPS, or both. With HTTP, messages can be encrypted only using NTLM or Kerberos encryption. With HTTPS, Secure Sockets Layer (SSL) is used for encryption. You can examine the configured listeners by typing **winrm enumerate winrm/config/ listener**. As Listing 3-2 shows, this lists the configuration details for configured listeners.

LISTING 3-2 Sample configuration for listeners

```
Listener
    Address = *
    Transport = HTTP
    Port = 80
    Hostname
```

```
Enabled = true
URLPrefix = wsman
CertificateThumbprint
ListeningOn = 127.0.0.1, 192.168.1.225
```

By default, your computer is likely to be configured to listen on any IP address. If so, you won't see any output. To limit WinRM to specific IP addresses, the computer's local loopback address (127.0.01) and assigned IPv4 and IPv6 addresses can be explicitly configured for listening. You can configure a computer to listen for requests on HTTP on all configured IP addresses by typing:

```
winrm create winrm/config/listener?Address=*+Transport=HTTP
```

You can listen for requests on HTTPS on all IP addresses configured on the computer by typing:

```
winrm create winrm/config/listener?Address=*+Transport=HTTPS
```

In this case, the * indicates all configured IP addresses. Note that the CertificateThumbprint property must be empty for the SSL configuration to be shared with another service.

You can enable or disable a listener for a specific IP address by typing:

```
winrm set winrm/config/listener?Address=IP:192.168.1.225+Transport=HTTP @
{Enabled="true"}
```

or

```
winrm set winrm/config/listener?Address=IP:192.168.1.225+Transport=HTTP @
{Enabled="false"}
```

You can enable or disable basic authentication on the client by typing:

```
winrm set winrm/config/client/auth @{Basic="true"}
```

or

```
winrm set winrm/config/client/auth @{Basic="false"}
```

You can enable or disable Windows authentication using either NTLM or Kerberos (as appropriate) by typing:

```
winrm set winrm/config/client @{TrustedHosts="<local>"}
```

or

```
winrm set winrm/config/client @{TrustedHosts=""}
```

In addition to managing WinRM at the command line, you can manage the service by using Group Policy. Keep in mind that Group Policy settings might override any other settings you enter.

CHAPTER 4

Using Exchange Management Shell

- Using Windows PowerShell   **97**
- Working with cmdlets   **103**
- Working with Exchange Management Shell   **108**
- Using a manual remote shell to work with Exchange   **122**

Microsoft Exchange Server 2013 includes Exchange Management Shell to complement the expanding role of Exchange Server administrators and developers. Exchange Management Shell is an extensible command-line environment for Exchange Server that builds on the existing framework provided by Windows PowerShell. When you install Exchange Server 2013 on a server, or when you install the Exchange Server management tools on a workstation, you install Exchange Management Shell as part of the process. This chapter introduces Windows PowerShell and its features and then details the available commands and options of Exchange Management Shell, which has changed considerably from its earlier implementations.

Using Windows PowerShell

Anyone with a UNIX background is probably familiar with the concept of a command shell. Most UNIX-based operating systems have several full-featured command shells available, such as C Shell and Bourne Shell (SH). Although Microsoft Windows operating systems have always had a command-line environment, they've lacked a full-featured command shell until Windows PowerShell was introduced.

Introducing Windows PowerShell

Not unlike the less sophisticated Windows command prompt, the UNIX command shells operate by executing built-in commands, external commands, and command-line utilities and then returning the results in an output stream as text. The output stream can be manipulated in various ways, including redirecting the output stream so that it can be used as input for another command. This process of redirecting one command's output to another command's input is called *piping*, and it is a widely used shell-scripting technique.

C Shell is one of the more sophisticated UNIX shells. In many respects, C Shell is a marriage of some of the best features of the C programming language and a full-featured UNIX shell environment. Windows PowerShell takes the idea of a full-featured command shell built on a programming language a step further. It does this by implementing a scripting language based on C# and an object model based on the Microsoft .NET Framework.

Basing the scripting language for Windows PowerShell on C# ensures that the scripting language can be easily understood by current C# developers and also allows new developers who work with PowerShell to advance to C#. Using an object model based on the .NET Framework allows Windows PowerShell to pass complete objects and all their properties as output from one command to another. The ability to redirect objects is extremely powerful and allows for a much more dynamic manipulation of a result set. For example, not only can you get the name of a particular user, but you can also get the entire related user object. You can then manipulate the properties of this user object as necessary by referring to the properties you want to work with by name.

Running and using Windows PowerShell

Windows PowerShell is built into Windows 8, Windows Server 2012, and later releases of the Windows operating system. Windows PowerShell has both a command-line environment and a graphical environment for running commands and scripts. The PowerShell console (powershell.exe) is available as a 32-bit or 64-bit environment for working with PowerShell at the command line. On 32-bit versions of Windows, you'll find the 32-bit executable in the %SystemRoot%\System32\WindowsPowerShell\v1.0 directory. On 64-bit versions of Windows, you'll find the 32-bit executable in the %SystemRoot%\SysWow64\WindowsPowerShell\v1.0 directory and the 64-bit executable in the %SystemRoot%\System32\WindowsPowerShell\v1.0 directory.

With Windows 8 or later and Windows Server 2012 RTM or R2, you can start the PowerShell console by using the Apps Search box. Type **powershell** in the Apps Search box, and then press Enter. Or you can tap or click Start and then choose Windows PowerShell. With Windows 7 and Windows Server 2008 R2, you can start Exchange Management Shell by tapping or clicking Start, pointing to All Programs, tapping or clicking Microsoft Exchange Server 2013, and then tapping or clicking Exchange Management Shell.

> **IMPORTANT** Exchange 2013 is optimized for 64-bit interfaces, and the related management tools can be run only on 64-bit versions of Windows. On 64-bit systems, the 64-bit version of PowerShell is started by default and the 32-bit PowerShell console is labeled as Windows PowerShell (x86). Don't use Windows PowerShell (x86) when working with Exchange 2013 from your management computer.

You can start Windows PowerShell from a Windows command shell (cmd.exe) by typing **powershell**. To exit Windows PowerShell and return to the command prompt, type **exit**. However, if you start Windows PowerShell from within a 32-bit command shell, the 32-bit Windows PowerShell console will be started—and that will cause problems when working with Exchange 2013. The 64-bit command shell is stored in the %SystemRoot%\System32 directory. The 32-bit command shell is stored in the %SystemRoot%\SysWow64 directory.

Usually, when the shell starts, you will see a message similar to the following:

```
Windows PowerShell
Copyright (C) 2012 Microsoft Corporation. All rights reserved.
```

You can disable this message by starting the shell with the -Nologo parameter, such as:

```
powershell -nologo
```

Figure 4-1 shows a PowerShell window. Typically, the window is 120 characters wide and displays 50 lines of text by default. When additional text is to be displayed in the window or you enter commands and the PowerShell console's window is full, the current text is displayed in the window and prior text is scrolled up. If you want to pause the display temporarily when a command is writing output, press Ctrl+S. Afterward, press Ctrl+S to resume or Ctrl+C to terminate execution.

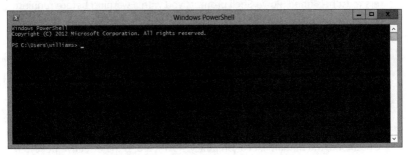

FIGURE 4-1 Working with Windows PowerShell.

When you start Windows PowerShell, the working environment is loaded automatically. Many features of the working environment come from profiles, which are a type of script that run when you start PowerShell. However, the working environment is also determined by imported modules, snap-ins, providers, command paths, file extensions, and file associations.

You can start Windows PowerShell without loading profiles using the -Noprofile parameter, such as:

```
powershell -noprofile
```

Whenever you work with scripts, you need to keep in mind the current execution policy and whether signed scripts are required. Execution policy controls whether and how you can run configuration files and scripts. Execution policy is a built-in security feature of Windows PowerShell that is set on a per-user basis in the Windows registry. Although the default configuration depends on which operating system and edition are installed, you can quickly determine the execution policy by typing **get-executionpolicy** at the PowerShell prompt.

The available execution policies, from least secure to most secure, are:

- **Bypass**   This policy bypasses warnings and prompts when scripts run. It is intended for use with programs that have their own security model or when a PowerShell script is built into a larger application.

- **Unrestricted**   This policy allows all configuration files and scripts to run whether they are from local or remote sources and regardless of whether they are signed or unsigned. However, if you run a configuration file or script from a remote resource, you are prompted with a warning that the file comes from a remote resource before the configuration file is loaded or the script runs.

- **RemoteSigned**   This policy requires all configuration files and scripts from remote sources to be signed by a trusted publisher. Configuration files and scripts on the local computer do not need to be signed. PowerShell does not prompt you with a warning before running scripts from trusted publishers.

- **AllSigned**   This policy requires all configuration files and scripts from all sources—whether local or remote—to be signed by a trusted publisher. Because of this requirement, configuration files and scripts on the local computer must be signed as configuration files, and scripts from remote computers must be signed. PowerShell prompts you with a warning before running scripts from trusted publishers.

- **Restricted**   This policy prevents PowerShell from loading configuration files and scripts. This means all configuration files and scripts, regardless of whether they are signed or unsigned. Because a profile is a type of script, profiles are not loaded either.

- **Undefined**   This policy removes the execution policy that is set for the current user scope. As a result, the execution policy set in Group Policy or for the LocalMachine scope is effective. If execution policy in all scopes is set to Undefined, the default execution policy, Restricted, is the effective policy.

IMPORTANT   By default, when you set execution policy, you are using the LocalMachine scope, which affects all users of the computer. You also can set the scope to CurrentUser so that the execution policy level is applied only to the currently logged on user.

You can use the Set-ExecutionPolicy cmdlet to change the preference for the execution policy. Changes to the policy are written to the registry. However, if the Turn On Script Execution setting in Group Policy is enabled for the computer or user, the user preference is written to the registry, but it is not effective, and Windows PowerShell displays a message explaining the conflict. You cannot use Set-ExecutionPolicy to override a group policy, even if the user preference is more restrictive than the policy setting.

To set the execution policy to require that all scripts have a trusted signature to execute, type the following command:

```
set-executionpolicy allsigned
```

To set the execution policy so that scripts downloaded from the web execute only if they are signed by a trusted source, type:

```
set-executionpolicy remotesigned
```

To set the execution policy to run scripts regardless of whether they have a digital signature and work in an unrestricted environment, type the following command:

```
set-executionpolicy unrestricted
```

The change occurs immediately and is applied to the local console or application session. Because the change is written to the registry, the new execution policy will be used whenever you work with PowerShell.

Running and using cmdlets

Windows PowerShell introduces the concept of a cmdlet (pronounced *commandlet*). A cmdlet is the smallest unit of functionality in Windows PowerShell. You can think of a cmdlet as a built-in command. Rather than being highly complex, most cmdlets are quite simple and have a small set of associated properties.

You use cmdlets the same way you use any other commands and utilities. Cmdlet names are not case sensitive. This means you can use a combination of both uppercase and lowercase characters. After starting Windows PowerShell, you can type the name of the cmdlet at the prompt, and it will run in much the same way as a command-line command.

For ease of reference, cmdlets are named using verb-noun pairs. As Table 4-1 shows, the verb tells you what the cmdlet does in general. The noun tells you what specifically the cmdlet works with. For example, the Get-Variable cmdlet gets a named Windows PowerShell environment variable and returns its value. If you don't specify which variable to get as a parameter, Get-Variable returns a list of all Windows PowerShell environment variables and their values.

TABLE 4-1 Common verbs associated with cmdlets and their meanings

CMDLET VERB	USAGE
Add	Adds an instance of an item, such as a history entry or snap-in
Clear	Removes the contents of an item, such as an event log or variable value
New	Creates a new instance of an item, such as a new mailbox
Remove	Removes an instance of an item, such as a mailbox
Enable	Enables a setting or mail-enables a recipient
Disable	Disables an enabled setting or mail-disables a recipient
Set	Modifies specific settings of an object
Get	Queries a specific object or a subset of a type of object, such as a specified mailbox or all mailbox users

You can work with cmdlets in several ways:

- Executing commands directly at the shell prompt
- Running commands from scripts
- Calling them from C# or other .NET Framework languages

You can enter any command or cmdlet you can run at the Windows PowerShell command prompt into a script by copying the related command text to a file and saving the file with the .ps1 extension. You can then run the script in the same way you would any other command or cmdlet.

> **NOTE** Windows PowerShell also includes a rich scripting language and allows the use of standard language constructs for looping, conditional execution, flow control, and variable assignment. Discussion of these features is beyond the scope of this book. A good resource is *Windows PowerShell 2.0 Administrator's Pocket Consultant* (Microsoft Press, 2009).

From the Windows command-line environment or a batch script, you can execute Windows PowerShell cmdlets with the -Command parameter. Typically, when you do this, you also want to suppress the Windows PowerShell logo and stop execution of profiles. After doing this, you can type the following command at a command prompt or insert it into a .BAT script:

```
powershell -nologo -noprofile -command get-service
```

Finally, when you are working with Windows PowerShell, the current directory is not part of the environment path in most instances. Because of this, you typically need to use "./" when you run a script in the current directory, such as:

```
./runtasks
```

Running and using other commands and utilities

Because Windows PowerShell runs within the context of the Windows command prompt, you can run all Windows command-line commands, utilities, and graphical applications from within Windows PowerShell. However, remember that the Windows PowerShell interpreter parses all commands before passing off the command to the command prompt environment. If Windows PowerShell has a like-named command or a like-named alias for a command, this command, and not the expected Windows command, is executed. (See the "Using cmdlet aliases" section later in this chapter for more information on aliases.)

Non–Windows PowerShell commands and programs must reside in a directory that is part of the PATH environment variable. If the item is found in the path, it is run. The PATH variable also controls where the Windows PowerShell looks for applications, utilities, and scripts. In Windows PowerShell, you can work with Windows environment variables using $env. To view the current settings for the PATH environment variable, type **$env:path**. To add a directory to this variable, use the following syntax:

```
$env:path += ";DirectoryPathToAdd"
```

where *DirectoryPathToAdd* is the directory path you want to add to the path, such as:

```
$env:path += ";C:\Scripts"
```

To have this directory added to the path every time you start Windows PowerShell, you can add the command line as an entry in your profile. Profiles store frequently used elements, including aliases and functions. Generally speaking, profiles are always loaded when you work with Windows PowerShell. Keep in mind that cmdlets are like built-in commands rather than standalone executables. Because of this, they are not affected by the PATH environment variable.

Working with cmdlets

Cmdlets provide the basic foundation for working with a computer from within the Windows PowerShell. Although there are many different cmdlets with many different available uses, cmdlets all have common features, which I'll examine in this section.

Using Windows PowerShell cmdlets

At the Windows PowerShell prompt, you can get a complete list of cmdlets available by typing **get-command**. However, the output lists both cmdlets and functions by name and definition. For cmdlets, the definition provided is the syntax, but the full syntax rarely fits on the line. A better way to get information about cmdlets is to use Get-Help.

If you type **get-help *-***, you get a list of all cmdlets, including a synopsis that summarizes the purpose of the cmdlet—which is much more useful than a list of commands. To get help documentation on a specific cmdlet, type **get-help** followed by the cmdlet name, such as:

```
get-help get-variable
```

Windows PowerShell uses online and updatable help files. Because of this, you may see only basic syntax for cmdlets and functions. To get full help details, you'll have to either use online help or download the help files to your computer. For online help, add the -online option to your get-help command, such as:

```
get-help get-variable -online
```

Use the Update-Help cmdlet to download and install the current help files from the Internet. Without parameters, Update-Help updates the help files for all modules installed on the computer. However, Update-Help:

- Downloads files only once a day
- Installs files only when they are newer than the ones on the computer
- Limits the total size of uncompressed help files to 1 GB

You can override these restrictions using the -Force parameter. Table 4-2 provides a list of cmdlets you'll commonly use for administration. Although many other cmdlets are available, these are the ones you're likely to use the most.

TABLE 4-2 Cmdlets commonly used for administration

CMDLET NAME	DESCRIPTION
Add-Computer, Remove-Computer, Stop-Computer, Restart-Computer	Adds or removes domain membership or stops or restarts a computer
Add-JobTrigger, Get-JobTrigger, New-JobTrigger, Set-JobTrigger	Cmdlets for adding, getting, creating, and setting triggers for scheduled jobs.
Checkpoint-Computer, Restore-Computer	Creates a system restore checkpoint for a computer, or restores a computer from a checkpoint
Compare-Object, Group-Object, Sort-Object, Select-Object, New-Object	Cmdlets for comparing, grouping, sorting, selecting, and creating objects
Connect-PSSession, Disconnect-PSSession	Connects or disconnects of PowerShell remote session.
ConvertFrom-SecureString, ConvertTo-SecureString	Cmdlets for creating or exporting secure strings
Get-Alias, New-Alias, Set-Alias, Export-Alias, Import-Alias	Cmdlets for getting, creating, setting, exporting, and importing aliases
Get-AuthenticodeSignature, Set-AuthenticodeSignature	Cmdlets for getting or setting the signature object associated with a file
Get-Command, Invoke-Command, Measure-Command, Trace-Command	Cmdlets for getting information about cmdlets, invoking commands, measuring the run time of commands, and tracing commands
Get-Counter	Gets performance counter data
Get-Credential	Gets a credential object based on a password
Get-Date, Set-Date	Gets or sets the current date and time
Get-EventLog, Write-EventLog, Clear-EventLog	Gets events, writes events, or clears events in an event log
Get-ExecutionPolicy, Set-ExecutionPolicy	Gets or sets the effective execution policy for the current shell
Get-Host	Gets information about the PowerShell host application
Get-HotFix	Gets the Quick Fix Engineering (QFE) updates that have been applied to a computer
Get-Location, Set-Location	Displays or sets the current working location

CMDLET NAME	DESCRIPTION
Get-Process, Start-Process, Stop-Process	Gets, starts, or stops processes on a computer
Get-PSDrive, New-PSDrive, Remove-PSDrive	Gets, creates, or removes a specified PowerShell drive
Get-ScheduledJob, Disable-ScheduledJob, Enable-ScheduledJob, Set-ScheduledJob	Cmdlets for getting, disabling, enabling, and setting scheduled jobs
Get-Service, New-Service, Set-Service	Gets, creates, or sets system services
Get-Variable, New-Variable, Set-Variable, Remove-Variable, Clear-Variable	Cmdlets for getting, creating, setting, and removing variables as well as for clearing variable values
Import-Counter, Export-Counter	Imports or exports performance counter log files
New-EventLog, Remove-EventLog, Limit-EventLog	Creates or removes a custom event log and event source, or sets the size and age limits for an event log
Read-Host, Write-Host, Clear-Host	Reads input from, writes output to, or clears the host window
Reset-ComputerMachinePassword	Changes and resets the machine account password that the computer uses to authenticate in a domain
Show-EventLog	Displays a computer's event logs in Event Viewer
Start-Sleep	Suspends shell or script activity for the specified period
Stop-Service, Start-Service, Suspend-Service, Resume-Service, Restart-Service	Cmdlets for stopping, starting, suspending, resuming, and restarting system services
Wait-Process	Waits for a process to be stopped before accepting input
Write-Output	Writes an object to the pipeline
Write-Warning	Displays a warning message

Using cmdlet parameters

All cmdlet parameters are designated with an initial dash (-). To reduce the amount of typing required, some parameters are position-sensitive, so you can sometimes pass parameters in a specific order without having to specify the parameter name.

For example, with Get-Service, you don't have to specify the -Name parameter, you can simply type:

```
get-service ServiceName
```

where *ServiceName* is the name of the service you want to examine, such as:

```
get-service MSExchangeIS
```

This command line returns the status of the Microsoft Exchange Information Store service. Because you can use wildcards, such as *, with name values, you can also type **get-service mse*** to return the status of all Microsoft Exchange–related services.

All cmdlets support the common set of parameters listed in Table 4-3. However, to use these parameters, you must run the cmdlet in such a way that these parameters are returned as part of the result set.

TABLE 4-3 Common cmdlet parameters

PARAMETER NAME	DESCRIPTION
Confirm	Pauses processes and requires the user to acknowledge the action before continuing. Cmdlets beginning with *Remove* and *Disable* have this parameter.
Debug	Provides programming-level debugging information about the operation.
ErrorAction	Controls the command behavior when an error occurs.
ErrorVariable	Sets the name of the variable (in addition to the standard error) in which to place objects for which an error has occurred.
OutBuffer	Sets the output buffer for the cmdlet.
OutVariable	Sets the name of the variable in which to place output objects.
Verbose	Provides detailed information about the operation.
WarningAction	Determines how a cmdlet responds to a warning message. Valid values are SilentlyContinue (suppress the warning and continue), Continue (display the warning and continue), Inquire (display the warning and prompt to confirm before continuing), and Stop (display the warning and halt execution). The default value is Continue.
WarningVariable	Sets the name of the variable (in addition to the standard error) in which to store warnings that have occurred.
WhatIf	Allows the user to view what would happen if a cmdlet were run with a specific set of parameters. Cmdlets beginning with Remove and Disable have this parameter.

Understanding cmdlet errors

When you work with cmdlets, you'll encounter two standard types of errors:

- **Terminating errors** Errors that halt execution
- **Nonterminating errors** Errors that cause error output to be returned but do not halt execution

With both types of errors, you'll typically see error text that can help you resolve the problem that caused it. For example, an expected file might be missing or you might not have sufficient permissions to perform a specified task.

Using cmdlet aliases

For ease of use, Windows PowerShell lets you create aliases for cmdlets. An alias is an abbreviation for a cmdlet that acts as a shortcut for executing the cmdlet. For example, you can use the alias *gsv* instead of the cmdlet name Get-Service.

Table 4-4 provides a list of commonly used default aliases. Although there are many other aliases, these are the ones you'll use most frequently.

TABLE 4-4 Commonly used cmdlet aliases

ALIAS	CMDLET
clear, cls	Clear-Host
Diff	Compare-Object
cp, copy	Copy-Item
Epal	Export-Alias
Epcsv	Export-Csv
Foreach	ForEach-Object
Fl	Format-List
Ft	Format-Table
Fw	Format-Wide
Gal	Get-Alias
ls, dir	Get-ChildItem
Gcm	Get-Command
cat, type	Get-Content
h, history	Get-History
gl, pwd	Get-Location
gps, ps	Get-Process
Gsv	Get-Service
Gv	Get-Variable

ALIAS	CMDLET
Group	Group-Object
Ipal	Import-Alias
Ipcsv	Import-Csv
R	Invoke-History
Ni	New-Item
Mount	New-PSDrive
Nv	New-Variable
rd, rm, rmdir, del, erase	Remove-Item
Rv	Remove-Variable
Sal	Set-Alias
sl, cd, chdir	Set-Location
sv, set	Set-Variable
Sort	Sort-Object
Sasv	Start-Service
Sleep	Start-Sleep
spps, kill	Stop-Process
Spsv	Stop-Service
write, echo	Write-Output

You can define additional aliases using the Set-Alias cmdlet. The syntax is:

```
set-alias aliasName cmdletName
```

where *aliasName* is the alias you want to use and *cmdletName* is the cmdlet for which you are creating an alias. The following example creates a "go" alias for the Get-Process cmdlet:

```
set-alias go get-process
```

To use your custom aliases whenever you work with Windows PowerShell, enter the related command line in your profile.

Working with Exchange Management Shell

Exchange Management Shell is a command-line management interface built on Windows PowerShell. You use Exchange Management Shell to manage any aspect of an Exchange Server 2013 configuration that you can manage in Exchange Admin Center. This means that you can typically use either tool to configure Exchange Server 2013. However, only Exchange Management Shell has the full complement of available commands, and this means that some tasks can be performed only at the shell prompt.

Running and using Exchange Management Shell

After you've installed the Exchange management tools on a computer, you can start to use Exchange Management Shell and the following techniques:

- With Windows 8 or later and Windows Server 2012 or later, you can start Exchange Management Shell by using the Apps Search box. Type **shell** in the Apps Search box, and then select Exchange Management Shell. Or tap or click Start and then choose Exchange Management Shell.

- With Windows 7 and Windows Server 2008 R2, you can start Exchange Management Shell by clicking Start, pointing to All Programs, clicking Microsoft Exchange Server 2013, and then clicking Exchange Management Shell.

Exchange Management Shell is designed to be run only on domain-joined computers. Whether you are logged on locally to an Exchange server or working remotely, this opens a custom Windows PowerShell console. The console does the following:

1. Connects to the closest Exchange 2013 server using Windows Remote Management (WinRM).

2. Performs authentication checks that validate your access to the Exchange 2013 server and determine the Exchange role groups and roles your account is a member of. You must be a member of at least one management role.

3. Creates a remote session with the Exchange 2013 server. A remote session is a runspace that establishes a common working environment for executing commands on remote computers.

Selecting the shell in this way starts Exchange Management Shell using your user credentials. This enables you to perform any administrative tasks allowed for your user account and in accordance with the Exchange role groups and management roles you're assigned. As a result, you don't need to run Exchange Management Shell in elevated, administrator mode, but you can. To do so, press and hold or right-click Exchange Management Shell, and then tap or click Run As Administrator.

If you examine the properties of the shortcut that starts the Exchange Management Shell, you'll see the actual command that runs when you start the shell is:

```
C:\Windows\System32\WindowsPowerShell\v1.0\powershell.exe -noexit -command
". 'C:\Program Files\Microsoft\Exchange Server\V15\bin\RemoteExchange.ps1';
Connect-ExchangeServer -auto -ClientApplication:ManagementShell "
```

As you can see, the command starts PowerShell, runs the RemoteExchange.ps1 profile file, and then uses the command Connect-ExchangeServer to establish the remote session. Note the parameters passed in for Connect-ExchangeServer. The -ClientApplication parameter specifies that client-side application is Exchange Management Shell. The -Auto parameter tells the cmdlet to automatically discover and try to connect to an appropriate Exchange 2013 server. Discovery works like this:

1. When you run the command on an Exchange 2013 server, the local server is tried first.

2. Next, the command tries to connect to a Client Access server in the current Active Directory site.

3. Finally, the command tries to connect to a Mailbox server in the current Active Directory site.

4. If no server is available, the command exits.

The RemoteExchange.ps1 profile file sets aliases, initializes Exchange global variables, and loads .NET assemblies for Exchange. It also modifies the standard PowerShell prompt so that it is scoped to the entire Active Directory forest and defines the following Exchange-specific functions:

- **Functions**   Allows you to list all available functions by typing **functions**.

- **Get-Exbanner**   Displays the Exchange Management Shell startup banner whenever you type **get-exbanner**.

- **Get-Exblog**   Opens Internet Explorer and accesses the Exchange blog at Microsoft whenever you type **get-exblog**.

- **Get-Excommand**   Allows you to list all available Exchange commands by typing **get-excommand**.

- **Get-Pscommand**   Allows you to list all available PowerShell commands by typing **get-pscommand**.

- **Get-Tip**   Displays the tip of the day whenever you type **get-tip**.

- **Quickref**   Opens Internet Explorer and allows you to download the Exchange Management Shell quick start guide whenever you type **quickref**.

The RemoteExchange.ps1 profile loads the ConnectFunctions.ps1 script, which defines a number of functions that enable AutoDiscover and Connect features. The functions include the following:

- Connect-ExchangeServer
- CreateOrGetExchangeSession
- Discover-EcpVirtualDirectoryForEmc
- Discover-ExchangeServer
- _AutoDiscoverAndConnect
- _CheckServicesStarted
- _ConnectToAnyServer
- _GetCAFEServers
- _GetCASServers
- _GetCurrentVersionServers
- _GetExchangeServersInSite
- _GetHostFqdn
- _GetHubMailboxUMServers
- _GetLocalForest
- _GetServerFqdnFromNetworkAddress
- _GetSites
- _GetWebServiceServers

- _GetURL
- _NewExchangeRunSpace
- _OpenExchangeRunSpace
- _PrintUsageAndQuit
- _SelectVdir

These functions are available for you to use whenever you work with Exchange Management Shell or have loaded the ConnectFunctions.ps1 script. However, only Connect-ExchangeServer, CreateOrGetExchangeSession, Discover-EcpVirtual-DirectoryForEmc and Discover-ExchangeServer are meant to be called directly. The other functions are helper functions.

When you are working with Exchange Management Shell or have run Connect-Functions.ps1, you can view the source for a function by typing **functions** followed by the name of the function, such as **functions connect-exchangeserver**.

If you want to access Exchange features from a manual remote shell (as discussed later in this chapter under "Using a manual remote shell to work with Exchange") or within scripts, you need to load the RemoteExchange.ps1 profile file. You can find an example of the command required to do this by viewing the properties of the shortcut for Exchange Management Shell. In the Properties dialog box, the Target text is selected by default. Press Ctrl+C to copy this text so that you can use it. For example, if you copy the Target text and paste it into an elevated command prompt (cmd.exe), you can access Exchange Management Shell and work with Exchange Server. If you copy the Target text and paste it into a script, you can be sure that the manual remote session is established when you run the script.

You also can customize the way Exchange Management Shell is initialized by editing the shortcut properties or by copying the shortcut that starts Exchange Management Shell and then editing the properties. With Windows 8 or later and Windows Server 2012 or later, one way to create a new shortcut for Exchange Management Shell is to do the following:

1. If an Exchange Management Shell shortcut is not pinned to the desktop taskbar, open the Start screen. Next, right-click Exchange Management Shell and then select Pin To Taskbar.

2. On the desktop, right-click the taskbar shortcut for Exchange Management Shell. This displays the Tasks dialog box.

3. In the Tasks dialog box, right-click Exchange Management Shell and then select Properties. This opens the Properties dialog box for the shortcut with the Shortcut tab selected.

4. Click in the Target box. The text should be selected automatically so you can copy it in the next step. If the text isn't selected, press Ctrl+A to select all of the related text.

5. Press Ctrl+C to copy the selected text and then click OK to close the Properties dialog box.

6. Right-click an open area of the desktop, select New, and then select Shortcut. This opens the Create Shortcut dialog box.

7. In the Create Shortcut dialog box, click in the Type The Location Of The Item box and then press Ctrl+V to paste the previously selected text.

8. Click Next. Type a name for the shortcut, such as Custom EMC. Click Finish to create the shortcut.

9. Run the shortcut with your custom options by double-clicking it on the desktop.

An extra command must always be added to the Target text. This additional command is Connect-ExchangeServer, a command enabled when the Connect-Functions.ps1 script runs. To customize the initialization of remote sessions, other parameters are available:

- **-ClearCache** A troubleshooting option that allows you to clear registry entries and exported modules and then re-create the registry settings and import modules. After you clear the cache, you can try to connect again using options you need.

  ```
  connect-exchangeserver -clearcache
  ```

- **-Forest** Allows you to specify a single part name or the fully qualified domain name (FQDN) of the Active Directory forest in which to perform discovery. You must be able to authenticate in the forest. User credentials you provide for the -Username parameter are not used for discovery. Use with -Auto.

  ```
  connect-exchangeserver -auto -forest ForestName
  ```

- **-Prompt** Prompts you for the FQDN of the Exchange server to connect to. If you use -Prompt with -Auto, you are prompted only if PowerShell cannot connect automatically. If you use -Prompt with -ServerFqdn, you are prompted only if PowerShell cannot connect to the specified server.

  ```
  connect-exchangeserver -auto -prompt
  ```

- **-ServerFqdn** Allows you to specify the FQDN of the Exchange server to connect to.

  ```
  connect-exchangeserver -serverfqdn ExServerFQDN
  ```

- **-Username** Allows you to specify the user name to use for authentication. You will be prompted for the user's password. You can also pass in a Credential object. Use with -ServerFqdn or -Auto.

  ```
  connect-exchangeserver -serverfqdn ExServerFQDN
  -username UserName
  ```

REAL WORLD When you are working with some cmdlets and objects in PowerShell, you might need to specify a credential for authentication. To do this, use Get-Credential to obtain a Credential object and save the result in a variable for later use. Consider the following example:

```
$cred = get-credential
```

PowerShell reads this command, prompts you for a user name and password, and then stores the credentials provided in the *$cred* variable. You also can specify that you want the credentials for a specific user in a specific domain. The following example requests the credentials for the ExAdmin account in the Pocket-Consultant.com domain:

```
$cred = get-credential -credential pocket-consulta\exadmin
```

A Credential object has UserName and Password properties that you can work with. Although the user name is stored as a regular string, the password is stored as a secure, encrypted string. Simply pass in the credential instead of the user name as shown in this example:

```
$cred = get-credential -credential pocket-consulta\exadmin
get-hotfix -credential $cred -computername mailserver18
```

IMPORTANT When you prompt for credentials, integrated Windows authentication is used for authentication. However, if the credentials are not set when prompted, such as when the user selects Cancel, Kerberos authentication is used with the user's default credentials.

REAL WORLD Where a domain name is required for credentials, you typically can use either the NET BIOS domain name or the DNS domain name. In the previous examples, I entered the NET BIOS domain name **pocket-consulta** rather than the DNS name **pocket-consultant.com**.

When you call Connect-ExchangeServer, the function does one of two things: It opens a remote session by using implicit credentials (the credentials of the user who is running Exchange Management Shell) or by using specified credentials (credentials you've explicitly provided). One of the final things Connect-ExchangeServer does is call _OpenExchangeRunSpace, which in turn calls _NewExchangeRunspace to establish the remote session.

In the script, the core code for _OpenExchangeRunSpace is:

```
$global:remoteSession = _NewExchangeRunspace $fqdn $credential $UseWIA
$SuppressError $ClientApplication $AllowRedirection
```

And the core code for _NewExchangeRunspace is:

```
$so = New-PSSessionOption -OperationTimeout $sessionOptionsTimeout
-IdleTimeout $sessionOptionsTimeout -OpenTimeout $sessionOptionsTimeout;

New-PSSession -ConnectionURI "$connectionUri" -ConfigurationName
Microsoft.Exchange -SessionOption $so
```

The code sample creates a global variable named *$remoteSession* to hold the remote session. A global variable is used to ensure that the session remains active and available when the script exits. The session is established using New-PSSession with a connection URI for a particular Exchange server. For example, if the Exchange server's FQDN is MailServer15.Cpandl.com, the connection URI is *https://mailserver15.cpandl.com/powershell*. The -ConfigurationName parameter sets the configuration namespace as Microsoft.Exchange (in place of the default Microsoft.PowerShell). The -SessionOption parameter sets session options that were defined previously using the New-PSSessionOption cmdlet. The session options include the operation timeout value, the idle timeout value, and the open session timeout value. By default, all three are set to 180,000 milliseconds (180 seconds) via the *$sessionOptionsTimeout* variable defined in the first section of the ConnectFunctions.ps1 script.

You can use the *MsExchEmsTimeout* environment variable to set the default time-out values. If you set this environment variable to a value of 900,000 milliseconds or less (15 minutes or less), the timeouts are set accordingly. If you set this environment variable to a value greater than 900,000 milliseconds, the timeout values revert to the 3-minute default value.

REAL WORLD When you connect to Exchange Admin Center in a browser, the browser version determines your experience level, and the location of your mailbox determines whether you see the console for Exchange 2007, Exchange 2010, or Exchange 2013. This is not the case when you are working with the shell. With the shell, the experience level is always set to FULL. Further, the HKLM:\SOFTWARE\ Microsoft\ExchangeServer\v15\Setup key in the registry is examined to determine the Exchange version and the build number, and then this information is used to set the client version compatibility level. Thus, a precise connection URI is set as *http://$fqdn /powershell?serializationLevel=Full;ExchClientVer=$clientVersion*.

Managing the PowerShell application

Microsoft Internet Information Services (IIS) handles every incoming request to a website within the context of a web application. A web application is a software program that delivers web content to users over HTTP or HTTPS. Each website has a default web application and one or more additional web applications associated with it. The default web application handles incoming requests that aren't assigned to other web applications. Additional web applications handle incoming requests that specifically reference a particular application.

When you connect to a server using a URL, such as *https://mailserver15.cpandl. com/powershell*, you are performing remote operations via the PowerShell appli-cation running on the web server providing Exchange services. Like all web ap-plications, the PowerShell application has a virtual directory associated with it. The virtual directory sets the application name and maps the application to the physical directory that contains the application's content.

You can manage the PowerShell application using IIS Manager GUI and Exchange Management Shell. The related commands for Exchange Management Shell are:

- **Get-PowerShellVirtualDirectory** Displays information about the Power-Shell application running on the web server providing services for Exchange.

```
Get-PowerShellVirtualDirectory [-Identity 'AppName']
[-DomainController 'DomainControllerName']
```

```
Get-PowerShellVirtualDirectory -Server 'ExchangeServerName'
[-DomainController 'DomainControllerName']
```

- **New-PowerShellVirtualDirectory**   Creates a new PowerShell application running on the web server providing services for Exchange.

```
New-PowerShellVirtualDirectory -Name 'AppName'
[-AppPoolId 'AppPoolName'] [-BasicAuthentication <$true | $false>]
[-CertificateAuthentication <$true | $false>] [-DomainController
'DomainControllerName'] [-ExternalUrl 'URL'] [-InternalUrl 'URL']
[-Path 'PhysicalDirectoryPath']
[-WindowsAuthentication <$true | $false>]
```

- **Remove-PowerShellVirtualDirectory**   Removes a specified PowerShell application running on the web server providing services for Exchange.

```
Remove-PowerShellVirtualDirectory -Identity 'AppName'
[-DomainController 'DomainControllerName']
```

- **Set-PowerShellVirtualDirectory**   Modifies the configuration settings for a specified PowerShell application running on the web server providing services for Exchange.

```
Set-PowerShellVirtualDirectory -Identity 'AppName'
[-BasicAuthentication <$true | $false>] [-CertificateAuthentication
<$true | $false>] [-DomainController 'DomainControllerName']
[-ExternalUrl 'URL'] [-InternalUrl 'URL']
[-LiveIdBasicAuthentication <$true | $false>]
[-WindowsAuthentication <$true | $false>]
```

At the Exchange Management Shell prompt, you can confirm the location of the PowerShell application by typing **get-powershellvirtualdirectory**.

GetPowerShellVirtualDirectory lists the name of the application, the associated directory and website, and the server on which the application is running, as shown in the following example:

```
Name                            Server
-------                         -------
PowerShell (Default Web Site)   CorpServer45
```

In this example, a standard configuration is being used where the application named *PowerShell* is running on Default Web Site on CorpServer45. You can use Set-PowerShellVirtualDirectory to specify the internal and external URL to use as well as the permitted authentication types. Authentication types you can enable or disable include basic authentication, Windows authentication, certificate authentication, and Live ID basic authentication. You can use New-PowerShellVirtualDirectory to create a new PowerShell application on the web server providing services for Exchange and Remove-PowerShellVirtualDirectory to remove a PowerShell application.

REAL WORLD Any change you make to the PowerShell virtual directory configuration requires careful pre-planning. For every potential change, you'll need to determine whether you need to modify the WinRM configuration and the PowerShell path in ConnectFunctions.ps1 scripts on management computers and Exchange servers, as well as the specific changes you'll need to make with regard to IIS on your Client Access servers.

Microsoft cautions against modifying the default configuration for the PowerShell virtual directory because any mistakes you make could prevent you from managing Exchange Server. Because Exchange configuration data is stored in Active Directory and the affected IIS metabase, you would need to be able to restore Exchange data in Active Directory and the affected IIS metabase to a previous state to recover.

Customizing Exchange Management Shell

Now that you know how the Exchange Management Shell environment works, you can more easily customize the shell to work the way you want it to. One way to do this is to modify the menu shortcut that starts Exchange Management Shell or create copies of this menu shortcut to change the way Exchange Management Shell starts. For example, if you want to connect to a named Exchange server rather than any available Exchange server, you can do the following:

1. In the Properties dialog box for the shortcut that starts Exchange Management Shell, the Target text is selected by default. Press the right arrow key to move to the end of the command text.

2. Delete -Auto and type **-ServerFqdn** followed by the FQDN of the Exchange server, such as **-ServerFQDN MailServer12.Cpandl.com**. Tap or click OK.

That said, this entire sequence of tasks is meant to simplify the task of establishing an interactive remote session with a single Exchange server. As implemented in the default configuration, you have a one-to-one, interactive approach for remote management, meaning you establish a session with a specific remote server and work with that specific server simply by executing commands.

When you are working with PowerShell outside of Exchange Management Shell, you might want to use the Enter-PSSession cmdlet to start an interactive session with an Exchange server or any other remote computer. The basic syntax is Enter-PSSession *ComputerName*, where *ComputerName* is the name of the remote computer, such as the following:

```
enter-pssession mailserver15
```

After you enter this command, the command prompt changes to show that you are connected to the remote computer, as shown in the following example:

```
[MailServer15]: PS C:\Users\wrstanek.cpandl\Documents>
```

Now, the commands that you type run on the remote computer just as if you had typed them directly on the remote computer. In most cases, you need to ensure you are running an elevated, administrator shell and that you pass credentials along in the session. When you connect to a server in this way, you use the standard PowerShell remoting configuration and do not go through the PowerShell application running on a web server. You can end the interactive session by using the command Exit-PSSession or typing **exit**.

To access an Exchange server in the same way as the ConnectFunctions.ps1 script, you need to use the -ConnectionURI parameter to specify the connection URI, the -ConfigurationName parameter to specify the configuration namespace, the -Authentication parameter to set the authentication type to use, and optionally, the -SessionOption parameter to set session options. Consider the following example:

```
enter-pssession -connectionURI http://mailserver12.cpandl.com/powershell
-ConfigurationName Microsoft.Exchange -Authentication Kerberos
```

Here, you set the connection URI as https://mailserver12.cpandl.com/powershell, set the configuration namespace as Microsoft.Exchange, and use Kerberos authentication with the implicit credentials of your user account. If you don't specify the authentication method, the default authentication method for WinRM is used. If you want to use alternate credentials, you can pass in credentials as shown in this example:

```
$cred = get-credential -credential pocket-consulta\williams

enter-pssession -connectionURI https://mailserver12.cpandl.com/powershell
-ConfigurationName Microsoft.Exchange -credential $cred
-Authentication Kerberos
```

Here, you set the connection URI as https://mailserver12.cpandl.com/powershell, set the configuration namespace as Microsoft.Exchange, and use alternate credentials. When PowerShell reads the Get-Credential command, you are prompted for the password for the specified account. Because the authentication type is not defined, the session uses the default authentication method for WinRM.

To put this all together, one way to create a script that runs on an Exchange server is to run the RemoteExchange.ps1 profile file and then run the ConnectFunctions.ps1 script to autoconnect to Exchange. The commands you insert into your script to do this are the following:

```
$s = $env:ExchangeInstallPath + "bin\RemoteExchange.ps1"
&$s
$t = $env:ExchangeInstallPath + "bin\ConnectFunctions.ps1"
&$t
```

Here, you define variables that point to the RemoteExchange.ps1 and ConnectFunctions scripts in the Exchange installation path, and then you use the & operator to invoke the scripts. The environment variable *ExchangeInstallPath* stores the location of the Exchange installation. If you enter the full path to a script, you don't need to assign the path to a variable and then invoke it. However, you then have a fixed path and might need to edit the path on a particular Exchange server. Be sure to run the script at an elevated, administrator PowerShell prompt.

To create a script that runs on your management computer and then executes commands remotely on an Exchange server, insert commands in your script to create a new session and then invoke commands in the session using the techniques discussed in the next section.

Performing one-to-many remote management

PowerShell also lets you perform one-to-many remote management. To do so, you must work with an elevated, administrator shell and can either invoke remote commands on multiple computers or establish remote sessions with multiple computers. When you remotely invoke commands, PowerShell runs the commands on the remote computers, returns all output from the commands, and establishes connections to the remote computers only for as long as is required to return the output. When you establish remote sessions, you can create persistent connections to the remote computers and then execute commands within the session. Any command you enter while working in the session is executed on all computers to which you are connected, whether this is one computer, ten computers, or a hundred computers.

> **TIP** As discussed in Chapter 1, "Exchange Server 2013 administration overview," WinRM must be appropriately configured on any computer you want to remotely manage. Although WinRM is configured on Exchange servers and most others computers running Windows 8 or later and Windows Server 2012 or later, WinRM listeners generally are not created by default. You can create the required listeners by running **winrm quickconfig**.

The following command entered as a single line invokes the Get-Service and Get-Process commands on the named servers:

```
invoke-command -computername MailServer12, MailServer21, MailServer32
-scriptblock {get-service; get-process}
```

The following command establishes a remote session with the named computers:

```
$s = new-PSSession -computername MailServer12, MailServer21, MailServer32
-Credential Cpandl\WilliamS
```

When you connect to a server in this way, you use the standard PowerShell remoting configuration and are not going through the PowerShell application running on a web server. After you establish the session, you can then use the $s session with Invoke-Command to return commands on all remote computers you are connected to. This example looks for stopped Exchange services on each computer:

```
invoke-command -session $s
-scriptblock {get-service mse* | where { $_.status -eq "stopped"}}
```

In this example, you pipe the output of Get-Service to the Where-Object cmdlet and filter based on the Status property. Because the $_ automatic variable operates on the current object in the pipeline, PowerShell examines the status of each service in turn and lists only those that are stopped in the output.

In addition to working with remote commands and remote sessions, some cmdlets have a ComputerName parameter that lets you work with a remote computer without using Windows PowerShell remoting. PowerShell supports remote background jobs as well. A background job is a command that you run asynchronously in an interactive or noninteractive session. When you start a background job, the command prompt returns immediately, and you can continue working while the job runs. For a complete discussion of these remoting features, see Chapter 4, "Using

Sessions, Jobs, and Remoting" in *Windows PowerShell 2.0 Administrator's Pocket Consultant* (Microsoft Press, 2009).

Troubleshooting Exchange Management Shell

Note that the ConnectionFunctions.ps1 script relies on your organization having a standard Exchange Server configuration. By default, Exchange is configured for management using HTTP with the URL *http://ServerName/powershell*. If you've modified the Web Server configuration on your Exchange servers to use a different path, such as might be required to enhance security, you need to update the connection URIs used in the ConnectionFunctions.ps1 script.

When you invoke the PowerShell application, the web server to which you connect runs the PowerShell plug-in (Pwrshplugin.dll) and the Exchange Authorization plug-in (Microsoft.Exchange.AuthorizationPlugin.dll). The PowerShell plug-in runs as a Microsoft.Exchange shell and has the following initialization parameters:

- PSVersion, which sets the PowerShell version as 3.0
- ApplicationBase, which sets the base path for the Exchange server as %ExchangeInstallPath%Bin
- AssemblyName, which sets the name of the .NET assembly to load as Microsoft.Exchange.Configuration.ObjectModel.dll

The Authorization plug-in handles Exchange authorization and authentication. Together, these plug-ins create an authorized shell environment for the remote session.

The physical directory for the PowerShell application is %ExchangeInstallPath%\ClientAccess\PowerShell. This application runs in the context of an application pool named MSExchangePowerShellAppPool. In a large organization, you might want to optimize settings for this and other application pools, as discussed in Chapter 9, "Managing Applications, Application Pools, and Worker Processes," in *Internet Information Services (IIS) 7.0 Administrator's Pocket Consultant* (Microsoft, 2007).

In the %ExchangeInstallPath%\ClientAccess\PowerShell directory on your server, you'll find a web.config file that defines the settings for the PowerShell application. This file contains a role-based access control (RBAC) configuration section that loads the assemblies and web controls for the application.

> **TIP** Microsoft recommends against changing the PowerShell application configuration. However, there's nothing magical or mystical about the PowerShell application or MSExchangePowerShellAppPool. You can re-create these features to enable remote management in alternate configurations, such as on nondefault websites or websites with alternate names. However, be sure to copy the PowerShell application's web.config file to the physical directory for your base application. Before you make any changes to a live production environment, you should plan and test your changes in a nonproduction test environment.

The Web server to which you connect processes your remote actions via the Exchange Control Panel (ECP) application running on the default website. With Exchange 2013, you see the ECP as Exchange Admin Center. The physical directory for this application is %ExchangeInstallPath%\ClientAccess\Ecp. This application runs in the context of an application pool named MSExchangeECPAppPool.

In the %ExchangeInstallPath%\ClientAccess\ECP directory on your server, you'll find a web.config file that defines the settings for the ECP application. This file contains an RBAC configuration section that loads the assemblies and web controls for the application.

Because of the interdependencies created by accessing Exchange via web applications, you'll want to examine related features as part of troubleshooting any issues you experience with remote sessions. Generally, your troubleshooting should follow these steps:

1. Examine the status and configuration of the WinRM on your local computer and the target Exchange server. The service must be started and responding.

2. Check the settings of any firewall running on your local computer, the target Exchange server, or any device between the two, such as a router with a firewall.

3. Check the status of the World Wide Web Publishing Service on the Exchange server. The service must be started and responding.

4. Check the configuration settings of the PowerShell and ECP applications on the web server. By default, the applications don't have access restrictions, but another administrator could have set restrictions.

5. Check the status of MSExchangePowerShellAppPool and MSExchangeECPApp-Pool. You might want to recycle the application pools to stop and then start them.

6. Check the configuration settings of MSExchangePowerShellAppPool and MSExchangeECPAppPool. By default, the application pools are configured to use only one worker process to service requests.

7. Check to ensure the PowerShell application's web.config file is present in the physical directory for the application, and also that the file has the appropriate settings.

8. Check to ensure the ECP application's web.config file is present in the physical directory for the application and also that the file has the appropriate settings.

Working with Exchange cmdlets

When you are working with Exchange Management Shell, additional Exchange-specific cmdlets are available. As with Windows PowerShell cmdlets, you can get help information on Exchange cmdlets:

- To view a list of all Exchange cmdlets, type **get-excommand** at the shell prompt.

- To view Exchange cmdlets related to a specific server role, type **get-help -role RoleName**, where RoleName is the name of the server role you want to examine. You can use the following role names:
  - *UM* for cmdlets related to the Unified Messaging server role
  - *Mailbox* for cmdlets related to the Mailbox server role
  - *ClientAccess* for cmdlets related to the Client Access server role

When you work with Exchange Management Shell, you'll often work with Get, Set, Enable, Disable, New, and Remove cmdlets (the groups of cmdlets that begin with these verbs). These cmdlets all accept the -Identity parameter, which identifies the unique object with which you are working.

Typically, a cmdlet that accepts the -Identity parameter has this parameter as its first parameter, allowing you to specify the identity, with or without the parameter name. When identities have names as well as aliases, you can specify either value as the identity. For example, you can use any of the following techniques to retrieve the mailbox object for the user William Stanek with the mail alias Williams:

```
get-mailbox -identity williams
get-mailbox -identity 'William Stanek'
get-mailbox Williams
get-mailbox "William Stanek"
```

With Get cmdlets, you typically can return an object set containing all related items simply by omitting the identity. For example, if you type **get-mailbox** at the shell prompt without specifying an identity, you get a list of all mailboxes in the enterprise (up to the maximum permitted to return in a single object set).

By default, all cmdlets return data in table format. Because there are often many more columns of data than fit across the screen, you might need to switch to Format-List output to see all of the data. To change to the Format-List output, redirect the output using the pipe symbol (|) to the Format-List cmdlet, as shown in this example:

```
get-mailbox -identity williams | format-list
```

You can abbreviate Format-List as *fl*, as in this example:

```
get-mailbox -identity williams | fl
```

Either technique typically ensures that you see much more information about the object or the result set than if you were retrieving table-formatted data.

Working with object sets and redirecting output

When you are working with PowerShell or Exchange Management Shell, you'll often need to redirect the output of one cmdlet and pass it as input to another cmdlet. You can do this using the pipe symbol. For example, if you want to view mailboxes for a specific mailbox database rather than all mailboxes in the enterprise, you can pipe the output of Get-MailboxDatabase to Get-Mailbox, as shown in this example:

```
get-mailboxdatabase -Identity "Engineering" | get-mailbox
```

Here, you use Get-MailboxDatabase to get the mailbox database object for the Engineering database. You then send this object to the Get-Mailbox cmdlet as input, and Get-Mailbox iterates through all the mailboxes in this database. If you don't perform any other manipulation, the mailboxes for this database are listed as output, as shown here:

Name	Alias	Server	ProhibitSendQuota
Administrator	Administrator	corpsvr127	unlimited
William S	williams	corpsvr127	unlimited
Tom G	tomg	corpsvr127	unlimited
David W	davidw	corpsvr127	unlimited
Kari F	karif	corpsvr127	unlimited
Connie V	conniev	corpsvr127	unlimited
Mike D	miked	corpsvr127	unlimited

You can also pipe this output to another cmdlet to perform an action on each individual mailbox in this database. If you don't know the name of the mailbox database you want to work with, enter **get-mailboxdatabase** without any parameters to list all available mailbox databases.

Using a manual remote shell to work with Exchange

Although the easiest way to work remotely with Exchange 2013 is to install the management tools on your computer, you can connect to and manage Exchange 2013 if you don't have the management tools installed. To do this, you can use a manual remote shell to connect to an Exchange 2013 server. However, you lose the benefits of the preconfigured tools which set up the environment and manage the Exchange connection for you. You also can use a manual remote shell to connect to and work with Exchange Online.

Preparing to use the remote shell

As you might expect, there are several prerequisites for creating a manual remote shell. The computer you use to connect an Exchange server must be running one of the following operating systems:

- Windows Server 2012 RTM or R2
- Windows Server 2008 R2 SP1
- Windows 8 or later
- Windows 7 SP1

The computer must have Windows Management Framework, which includes Windows PowerShell and WinRM, and Microsoft .NET Framework 4.5. Although Windows Server 2012 RTM or R2 and Windows 8 or later include these components, Windows 7 SP1 and Windows Server 2008 R2 SP1 do not.

> **REAL WORLD** When you install the Client Access server role for Exchange 2013, the server is configured automatically with a Windows PowerShell gateway that is configured as a proxy service. This proxy service allows you to run remote commands in web browsers and in remote sessions. Whenever you work with Exchange Admin Center or Exchange Management Shell, the commands are executed via this proxy—even if you logged on locally.

Before you can work remotely, WinRM must be running and the authentication mechanisms you want to use must be enabled. Because Exchange Online uses Basic authentication, you may need to enable this. At an elevated, administrator Power-Shell prompt, enter the following commands to check the status of WinRM:

```
get-service "winrm"
```

If WinRM isn't running, start the service by entering:

```
start-service "winrm"
```

Next, ensure that the authentication mechanisms you want to use are enabled for use with WinRM. To do this, enter the following command:

```
winrm get winrm/config/client/auth
```

Although you are working in the PowerShell window, this command is passed through to the command prompt and the output states the status of available authentication mechanisms:

```
Auth
    Basic = false
    Digest = true
    Kerberos = true
    Negotiate = true
    Certificate = true
    CredSSP = false
```

If Basic authentication isn't enabled and you want to work with Exchange Online, you must enable it. Unfortunately, there's no easy way to pass a complex command through to the command prompt. Because of this, you'll need to open an elevated command prompt and then enter the following command:

```
winrm set winrm/config/client/auth '@{Basic="true"}'
```

IMPORTANT   Exchange Management Shell and Exchange Admin Center require integrated Windows authentication. Exchange Online uses Basic authentication.

Once you've ensured WinRM is running and configured appropriately, you can check the status of script execution by entering the following command at the PowerShell prompt:

```
Get-ExecutionPolicy
```

Windows PowerShell script execution must be enabled on your computer. Typically, you'll want to use the RemoteSigned execution policy. If so, enter the following command at an elevated, administrator PowerShell prompt:

```
Set-ExecutionPolicy RemoteSigned
```

When you connect to a remote Exchange server, you can use your current network credentials or you can specify another set of credentials. Either way, the user account that you want to use for remote management must be a member of a management role group or be enabled for remote shell.

By default, when you create a new mailbox user for Exchange 2013 or Exchange Online, the mailbox user has remote PowerShell enabled. You can view the access status for all users in the Exchange organization by entering the following command:

```
Get-User -ResultSize unlimited |
Format-Table Name,DisplayName,RemotePowerShellEnabled
```

If you want to display a list of only users who don't have access, you could filter the results for this value by running the following command instead:

```
Get-User -ResultSize unlimited -Filter {RemotePowerShellEnabled -eq $false}
```

Set the filtered value to $true if you want to see a list of only users who have access. You can check the access status of a specific user as well by specifying the SAM account name, display name, or login name of the user, as shown in these examples:

```
Get-User "williams" | Format-List RemotePowerShellEnabled
```

```
Get-User "William Stanek" | Format-List RemotePowerShellEnabled
```

```
Get-User "williams@pocket-consultant.com" | Format-List
RemotePowerShellEnabled
```

Connecting manually to Exchange 2013 servers

In an elevated, administrator Windows PowerShell window, you can establish a connection to the remote Exchange server using a PowerShell session. When your management computer is joined to the domain, you can use either HTTP or HTTPS with Kerberos authentication to establish the session. However, HTTPS is normally disabled by default in the client configuration. The basic syntax is:

```
$Session = New-PSSession -ConfigurationName Microsoft.Exchange
-ConnectionUri http://Exchange2013CASName/PowerShell/
-Authentication Kerberos
```

where *Exchange2013CASName* is the host name or FQDN of the Exchange 2013 Client Access server to which you want to connect and *PowerShell* is the name of the PowerShell virtual directory on the server, such as:

```
$Session = New-PSSession -ConfigurationName Microsoft.Exchange
-ConnectionUri http://mailserver35.pocket-consultant.com/PowerShell/
-Authentication Kerberos
```

With Kerberos authentication, your current credentials are used to establish the session. Keep in mind that with Kerberos authentication you must use the server name or the FQDN and cannot use an IP address.

If you want to use an authentication mechanism other than Kerberos or your computer isn't connected to a domain, you must use HTTPS as the transport (or the destination server must be added to the TrustedHosts configuration settings for WinRM, and HTTP must be enabled in the client configuration). You also must explicitly pass in a credential using the -Credential parameter.

You also can specify the authentication mechanism, such as Basic, Digest, or Negotiate. All communications are encrypted with HTTPS. The modified syntax is then:

```
$Session = New-PSSession -ConfigurationName Microsoft.Exchange
-ConnectionUri https://Exchange2013CASNameOrIP/PowerShell/
-Authentication Negotiate -Credential Credential
```

where *Exchange2013CASNameOrIP* is the FQDN or IP address of the Exchange 2013 Client Access server to which you want to connect, *PowerShell* is the name of the PowerShell virtual directory on the server, and *Credential* sets the user name under which the session is established. Consider the following example:

```
$Session = New-PSSession -ConfigurationName Microsoft.Exchange
-ConnectionUri https://mailserver35.pocket-consultant.com/PowerShell/
-Authentication Negotiate -Credential pocket-consulta\williams
```

Here, you establish a session with MailServer35 using integrated Windows authentication and store this session in the $Session object. As you are passing in a credential for Williams, you are prompted for and must enter the account password. You also can store the credential in a Credential object and then use Get-Credential to request the credentials. The syntax then becomes:

```
$Cred = Get-Credential
$Session = New-PSSession -ConfigurationName Microsoft.Exchange
-ConnectionUri https://mailserver35.pocket-consultant.com/PowerShell/
-Authentication Negotiate -Credential $Cred
```

> **IMPORTANT** Regardless of whether you use Kerberos or another authentication mechanism, the Exchange server's SSL certificate must contain a common name (CN) that matches the identifier you are using. Otherwise, you won't be able to connect.

Connecting manually to Exchange Online

Connecting manually to Exchange Online is similar to connecting manually to on-premises servers running Exchange 2013. In an elevated, administrator Windows PowerShell window, you can establish a connection to Exchange Online using a PowerShell session. You can use a stand-alone computer or a domain-joined computer that meets the requirements discussed earlier under "Preparing to use the remote shell."

The basic syntax for connecting manually to Exchange Online is:

```
$Cred = Get-Credential
$Session = New-PSSession -ConfigurationName Microsoft.Exchange
-ConnectionUri https://ps.outlook.com/powershell/
-Authentication Basic -Credential $Cred -AllowRedirection
```

Here, you use HTTPS with Basic authentication for the session and establish a connection to the Exchange Online URL provided by Microsoft, which typically is *https://ps.outlook.com*. To establish the connection, you must pass in your Exchange Online user name and password. This example stores credentials in a Credential object and then uses Get-Credential to prompt for the required credentials. You also could specify the credentials explicitly, as shown here:

```
$Session = New-PSSession -ConfigurationName Microsoft.Exchange
-ConnectionUri https://ps.outlook.com/powershell/
-Authentication Basic -Credential wrs@pocketconsultant.onmicrosoft.com
-AllowRedirection
```

Here, you are prompted for the password for the account.

NOTE When you work with Exchange Online, keep in mind that not all of the cmdlets are available as compared to an on-premises installation. This is because the operating environments are different. Exchange Online runs on Windows Azure. You can connect to and work directly with the Microsoft Online service and Windows Azure as discussed in the section of Chapter 6, "User and contact administration" titled "Understanding on-premises and online recipient management."

Managing remote sessions

After you establish a session with an Exchange 2013 server or Exchange Online, you must import the server-side PowerShell session into your client-side session by running the following command:

```
Import-PSSession $Session
```

You can then work with the remote server.

When you are finished, you should disconnect the remote shell from Exchange server. It's important to note that, beginning with Windows PowerShell 3.0, sessions are persistent by default. When you disconnect from a session, any command or scripts that are running in the session continue running, and you can later reconnect to the session to pick up where you left off. You also can reconnect to a session if you were disconnected unintentionally, such as by a temporary network outage.

IMPORTANT With Exchange Online, each account can have only three connections to sever-side sessions at a time. If you close the PowerShell window without disconnecting from the session, the connection remains open for 15 minutes and then disconnects.

To disconnect a session without stopping commands or releasing resources, run the following command:

```
Disconnect-PSSession $Session
```

The $Session object was instantiated when you created the session. As long as you don't exit the PowerShell window in which this object was created, you can use this object to reconnect the session by entering:

```
Connect-PSSession $Session
```

When you are completely finished with the session, you should remove it. Removing a session stops any commands or scripts that are running, ends the session, and releases the resources the session was using. Remove a session by running the following command:

```
Remove-PSSession $Session
```

CHAPTER 5

Managing Exchange Server 2013 clients

A s a Microsoft Exchange administrator, you need to know how to configure and maintain Exchange clients. With Microsoft Exchange Server 2013 and Exchange Online, you can use any mail client that supports standard mail protocols. For ease of administration, however, you'll want to choose specific clients for users. I recommend focusing on Microsoft Office Outlook 2007 and later and Outlook Web App (OWA) as your clients of choice. Each client supports a slightly different set of features and messaging protocols, and each client has its advantages and disadvantages, including the following:

- With Outlook 2007 or later, you get a full-featured client that on-site, off-site, and mobile users can use. Outlook 2007 or later is part of the Microsoft Office system of applications. They are the only mail clients that support the latest messaging features in Exchange Server. Corporate and workgroup users often need their rich support for calendars, scheduling, voice mail, and email management. Only Microsoft Office Outlook 2010 and Outlook 2013 support calendar sharing and other enhancements available with Exchange 2010 and Exchange 2013.

- With Outlook Web App, you get a mail client that you can access securely through a standard web browser. With Microsoft Internet Explorer 9.0, Internet Explorer 10.0, Firefox 17 or later, and Chrome 24 or later, Outlook Web App supports many of the features found in Outlook 2007 and later, including calendars, scheduling, and voice mail. With other browsers, the client functionality remains the same, but some features might not be supported. You don't need to configure Outlook Web App on the client, and it's ideal for users who want to access email while away from the office.

Outlook 2007 and later versions are the most common Exchange clients for corporate and workgroup environments. With the Outlook Anywhere feature of Exchange, which eliminates the need for a virtual private network (VPN) to securely access Exchange Server over the Internet by using a remote procedure call (RPC) over Secure Hypertext Transfer Protocol (HTTPS) connection, Outlook 2007 and later versions might also be your clients of choice for off-site and mobile users. With Exchange 2013 and Exchange Online, Outlook Anywhere is enabled by default.

This chapter shows you how to manage Outlook 2007 and later. For ease of reference, I will refer to Outlook 2007 and later simply as Outlook, unless I need to differentiate between them.

Configuring mail support for Outlook

You can install Outlook as a client on a user's computer. This section looks at the following topics:

- Understanding address lists, offline address books, and autodiscover
- Configuring Outlook for the first time
- Adding Internet mail accounts to Outlook
- Reconfiguring Outlook mail support

Unless specified otherwise, the procedures in this section work with desktop computers running Windows 7 or later as well as server operating systems running Windows Server 2008 R2 or later. Additionally, unless noted otherwise, the procedures work with Outlook 2007, Outlook 2010, and Outlook 2013.

Understanding address lists, offline address books, and autodiscover

Address lists are collections of recipients in an Exchange organization. Offline address books (OABs) are copies of address lists that are downloaded and cached on a computer so an Outlook user can access the address book while disconnected from the Exchange organization.

Every Exchange organization has a global address list and a default OAB. In the Exchange organization, address lists reside in Active Directory. If mobile users are disconnected from the Internet, they are unable to access the address lists stored on Exchange Online. If mobile users are disconnected from the corporate network, they are unable to access the address lists stored on Exchange 2013. To allow users to continue working when disconnected from the network, Exchange 2013 and Exchange Online generate offline address books and make them accessible to Outlook clients so that they can be downloaded and cached for use while working offline.

Although Exchange 2013 and Exchange Online continue to support public folders, public folders are not required for access to the global address list or the OAB. Exchange 2013 and Exchange Online provide these features through a web-based distribution point. Outlook clients use the web-based distribution point to obtain the global address list and the OAB automatically.

Exchange Online largely manages the default address lists and OABs automatically. On-premises Exchange, however, includes many configuration options, as discussed in the remainder of this section. For more information on global address lists and OABs, see "Managing online address lists" and "Managing offline address books" in Chapter 8, "Working with distribution groups and address lists."

A designated Mailbox server, referred to as the *generation server,* is responsible for creating and updating the OABs. OAB data is produced by the Microsoft Exchange OABGen Service and stored in a special arbitration mailbox with the persisted capability "OrganizationCapabilityOABGen." When a client initiates an OAB distribution request, the request is directed through a Client Access server that routes the request to the Mailbox server hosting the OAB data. The OAB data is then distributed directly from the Mailbox server to the client.

Outlook 2007 and later as well as some mobile devices use the Autodiscover service to automatically configure themselves for access to Exchange. Outlook relies on DNS lookups to locate a host service (SRV) resource record for the Autodiscover service, then uses the user's credentials to authenticate to Active Directory and search for the Autodiscover connection points. After retrieving the connection points, the client connects to the first Client Access server in the list and obtains the profile information. The connection point uses the globally unique identifier (GUID) for the user's mailbox plus the at symbol (@) and the domain portion of the user's primary SMTP address. The profile information includes the user's display name, the location of the user's mailbox server, connection settings for internal and external connectivity, Outlook Anywhere settings, and the URLs for Outlook features including those for free-busy data, the OAB, and Unified Messaging.

When you install a Client Access server, an Autodiscover virtual directory is created on the default website in Internet Information Services (IIS), and an internal URL is set up for automatic discovery and other features, such as the OAB (which can be automatically discovered as well). Typically, the Autodiscover URL is either *https://*domain*/autodiscover/autodiscover.xml* or *https://autodiscover.*domain */autodiscover/autodiscover.xml,* where *domain* is your organization's primary SMTP domain address, such as *https://autodiscover.pocket-consultant.com/autodiscover /autodiscover.xml.* When you deploy multiple Client Access servers, a connection point is created for each. This connection point stores the server's fully qualified domain name (FQDN) in the form *https://*servername*/autodiscover/autodiscover.xml,* where *servername* is the FQDN of the Client Access server, such as *https://server18. pocket-consultant.com/autodiscover/autodiscover.xml.*

The OAB virtual directory is the web-based distribution point for the OAB. By default, when you install a Client Access server, this directory is created on the default website in IIS and configured for internal access. You can specify an external URL as well. Typically, the internal URL is set as *https://*servername*/OAB,* where *servername* is the FQDN of the Client Access server, such as *https://server18.pocket-consultant. com/OAB.*

For Outlook Anywhere to be automatically configured by using the Autodiscover service, external users running Outlook 2007 or later clients must have a valid Secure Sockets Layer (SSL) certificate on the Internet-facing Client Access server that includes both the common name, such as mail.pocket-consultant.com, and a Subject Alternative name for the Autodiscover service, such as autodiscover.pocket-consultant.com. Also, the external URLs for the offline address book, Exchange Web Services, and Outlook Anywhere must be configured.

To configure the external URL for the OAB, you can use the -ExternalUrl parameter of the Set-OABVirtualDirectory cmdlet. In the following example, you set the OAB external URL and configure it for use with SSL:

```
Set-OABVirtualDirectory -identity "CASServer01\OAB (Default Web Site)"
-externalurl https://mail.pocket-consultant.com/OAB -RequireSSL $true
```

To configure the external URL for Exchange Web Services, you can use the -ExternalUrl parameter of the Set-WebServicesVirtualDirectory cmdlet. The following example sets the Exchange Web Services external URL and configures it for use with basic authentication:

```
Set-WebServicesVirtualDirectory -identity "CASServer01\EWS (Default Web
Site)" -externalurl https://mail.pocket-consultant.com/EWS/Exchange.asmx
-BasicAuthentication $True
```

To configure the external host name for Outlook Anywhere, you can use the -ExternalHostname parameter of Set-OutlookAnywhere. The following example sets the external host name and configures authentication:

```
Set-OutlookAnywhere -Server CASServer01 -ExternalHostname
"mail.pocket-consultant.com" -ExternalClientAuthenticationMethod Negotiate
-InternalClientAuthenticationMethod NTLM
-IISAuthenticationMethods Basic, NTLM, Negotiate
-SSLOffloading $False
```

Once you've configured Autodiscover, OAB, and EWS, you can test these services by using Test-OutlookWebServices. Here is an example:

```
Test-OutlookWebServices -ClientAccessServer "CASServer01"
```

Configuring Outlook for the first time

You can install Outlook as a standalone product or as part of Microsoft Office. Outlook can be used to connect to the following types of email servers:

- **Microsoft Exchange** Connects directly to Exchange Server, Exchange Online, or both; best for users who are connected to the organization's network. Users will have full access to Exchange. If users plan to connect to Exchange using Outlook Anywhere, this is the option to choose as well. With Exchange, users can check mail on an email server and access any private or public folders to which they have been granted permissions. If you define a personal folder and specify that new email messages should be delivered to it, messages can be delivered to a personal folder on a user's computer.

- **POP3** Connects to Exchange 2013 or another POP3 email server through the Internet; best for users who are connecting from a remote location, such as a home or a remote office, using dial-up or broadband Internet access. With POP3, users can check mail on an email server and download it to their inboxes. Users can't, however, synchronize mailbox folders or access private or public folders on the server. By using advanced configuration settings, the user can elect to download the mail and leave it on the server for future use. By leaving the mail on the server, the user can check mail in Outlook Web App or on a home computer and then still download it to an office computer later.

- **IMAP4** Connects to Exchange 2013 or another IMAP4 email server through the Internet; best for users who are connecting from a remote location, such as a home or a remote office, using dial-up or broadband Internet access. It's also well suited for users who have a single computer, such as a laptop, that they use to check mail both at the office and away from it. With IMAP4, users can check mail on an email server and synchronize mailbox folders. Users can also download only message headers and then access each message individually to download it. Unlike POP3, IMAP4 has no option to leave mail on the server. IMAP4 also lets users access public and private folders on an Exchange server.

- **ActiveSync** Connects to an Exchange ActiveSync compatible service, such as Outlook.com, through the Internet; best as an additional email configuration option. Users can have an external email account with a web-based email service that they can check in addition to corporate email.

- **Additional server types** Connects to a third-party mail server or other services, such as Outlook Mobile Text Messaging. If your organization has multiple types of mail servers, including Exchange Server, you'll probably want to configure a connection to Exchange Server first and then add more email account configurations later.

To begin, log on to the computer as the user whose email you are configuring or have the user log on. If the computer is part of a domain, log on using the user's domain account. If you are configuring email for use with a direct Exchange 2013 or Exchange Online connection rather than a POP3, IMAP4, or ActiveSync connection, ensure that the user's mailbox has been created. If the user's mailbox has not been created, auto-setup will fail, as will the rest of the account configuration.

The first time you start Outlook, the application runs the Welcome Wizard. You can use the Welcome Wizard to configure email for Exchange, POP3, IMAP4, and ActiveSync mail servers, as discussed in the sections that follow.

First-time configuration: Connecting to Exchange Server

With Outlook 2007 or later, you can use the Welcome Wizard to configure email for Exchange 2013 or Exchange Online in Outlook by completing the following steps:

1. Start Outlook and tap or click Next on the Welcome page. The procedure is nearly identical whether you are working with Outlook 2007, Outlook 2010, or Outlook 2013.

2. When prompted to indicate whether you would like to configure an email account, verify that Yes is selected, and then tap or click Next.

3. The next page of the wizard varies depending on the computer's current configuration:

- For computers that are part of a domain and for users that have an existing Exchange Server mailbox, the wizard uses the Autodiscover feature to automatically discover the required account information.

- For computers that are part of a domain and for users without an on-premises Exchange mailbox, leave the wizard open, create the user's Exchange mailbox, and then proceed with the wizard once the mailbox is automatically discovered.

- For all other configurations, including computers that are part of a workgroup and computers on which you are logged on locally, Outlook assumes you want to configure an Internet email account for the user. Enter the user's account name, email address, and password. Then type and confirm the user's password (see Figure 5-1).

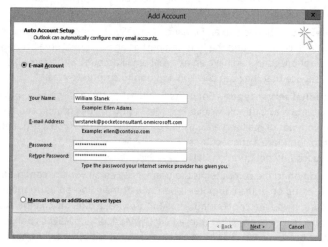

FIGURE 5-1 Although the wizard can automatically fill in account information when you are logged on to a domain, the wizard does not do this for other configurations.

4. After you tap or click Next, the wizard uses the new Auto Account Setup feature to automatically discover the rest of the information needed to configure the account and then uses the settings to log on to the server. If the auto-configuration and server logon are successful, tap or click Finish and skip the remaining steps in this procedure. The wizard then sets up the user's Exchange mailbox on the computer as appropriate.

5. If auto-configuration is not successful, tap or click Next so that the wizard can attempt to establish an unencrypted connection to the server. If the auto-configuration and server logon are successful this time, tap or click Finish, and then skip the remaining steps in this procedure.

6. If auto-configuration fails twice, you'll see a prompt to confirm the user's email address. If the email address is incorrect, correct it, and then tap or

click Retry. If the auto-configuration and server logon are successful this time, tap or click Finish, and then skip the remaining steps in this procedure.

7. If all attempts at auto-configuration fail, you can try to configure settings manually (and might also want to confirm that the Autodiscover service is working properly). Tap or click Next. On the Choose Service page, select a service. Tap or click Next. On the next wizard page, complete the necessary information for the type of email service you selected. If necessary, tap or click More Settings, and then use the Properties dialog box to configure the additional required settings. When you are finished, tap or click OK to close the Properties dialog box. Tap or click Next, and then tap or click Finish to complete the mail configuration.

First-time configuration: Connecting to Internet email servers

When a user is logged on to a domain, Outlook automatically attempts to configure itself for use with the user's Exchange mailbox as part of its initial configuration. This configuration works for internal users but not for remote users who need or prefer to access Exchange using POP3 or IMAP4 (rather than Outlook Anywhere). For these users, you can complete the first-time configuration of Outlook by following these steps:

1. In the Welcome Wizard, when you are prompted to indicate whether you would like to configure an email account, verify that Yes is selected, and then tap or click Next.

2. Select the manual setup option. In Outlook 2007 and Outlook 2010, this checkbox is labeled as Manually Configure Server Settings Or Additional Server Types. In Outlook 2010, this checkbox is labeled as Manual Setup Or Additional Server Types. Tap or click Next.

3. On the Choose Service page, choose the service to use. In Outlook 2007 and Outlook 2010, choose Internet E-Mail as the service. In Outlook 2013, choose POP Or IMAP as the service. Tap or click Next.

4. In the Your Name text box, type the name to appear in the From field of outgoing messages for this user, such as **William Stanek**.

5. In the E-Mail Address text box, type the email address of the user. Be sure to type the email user name as well as the domain name, such as **williams@ pocket-consultant.com**.

6. From the Account Type list, select POP3 or IMAP4 as the type of protocol to use for the incoming mail server. The advantages and disadvantages of these protocols are as follows:

   ▪ POP3 is used to check mail on an email server and download it to the user's inbox. The user can't access private or public folders on the server. By using advanced configuration settings, the user can elect to download email and leave it on the server for future use. By leaving the email on the server, the user can check a message on a home computer and still download it to an office computer later.

- IMAP4 is used to check mail on an email server and download message headers. The user can then access each email individually and download it. Unlike POP3, IMAP4 has no option to leave mail on the server. IMAP4 also lets users access public and private folders on an Exchange server. It is best suited for users who have a single computer, such as a laptop, that they use to check mail both at the office and away from it.

7. Enter the FQDN for the incoming and outgoing mail servers. Although these entries are often the same, some organizations have different incoming and outgoing mail servers. If you are not certain of your mail servers' FQDN, contact your network administrator.

   NOTE If you're connecting to Exchange with POP3 or IMAP4, you should enter the FQDN for the Exchange server rather than just the host name. For example, you would use MailServer.pocket-consultant.com instead of MailServer. This ensures Outlook will be able to find the Exchange server.

8. Under Logon Information, type the user's logon name and password. If the mail server requires secure logon, select the Require Logon Using Security Password Authentication check box.

9. To verify the settings, tap or click Test Account Settings. Outlook verifies connectivity to the Internet and then logs on to the Mail server. Next, Outlook sends a test message to the specified mail server. If the test fails, note the errors and make corrections as necessary.

10. If necessary, tap or click More Settings. Use the Properties dialog box to configure the additional required settings, and then tap or click OK. When you are ready to continue, tap or click Next, and then tap or click Finish to complete the configuration.

Configuring Outlook for Exchange

If you didn't configure Outlook to use Exchange the first time it was started, don't worry: You can change the Outlook configuration to use Exchange. It does take a bit of extra work, however.

To get started, close Outlook if it is started, and then follow these steps to configure Outlook to use Exchange:

1. Start the Mail utility. In Control Panel, tap or click Small Icons on the View By list, and then start the Mail app by tapping or clicking its icon.

2. If your computer doesn't have any current mail profiles, you see the profiles view of the Mail dialog box. Here, you need to create a mail profile before you can add an account. Tap or click Add. In the New Profile dialog box, type a name for the mail profile, such as Outlook, and then tap or click OK. This starts the Add Account Wizard.

3. If your computer has a default mail profile, you see the Mail Setup–Outlook dialog box. In the Mail Setup–Outlook dialog box, tap or click E-Mail Accounts. The Accounts Settings dialog box appears. In the Account Settings

dialog box, the E-Mail tab is selected by default. Tap or click New. This starts the Add Account Wizard.

4. Follow steps 3–7 outlined previously in the "First-time configuration: Connecting to Exchange Server" section.

5. When you finish the previous procedure, close all the open dialog boxes, and then start Outlook.

Adding Internet mail accounts to Outlook

Through email account configuration, each mail profile for Outlook supports only one Exchange Server account at a time. If you need access to multiple Exchange Server mailboxes in the same mail profile, you must configure access to these mailboxes as discussed in the section "Accessing multiple Exchange mailboxes" later in the chapter.

Although you can configure only one Exchange email account for each mail profile, Outlook allows you to retrieve mail from both Exchange Online and Exchange Server as well as from multiple Internet servers. For example, you can configure Outlook to check mail on the corporate Exchange server, a personal account with an ActiveSync compatible service, and Exchange Online.

You can add Internet mail accounts to Outlook. In Outlook 2007, complete the following steps:

1. To display the Account Settings dialog box, select Tools, and then select Account Settings.

2. In the Account Settings dialog box, the E-Mail tab is selected by default. Tap or click New.

3. On the Choose E-Mail Service page, select Microsoft Exchange, POP3, IMAP, Or HTTP, and then tap or click Next.

4. Follow steps 2–10 outlined previously in the "First-time configuration: Connecting to Internet email servers" section.

In Outlook 2010, tap or click the Office button, tap or click Account Settings, and then select Add Account. Follow steps 4–10 outlined previously in the "First-time Configuration: Connecting to Internet email servers" section.

In Outlook 2013, on the File pane, select Add Account. Follow steps 4–10 outlined previously in the "First-time configuration: Connecting to Internet email servers" section.

Repairing and changing Outlook mail accounts

When you first configure Outlook on a computer, you can configure it to connect to an Exchange server, to Exchange Online, to Internet email, or to another email server. With Exchange Server, Outlook uses MAPI to connect to the RPC Client Access service on the appropriate Client Access server, and the RPC Client Access service connects Outlook to the appropriate Mailbox server for the user by proxying or redirecting the connection as necessary. Outlook clients remain connected to the Client Access server. They use the RPC Client Access service as the MAPI endpoint, and the Address Book service as the Active Directory endpoint. The Client Access server that is proxying or redirecting the connection for them then communicates with the appropriate Mailbox server using MAPI/RPC.

Because of this connection process, the underlying infrastructure is transparent to users—they are connected automatically to their mailboxes. If a user's mailbox is moved to a different server within the Exchange organization, the user is connected to this server automatically the next time he or she starts Outlook. If, for some reason, a user has a problem connecting to Exchange or needs to update configuration settings, you can use a repair operation. Repairing the user's account restarts the Auto Account Setup feature.

With non-Exchange servers, access to email very much depends on the account and server configuration remaining the same. If the account or server configuration changes, the account configuration in Outlook must be updated. The easiest way to do this is with a repair operation.

To start a repair, follow these steps:

1. Log on as the domain account of the user for whom you are repairing email.

2. In Outlook 2007, to display the Account Settings dialog box, select Tools, and then select Account Settings. In Outlook 2010, tap or click the Office button, tap or click Account Settings, and then select the Account Settings option. In Outlook 2013, on the File pane, tap or click Account Settings, and then select the Account Settings option.

3. In the Account Settings dialog box, the E-Mail tab lists all currently configured email accounts by name. Select the account to repair, and then tap or click Repair.

4. On the Auto Account Setup page, check the account settings. With Exchange accounts for domain users and with Exchange Online, you cannot change the displayed information. With other accounts, you can modify the user's email address and password, as necessary.

5. When you tap or click Next, the Repair E-Mail Account Wizard contacts the mail server and tries to determine the correct account settings. If the auto-configuration and server logon are successful, tap or click Finish. Skip the remaining steps in this procedure.

6. If auto-configuration is not successful, tap or click Next so that the wizard can attempt to establish an unencrypted connection to the server. If the auto-configuration and server logon are successful this time, tap or click Finish, and then skip the remaining steps in this procedure. You must restart Outlook.

   NOTE You may be prompted to confirm the user's credentials. If so, type the user's password, select the Remember My Credentials checkbox, and then tap or click OK.

7. If auto-configuration fails twice, you can try to configure settings manually. Select the manual setup option, and then tap or click Next.

8. Use the fields provided to update the mail account configuration. If you need to configure additional settings beyond the user, server, and logon information, tap or click More Settings, and then use the Properties dialog box to configure the additional required settings. When you are finished, tap or click OK to close the Properties dialog box.

9. To check the new settings tap or click Test Account Settings.

10. Tap or click Next, and then tap or click Finish.

In some cases, if you've incorrectly configured Exchange, you might not be able to start Outlook and access the Account Settings dialog box. In this case, you can repair the settings using the following procedure:

1. Start the Mail utility. In Control Panel, tap or click Small Icons on the View By list, and then start the Mail app by tapping or clicking its icon or by double-tapping or double-clicking its icon.

2. In the Mail Setup–Outlook dialog box, tap or click E-Mail Accounts. The Accounts Settings dialog box appears.

3. In the Account Settings dialog box, the E-Mail tab is selected by default. Tap or click the incorrectly configured Exchange account, and then do one of the following:

   - Tap or click Change to modify the Exchange settings using the techniques discussed previously.

   - Tap or click Remove to remove the Exchange settings so that they are no longer used by Outlook.

4. When you are finished, close the Mail Setup–Outlook dialog box, and then start Outlook.

For POP3 or IMAP4, you can change a user's email configuration at any time by completing the following steps:

1. In Outlook 2007, to display the Account Settings dialog box, select Tools, and then select Account Settings. In Outlook 2010, tap or click the Office button, tap or click Account Settings, and then select the Account Settings option. In Outlook 2013, on the File pane, tap or click Account Settings, and then select the Account Settings option.

2. In the Account Settings dialog box, the E-Mail tab lists all currently configured email accounts by name. Select the account you want to work with, and then tap or click Change.

3. Use the fields provided to update the mail account configuration. If you need to configure additional settings beyond the user, server, and logon information, tap or click More Settings, and then use the Properties dialog box to configure the additional required settings. When you are finished, tap or click OK to close the Properties dialog box.

4. To check the new settings, tap or click Test Account Settings.

5. Tap or click Next, and then tap or click Finish.

Leaving mail on the server with POP3

If the user connects to an Internet email server, an advantage of POP3 is that it lets a user leave mail on the server. By doing this, the user can check mail on a home computer and still download it to an office computer later.

With Outlook, you can configure POP3 accounts to leave mail on the server by completing the following steps:

1. Start Outlook. In Outlook 2007, on the Tools menu, tap or click Account Settings. In Outlook 2010, tap or click the Office button, tap or click Account Settings, and then select the Account Settings option. In Outlook 2013, on the File pane, tap or click Account Settings, and then select the Account Settings option.

2. In the Account Settings dialog box, select the POP3 mail account you want to modify, and then tap or click Change.

3. Tap or click More Settings to display the Internet E-Mail Settings dialog box.

4. In the Internet E-Mail Settings dialog box, tap or click the Advanced tab, as shown in Figure 5-2.

FIGURE 5-2 Using the Advanced tab to configure how and when mail should be left on the server with POP3 mail accounts.

5. Use the options below Delivery to configure how and when mail should be left on the server. To enable this option, select the Leave A Copy Of Messages On The Server check box. The additional options depend on the client configuration. Options you might see include the following:

    ■ **Remove From Server After *N* Days**   Select this option if the user will be connecting to an Internet service provider (ISP) and you want to delete messages from the server after a specified number of days. By deleting ISP mail periodically, you ensure that the mailbox size doesn't exceed the limit.

- **Remove From Server When Deleted From "Deleted Items"**   Select this option to delete messages from the server when the user deletes them from the Deleted Items folder. You'll see this option with Internet-only Outlook configurations.

6. Tap or click OK when you've finished changing the account settings.

7. Tap or click Next, and then tap or click Finish. Tap or click Close to close the Account Settings dialog box.

Checking private and public folders with IMAP4 and UNIX mail servers

With IMAP4, you can check public and private folders on a mail server. This option is enabled by default, but the default settings might not work properly with UNIX mail servers.

With Outlook, you can check or change the folder settings used by IMAP4 by completing the following steps:

1. Start Outlook. In Outlook 2007, on the Tools menu, tap or click Account Settings. In Outlook 2010, tap or click the Office button, tap or click Account Settings, and then select the Account Settings option. In Outlook 2013, on the File pane, tap or click Account Settings, and then select the Account Settings option.

2. In the Account Settings dialog box, select the IMAP4 mail account you want to modify and then tap or click Change.

3. Tap or click More Settings to display the Internet E-Mail Settings dialog box.

4. In the Internet E-Mail Settings dialog box, tap or click the Advanced tab, as shown in Figure 5-3.

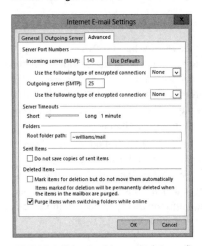

FIGURE 5-3 Using the Advanced tab to configure how folders are used with IMAP4 mail accounts.

5. If the account connects to a UNIX mail server, enter the path to the mailbox folder on the server, such as **~williams/mail**—don't end the folder path with a forward slash (/)—and then tap or click OK.

6. Tap or click Next, and then tap or click Finish.

Managing the Exchange configuration in Outlook

Whenever you use Outlook to connect to Exchange, you have several options for optimizing the way mail is handled. These options include the following:

- Email delivery and processing
- Remote mail
- Scheduled connections
- Multiple mailboxes

Each of these options is examined in this section.

Managing delivery and processing email messages

When Outlook uses Exchange, you have strict control over how email is delivered and processed. Exchange mail can be delivered in one of two ways:

- To server mailboxes with local copies
- To personal folders

Exchange mail can be processed by any of the information services configured for use in Outlook. These information services include the following:

- Microsoft Exchange
- Internet email

Let's look at how you use each of these delivery and processing options.

Using server mailboxes

When you are using Outlook 2007 or later with Exchange 2013 or Exchange Online, server mailboxes with local copies are the default configuration option. With server mailboxes, new email is delivered to a mailbox on the Exchange server, and users can view or receive new mail only when they're connected to Exchange. When users are connected to Exchange, Outlook retrieves their mail and stores a local copy on their computer in addition to the email stored on Exchange.

The local copy of a user's mail is stored in an offline folder .ost file. With Windows 7 or with Windows 8 and later, the default location of a .ost file is *%LocalAppData%*\Microsoft\Outlook, where *%LocalAppData%* is a user-specific environment variable that points to a user's local application data. Using server mailboxes offers users protected storage and the ability to have a single point of recovery in case something happens to their computers.

Using personal folders

An alternative to using server mailboxes is to use personal folders. Personal folders are stored in a .pst file on the user's computer. With personal folders, you can specify that mail should be delivered to the user's inbox and stored on the server or that mail should be delivered only to the user's inbox. Users have personal folders when Outlook is configured to use Internet email or other email servers. Users might also have personal folders if the auto-archive feature is used to archive messages.

> **REAL WORLD** With Windows 7 or with Windows 8 and later, the default location of a .pst file is *%LocalAppData%*\Microsoft\Outlook, where *%LocalAppData%* is a user-specific environment variable that points to a user's local application data. Personal folders are best suited for mobile users who check mail through dial-up connections and who might not be able to use a dial-up connection to connect directly to Exchange.
>
> Users with personal folders lose the advantages that server-based folders offer— namely, protected storage and the ability to have a single point of recovery in case of failure. In addition, .pst files have many disadvantages. They get corrupted more frequently and, on these occasions, you must use the Inbox Repair Tool to restore the file. If the hard disk on a user's computer fails, you can recover the mail only if the .pst file has been backed up. Unfortunately, most workstations aren't backed up regularly (if at all), and the onus of backing up the .pst file falls on the user, who might or might not understand how to do this.

DETERMINING THE PRESENCE OF PERSONAL FOLDERS

You can determine the presence of personal folders by following these steps:

1. Start Outlook. In Outlook 2007, on the Tools menu, tap or click Account Settings. In Outlook 2010, tap or click the Office button, tap or click Account Settings, and then select the Account Settings option. In Outlook 2013, on the File pane, tap or click Account Settings, and then select the Account Settings option.

2. In the Account Settings dialog box, tap or click the Data Files tab.

3. The location of the data file associated with each email account is listed. If the file name ends in .pst, the account is using a personal folder.

CREATING NEW OR OPENING EXISTING PERSONAL FOLDERS

If personal folders aren't available and you want to configure them, follow these steps:

1. Start Outlook. In Outlook 2007, on the Tools menu, tap or click Account Settings. In Outlook 2010, tap or click the Office button, tap or click Account Settings, and then select the Account Settings option. In Outlook 2013, on the File pane, tap or click Account Settings, and then select the Account Settings option.

2. In the Account Settings dialog box, tap or click the Data Files tab.

3. Tap or click Add. If the New Outlook Data File dialog box appears, Office Outlook Personal Folders File (.pst) should be selected by default. Tap or click OK.

4. Use the Create Or Open Outlook Data File dialog box, as shown in Figure 5-4, to create a new .pst file or open an existing .pst file:

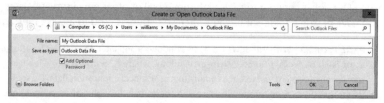

FIGURE 5-4 Using the Create Or Open Outlook Data File dialog box to search for an existing .pst file or to create a new one.

- To create a new .pst file in the default folder, type a name for the Outlook data file in the text box provided or accept the default value. To secure the file and ensure only a person with this password can access the file, select the Add Optional Password checkbox. In the Create Microsoft Personal Folders dialog box, specify a password, verify the password for the .pst file, and tap or click OK.

- To create a new .pst file in a nondefault folder, tap or click Browse Folders to show the folder view if it is hidden. Browse for the folder you want to use, type the file name in the text box provided or accept the default value, and then tap or click OK. Optionally, select the Add Optional Password checkbox. In the Create Microsoft Personal Folders dialog box, specify a password, verify the password for the .pst file, and tap or click OK.

- To open an existing .pst file, tap or click Browse Folders to show the folder view if it is hidden. Browse to the folder containing the .pst file. Select the .pst file, and then tap or click OK. In the Personal Folders dialog box, use the options provided to change the current password or compact the personal folder, and then tap or click OK.

NOTE It is important to be aware that Exchange Server does not ship with any password recovery utility for .pst files. If a user sets a password on a .pst file and forgets it, the Exchange administrator has no way to reset it. You might find third-party vendors who make password-cracking or recovery tools, but they are not guaranteed to work and they are not supported by Microsoft.

5. Tap or click Close. The personal folder you've selected or created is displayed in the Outlook folder list. You should see related subfolders as well.

DELIVERING MAIL TO PERSONAL FOLDERS

When you configure mail to be delivered to a personal folder, Outlook saves email messages only locally on the computer. As a result, Outlook removes the messages from Exchange Server after delivery and you can access the messages only on the currently logged-on computer.

If you want mail to be delivered to a personal folder, complete the following steps:

1. Start Outlook. In Outlook 2007, on the Tools menu, tap or click Account Settings. In Outlook 2010, tap or click the Office button, tap or click Account Settings, and then select the Account Settings option. In Outlook 2013, on the File pane, tap or click Account Settings, and then select the Account Settings option.

2. In the Account Settings dialog box, tap or click the Data Files tab.

3. Select the .pst file to use in the list of data files provided, and then tap or click Set As Default.

4. When prompted to confirm, tap or click Yes, and then tap or click Close.

5. Exit and restart Outlook. Outlook will now use personal folders.

If you want mail to resume using server-stored mail, complete the following steps:

1. Start Outlook. In Outlook 2007, on the Tools menu, tap or click Account Settings. In Outlook 2010, tap or click the Office button, tap or click Account Settings, and then select the Account Settings option. In Outlook 2013, on the File pane, tap or click Account Settings, and then select the Account Settings option.

2. In the Account Settings dialog box, tap or click the Data Files tab.

3. Select the .ost file to use in the list of data files provided, and then tap or click Set As Default.

4. When prompted to confirm, tap or click OK, and then tap or click Close.

5. Exit and restart Outlook. Outlook will now use personal folders.

Repairing .pst data files

When Outlook uses personal folders, you can use the Inbox Repair tool (scanpst.exe) to analyze and repair corrupted data files. This tool is stored in the *%SystemDrive%* Program Files\Microsoft Office\Office*Version* folder, where *Version* is the internal version of Office you are using, such as Office15 for Outlook 2013. If a .pst file won't open or is damaged, you can use the Inbox Repair tool to repair it by completing the following these steps:

1. Exit Outlook. Open the Office folder in File Explorer and then double-tap or double-click the Inbox Repair tool (scanpst.exe).

2. Tap or click Browse. In the Select File To Scan dialog box, browse to the folder where .pst files are stored, select the .pst file you want to work with, and then tap or click Open. By default, .pst files are stored in *%LocalAppData%* Microsoft\Outlook, where *%LocalAppData%* is a user-specific environment variable that points to a user's local application data.

3. Tap or click Start, and the Inbox Repair tool will begin analyzing the file. The larger the file the longer the analysis will take.

4. If errors are found, click Repair to start the repair process. The Inbox Repair tool will create a copy of the .pst file before attempting the repair operation. During the repair, the Inbox Repair tool will rebuild the .pst file.

5. Start Outlook with the profile that contains the .pst file that you repaired. Press Ctrl+6 to display the Folder List view and look for a folder named Recovered Personal Folders. This folder contains the default Outlook folders as well as a Lost And Found folder, which contains any items recovered by the Inbox Repair tool.

6. Create a new .pst data file to store your mail items. Drag the items from the Lost And Found folder into the appropriate folder under the new Personal folders. When you've moved all the items, you can remove the Recovered Personal Folders.

7. The Inbox Repair tool creates a backup of the original .pst file and names it with the .bak file extension. By default this file is stored in the same location as the original .pst file. If you make a copy of this file and name it with a .pst extension, you may be able to recover additional items. To do this, add the .pst file to the mail profile, and then move any additional mail items from this old .pst file to the new data file created in step 6.

Repairing .ost data files

When Outlook uses server mailboxes, .ost data files contain copies of information saved on the server. If an .ost file won't open or is damaged, you can re-create the file by completing the following steps:

1. Exit Outlook. Start the Mail utility. Press the Windows key +I and then tap or click Control Panel. In Control Panel, tap or click Small Icons on the View By list, and then start the Mail app by tapping or clicking its icon or double-tapping or double-clicking its icon.

2. In the Mail Setup–Outlook dialog box, tap or click E-Mail Accounts. The Accounts Settings dialog box appears.

3. In the Account Settings dialog box, tap or click the Data Files tab.

4. Select the Exchange account and then click Open File Location. This opens File Explorer to the location of the data file. Note this location. By default, .ost files are stored in *%LocalAppData%*\Microsoft\Outlook, where *%LocalAppData%* is a user-specific environment variable that points to a user's local application data.

5. Close the Account Settings and Mail Setup dialog boxes. In File Explorer, press and hold or right-click the .ost file, and then click Delete. If you are unable to delete the file, make sure all mail and Office windows are closed.

6. Start Outlook. Download a copy of the mail items again to automatically re-create the .ost file.

Accessing multiple Exchange mailboxes

Earlier in the chapter, I discussed how users could check multiple Internet mail accounts in Outlook. You might have wondered whether users could check multiple Exchange mailboxes as well—and they can. Users often need to access multiple Exchange mailboxes for many reasons:

- Help desk administrators might need access to the help desk mailbox in addition to their own mailboxes.
- Managers might need temporary access to the mailboxes of subordinates who are on vacation.
- Project team members may need to access mailboxes set up for long-term projects.
- Resource mailboxes might need to be set up for accounts payable, human resources, corporate information, and so on.

Normally, a one-to-one relationship exists between user accounts and Exchange mailboxes. You create a user account and add a mailbox to it; only this user can access the mailbox directly through Exchange. To change this setup, you must change the permissions on the mailbox. One way to change mailbox access permissions is to do the following:

1. Log on to Exchange as the owner of the mailbox.
2. Delegate access to the mailbox to one or more additional users.
3. Have users with delegated access log on to Exchange and open the mailbox.

The sections that follow examine each of these steps in detail.

Logging on to Exchange as the mailbox owner

Logging on to Exchange as the mailbox owner allows you to delegate access to the mailbox. Before you can do this, however, you must complete the following steps:

1. Log on as the user or have the user log on for you.
2. Start Outlook. Make sure that mail support is configured to use server mailboxes. If necessary, configure this support, which creates the mail profile for the user.
3. After you configure Outlook to use Exchange, you should be able to log on to Exchange as the mailbox owner.

TIP With multiple mailbox users, you should configure the mailbox to deliver mail to the server rather than to a personal folder. In this way, the mail can be checked by one or more mailbox users.

Delegating mailbox access

After you've logged on as the mailbox owner, you can delegate access to the mailbox by completing these steps:

1. Start Outlook. Do one of the following:

- In Outlook 2007, on the Tools menu, tap or click Account Settings. On the Delegates tab or in the Delegates dialog box, tap or click Add.

- In Outlook 2010, tap or click the Office button, tap or click Account Settings, and then select the Account Settings option. On the Delegates tab or in the Delegates dialog box, tap or click Add.

- In Outlook 2013, on the File pane, tap or click Account Settings, and then select the Delegate Access option. In the Delegates dialog box, tap or click Add.

2. The Add Users dialog box appears. To add users, double-tap or double-click the name of a user who needs access to the mailbox. Repeat this step as necessary for other users, and then tap or click OK when you're finished.

3. In the Delegate Permissions dialog box, assign permissions to the delegates for the Calendar, Tasks, Inbox, Contacts, and Notes. The available permissions include

   - **None**   No permissions
   - **Reviewer**   Grants read permission only
   - **Author**   Grants read and create permissions
   - **Editor**   Grants read, create, and modify permissions

   NOTE If the user needs total control over the mailbox, you should grant the user Editor permission for all items.

4. Tap or click OK twice. These changes go into effect when the user restarts Outlook.

Delegated users can access the mailbox and send mail on behalf of the mailbox owner. To change this behavior, set folder permissions as described later in the "Granting permission to access folders without delegating access" section.

Opening additional Exchange mailboxes

The final step is to let Exchange Server know about the additional mailboxes the user can open. To do this, follow these steps:

1. Have the user who will be accessing additional mailboxes log on and start Outlook.

2. In Outlook 2007, on the Tools menu, tap or click Account Settings. In Outlook 2010, tap or click the Office button, tap or click Account Settings, and then select the Account Settings option. In Outlook 2013, on the File pane, tap or click Account Settings, and then select the Account Settings option.

3. Select the Microsoft Exchange Server account, and then tap or click Change.

4. In the Change Account dialog box, tap or click More Settings.

5. In the Microsoft Exchange dialog box, on the Advanced tab, tap or click Add. Type the name of a mailbox to open. Generally, this is the same name as the mail alias for the user or account associated with the mailbox. Tap or click OK. Repeat this step to add other mailboxes.

6. Tap or click Next, and then tap or click Finish.

7. Tap or click Close. The additional mailboxes are displayed in the Outlook folder list.

Granting permission to access folders without delegating access

When a mailbox is stored on the server, you can grant access to individual folders in the mailbox. Granting access in this way allows users to add the mailbox to their mail profiles and work with the folder. Users can perform tasks only for which you've granted permission.

To grant access to folders individually, follow these steps:

1. Press and hold or right-click the folder for which you want to grant access, and then select Properties. In the Properties dialog box, select the Permissions tab, as shown in Figure 5-5.

FIGURE 5-5 Granting access to a folder through the Permissions tab.

2. The Name and Permission Level lists display account names and their permissions on the folder. Two special names might be listed:

- **Default**   Provides default permissions for all users.

- **Anonymous**   Provides permissions for anonymous users, such as those who anonymously access a published public folder through the web.

3. To grant permission that differs from the default permission, tap or click Add.

4. In the Add Users dialog box, double-tap or double-click the name of a user who needs access to the mailbox. Tap or click Add to put the name in the Add Users list. Repeat this step as necessary for other users, and tap or click OK when finished.

5. In the Name and Role lists, select one or more users whose permissions you want to modify. Then use the Roles list to assign permissions or select individual permission items. The roles are defined as follows:

- **Owner** Grants all permissions in the folder. Users with this role can create, read, modify, and delete all items in the folder. They can create subfolders and change permissions on folders as well.

- **Publishing Editor** Grants permission to create, read, modify, and delete all items in the folder. Users with this role can create subfolders as well.

- **Editor** Grants permission to create, read, modify, and delete all items in the folder.

- **Publishing Author** Grants permission to create and read items in the folder, to modify and delete items the user created, and to create subfolders.

- **Author** Grants permission to create and read items in the folder and to modify and delete items the user created.

- **Nonediting Author** Grants permission to create and read items in the folder.

- **Reviewer** Grants read-only permission.

- **Contributor** Grants permission to create items but not to view the contents of the folder.

- **None** Grants no permission in the folder.

6. When you're finished granting permissions, tap or click OK.

Using mail profiles to customize the mail environment

The mail profile used with Outlook determines which information services are available and how they are configured. A default mail profile is created when you install and configure Outlook for the first time. This mail profile is usually called Outlook.

The active mail profile defines the mail setup for the user who is logged on to the computer. You can define additional profiles for the user as well. You can use these additional profiles to customize the user's mail environment for different situations. Here are two scenarios:

- A manager needs to check the Technical Support and Customer Support mailboxes only on Mondays when she writes summary reports. On other days, the manager doesn't want to see these mailboxes. To solve this problem, you create two mail profiles: Support and Standard. The Support profile displays the manager's mailbox as well as the Technical Support and Customer Support mailboxes. The Standard profile displays only the manager's mailbox. The manager can then switch between these mail profiles as necessary.

- A laptop user wants to check Exchange mail directly while connected to the LAN. When at home, the user wants to use remote mail with scheduled connections. On business trips, the user wants to use SMTP and POP3. To solve this problem, you create three mail profiles: On-Site, Off-Site, and Home. The On-Site profile uses the Exchange Server service with a standard configuration.

The Off-Site profile configures Exchange Server for remote mail and scheduled connections. The Home profile uses the Internet mail service instead instead of the Exchange information service.

Common tasks you'll perform to manage mail profiles are examined in this section.

Creating, copying, and removing mail profiles

You manage mail profiles through the Mail utility. To access this utility and manage profiles, follow these steps:

1. Start the Mail utility. Press the Windows key +I, and then tap or click Control Panel. In Control Panel, tap or click Small Icons on the View By list, and then start the Mail app by tapping or clicking its icon or by double-tapping or double-clicking its icon.

2. In the Mail Setup–Outlook dialog box, tap or click Show Profiles.

3. As Figure 5-6 shows, you should see a list of mail profiles for the current user. Mail profiles for other users aren't displayed. You can now perform the following actions:

   - Tap or click Add to create a new mail profile using the Account Settings Wizard.

   - Delete a profile by selecting it and tapping or clicking Remove.

   - Copy an existing profile by selecting it and tapping or clicking Copy.

   - View a profile by selecting it and tapping or clicking Properties.

FIGURE 5-6 Using the Mail dialog box to add, remove, or edit mail profiles.

Selecting a specific profile to use on startup

You can configure Outlook to use a specific profile on startup or to prompt for a profile to use.

To start with a specific profile, follow these steps:

1. Start the Mail utility. Press the Windows key +I, and then tap or click Control Panel. In Control Panel, tap or click Small Icons on the View By list, and then

start the Mail app by tapping or clicking its icon or by double-tapping or double-clicking its icon.

2. In the Mail Setup–Outlook dialog box, tap or click Show Profiles.

3. Select Always Use This Profile, and then use the drop-down list to choose the startup profile. Tap or click OK.

To prompt for a profile before starting Outlook, follow these steps:

1. Start the Mail utility. Press the Windows key +I, and then tap or click Control Panel. In Control Panel, tap or click Small Icons on the View By list, and then start the Mail app by tapping or clicking its icon or by double-tapping or double-clicking its icon.

2. In the Mail Setup–Outlook dialog box, tap or click Show Profiles.

3. Select Prompt For A Profile To Be Used, and then tap or click OK.

The user will be prompted for a profile the next time Outlook is started.

User and contact administration

Often, one of your primary tasks as a Microsoft Exchange administrator is to manage user accounts and contacts. User accounts enable individual users to log on to the network and access network resources. In Active Directory, users are represented by User and InetOrgPerson objects. User objects represent standard user accounts; InetOrgPerson objects represent user accounts imported from non-Microsoft Lightweight Directory Access Protocol (LDAP) or X.500 directory services. User and InetOrgPerson are the only Active Directory objects that can have Exchange mailboxes associated with them. Contacts, on the other hand, are people who you or others in your organization want to get in touch with. Contacts can have street addresses, phone numbers, fax numbers, and email addresses associated with them. Unlike user accounts, contacts don't have network logon privileges.

Understanding users and contacts

In Active Directory, users are represented as objects that can be mailbox-enabled or mail-enabled. A *mailbox-enabled* user account has an Exchange mailbox associated with it. Mailboxes are private storage areas for sending and receiving mail. A user's display name is the name Exchange presents in the global address list.

Another important identifier for mailbox-enabled user accounts is the Exchange alias. The alias is the name that Exchange associates with the account for addressing mail. When your mail client is configured to use Microsoft Exchange Server, you can type the alias or display name in the To, Cc, or Bcc text boxes of an email message and have Exchange Server resolve the alias or name to the actual email address.

Although you'll likely configure most Windows user accounts as mailbox-enabled, user accounts don't have to have mailboxes associated with them. You can create user accounts without assigning mailboxes. You can also create user accounts that are *mail-enabled* rather than mailbox-enabled, which means that the account has an off-site email address associated with it but doesn't have an actual mailbox. Mail-enabled users have Exchange aliases and display names that Exchange Server can resolve to actual email addresses. Internal users can send a message to the mail-enabled user account using the Exchange display name or alias and the message will be directed to the external address. Users outside the organization can use the Exchange alias to send mail to the user.

It's not always easy to decide when to create a mailbox for a user. To better understand the decision-making process, consider the following scenario:

1. You've been notified that two new users, Elizabeth and Joe, will need access to the domain.

2. Elizabeth is a full-time employee who starts on Tuesday. She'll work on site and needs to be able to send and receive mail. People in the company need to be able to send mail directly to her.

3. Joe, on the other hand, is a consultant who is coming in to help out temporarily. His agency maintains his mailbox, and he doesn't want to have to check mail in two places. However, people in the company need to be able to contact him, and he wants to be sure that his external address is available.

4. You create a mailbox-enabled user account for Elizabeth. Afterward, you create a mail-enabled user account for Joe, ensuring that his Exchange information refers to his external email address.

Mail-enabled users are one of several types of custom recipients that you can create in Exchange Server. Another type of custom recipient is a *mail-enabled* contact. You create a mail-enabled contact so that users can more easily send email to that contact. A mail-enabled contact has an external email address.Microsoft Exchange Server 2013 has in-place archiving for user mailboxes, which is designed to replace the need for personal stores in Outlook. An in-place archive is an alternative storage location for historical message data that is seamlessly accessible to a user in Microsoft Outlook 2007 and later and Outlook Web App.

The in-place archive is created as an additional mailbox and is referred to as an archive mailbox. Users can easily move and copy mail data between a primary mailbox and an archive mailbox. Because in-place archiving is a premium feature, an enterprise license is required for each user with an archive mailbox. For more information, see "Creating and using archive mailboxes" in Chapter 7 "Mailbox administration."

Understanding the basics of email routing

Exchange uses email addresses to route messages to mail servers inside and outside the organization. When routing messages internally, Mailbox servers use mail connectors to route messages to other Exchange servers, as well as to other types of mail servers that your company might use. Two standard types of connectors are used:

- **Send connectors**   Control the flow of outbound messages
- **Receive connectors**   Control the flow of inbound messages

Send and Receive connectors use Simple Mail Transfer Protocol (SMTP) as the default transport and provide a direct connection among Mailbox servers in an on-premises Exchange organization. Edge Transport servers can also receive mail from and send mail to other types of mail servers.

You can use these connectors to connect Mailbox servers in an organization. When routing messages outside the company, Mailbox servers and Edge Transport servers use mail gateways to transfer messages. The default gateway is SMTP.

Online-only deployments work in much the same way, except that mail is routed through the Exchange Online organization. Here, Exchange Online Protection handles transport.

In hybrid deployments, mailboxes can reside in the on-premises Exchange organization and in an Exchange Online organization. Messages are sent between the organizations transparently and appear as internal messages. To enhance security, messages are encrypted and transferred between the organizations using Transport Layer Security (TLS).

Exchange Server 2013 uses directory-based recipient resolution for all messages that are sent from and received by users throughout an Exchange organization. The Exchange component responsible for recipient resolution is the Categorizer. The Categorizer must be able to associate every recipient in every message with a corresponding recipient object in Active Directory.

All senders and recipients must have a primary SMTP address. If the Categorizer discovers a recipient that does not have a primary SMTP address, it will determine what the primary SMTP address should be or replace the non-SMTP address. Replacing a non-SMTP address involves encapsulating the address in a primary SMTP address that will be used while transporting the message.

IMPORTANT   Non-SMTP email address formats include fax, X.400, and the legacy Exchange format (EX). The Categorizer encapsulates email addresses using non-SMTP formats in the Internet Mail Connector Encapsulated Addressing (IMCEA) format. For example, the Categorizer encapsulates the fax address, FAX-888-555-1212, as IMCEAFAX-888-555-1212@yourdomain.com. Any email address that is longer than what SMTP allows is transmitted as an extended property in the XExch50 field, provided the name part of the address and domain part of the address don't exceed the allowed limits. The maximum allowed length for an email address in Exchange is 571 characters, 315 characters for the name part of the address, 255 characters for the domain name, and the @ sign character that separates the two name parts.

In addition to primary SMTP email addresses, you can configure alternative recipients and forwarding addresses for users and public folders. If there is an alternative recipient or forwarding address, redirection is required during categorization. You specify the addresses to which messages will be redirected in Active Directory, and redirection history is maintained with each message.

Understanding on-premises and online recipient management

Exchange Management Shell provides many commands for working with mailbox-enabled users, mail-enabled users, and contacts. The main commands you'll use are shown in the following list:

MAILBOX-ENABLED USER	MAIL-ENABLED USERS	CONTACTS
Connect-Mailbox	Disable-MailUser	Disable-MailContact
Disable-Mailbox	Enable-MailUser	Enable-MailContact
Enable-Mailbox	Get-MailUser	Get-MailContact
Get-Mailbox	New-MailUser	New-MailContact
New-Mailbox	Remove-MailUser	Remove-MailContact
Remove-Mailbox	Set-MailUser	Set-MailContact
Set-Mailbox		

Because Exchange organizations can be on-premises, online, or a hybrid of the two, working with recipients is more complex than it used to be, especially when it comes to creating recipients. Normally, to work with the recipient you access the organization where the recipient should be or has been created. For example, if a mailbox was created in the on-premises Exchange organization, you connect to the on-premises organization and work with the mailbox using the on-premises implementation of Exchange Admin Center or Exchange Management Shell. If a mailbox was created in the online Exchange organization, you connect to the online organization and work with the mailbox using the online implementation of Exchange Admin Center or Exchange Management Shell.

With hybrid deployments, however, you can synchronize users from on-premises Active Directory to Exchange Online. You do this using the hybrid deployment tools. When you run the sync tool for the first time, it copies all of the user accounts, contacts, and groups from Active Directory to Exchange Online. The domains in your organization are then synchronized automatically, so you need to re-run the sync tool only if you add, remove, or rename domains.

Although accounts for synced users are created in the Exchange Online organization, they are not activated for online use, which means they don't have access to the online features and also haven't been licensed. If you want to create an online mailbox for a synced user, you also must activate the account before the grace period expires. If the user has a local mailbox and you want to move it to Exchange Online, you run the Mailbox Migration Wizard. This wizard configures forwarding of the user's local mailbox to Exchange Online and then copies the user's mailbox data to Exchange Online. Moving and migrating mailboxes is discussed in more detail in Chapter 7 "Mailbox administration."

To create a new synced mailbox user, you have several options. One option is as follows:

1. Create the user account in Active Directory Users And Computers.

2. Wait for the account to be synchronized with the Exchange Online organization.

3. Access the Exchange Online organization. Next, either create the mailbox for the user or migrate the user's existing mailbox to Exchange Online. If you create a mailbox for the user, keep the following in mind:

   ■ For Exchange Admin Center, this means using the online console for administration. In a synchronized hybrid deployment, you can access the online console from an on-premises console. Tap or click the Office 365 option. In Office 365 Admin Center, tap or click Admin and then select Exchange. This opens the Exchange Online version of Exchange Admin Center.

   ■ For Exchange Management Shell, you access the Exchange Online organization by establishing a remote session with Exchange Online as discussed in "Connecting manually to Exchange Online" in Chapter 4 "Using Exchange Management Shell."

4. Using Office 365 Admin, activate the synced user and assign a license. When you assign a license, a mailbox is created automatically for the user.

The second option for creating a new synced mailbox user is to use the New-RemoteMailbox cmdlet. In this method, you access the on-premises Exchange organization in Exchange Management Shell and then use New-RemoteMailbox to create an enabled and synced mailbox user, which means:

■ A mail-enabled user is created in on-premises Active Directory.

■ An associated mailbox is created in Exchange Online.

NOTE Don't forget, you'll also need to assign the user a mailbox plan.

The basic syntax for the RemoteMailbox cmdlets are as follows:

■ **New-RemoteMailbox** Creates a mail-enabled user in on-premises Active Directory and a mailbox in Exchange Online.

```
New-RemoteMailbox -Name CommonName [-Alias ExchangeAlias]
[-ArbitrationMailbox ModeratorMailbox] [-Archive <$true
| $false>] [-DisplayName Name] [-DomainController FullyQualifiedName]
[-FirstName FirstName] [-Initials Initials] [-LastName LastName]
[-ModeratedBy Moderators] [-ModerationEnabled <$true | $false>]
[-OnPremisesOrganizationalUnit OUName] [-OverrideRecipientQuotas
```

```
<$true | $false>] [-Password Pwd] [-PrimarySmtpAddress SmtpAddress]
[-RemotePowerShellEnabled <$true |$false>] [-RemoteRoutingAddress
ProxyAddress] [-ResetPasswordOnNextLogon <$true | $false>]
[-SamAccountName PreWin2000Name] [-SendModerationNotifications <Never
| Internal | Always>] [-UserPrincipalName LoginName]
```

- **Enable-RemoteMailbox**   Creates an online mailbox for a user already created in on-premises Active Directory.

```
Enable-RemoteMailbox -Identity UserId [-Alias ExchangeAlias]
[-DisplayName DisplayName] [-DomainController DomainControllerName]
[-PrimarySmtpAddress SmtpAddress] [-RemoteRoutingAddress
ProxyAddress]
```

- **Disable-RemoteMailbox**   Removes an online mailbox but keeps the user account in on-premises Active Directory.

```
Disable-RemoteMailbox -Identity UserId [-Archive <$true | $false>]
[-DomainController DomainControllerName] [-IgnoreDefaultScope<$true |
$false>] [-IgnoreLegalHold <$true | $false>]
```

- **Remove-RemoteMailbox**   Removes an online mailbox and the related account in on-premises Active Directory.

```
Remove-RemoteMailbox -Identity UserId [-Archive <$true | $false>]
[-DomainController DomainControllerName] [-IgnoreDefaultScope<$true |
$false>] [-IgnoreLegalHold <$true | $false>]
```

Regardless of which approach you use to create new mailbox users in Exchange Online, you must license these mailbox users in Office 365. You do this by associating a mailbox plan with each mailbox user. Using the graphical tools, you can associate mailbox plans when you are creating mailbox users or afterward by editing the account properties. In a remote session with Exchange Online, you can use the -MailboxPlan parameter with the New-Mailbox cmdlet to do the same. However, at the time of this writing, there are no mailbox plan parameters for any of the RemoteMailbox cmdlets. (Hopefully, this oversight will be corrected by the time you read this.) When you assign mailbox plans, you need to ensure you have enough licenses. You purchase and assign licenses using Office 365 Admin Center. Select Licensing in the feature pane to see the subscription and licensing options. On the Subscriptions tab, tap or click a subscription link to purchase additional licenses for that plan. On the Licenses tab, as shown in Figure 6-1, you see a summary of the number of valid, expired, and assigned licenses for each plan being used.

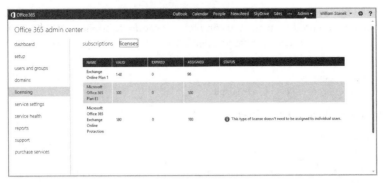

FIGURE 6-1 Accessing the Licensing node to work with subscriptions and licensing.

Office 365 will allow you to assign more mailbox plans than you have licenses for. However, after the initial grace period, problems will occur. For example, mail data for unlicensed mailboxes may become unavailable. Remember, the number of valid licenses shouldn't exceed the number of assigned licenses.

You activate and license synced users in Office 365 as well. Under Users And Groups > Active Users, select the check boxes for the users you want to activate and license and then select Activate Synced Users. Next, specify the work location for the users, such as United States. Under Assign Licenses, select the mailbox plan to assign. Finally, select Activate.

The Office 365 service, its settings, and accounts are all manageable from Windows PowerShell. Every account you create in the online environment is in fact created in the online framework within which Office 365 and Exchange Online operate. This framework is called Windows Azure, and like Windows Server, it uses Active Directory to provide its directory services.

Before you can manage Office 365, its settings, and accounts from Windows PowerShell, you must install the Windows Azure Active Directory module (which is available at the Microsoft Download Center: *http://go.microsoft.com/fwlink /p/?linkid=236297*). Any computer capable of running Exchange 2013 or acting as a management server can run this module, provided .NET framework 3.51 and the Microsoft Online Services Sign-in Assistant version 7.0 or later are installed. At the time of this writing, the sign-in assistant was available at *http://go.microsoft.com /fwlink/?LinkId=286152*. Be sure to download and install only the 64-bit versions of the module and the sign-in assistant.

After you download and install the required components, the Windows Azure Active Directory module is available for your use. This module also is referred to as the Microsoft Online module. Although Windows PowerShell 3.0 or later can implicitly import modules, you must explicitly import this module with PowerShell 2.0. After you import the module, if necessary, you can connect to the Windows Azure and Microsoft Online Services using the Connect-MSOLService cmdlet.

Because you'll typically want to store your credentials in a Credential object rather than be prompted for them, the complete procedure to connect to Microsoft Online Services by using Windows PowerShell 2.0 is:

```
import-module msonline
$cred = get-credential
connect-msolservice -credential:$cred
```

Or, by using Windows PowerShell 3.0 or later:

```
$cred = get-credential
connect-msolservice -credential:$cred
```

After connecting to the service, you can use the available commands to manage online settings and objects. For example, if you want to get a list of user accounts that have been created in the online service along with their licensing status, enter **get-msoluser**. The results will be similar to the following:

```
UserPrincipalName                    DisplayName            isLicensed
-----------------                    -----------            ----------
wrstanek@pocketconsultant.onmicrosof... William Stanek       True
valeryv@pocketconsultant.onmicrosoft... Valery Ushakov       False
```

Enter **get-help *msol*** to get a list of commands specific to Microsoft Online Services.

Managing user accounts and mail features

With Exchange Server 2013, Exchange Admin Center and Exchange Management Shell are the primary administration tools you use to manage mailboxes, distribution groups, and mail contacts. You can use these tools to create and manage mail-enabled user accounts, mailbox-enabled user accounts, and mail-enabled contacts, as well as any other configurable aspect of Exchange Server.

The sections that follow examine techniques to manage user accounts and the Exchange features of those accounts whether you are working with either on-premises Exchange organizations or Exchange Online. In a hybrid environment, you always manage domain user accounts and their mailboxes using the on-premises Exchange tools. Your changes are then synced to the online environment.

> **NOTE** Domain administrators can create user accounts and contacts using Active Directory Users And Computers. If any existing user accounts need to be mail-enabled or mailbox-enabled, you perform these tasks using the Exchange management tools. If existing contacts need to be mail-enabled, you also perform this task using the Exchange management tools.

Finding existing mailboxes, contacts, and groups

You work with recipients where they were created, which can be either in an on-premises Exchange organization or in Exchange Online. You can view current mailboxes, mail-enabled users, contacts, and groups by following these steps:

1. Open Exchange Admin Center using one of the following techniques:

   - For on-premises Exchange, open your web browser and then enter the secure URL for Exchange Admin Center, such as *https://mailserver48.cpandl.com/ecp*.

   - For online Exchange, open your web browser and then enter the secure URL for Office 365 Admin Center, such as *https://portal.microsoftonline.com/admin/default.aspx*. In Office 365 Admin Center, tap or click Admin and then select Exchange. This opens the Exchange Online version of Exchange Admin Center.

2. As shown in Figure 6-2, select Recipients in the feature pane and then select the related Mailboxes, Groups, or Contacts tab, as appropriate for the type of recipient you want to work with.

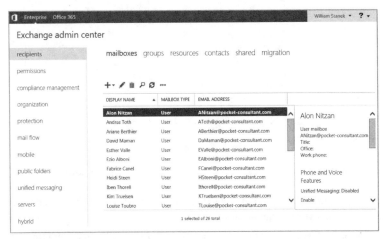

FIGURE 6-2 Accessing the Recipients node to work with mailboxes, distribution groups, and mail contacts.

3. By default all recipients of the selected type are displayed. With mailboxes this means that user mailboxes, linked user mailboxes, legacy user mailboxes, and remote user mailboxes are displayed. If you want to display the recipient subtype, tap or click More and then select Add/Remove Columns. In the Add/Remove Columns dialog box, select Recipient Type and then select OK.

4. If you want to filter recipients based on attributes, tap or click More and then select Advanced Search.

   You can then filter by alias, display name, department, email addresses, first name, last name, and recipient type. The Recipient Types condition allows you to filter the results for specific recipient subtypes, such as only remote mailbox users.

   You can add conditions that allow you to filter results based on city, state, country, office, title, group membership, and more. To do this, select More Options and then select Add Condition.

5. By default, Exchange Admin Center displays only three columns of information for each recipient, including the display name, mailbox type, and email

address. To customize the columns of information displayed, tap or click More. Use the options provided in the Add/Remove Columns dialog box, shown in Figure 6-3, to configure the columns to use, and then tap or click OK.

FIGURE 6-3 Customizing the list of columns to display using the options provided.

In Exchange Management Shell, you can find mailboxes, contacts, and groups by using the following commands:

- **Get-User** Use the Get-User cmdlet to retrieve all users in the forest that match the specified conditions.

```
Get-User [-Identity UserId | -Anr Identifier]
[-AccountPartition PartitionId]
[-Arbitration <$true | $false>] [-Credential Credential]
[-DomainController DomainControllerName] [-Filter FilterString]
[-IgnoreDefaultScope <$true | $false>] [-Organization OrgName]
[-OrganizationalUnit OUName] [-PublicFolder <$true | $false>]
[-ReadFromDomainController <$true | $false>] [-RecipientTypeDetails
Details] [-ResultSize Size] [-SortBy String]
```

- **Get-Contact** Use the Get-Contact cmdlet to retrieve information about a specified contact or contacts.

```
Get-Contact [-Identity ContactId | -Anr ContactID] [-AccountPartition
PartitionId] [-Credential Credential] [-DomainController
DCName] [-Filter FilterString] [-IgnoreDefaultScope <$true
| $false>] [-Organization OrgName] [-OrganizationalUnit OUName]
[-ReadFromDomainController <$true | $false>]
[-RecipientTypeDetails Details] [-ResultSize Size] [-SortBy Value]
```

- **Get-Group** Use the Get-Group cmdlet to query for existing groups.

```
Get-Group [-Identity GroupId | -Anr GroupID]
[-AccountPartition PartitionId] [-Credential Credential]
[-DomainController FullyQualifiedName] [-Filter FilterString]
[-IgnoreDefaultScope <$true | $false>] [-Organization OrgName]
[-OrganizationalUnit OUName] [-ReadFromDomainController <$true |
$false>] [-RecipientTypeDetails {"Contact" | "MailContact" |
"MailUser" | "RoleGroup" | "User" | "UserMailbox" | ... }]
[-ResultSize Size] [-SortBy Value]
```

- **Get-RemoteMailbox** Use the Get-RemoteMailbox cmdlet to get details for mail-enabled users in on-premises Active Directory that have mailboxes in Exchange Online.

```
Get-RemoteMailbox [-Identity UserId | -Anr Identifier] [-Alias
ExchangeAlias] [-Archive <$true | $false>] [-DomainController
DomainControllerName] [-OnPremisesOrganizationalUnit OUName]
[-ReadFromDomainController DomainControllerName]
[-ResultSize NumResults]
```

Finding synced, unlicensed, inactive, and blocked users

When you are working with hybrid organizations, users can be synced from Active Directory to Exchange Online. These synced users can have mailboxes on-premises or in Exchange Online. If you need to view all the synced users, determine where a synced user's mailbox is located, or perform other tasks with synced users, you can use a custom filter. To create a custom filter for synced users, complete the following steps:

1. Open Office 365 Admin Center. Select Users And Groups in the feature pane, and the Active Users option will be selected by default.

2. Tap or click Filter. Next, in the Filter drop-down list, select New View.

3. On the New View page, enter a name for the view, such as Synced Users.

4. Select the Synchronized Users Only checkbox and then select Save.

5. Select the view you just created in the Filter drop-down list. You should now see a list of synced users.

Custom views that you create are persistent and as such will be available each time you log in to Office 365 Admin Center. To change the options of a custom view, display the view by selecting it in the Filter drop-down list and then select Edit View in the Filter drop-down list.

If you no longer want a custom view, you can delete it. Display the view by selecting it in the Filter drop-down list and then select Delete View in the Filter drop-down list. When prompted to confirm, select Yes and then select Close.

A synced user is only one type of user you may want to find in an Exchange Online organization. You also may want to find:

- **Unlicensed users**   These users haven't been assigned an Exchange Online license. Although there is a grace period for licensing after creating a mailbox user online, the user may lose mailbox data after the grace period expires.

- **Inactive users**   These users have been deleted by an admin, which puts them in inactive status for a period of 30 days. When the recovery period expires, the account and any unprotected data is removed.

- **Blocked users**   These users cannot sign in and the related accounts are blocked, such as may happen when a user's password expires.

- **Users with errors**   These users have errors associated with their accounts.

You can find blocked users, unlicensed users, or users with errors by completing the following steps:

1. Open Office 365 Admin Center. Select Users And Groups in the feature pane, and the Active Users option will be selected by default.

2. Tap or click Filter. Next, in the Filter drop-down list, select Sign-in Blocked Users, Unlicensed Users, or Users With Errors as appropriate.

In Office 365 Admin Center, you can find inactive users by selecting Users And Groups in the feature pane and then selecting the Deleted Users tab.

Creating mailbox-enabled and mail-enabled user accounts

Generally speaking, you need to create a user account for each user who wants to use network resources. The following sections explain how to create domain user accounts that are either mailbox-enabled or mail-enabled, and how to add a mailbox to an existing user account. If a user needs to send and receive email, you need to create a new mailbox-enabled account for the user or add a mailbox to the user's existing account. Otherwise, you can create a mail-enabled account.

Understanding logon names and passwords

Before you create a domain user account, you should think for a moment about the new account's logon name and password. You identify all domain user accounts with a logon name. This logon name can be (but doesn't have to be) the same as the user's email address. In Windows domains, logon names have two parts:

- **User name**   The account's text label
- **User domain**   The domain where the user account exists

For the user Williams whose account is created in pocket-consultant.com, the full logon name for Windows is williams@pocket-consultant.com.

User accounts can also have passwords and public certificates associated with them. *Passwords* are authentication strings for an account. *Public certificates* combine a public and private key to identify a user. You log on with a password by typing the password. You log on with a public certificate by using a smart card and a smart card reader.

Although Windows displays user names to describe privileges and permissions, the key identifiers for accounts are security identifiers (SIDs). SIDs are unique identifiers that Windows generates when you create accounts. SIDs consist of the domain's security ID prefix and a unique relative ID. Windows uses these identifiers to track accounts independently from user names. SIDs serve many purposes; the two most important are to allow you to easily change user names and to allow you to delete accounts without worrying that someone could gain access to resources simply by re-creating an account with the same user name.

When you change a user name, you tell Windows to map a particular SID to a new name. When you delete an account, you tell Windows that a particular SID is no longer valid. Afterward, even if you create an account with the same user name, the new account won't have the same privileges and permissions as the previous one because the new account will have a new SID.

Creating mail-enabled user accounts

Mail-enabled users are defined as custom recipients in Exchange Server. They have an Exchange alias and an external email address, but they do not have an Exchange mailbox. All email messages sent to a mail-enabled user are forwarded to the remote email address associated with the account.

In Exchange Admin Center, mail-enabled users are listed as Mail Users under Recipients > Contacts. You can manage mail-enabled users through Exchange Admin Center and Exchange Management Shell.

> **NOTE** With on-premises Exchange, you have two options for mail-enabled users and contacts that are no longer needed. You can disable or delete the mail-enabled user or contact. With Exchange online, your only option is to delete the mail-enabled user or contact.

You can create a new mail-enabled user by completing the following steps:

1. In Exchange Admin Center, select Recipients in the feature pane and then select Contacts.

2. Tap or click New and then select Mail User. This opens the New Mail User dialog box. Figure 6-4 shows on-premises Exchange options on the left and Exchange online options on the right.

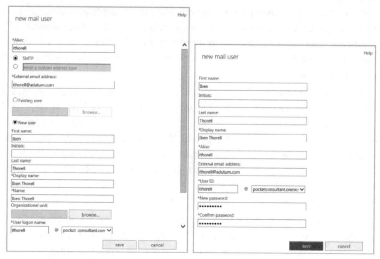

FIGURE 6-4 Configuring the mail-enabled user's settings.

3. If you are working with on-premises Exchange, select New User.

4. Type the user's first name, middle initial, and last name in the text boxes provided. These values are used to create the Display Name entry (as well as the Active Directory name with on-premises Exchange).

5. The Display Name and Name properties can't exceed 64 characters. As necessary, make changes to the Display Name, Name, or both text boxes. For example, you might want to type the name in LastName FirstName Middle-Initial format or in FirstName MiddleInitial LastName format.

   IMPORTANT The difference between the Display Name and the Name properties is subtle but important. The Display Name property sets the name displayed in Exchange and Outlook. The Name property sets the display name in Active Directory and is the Common Name (CN) value associated with the user.

6. In the Alias text box, type an alias for the mail-enabled user. This alias should uniquely identify the mail-enabled user in the Exchange organization. Alias names cannot contain spaces.

7. In the External Email Address text box, type the mail user's external email address. By default, the address is configured as a standard SMTP email address. If you are working with on-premises Exchange, you can specify a custom address type by selecting the related option and then entering a prefix that identifies the custom type. Use X.400, GroupWise or Lotus Notes for X.400, GroupWise, and Lotus Notes address types respectively.

8. With on-premises Exchange, the user account is created in the default user container, which typically is the Users container. Because you'll usually need to create new user accounts in a specific organizational unit rather than in the Users container, click Browse to the right of the Organizational Unit text box. In the Select Organizational Unit dialog box, choose the location where you want to store the account and then click OK.

9. In the User ID or User Logon Name text box, type the user's logon name. Use the drop-down list to select the domain with which you want to associate the account. This sets the fully qualified logon name, such as williams@pocket-consultant.com.

10. Type and then confirm the password for the account. This password must follow the conventions of your organization's password policy. Typically, this means that the password must include at least eight characters and must use three of the four available character types: lowercase letters, uppercase letters, numbers, and symbols.

11. With on-premises Exchange you can select Require Password Change On Next Logon check box to ensure that the user changes the password at next logon.

12. Tap or click Save. Exchange Admin Center creates the new mail-enabled user.

If an error occurs, the user will not be created. You will need to tap or click OK, correct the problem, and then tap or click Save again. Consider the error example shown in Figure 6-5. In this instance, the user logon name/user ID was already in use so the user couldn't be created.

error

The value "ithorell@pocket-consultant.com" of property "UserPrincipalName" is used by another recipient object "pocket-consultant.com/Users/Iben Thorell". Please specify a unique value.

Click here for help...

ok

FIGURE 6-5 An error occurs when a user's principal name is already in use.

You can list all mail-enabled users by typing **get-mailuser** at the Exchange Management Shell prompt. Sample 6-1 provides the full syntax and usage for Get-MailUser.

SAMPLE 6-1 Get-MailUser cmdlet syntax and usage

Syntax

```
Get-MailUser [-Identity Identifier | -Anr Name] [-AccountPartition
PartitionId] [-Credential Credential] [-DomainController DCName]
[-Filter FilterString] [-IgnoreDefaultScope {$true | $false}]
[-Organization OrgName] [-OrganizationalUnit OUName]
  [-ReadFromDomainController {$true | $false}] [-ResultSize Size]
  [-SortBy Value]
```

Usage

```
Get-MailUser -Identity "aaronl" | fl

Get-MailUser -OrganizationalUnit "marketing" | fl
```

NOTE By default, Get-MailUser lists the name and recipient type for matches. In the example, fl is an alias for Format-List and is used to get detailed information about matching entries.

You can create a new mail-enabled user account using the New-MailUser cmdlet. Sample 6-2 shows the syntax and usage. When prompted, provide a secure password for the user account.

NOTE The syntax and usage are entered on multiple lines for ease of reference. You must enter the command-line values for a cmdlet on a single line.

SAMPLE 6-2 New-MailUser cmdlet syntax and usage

Syntax

```
New-MailUser -Name CommonName -ExternalEmailAddress EmailAddress
[-Password Password] [-UserPrincipalName LoginName] {AddtlParams1}

New-MailUser -Name CommonName -FederatedIdentity FederatedId
-WindowsLiveID WindowsLiveId [-EvictLiveId <$true | $false>]
[-ExternalEmailAddress EmailAddress] [-NetID NetID] {AddtlParams2}

New-MailUser -Name CommonName -FederatedIdentity FederatedId
-MicrosoftOnlineServicesID WindowsLiveId [-NetID NetID] {AddtlParams2}

New-MailUser -Name CommonName -ImportLiveId <$true | $false>
-WindowsLiveID WindowsLiveId [-ExternalEmailAddress EmailAddress]
[-UsageLocation CountryInfo] {AddtlParams2}

New-MailUser -Name CommonName [-MicrosoftOnlineServicesID WindowsLiveId]
{AddtlParams2}

New-MailUser -Name CommonName -MicrosoftOnlineServicesID WindowsLiveId
-Password Password [-ExternalEmailAddress EmailAddress] [-UsageLocation
CountryInfo] {AddtlParams2}

New-MailUser -Name CommonName -Password Password -WindowsLiveID
WindowsLiveId [-EvictLiveId <$true | $false>] [-ExternalEmailAddress
EmailAddress] [-UsageLocation CountryInfo] {AddtlParams2}

New-MailUser -Name CommonName -UseExistingLiveId <$true | $false>
-WindowsLiveID WindowsLiveId [-BypassLiveId <$true | $false>]
[-ExternalEmailAddress EmailAddress] [-NetID NetID]
[-UsageLocation CountryInfo] {AddtlParams2}

{AddtlParams1}
[-Alias ExchangeAlias] [-ArbitrationMailbox ModeratorMailbox]
[-DisplayName Name] [-DomainController FullyQualifiedName] [-FirstName
FirstName] [-Initials Initials] [-LastName LastName]
[-MacAttachmentFormat <BinHex | UuEncode | AppleSingle | AppleDouble>]
```

```
[-MessageBodyFormat <Text | Html | TextAndHtml>] [-MessageFormat <Text |
Mime>] [-ModeratedBy Moderators] [-ModerationEnabled <$true | $false>]
[-Organization OrgName] [-OrganizationalUnit OUName] [-PrimarySmtpAddress
}SmtpAddress] [-ResetPasswordOnNextLogon <$true | $false>]
}[-SamAccountName PreWin2000Name] [-SendModerationNotifications <Never |
Internal | Always>] [-UsageLocation CountryInfo] [-UsePreferMessageFormat
<$true | $false>]

{AddtlParams2}
[-Alias ExchangeAlias] [-ArbitrationMailbox ModeratorMailbox]
[-DisplayName Name] [-DomainController FullyQualifiedName] [-FirstName
FirstName] [-Initials Initials] [-LastName LastName] [-ModeratedBy
Moderators] [-ModerationEnabled <$true | $false>] [-Organization OrgName]
[-OrganizationalUnit OUName] [-PrimarySmtpAddress SmtpAddress]
[-RemotePowerShellEnabled <$true | $false>] [-ResetPasswordOnNextLogon
<$true | $false>] [-SamAccountName PreWin2000Name]
[-SendModerationNotifications <Never | Internal | Always>]
```

Usage

```
New-MailUser -Name "Frank Miller" -Alias "Frankm"
-OrganizationalUnit "cpandl.com/Technology"
-UserPrincipalName "Frankm@cpandl.com" -SamAccountName "Frankm"
-FirstName "Frank" -Initials "" -LastName "Miller"
-ResetPasswordOnNextLogon $false
-ExternalEmailAddress "SMTP:Frankm@hotmail.com"
```

Mail-enabling existing user accounts

When a user already has an account in Active Directory, you can mail-enable the account using Exchange Admin Center and Exchange Management Shell. In Exchange
Admin Center for your on-premises organization, you can mail-enable an existing
user account by completing the following steps:

1. Select Recipients in the feature pane and then select Contacts.

2. Tap or click New and then select Mail User. This opens the New Mail User
   dialog box.

3. In the Alias text box, type an alias for the mail-enabled user. This alias should
   uniquely identify the mail-enabled user in the Exchange organization. Alias
   names cannot contain spaces.

4. In the External Email Address text box, type the mail user's external email
   address. By default, the address is configured as a standard SMTP email
   address. If you are working with on-premises Exchange, you can specify a
   custom address type by selecting the related option and then entering a
   prefix that identifies the custom type. Use X.400, GroupWise or Lotus Notes
   for X.400, GroupWise, and Lotus Notes address types respectively.

5. The Existing User option is selected by default, as shown in Figure 6-6. Tap or
   click Browse. This displays the Select User dialog box.

FIGURE 6-6 Configuring mail for an existing user.

6. In the Select User dialog box, select the user account you want to mail-enable and then tap or click OK. User accounts that are not yet mail-enabled or mailbox-enabled for the current domain are listed by name and organizational unit.

7. Tap or click Save. Exchange Admin Center mail-enables the user account you previously selected. If you're working in a synced, hybrid organization, the mail-enabled user will be synced to Exchange Online as well. If an error occurs, the user account will not be mail-enabled. You will need to correct the problem and repeat this procedure. Tap or click Finish.

You can mail-enable an existing user account using the Enable-MailUser cmdlet. Sample 6-3 shows the syntax and usage. For the identity parameter, you can use the user's display name, logon name, or user principal name.

SAMPLE 6-3 Enable-MailUser cmdlet syntax and usage

Syntax

```
Enable-MailUser -Identity Identity -ExternalEmailAddress EmailAddress
[-Alias ExchangeAlias] [-DisplayName Name] [-DomainController
FullyQualifiedName] [-MacAttachmentFormat <BinHex | UuEncode |
AppleSingle | AppleDouble>] [-MessageBodyFormat <Text | Html |
TextAndHtml>] [-MessageFormat <Text | Mime>] [-PrimarySmtpAddress
SmtpAddress] [-UsePreferMessageFormat <$true | $false>]
```

Usage

```
Enable-MailUser -Identity "cpandl.com/Marketing/Frank Miller"
-Alias "Frankm" -ExternalEmailAddress "SMTP:Frankm@hotmail.com"
```

Managing mail-enabled user accounts

You can manage mail-enabled users in several ways. If a user account should no longer be mail-enabled, you can disable mail forwarding. To disable mail forwarding in Exchange Admin Center for your on-premises organization, select Recipients in the feature pane and then select the Contacts tab. Next, select the user you want to disable. Click the More button (the button with three dots) and then select Disable. When prompted to confirm, select Yes. If you're working in a synced, hybrid organization, this change will be synced to Exchange Online as well.

At the Exchange Management Shell prompt, you can disable mail forwarding using the Disable-MailUser cmdlet, as shown in Sample 6-4.

SAMPLE 6-4 Disable-MailUser cmdlet syntax and usage

Syntax

```
Disable-MailUser -Identity Identity [-DomainController
FullyQualifiedName] [-IgnoreDefaultScope {$true | $false}]
```

Usage

```
Disable-MailUser -Identity "Frank Miller"
```

If you no longer need a mail-enabled user account, you can permanently remove it from Active Directory. To remove a mail-enabled user account in Exchange Admin Center for your on-premises organization, select the mail user and then select the Delete option. When prompted to confirm, tap or click Yes. If you're working in a synced, hybrid organization, this change will be synced to Exchange Online as well.

At the Exchange Management Shell prompt, you can remove a mail-enabled user account by using the Remove-MailUser cmdlet, as shown in Sample 6-5.

SAMPLE 6-5 Remove-MailUser cmdlet syntax and usage

Syntax

```
Remove-MailUser -Identity "Identity" [-DomainController DCName]
[-IgnoreDefaultScope {$true | $false}]
[-KeepWindowsLiveID {$true | $false}]
```

Usage

```
Remove-MailUser -Identity "Frank Miller"
```

Creating domain user accounts with mailboxes

You can create a new domain user account with a mailbox in several ways. If you are using a hybrid configuration and want the user created in Active Directory and the mailbox created in Exchange online, you can use the techniques discussed earlier under "Understanding on-premises and online recipient management." Otherwise, you can create a new domain user account and a mailbox for that account using only your on-premises Exchange administration tools. To do this, complete the following steps:

1. In Exchange Admin Center, select Recipients in the feature pane and then select Mailboxes.

2. Tap or click New and then select User Mailbox. This opens the New User Mailbox dialog box, shown in Figure 6-7.

FIGURE 6-7 Creating a new domain user account with a mailbox.

3. In the Alias text box, type an alias for the mailbox user. This alias should uniquely identify the user in the Exchange organization. Alias names cannot contain spaces.

   NOTE The alias and domain suffix are combined to create the email address for the user. For example, if the alias is tedc and the domain suffix is pocket-consultant.com, the email address is set as tedc@pocket-consultant.com.

4. Select New User. Type the user's first name, middle initial, and last name in the text boxes provided. These values are used to create the Display Name entry as well as the Active Directory name with on-premises Exchange.

5. The Display Name and Name properties can't exceed 64 characters. As necessary, make changes to the Display Name, Name, or both text boxes. For example, you might want to type the name in LastName FirstName Middle-Initial format or in FirstName MiddleInitial LastName format.

   IMPORTANT The difference between the Display Name and the Name properties is subtle but important. The Display Name property sets the name displayed in Exchange and Outlook. The Name property sets the display name in Active Directory and is the Common Name (CN) value associated with the user.

6. The user account is created in the default user container, which typically is the Users container. Because you'll usually need to create new user accounts in a specific organizational unit rather than in the Users container,

click Browse to the right of the Organizational Unit text box. In the Select An Organizational Unit dialog box, shown in Figure 6-8, choose the location to store the account and then click OK.

FIGURE 6-8 Selecting the organizational unit for the new user.

7. In the User Logon Name text box, type the user's logon name. Use the drop-down list to select the domain with which you want to associate the account. This sets the fully qualified logon name, such as msandberg@pocket-consul-tant.com.

8. Type and then confirm the password for the account. This password must follow the conventions of your organization's password policy. Typically, this means that the password must include at least eight characters and must use three of the four available character types: lowercase letters, uppercase letters, numbers, and symbols.

9. You can select the Require Password Change On Next Logon check box to ensure that the user changes the password at next logon.

10. Tap or click More Options. At this point, you do the following:

- **Specify the mailbox database** Exchange uses the mailbox provisioning load balancer to select a database to use when you create a mailbox and do not specify the mailbox database to use. If you want to specify the database to use, tap or click Browse to the right of the Mailbox Database box. In the Select Mailbox Database dialog box, you'll see a list of available mailbox databases listed by name, server, and Exchange version. Select the mailbox database to use and then select OK.

- **Create an archive mailbox** If you want to create an archive mailbox for the user, select the related check box. Items in the user's mailbox will be moved automatically to the archive mailbox based on the default retention policy. You also can chose a mailbox database for the archive. If you don't chose a mailbox database for the archive, Exchange chooses one for you.

- **Assign an address book policy**   By default, a user has access to the full address book information in the organization. Using address book policies, you can create customized address books. To apply an available policy, select it from the drop-down list.

11. Tap or click Save. Exchange Admin Center creates the new mailbox user. If an error occurs, neither the user nor the mailbox will be created. You will need to tap or click OK, correct the problem, and then tap or click Save again.

Creating the user account and mailbox isn't necessarily the final step. You might also want to do the following:

- Add detailed contact information for the user, such as a business phone number and title
- Add the user to security and distribution groups
- Enable or disable mailbox features for the account
- Modify the user's default delivery options, storage limits, and restrictions on the account
- Associate additional email addresses with the account

NOTE   For all mailbox-enabled accounts, an SMTP email address is configured automatically. You can also add more addresses of the same type. For example, if Brian Johnson is the company's human resources administrator, he might have the primary SMTP address of brianj@pocket-consultant.com and an alternate SMTP address of resumes@pocket-consultant.com.

You may also want to apply appropriate policies to the mailbox. Various types of policies control how users access their mailboxes and how mailbox data is stored. These policies include:

- **Address book policy**   Controls access to the address book information in the organization and allows you to create custom views for various users. A default address book policy is not created when you install Exchange 2013. You can check to see if any address book policies have been created by entering **get-addressbookpolicy** in Exchange Management Shell.

- **Mobile device mailbox policy**   Controls security settings for mobile devices. When you install Exchange Server, a default mobile device mailbox policy is created and applied automatically to all new mailboxes you create unless you specify a different policy to use. To view the settings for the default policy, enter **get-mobiledevicemailboxpolicy –identity "Default"** in Exchange Management Shell.

- **Retention policy**   Specifies the delete and move-to-archive rules that are applied to items in mailboxes. Exchange Server 2013 uses retention policies and retention tags as part of the Messaging Records Management feature. When you install Exchange 2013 a default retention policy is created but is not applied to new mailboxes by default. Therefore, you must explicitly assign a retention policy. To view the settings for the default policy, enter **get-retentionpolicy –identity "Default MRM Policy" | fl** in Exchange Management Shell.

- **Role assignment policy** Controls management roles assigned to users. When you install Exchange Server, a default role assignment policy is created and applied automatically to all new mailboxes you create unless you specify a different policy to use. To view the settings for the default policy, enter **get-roleassignmentpolicy –identity "Default Role Assignment Policy"** in Exchange Management Shell.

- **Sharing policy** Controls how users can share calendar and contact information with users outside your organization. When you install Exchange Server, a default sharing policy is created and applied automatically to all new mailboxes you create unless you specify a different policy to use. To view the settings for the default policy, enter **get-sharingpolicy –identity "Default Sharing Policy"** in Exchange Management Shell.

In Exchange Management Shell, you can create a user account with a mailbox by using the New-Mailbox cmdlet. Sample 6-6 provides the syntax and usage. When you are prompted, enter a secure password for the new user account.

SAMPLE 6-6 New-Mailbox cmdlet syntax and usage

Syntax

```
New-Mailbox -Name Name -Password Password -UserPrincipalName
UserNameAndSuffix {AddtlParams} {CommonParams} {ModParams}

New-Mailbox -Name Name -Room <$true | $false> [-Office OfficeName]
[-Password Password] [-Phone PhoneNumber] [-ResourceCapacity Capacity]
[-UserPrincipalName UserNameAndSuffix] {CommonParams} {ModParams}

New-Mailbox -Name Name -Password Password -WindowsLiveID WindowsLiveId
[-EvictLiveId <$true | $false>] {AddtlParams} {CommonParams}
{ModParams}

New-Mailbox -Name Name -UseExistingLiveId <$true | $false> -WindowsLiveID
WindowsLiveId [-BypassLiveId <$true | $false>] [-NetID NetID]
{AddtlParams} {CommonParams} {ModParams}

New-Mailbox -Name Name -UserPrincipalName UserNameAndSuffix [-MailboxPlan
MailboxPlanId] {CommonParams} {ModParams}

New-Mailbox -Name Name -AccountDisabled <$true | $false> [-MailboxPlan
MailboxPlanId] [-Password Password] [-UsageLocation Location]
[-UserPrincipalName UserNameAndSuffix] {CommonParams} {ModParams}

New-Mailbox -Name Name -ImportLiveId <$true | $false> -WindowsLiveID
WindowsLiveId {AddtlParams} {CommonParams} {ModParams}

New-Mailbox -Name Name -RemovedMailbox RemovedMailboxId [-MailboxPlan
MailboxPlanId] [-Password Password] {CommonParams} {ModParams}
```

```
New-Mailbox -Name Name -FederatedIdentity FederatedId -WindowsLiveID
WindowsLiveId [-EvictLiveId <$true | $false>] [-NetID NetID]
{AddtlParams} {CommonParams}

New-Mailbox -Name Name -FederatedIdentity FederatedId
-MicrosoftOnlineServicesID WindowsLiveId [-NetID NetID]
{AddtlParams} {CommonParams}

New-Mailbox -Name Name -ArchiveDomain SmtpDomain -Password Password
-UserPrincipalName UserNameAndSuffix [-MailboxPlan MailboxPlanId]
[-RemoteArchive <$true | $false>] [-RemovedMailbox RemovedMailboxId]
{CommonParams} {ModParams}

New-Mailbox -Name Name -MicrosoftOnlineServicesID WindowsLiveId -Password
Password {AddtlParams} {CommonParams} {ModParams}

New-Mailbox -Name Name [-UserPrincipalName UserNameAndSuffix]
{CommonParams} {ModParams}

New-Mailbox -Name Name -LinkedDomainController DCName -LinkedMasterAccount
Identity [-LinkedCredential Credential] [-UserPrincipalName
UserNameAndSuffix] {CommonParams} {ModParams}

New-Mailbox -Name Name -Equipment <$true | $false> [-Password Password]
[-UserPrincipalName UserNameAndSuffix] {CommonParams} {ModParams}

New-Mailbox -Name Name -Shared <$true | $false> [-Password Password]
[-UserPrincipalName UserNameAndSuffix] {CommonParams} {ModParams}

New-Mailbox -Name Name [-Password Password] [-UserPrincipalName
UserNameAndSuffix] {CommonParams} {ModParams}

New-Mailbox -Name Name -Arbitration <$true | $false> -UserPrincipalName
UserNameAndSuffix [-Password Password] {CommonParams}

New-Mailbox -Name Name [-Password Password] [-UserPrincipalName
UserNameAndSuffix] {CommonParams} {ModParams}

New-Mailbox -Name Name -Discovery <$true | $false> [-Password Password]
[-UserPrincipalName UserNameAndSuffix] {CommonParams}

New-Mailbox -Name Name -EnableRoomMailboxAccount <$true | $false>
-Room <$true | $false> [-MicrosoftOnlineServicesID WindowsLiveId]
[-RoomMailboxPassword Password] [-UserPrincipalName UserNameAndSuffix]
{CommonParams}

New-Mailbox -Name Name -PublicFolder <$true | $false> [-HoldForMigration
<$true | $false>] [-IsExcludedFromServingHierarchy <$true | $false>]
{CommonParams}
```

```
{AddtlParams}

[-MailboxPlan PlanID] [-RemovedMailbox RemovedMailboxId]
[-UsageLocation Location]

{ModParams}
[-ArbitrationMailbox ModeratorMailbox] [-ModeratedBy Moderators]
[-ModerationEnabled <$true | $false>] [-SendModerationNotifications
<Never | Internal | Always>]

{CommonParams}
[-ActiveSyncMailboxPolicy MailboxPolicyId] [-AddressBookPolicy ABPolicyId]
[-Alias ExchangeAlias] [-Archive {$true | $false}] [-ArchiveDatabase
DatabaseId] [-Database DatabaseId] [-DisplayName Name]
[-DomainController DCName] [-ExternalDirectoryObjectID ObjectID]
[-FirstName FirstName] [-ImmutableId Id] [-Initials Initials] [-LastName
LastName] [-ManagedFolderMailboxPolicy MailboxPolicyId]
[-ManagedFolderMailboxPolicyAllowed {$true | $false}]
[-Organization OrgName] [-OrganizationalUnit OUName]
[-OverrideRecipientQuotas {$true | $false}] [-PrimarySmtpAddress
SmtpAddress] [-QueryBaseDNRestrictionEnabled <$true | $false>]
[-RemoteAccountPolicy PolicyId] [-RemotePowershellEnabled
<$true | $false>] [-ResetPasswordOnNextLogon <$true | $false>]
[-RetentionPolicy PolicyId] [-RoleAssignmentPolicy PolicyId]
[-SamAccountName PreWin2000Name] [-SharingPolicy PolicyId]
[-TargetAllMDBs <$true | $false>] [-ThrottlingPolicy PolicyId]
```

Usage

```
New-Mailbox -Name "Shane S. Kim" -Alias "shanek"
-OrganizationalUnit "cpandl.com/Engineering"
-Database "Engineering Primary"
-UserPrincipalName "shanek@cpandl.com" -SamAccountName "shanek"
-FirstName "Shane" -Initials "S" -LastName "Kim"
-ResetPasswordOnNextLogon $true -Archive $true
```

Creating online user accounts with mailboxes

You can create user accounts with mailboxes in Exchange Online. These accounts are then available in the online organization.

To create an online user account, follow these steps:

1. From the dashboard in Office 365 Admin Center, select Add New Users. This starts the New User Wizard, shown in Figure 6-9.

FIGURE 6-9 Providing the name details for the new user.

2. Type the user's first name and last name in the text boxes provided. These values are used to create the Display Name entry.

3. The Display Name and Name properties can't exceed 64 characters. As necessary, make changes to the Display Name. For example, you might want to type the name in LastName FirstName format or in FirstName LastName format.

4. In the User Name text box, type the user's logon name. Use the drop-down list to select the domain with which you want to associate the account. This sets the fully qualified logon name, such as msandberg@pocket-consultant. com (which is referred to as the logon ID with Exchange Online).

5. Tap or click Next. On the Settings page, specify a user location, such as United States. Note that due to certain licensing restrictions some online features may not be available in certain locations.

6. Tap or click Next. On the Assign Licenses page, select a license to assign to the user.

IMPORTANT The available licenses will depend on the license types previously purchased for your organization. While you don't have to assign a license when you create a user, users are assigned a mailbox only when you assign a license. Therefore, if you don't assign a license, no mailbox is created for the user.

7. Tap or click Next. When you tap or click Create, Office 365 Admin Center creates the new online user. On the Results page, shown in Figure 6-10, note the full user name and temporary password assigned to the user and then tap or click Finish.

FIGURE 6-10 Confirming the account creation.

Creating the online user account and mailbox isn't necessarily the final step. You might also want to do the following:

- Add detailed contact information for the user, such as a business phone number and title
- Add the user to security and distribution groups
- Enable or disable mailbox features for the account
- Modify the user's default delivery options, storage limits, and restrictions on the account
- Associate additional email addresses with the account

In Exchange Management Shell, you can create an online user account using the New-Mailbox cmdlet. Keep in mind that a mailbox is created only when you use the -MailboxPlan parameter to assign a mailbox plan to the new user.

Adding mailboxes to existing domain user accounts

You don't have to create an Exchange mailbox when you create a user account. You can create a mailbox for a user account any time you determine the mailbox is needed.

You can add a mailbox to an existing domain user account in several ways. If you are using a hybrid configuration and want the mailbox created in Exchange Online, you can use the techniques discussed earlier under "Understanding on-premises and online recipient management." Otherwise, you can add a mailbox to a domain user account using only your on-premises Exchange administration tools. To do this, complete the following steps:

1. In Exchange Admin Center, select Recipients in the feature pane and then select Mailboxes.

2. Tap or click New and then select User Mailbox. This opens the New User Mailbox dialog box, shown in Figure 6-11.

FIGURE 6-11 Adding a mailbox to an existing domain user account.

3. In the Alias text box, type an alias for the mailbox user. This alias should uniquely identify the user in the Exchange organization. Alias names cannot contain spaces.

NOTE The alias and domain suffix are combined to create the email address for the user. For example, if the alias is tedc and the domain suffix is pocket-consultant.com, the email address is set as tedc@pocket-consultant.com.

4. The Existing User option is selected by default. Tap or click Browse. This displays the Select User dialog box.

5. In the Select User dialog box, shown in Figure 6-12, select the user account you want to mailbox-enable and then tap or click OK. User accounts that are not yet mail-enabled or mailbox-enabled for the current domain are listed by name and organizational unit.

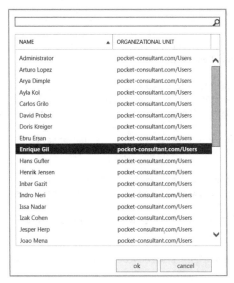

FIGURE 6-12 Finding the user account you want to mailbox-enable.

6. Tap or click More Options. You can now:

- **Specify the mailbox database** Exchange uses the mailbox provisioning load balancer to select a database to use when you create a mailbox and do not specify the mailbox database to use. If you want to specify the database to use, tap or click Browse to the right of the Mailbox Database box. In the Select Mailbox Database dialog box, you'll see a list of available mailbox databases listed by name, server, and Exchange version. Select the mailbox database to use and then click OK.

- **Create an archive mailbox** If you want to create an archive mailbox for the user, select the related check box. Items in the user's mailbox will be moved automatically to the archive mailbox based on the default retention policy. You also can choose a mailbox database for the archive. If you don't choose a mailbox database for the archive, Exchange chooses one for you.

- **Assign an address book policy** By default, a user has access to the full address book information in the organization. Using address book policies, you can create customized address books. To apply an available policy, select it from the drop-down list.

7. Tap or click Save. Exchange Admin Center creates the mailbox for the selected user. If an error occurs, the mailbox will not be created. You will need to tap or click OK, correct the problem, and then tap or click Save again.

In Exchange Management Shell, you can add a mailbox to individual user accounts using the Enable-Mailbox cmdlet. Sample 6-7 provides the syntax and usage. If you want to create mailboxes for multiple accounts, you need to enter a separate command for each account.

SAMPLE 6-7 Enable-Mailbox cmdlet syntax and usage

Syntax

Enable-Mailbox [-AccountDisabled <$true | $false>] [-MailboxPlan
MailboxPlanId] [-UsageLocation **Location**] {AddtlParams} {CommonParams}

Enable-Mailbox -LinkedDomainController **DCName** -LinkedMasterAccount **Identity**
[-Database **DatabaseId**] [-LinkedCredential **Credential**]
[-TargetAllMDBs <$true | $false>] {CommonParams}

Enable-Mailbox -Discovery <$true | $false> [-Database **DatabaseId**]
[-TargetAllMDBs <$true | $false>] {CommonParams}

Enable-Mailbox [-AccountDisabled <$true | $false>] [-MailboxPlan
MailboxPlanId] [-UsageLocation **Location**] {AddtlParams} {CommonParams}

Enable-Mailbox -Equipment <$true | $false> [-AccountDisabled <$true |
$false>] {AddtlParams} {CommonParams}

Enable-Mailbox -Room <$true | $false> [-AccountDisabled <$true | $false>]
{AddtlParams} {CommonParams}

Enable-Mailbox -PublicFolder <$true | $false> [-Database **DatabaseId**]
[-HoldForMigration <$true | $false>] {CommonParams}

Enable-Mailbox -Arbitration <$true | $false> [-Database **DatabaseId**]
[-TargetAllMDBs <$true | $false>] {CommonParams}

Enable-Mailbox -Shared <$true | $false> [-AccountDisabled <$true | $false>]
{AddtlParams} {CommonParams}

Enable-Mailbox [-Archive <$true | $false>] [-ArchiveDatabase **DatabaseId**]
[-ArchiveGuid <Guid>] [-ArchiveName <MultiValuedProperty>]
[-BypassModerationCheck <$true | $false>] {CommonParams}

Enable-Mailbox -ArchiveDomain **SmtpDomain** [-RemoteArchive <$true |
$false>] {CommonParams}

{AddtlParams}

[-BypassModerationCheck <$true | $false>] [-Database DatabaseId]
[-TargetAllMDBs <$true | $false>]

{CommonParams}
[-ActiveSyncMailboxPolicy **MailboxPolicyId**] [-Alias **ExchangeAlias**]
[-DisplayName **Name**] [-DomainController **FullyQualifiedName**]
[-ManagedFolderMailboxPolicy **MailboxPolicyId**]
[-ManagedFolderMailboxPolicyAllowed {$true | $false}]
[-OverrideRecipientQuotas {$true | $false}]
[-PrimarySmtpAddress **SmtpAddress**]
[-RetentionPolicy **PolicyId**] [-RoleAssignmentPolicy **PolicyId**]

```
Enable-Mailbox -Identity "cpandl.com/Engineering/Oliver Lee"
-Alias "Oliverl" -Database "Engineering Primary"
```

Setting or changing the common name and logon name for domain user accounts

All domain user accounts have a common name stored in Active Directory and a logon name used for logging on to the domain. These names can be different from the mailbox display name and mailbox alias used by Exchange Server.

You can set this information for a domain user account by completing the following steps:

1. In Exchange Admin Center, select Recipients in the feature pane and then select Mailboxes.

2. Double-tap or double-click the mailbox entry for the user with which you want to work. This opens a properties dialog box for the user.

3. On the General page, shown in Figure 6-13, use the following text boxes to set the user's common name and logon name:

   - **First Name, Initials, Last Name**   Sets the user's full name.
   - **Name**   Sets the user's display name as seen in logon sessions and in Active Directory.
   - **User Logon Name**   Sets the user's logon name.

4. Tap or click Save to apply your changes.

FIGURE 6-13 Changing the user's naming information for Active Directory.

Setting or changing contact information for user accounts

You can set contact information for a user account by completing the following steps:

1. In Exchange Admin Center, select Recipients in the feature pane and then select Mailboxes.

2. Double-tap or double-click the mailbox entry for the user with which you want to work.

3. On the Contact Information page, use the text boxes provided to set the user's business address or home address. Normally, you'll want to enter the user's business address. This way, you can track the business locations and mailing addresses of users at various offices.

   NOTE You need to consider privacy issues before entering private information, such as home addresses and home phone numbers, for users. Discuss the matter with the appropriate groups in your organization, such as the human resources and legal departments. You might also want to get user consent before releasing home addresses.

4. Use the Work Phone, Mobile Phone, and Fax text boxes to set the user's primary business telephone, mobile phone, and fax numbers.

5. Tap or click More Options. Use the Office text box to set the user's office and the Web Page text box to set the URL of the user's home page, which can be on the Internet or the company intranet.

6. On the Organization page, as appropriate, type the user's title, department, and company.

7. To specify the user's manager, tap or click Browse. In the Manager dialog box, select the user's manager and then tap or click OK. When you specify a manager, the user shows up as a direct report in the manager's account. Tap or click Save to apply the changes.

Changing logon ID or logon domain for online users

For Exchange Online, the fully-qualified logon ID is the user's name followed by the @ symbol and the user's logon domain. You can modify this information for an online user account by completing the following steps:

1. In the dashboard for Office 365 Admin Center, select Users And Groups in the feature pane and then select Active Users.

2. Double-tap or double-click the mailbox entry for the user with which you want to work. This opens a properties dialog box for the user.

3. On the Details page, use the User Name text boxes to set the user's logon name and domain.

4. Tap or click Save to apply your changes.

Changing a user's Exchange Server alias and display name

Each mailbox has an Exchange alias and display name associated with it. The Exchange alias is used with address lists as an alternative way of specifying the user in the To, Cc, or Bcc text boxes of an email message. The alias also sets the primary SMTP address associated with the account.

> **TIP** Whenever you change the Exchange alias in an on-premises organization, a new email address is generated and set as the default address for SMTP. The previous email addresses for the account aren't deleted. Instead, these remain as alternatives to the defaults. To learn how to change or delete these additional email addresses, see "Adding, changing, and removing email and other addresses" later in this chapter.

With Exchange Online, changing a user's Exchange alias doesn't normally change the primary SMTP address for the user.

To change the Exchange alias and mailbox name on a user account, complete the following steps:

1. In Exchange Admin Center, select Recipients in the feature pane and then select Mailboxes.

2. Double-tap or double-click the mailbox entry for the user with which you want to work.

3. On the General page, the Display Name text box sets the mailbox name. Change this text box if you'd like the mailbox to have a different display name.

4. The Alias text box sets the Exchange alias. If you'd like to assign a new alias, enter the new Exchange alias in this text box.

5. Tap or click Save.

> **NOTE** Often, the user logon name and the Exchange alias are set to the same value. If you've implemented this practice in your organization, you may also want to modify the user logon name. However, this is not a best practice when security is a concern.

Adding, changing, and removing email and other addresses

When you create a mailbox-enabled user account, default email addresses are created. Any time you update the user's Exchange alias in an on-premises Exchange organization, a new default email address is created. However, the old addresses aren't deleted. They remain as alternative email addresses for the account.

With Exchange Online, changing a user's Exchange alias doesn't normally change the email address for the user. You can, however, modify the primary SMTP address or add additional SMTP addresses.

Exchange also allows you to create non-SMTP addresses for users:

- Exchange Unified Messaging (EUM) addresses used by the Unified Messaging service to locate UM-enabled users within the Exchange organization

- Custom addresses for legacy Exchange (Ex) as well as these non-Exchange mail organizations: X.400, X.500, MSMail, CcMail, Lotus Notes, and Novell GroupWise

To add, change, or remove an email or other address, follow these steps:

1. In Exchange Admin Center, select Recipients in the feature pane and then select Mailboxes.

2. Double-tap or double-click the mailbox entry for the user with which you want to work.

3. On the Email Address page, shown in Figure 6-14, you can use the following techniques to manage the user's email addresses:

FIGURE 6-14 Configuring the email addresses for the user account.

- **Create a new SMTP address** Tap or click Add. Because the address type SMTP is selected by default, enter the SMTP email address, and then tap or click OK to save your changes.

- **Create a new EUM address** Tap or click Add, and then select the EUM option. Enter the custom address or extension. Next, tap or click Browse and then select a dial plan. Tap or click OK to save your changes.

- **Create a custom address** Tap or click Add, and then select the Custom Address Type option. Enter the custom address type in the text box provided. Valid types include: X.400, X.500, EUM, MSMail, CcMail, Lotus Notes, and NovellGroupWise. Next, enter the custom address. This address must comply with the format requirements for the address type. Tap or click OK to save your changes.

TIP Use SMTP as the address type for standard Internet email addresses. For custom address types, such as X.400, you must enter the address in the proper format.

- **Edit an existing address** Double-tap or double-click the address entry, or select the entry and then select Edit on the toolbar. Modify the settings in the Address dialog box, and then tap or click OK.

- **Delete an existing address**   Select the address, and then tap or click Remove.

NOTE   You can't delete the primary SMTP address without first promoting another email address to the primary position. Exchange Server uses the primary SMTP address to send and receive messages.

Setting a default reply address for a user account

Each email address type has one default reply address. This email address sets the value of the Reply To text box. To change the default reply address, follow these steps:

1. In Exchange Admin Center, select Recipients in the feature pane and then select Mailboxes.

2. Double-tap or double-click the mailbox entry for the user with which you want to work.

3. On the Email Address page, current default email addresses are highlighted with bold text. Email addresses that aren't highlighted are used only as alternative addresses for delivering messages to the current mailbox.

4. To change the current default settings, select an email address that isn't highlighted and then tap or click Edit.

5. In the Email Address dialog box, select the Make This The Reply Address checkbox. Tap or click OK to save the changes.

Changing a user's web, wireless service, and protocol options

When you create user accounts with mailboxes, global settings determine the web, wireless services, and protocols that are available. You can change these settings for individual users at any time by completing the following steps:

1. In Exchange Admin Center, select Recipients in the feature pane and then select Mailboxes.

2. Double-tap or double-click the mailbox entry for the user with which you want to work.

3. Tap or click the Mailbox Features tab. As shown in Figure 6-15, configure the following web, wireless services, and protocols for the user:

   - **Exchange ActiveSync**   Allows the user to synchronize the mailbox and to browse wireless devices. Properties allow you to specify an Exchange ActiveSync policy. When you enable Exchange ActiveSync, the account uses the default mobile device mailbox policy. To set an alternative policy, tap or click the related View Details option.

   - **Outlook Web App**   Permits the user to access the mailbox with a web browser. Properties allow you to specify an Outlook Web App mailbox policy.

   - **Unified Messaging**   Allows the user to access unified messaging features, such as the voice browser. In a standard configuration of Exchange

2013, all new mailbox users have unified messaging enabled. However, a default UM Mailbox policy is required to fully activate the feature. If one hasn't been assigned, tap or click Enable to display a dialog box where you can specify the required policy.

- **MAPI**   Permits the user to access the mailbox with a Messaging Application Programming Interface (MAPI) email client.

- **POP3**   Permits the user to access the mailbox with a Post Office Protocol version 3 (POP3) email client.

- **IMAP4**   Permits the user to access the mailbox with an Internet Message Access Protocol version 4 (IMAP4) email client.

- **Litigation Hold**   Indicates whether a mailbox is subject to litigation hold where users can delete mail items but the items are retained by Exchange. Properties allow you to provide a note to users about litigation hold and the URL of a webpage where they can learn more.

- **Archive**   Indicates whether an in-place archive mailbox has been created for the user. When you enable an in-place archive, you can specify the mailbox database to use. Properties allow you to specify the name of the folder in the user's mailbox that contains the archive. You also can set an archive quota limit and warning value.

FIGURE 6-15 Changing wireless service and protocol options for users in the Properties dialog box for each user.

4. Select an option and then tap or click Enable or Disable, as appropriate, to change the status. If an option has required properties, you'll be prompted to configure these properties when you enable the option. If an option has

additional configurable properties, tap or click the related View Details option to configure them.

5. Tap or click Save to close the Properties dialog box.

Requiring domain user accounts to change passwords

Group Policy settings typically require users to periodically change their passwords. Sometimes, you might have to ensure that a user changes her password the next time she logs on. For example, if you have to reset a password and give it to the user over the phone, you might want the user to change the password the next time she logs on.

To set a user account to require the password be changed on next logon complete the following steps:

1. In Exchange Admin Center, select Recipients in the feature pane and then select Mailboxes.

2. Double-tap or double-click the mailbox entry for the user with which you want to work.

3. On the General page, select the Require Password Change On Next Logon check box. Tap or click OK.

You can use the Set-User cmdlet to perform the same task, following the syntax shown in Sample 6-8.

SAMPLE 6-8 Requiring a user password change

Syntax
```
Set-User -Identity UserIdentity
-ResetPasswordOnNextLogon <$false|$true>
```

Usage
```
Set-User -Identity "Oliver Lee" -ResetPasswordOnNextLogon $true
```

Deleting mailboxes from user accounts

When you disable a mailbox for a domain user account using the Exchange management tools, you permanently remove all Exchange attributes from the user object in Active Directory and mark the primary mailbox for deletion. Exchange Server then deletes the mailbox according to the retention period you set on the account or on the mailbox database. Because you only removed the user account's Exchange attributes, the user account still exists in Active Directory.

In Exchange Admin Center, you can delete a mailbox from a domain user account and delete all related Exchange attributes by completing the following steps:

1. In Exchange Admin Center, select Recipients in the feature pane and then select Mailboxes.

2. Select the mailbox entry for the user with which you want to work.

3. Select the More button (the button with three dots) and then select Disable.

4. When prompted to confirm this action, select Yes. The mailbox is then in the disconnected state and will be removed when the retention period expires. If the account was subject to litigation hold, mail items subject to litigation hold are preserved as recoverable items until the litigation hold period expires.

If you remove the Exchange Online license for an online user account, the user's account is marked as an unlicensed account. Exchange Online deletes mailboxes from unlicensed accounts automatically after the grace period expires. By default, this grace period is 30 days. As with on-premises Exchange, retention hold, archiving and litigation hold settings determine whether some or any mailbox data is held.

You can remove a license from an online user account by completing the following steps:

1. In the dashboard for Office 365 Admin Center, select Users And Groups.
2. Select the user whose license you want to remove and then tap or click Edit.
3. On the Assign Licenses page, uncheck the box for the license that you want to remove.
4. When prompted to confirm this action, select Yes. The license that was previously assigned to this user will become available to be assigned to another user.

You can use the Disable-Mailbox cmdlet to delete mailboxes while retaining the user accounts as well. Sample 6-9 shows the syntax and usage.

SAMPLE 6-9 Disable-Mailbox cmdlet syntax and usage

Syntax

```
Disable-Mailbox -Identity Identifier [-DomainController DCName]
```

Usage

```
Disable-Mailbox -Identity "Oliver Lee"
```

Deleting user accounts and their mailboxes

When you delete a domain user account and its mailbox using the Exchange management tools, you permanently remove the account from Active Directory and mark the primary mailbox for deletion. Exchange Server then deletes the mailbox according to the retention period you set on the account or on the mailbox database. Further, if the account was subject to litigation hold, mail items subject to litigation hold are preserved as recoverable items until the litigation hold period expires.

After you delete an account, you can't create an account with the same name and have the account automatically retain the same permissions as the original account. This is because the SID for the new account won't match the SID for the old account. However, that doesn't mean that after you delete an account, you can never again create an account with that same name. For example, a person might leave the company only to return a short while later. You can create an account using the same naming convention as before, but you'll have to redefine the permissions for that account.

Because deleting built-in accounts could have far-reaching effects on the domain, Windows doesn't let you delete built-in user accounts. In Exchange Admin Center, you can remove other types of accounts and the mailboxes associated with those accounts by following these steps:

1. In Exchange Admin Center, select Recipients in the feature pane and then select Mailboxes.

2. Select the user that you want to delete and then click Delete.

3. When prompted to confirm this action, select Yes.

NOTE Because Exchange security is based on domain authentication, you can't have a mailbox without an account. If you still need the mailbox for an account you want to delete, you can disable the account using Active Directory Users And Computers. Disabling the account in Active Directory prevents the user from logging on, but you can still access the mailbox if you need to. To disable an account, press and hold or right-click the account in Active Directory Users And Computers and then select Disable Account. If you don't have permissions to use Active Directory Users And Computers, ask a domain administrator to disable the account for you.

IMPORTANT If your organization synchronizes user accounts to Exchange Online from your on-premises Active Directory environment, you must delete and restore synced user accounts using the on-premises tools. You can't delete or restore them in the online organization.

If you delete the corresponding Office 365 user account for a mailbox, the online user's mailbox is marked for deletion and the account is marked as a deleted account.

Deleted online users aren't removed immediately. Instead, the accounts are inactivated and marked for deletion. By default, the retention period is 30 days. When the retention period expires, a user and all related data is permanently deleted and is not recoverable. As with on-premises Exchange, retention hold, archiving, and litigation hold settings determine whether some or any mailbox data is held.

You can delete an online user account by completing the following steps:

1. In the dashboard for Office 365 Admin Center, select Users And Groups.

2. Select the user whose license you want to remove and then tap or click Delete.

3. When prompted to confirm this action, select Yes. The license that was previously assigned to this user will become available to be assigned to another user.

You can use the Remove-Mailbox cmdlet to delete user accounts as well. Sample 6-10 shows the syntax. By default, the -Permanent flag is set to $false and mailboxes are retained in a disconnected state according to the mailbox retention policy. If you set the -Permanent flag to $true, the mailbox is removed from Exchange.

SAMPLE 6-10 Remove-Mailbox cmdlet syntax and usage

Syntax

```
Remove-Mailbox -Identity UserIdentity {AddtlParams}

Remove-Mailbox -Database DatabaseId -StoreMailboxIdentity StoreMailboxId
{AddtlParams}

{AddtlParams}
[-Arbitration <$false|$true>] [-DomainController DCName]
[-IgnoreDefaultScope {$true | $false}] [-KeepWindowsLiveID {$true |
$false}] [-Permanent <$false|$true>]
[-RemoveLastArbitrationMailboxAllowed {$true | $false}]
```

Usage

```
Remove-Mailbox -Identity "Oliver Lee"

Remove-Mailbox -Identity "Oliver Lee" -Permanent $true
```

Managing contacts

Contacts represent people with whom you or others in your organization want to get in touch. Contacts can have directory information associated with them, but they don't have network logon privileges.

The only difference between a standard contact and a mail-enabled contact is the presence of email addresses. A mail-enabled contact has one or more email addresses associated with it; a standard contact doesn't. When a contact has an email address, you can list the contact in the global address list or other address lists. This allows users to send messages to the contact.

In Exchange Admin Center, mail-enabled contacts and mail-enabled users are both listed in the Mail Contact node. Mail-enabled contacts are listed with the recipient type Mail Contact, and mail-enabled users are listed with the recipient type Mail User.

Creating mail-enabled contacts

You can create and mail-enable a new contact by completing the following steps:

1. In Exchange Admin Center, select Recipients in the feature pane and then select Contacts.

2. Tap or click New and then select Mail Contact. This opens the New Mail Contact dialog box. Figure 6-16 shows on-premises Exchange options on the left and Exchange Online options on the right.

3. Type the contact's first name, middle initial, and last name in the text boxes provided. These values are used to automatically create the following entries:

   - **Name** The common name is displayed in Active Directory (and only applies with on-premises Exchange).

   - **Display Name** The Display Name is displayed in the global address list and other address lists created for the organization. It is also used when addressing email messages to the contact.

FIGURE 6-16 Creating a new mail contact for the Exchange organization

4. Enter the Exchange alias for the contact. Aliases provide an alternative way of addressing users and contacts in To, Cc, and Bcc text boxes of email messages.

5. In the External Email Address text box, enter the address to associate with the contact. With on-premises Exchange, you can use both SMTP and non-SMTP addresses. With online Exchange, only standard SMTP addresses are accepted.

> **NOTE** For non-SMTP addresses, the dialog box requires that you use a prefix that identifies the address type and that the address format comply to the rules for that type. Use the prefix X400: for X.400 addresses, the prefix X500: for X.500 addresses, the prefix MSMAIL: for MSMail addresses, the prefix CCMAIL: for CcMail addresses, the prefix LOTUSNOTES: for Lotus Notes, and the prefix NOVELLGROUP-WISE: for NovellGroupWise.

6. The Organizational Unit text box shows where in Active Directory the contact will be created. By default, this is the Users container in the current domain. Because you'll usually need to create new contacts in a specific organizational unit rather than in the Users container, tap or click Browse. Use the Select An Organizational Unit dialog box to choose the location in which to store the contact, and then tap or click OK.

7. Tap or click Save. Exchange Admin Center creates the new contact and mail-enables it. If an error occurs, the contact will not be created. You will need to correct the problem and repeat this procedure.

In Exchange Management Shell, you can create a new mail-enabled contact using the New-MailContact cmdlet. Sample 6-11 provides the syntax and usage.

SAMPLE 6-11 New-MailContact cmdlet syntax and usage

Syntax

```
New-MailContact -Name Name -ExternalEmailAddress TYPE:EmailAddress
[-ArbitrationMailbox ModeratorMailbox] [-Alias ExchangeAlias]
[-DisplayName Name] [-DomainController DCName] [-FirstName FirstName]
[-Initials Initials] [-LastName LastName] [-MacAttachmentFormat <BinHex |
UuEncode | AppleSingle | AppleDouble>] [-MessageBodyFormat <Text | Html |
TextAndHtml>] [-MessageFormat <Text | Mime>] [-ModeratedBy Moderators]
[-ModerationEnabled <$true | $false>] [-Organization OrgName]
[-OrganizationalUnit OUName] [-PrimarySmtpAddress
SmtpAddress] [-SendModerationNotifications <Never | Internal | Always>]
[-UsePreferMessageFormat <$true | $false>]
```

Usage

```
New-MailContact -ExternalEmailAddress "SMTP:wendywheeler@msn.com"
 -Name "Wendy Wheeler" -Alias "WendyWheeler"
 -OrganizationalUnit "cpandl.com/Corporate Services"
 -FirstName "Wendy" -Initials "" -LastName "Wheeler"
```

In Exchange Management Shell, you can mail-enable an existing contact using the Enable-MailContact cmdlet. Sample 6-12 provides the syntax and usage.

SAMPLE 6-12 Enable-MailContact cmdlet syntax and usage

Syntax

```
Enable-MailContact -Identity ContactId -ExternalEmailAddress EmailAddress
[-Alias ExchangeAlias] [-DisplayName Name] [-DomainController
FullyQualifiedName] [-MacAttachmentFormat <BinHex | UuEncode |
AppleSingle | AppleDouble>] [-MessageBodyFormat <Text | Html |
TextAndHtml>] [-MessageFormat <Text | Mime>] [-PrimarySmtpAddress
SmtpAddress] [-UsePreferMessageFormat <$true | $false>]
```

Usage

```
Enable-MailContact -Identity "cpand.com/Sales/John Smith"
 -ExternalEmailAddress "SMTP:johnsmith@pocket-consultant.com"
 -Alias "JohnSmith" -DisplayName "John Smith"
```

Setting or changing a contact's name and alias

Mail-enabled contacts can have the following name components:

- **First Name, Initials, Last Name**   The first name, initials, and last name of the contact

- **Common Name**   The name used in Active Directory for on-premises contacts

- **Display Name**   The name displayed in the global address list

- **Alias**   The Exchange alias for the contact

You can set or change name and alias information for a mail-enabled contact or user by completing the following steps:

1. In Exchange Admin Center, select Recipients in the feature pane and then select Contacts.

2. Double-tap or double-click the name of the mail-enabled contact or user you want to work with. The Properties dialog box appears.

3. On the General tab, use the textboxes provided to update the first name, middle initial, and last name as necessary. Changes you make will update the display name but not the common name. Therefore, as necessary, use the Name text box to update the common name.

4. With mail-enabled contacts, the Alias text box sets the Exchange alias. If you'd like to assign a new alias, enter the new Exchange alias in this text box.

5. With mail-enabled users, the User Logon Name text box sets the name used to log on to the domain and also sets the domain suffix.

6. Tap or click Save to apply your changes.

Setting additional directory information for contacts

You can set additional directory information for a mail-enabled contact or user by completing the following steps:

1. In Exchange Admin Center, select Recipients in the feature pane and then select Contacts.

2. Double-tap or double-click the name of the mail-enabled contact or user you want to work with. The Properties dialog box appears.

3. On the Contact Information page, use the text boxes provided to set the contact's business address or home address. Normally, you'll want to enter the contact's business address. This way, you can track the business locations and mailing addresses of contacts at various offices.

   NOTE You need to consider privacy issues before entering private information, such as home addresses and home phone numbers, for users. Discuss the matter with the appropriate groups in your organization, such as the human resources and legal departments. You might also want to get user consent before releasing home addresses.

4. Use the Work Phone, Mobile Phone, and Fax text boxes to set the contact or user's primary business telephone, mobile phone, and fax numbers.

5. Use the Office text box to set the user's Office and the Notes text box to add any important notes about the contact.

6. On the Organization page, as appropriate, type the contact or user's title, department, and company.

7. To specify the contact or user's manager, tap or click Browse. In the Manager dialog box, select the manager and then tap or click OK. When you specify a manager, the contact or user shows up as a direct report in the manager's account. Tap or click Save to apply the changes.

Changing email addresses associated with contacts

Mail-enabled contacts and users have several types of email addresses associated with them:

- An internal, automatically generated email address used for routing within the organization
- An external email address to which mail routed internally is forwarded for delivery

With mail-enabled contacts, you can only use SMTP email addresses. You can change the SMTP email addresses associated with a mail-enabled contact by completing the following steps:

1. In Exchange Admin Center, select Recipients in the feature pane and then select Contacts.

2. Double-tap or double-click the name of the mail-enabled contact you want to work with. The Properties dialog box appears.

3. On the General page, the external SMTP email address of the mail-enabled contact is listed. This is the primary SMTP email address for the mail-enabled contact. As necessary, enter a new email address.

   NOTE The primary email address is listed with the prefix SMTP. When you enter a new email address, you aren't required to enter this prefix. Thus, you could enter SMTP:williams@treyresearch.net or williams@treyresearch.net.

4. On the Email Addresses page, the primary SMTP email address is listed along with the internal email address. You can use the following techniques to manage the internal addresses:

   - **Create an alternative internal address**   Tap or click Add. Specify the internal email address to use by entering the Exchange alias and then selecting the domain for this internal address. Tap or click OK.

   - **Edit an existing address**   Double-tap or double-click the address entry, or tap or click Edit on the toolbar. Modify the address settings as necessary, and then tap or click OK.

   - **Delete an existing address**   Select the address, and then tap or click Remove.

5. Tap or click Save to apply your changes.

With mail-enabled users, you can use SMTP and non-SMTP email addresses. You can change the email addresses associated with a mail-enabled user by completing the following steps:

1. In Exchange Admin Center, select Recipients in the feature pane and then select Contacts.

2. Double-tap or double-click the name of the mail-enabled user you want to work with. The Properties dialog box appears.

3. On the Email Addresses page, you can use the following techniques to manage the mail-enabled user's email addresses:

- **Create a new SMTP address** Tap or click Add. Because the address type SMTP is selected by default, enter the SMTP email address, and then tap or click OK to save your changes.

- **Create a custom address** Tap or click Add, and then select the Custom Address Type option. Enter the custom address type in the text box provided. Valid types include: X.400, X.500, EUM, MSMail, CcMail, Lotus Notes, and NovellGroupWise. Next, enter the custom address. This address must·comply with the format requirements for the address type. Tap or click OK to save your changes.

- **Edit an existing address** Double-tap or double-click the address entry, or select the entry and then select Edit on the toolbar. Modify the settings in the Address dialog box, and then tap or click OK.

- **Delete an existing address** Select the address, and then tap or click Remove.

NOTE You can't delete the primary SMTP address without first promoting another email address to the primary position. Exchange Server uses the primary SMTP address to send and receive messages.

4. The external email address of the mail-enabled user is also listed on the Email Addresses page. This is the primary email address for the mail user or contact. As necessary, select an alternative email address to be the primary.

5. Tap or click Save to apply your changes.

Disabling contacts and removing Exchange attributes

With on-premises Exchange, you have two options for mail-enabled users and contacts that are no longer needed. You can disable the mail-enabled user or contact, or you can delete the mail-enabled user or contact. With Exchange Online, your only option is to delete the mail-enabled user or contact.

When you disable a contact using the on-premises Exchange management tools, you permanently remove the contact from the Exchange database, but you do not remove it from Active Directory.

In Exchange Admin Center, you can disable mail-enabled contacts by following these steps:

1. In Exchange Admin Center, select Recipients in the feature pane and then select Contacts.
2. Select the contact that you want to disable.
3. Click the More button (the button with three dots) and then select Disable.
4. When prompted to confirm this action, select Yes.

You can use the Disable-MailContact cmdlet to remove Exchange attributes from contacts while retaining the contact in Active Directory. Sample 6-13 shows the syntax and usage.

SAMPLE 6-13 Disable-MailContact cmdlet syntax and usage

Syntax

```
Disable-MailContact -Identity ContactIdentity
```

Usage

```
Disable-MailContact -Identity "David So"
```

Later, if you want to re-enable the contact, you can do this using the Enable-MailContact cmdlet.

Deleting contacts

When you delete a mail-enabled user or contact from Exchange Online, the mail-enabled user or contact is permanently removed from Exchange Online. When you delete a contact using the on-premises Exchange management tools, you permanently remove it from Active Directory and from the Exchange database. In Exchange Admin Center, you can delete contacts by following these steps:

1. In Exchange Admin Center, select Recipients in the feature pane and then select Contacts.
2. Select the contact that you want to delete and then click Delete.
3. When prompted to confirm this action, select Yes.

You can use the Remove-MailContact cmdlet to delete contacts as well. Sample 6-14 shows the syntax and usage.

SAMPLE 6-14 Remove-MailContact cmdlet syntax and usage

Syntax

```
Remove-MailContact -Identity ContactIdentity
```

Usage

```
Remove-MailContact -Identity "Henrik Larsen"
```

Mailbox administration

The difference between a good Microsoft Exchange Server administrator and a great one is the attention he or she pays to mailbox administration. Mailboxes are private storage places for messages you've sent and received, and they are created as part of private mailbox databases in Exchange. Mailboxes have many properties that control mail delivery, permissions, and storage limits. You can configure most mailbox settings on a per-mailbox basis. However, with Exchange Online, some settings are configured for all users of the service while other settings are fixed as part of the service and cannot be changed. With on-premises Exchange, you cannot change some settings without moving mailboxes to another mailbox database or changing the settings of the mailbox database itself. For example, with on-premises Exchange, you set the storage location on the file system, the storage limits, the deleted item retention, and the default offline address book on a per-mailbox-database basis. Keep this in mind when performing capacity planning and when deciding which mailbox location to use for a particular mailbox.

Creating special-purpose mailboxes

Exchange Server 2013 and Exchange Online make it easy to create several special-purpose mailbox types, including the following:

- **Room mailbox**   A room mailbox is a mailbox for room scheduling.
- **Equipment mailbox**   An equipment mailbox is a mailbox for equipment scheduling.
- **Linked mailbox**   A linked mailbox is a mailbox for a user from a separate, trusted forest.
- **Forwarding mailbox**   A forwarding mailbox is a mailbox that can receive mail and forward it off site.
- **Archive mailbox**   An archive mailbox is used to store a user's messages, such as might be required for executives and needed by some managers.

- **Arbitration mailbox**   An arbitration mailbox is used to manage approval requests, such as may be required for handling moderated recipients and distribution group membership approval.

- **Discovery mailbox**   A Discovery mailbox is the target for Discovery searches and can't be converted to another mailbox type after it's created. In-Place eDiscovery is a feature of Exchange 2013 that allows authorized users to search mailboxes for specific types of content that might be required to meet legal discovery requirements.

- **Shared mailbox**   A shared mailbox is a mailbox that is shared by multiple users, such as a general mailbox for customer inquiries.

- **Public folder mailbox**   A public folder mailbox is a shared mailbox for storing public folder data.

The sections that follow discuss techniques for working with these special-purpose mailboxes.

Using room and equipment mailboxes

You use room and equipment mailboxes for scheduling purposes only. You'll find that:

- Room mailboxes are useful when you have conference rooms, training rooms, and other rooms for which you need to coordinate the use.

- Equipment mailboxes are useful when you have projectors, media carts, or other items of equipment for which you need to coordinate the use. Every room and equipment mailbox must have a separate user account associated with it. Although these accounts are required so that the mailboxes can be used for scheduling, the accounts are disabled by default so that they cannot be used for logon. To ensure that the resource accounts do not get enabled accidentally, you need to coordinate closely with other administrators in your organization.

IMPORTANT   Each room or piece of equipment must have a separate user account. This is necessary to track the unique free/busy data for each resource.

NOTE   Exchange Admin Center doesn't show the enabled or disabled status of user accounts. The only way to check the status is to use domain administration tools.

Because the number of scheduled rooms and amount of equipment grows as your organization grows, you'll want to carefully consider the naming conventions you use with rooms and equipment:

- With rooms, you may want to use display names that clearly identify the rooms' physical locations. For example, you might have rooms named "Conference Room B on Fifth Floor" or "Building 83 Room 15."

- With equipment, you may want the display name to identify the type of equipment, the equipment's characteristics, and the equipment's relative location. For example, you might have equipment named "NEC HD Projector at Seattle Office" or "Fifth Floor Media Cart."

As with standard user mailboxes, room and equipment mailboxes have contact information associated with them (see Figure 7-1). To make it easier to find rooms and equipment, you should provide as much information as possible. If a room has a conference or call-in phone, be sure to provide this phone number. Also, provide location details that help people find the conference room and specify the room capacity. The phone, location, and capacity are displayed in Microsoft Office Outlook.

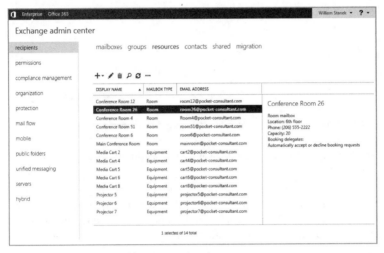

FIGURE 7-1 Mailboxes created for rooms and equipment.

After you've set up mailboxes for your rooms and equipment, scheduling the rooms and equipment is straightforward. In Exchange, room and equipment availability is tracked using free/busy data. In Outlook, a user who wants to reserve rooms, equipment, or both simply makes a meeting request that includes the rooms and equipment that are required for the meeting.

The steps to schedule a meeting and reserve equipment are as follows:

1. Create a meeting request:
   - In Outlook 2007, tap or click New, and then select Meeting Request. Or press Ctrl+Shift+Q.
   - In Outlook 2010 or Outlook 2013, tap or click New Items, and then select Meeting. Or press Ctrl+Shift+Q.

2. In the To text box, invite the individuals who should attend the meeting by typing their display names, Exchange aliases, or email addresses, as appropriate (see Figure 7-2).

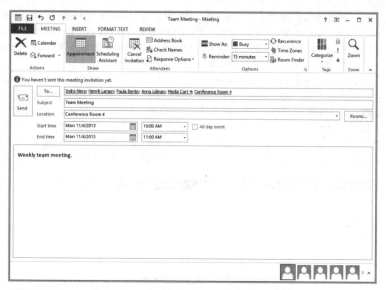

FIGURE 7-2 You can schedule a meeting that includes a reserved room and reserved equipment.

3. Type the display name, Exchange alias, or email address for any equipment you need to reserve.

4. Tap or click Rooms to the right of the Location text box. The Select Rooms dialog box appears, as shown in Figure 7-3. By default, the Select Rooms dialog box uses the All Rooms address book. Rooms are added to this address book automatically when you create them.

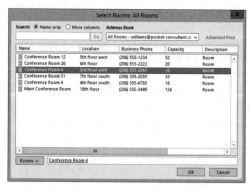

FIGURE 7-3 Selecting a room to use for the meeting.

5. Double-tap or double-click the room you'd like to use. This adds the room to the Rooms list. Tap or click OK to close the Select Rooms dialog box.

6. In the Subject text box, type the meeting subject.

7. Use the Start Time and End Time options to schedule the start and end times for the meeting.

8. Tap or click Scheduling Assistant to view the free/busy data for the invited users and the selected resources. Use the free/busy data to make changes if necessary.

9. Type a message to accompany the meeting request, then tap or click Send.

Exchange can be configured to accept booking requests automatically, based on availability, or to route requests through delegates, such as office administrators, who review requests. Although small organizations might not need coordinators for rooms and equipment, most large organizations will need coordinators to prevent conflicts.

Both on-premises Exchange and Exchange Online provide additional booking options that can help to reduce conflicts (see Figure 7-4). The booking options are the same for both rooms and equipment. The options allow you to:

- Specify whether repeat bookings are allowed. By default, repeat bookings are allowed. If you disable the related settings, users won't be able to schedule repeating meetings.

- Specify whether the room or equipment can be scheduled only during working hours. By default, this option is disabled, which allows rooms and equipment to be scheduled for use at any time. The standard working hours are defined as 8:00 A.M. to 5:00 P.M. Monday through Friday but can be changed using the Calendaring options in Outlook.

- Specify the maximum number of days in advance the room or equipment can be booked. By default, rooms and equipment can be booked up to 180 days in advance. You can change the default to any value from 0 to 1080. A value of 0 removes the lead time restriction completely.

- Specify the maximum duration that the room or equipment can be reserved. By default, rooms and equipment can be reserved for up to 24 hours, which allows for preparation and maintenance that may be required. You can change the default to any value from 0 to 35791394.1. A value of 0 removes the duration restriction completely.

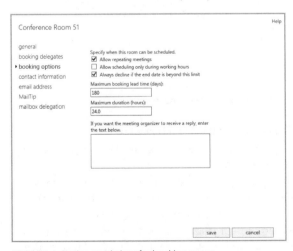

FIGURE 7-4 Setting restrictions for booking rooms.

You can configure booking options after you create the room or equipment mailbox. In Exchange Admin Center, navigate to Recipients > Resources and then double-tap or double-click the resource you want to configure. Next, in the properties dialog box for the resource, select Booking Options. After you change the booking options, tap or click Save to apply the changes.

Creating room mailboxes

In Exchange Admin Center, room mailboxes are displayed under Recipients > Resources. In Exchange Management Shell, you can find all room mailboxes in the organization by entering:

```
Get-Mailbox -ResultSize unlimited -Filter {(RecipientTypeDetails
-eq 'RoomMailbox')}
```

You can create room mailboxes by completing the following steps:

1. In Exchange Admin Center, select Recipients in the feature pane and then select Resources.

2. Tap or click New, and then select Room Mailbox. This opens the New Room Mailbox dialog box. Figure 7-5 shows on-premises Exchange options on the left and Exchange Online options on the right.

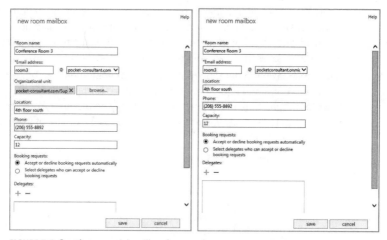

FIGURE 7-5 Creating a special mailbox for a conference room.

3. Type a descriptive display name in the Room Name text box.

4. In the Email Address text box, type the Exchange alias. The Exchange alias is used to set the default email address.

5. Use the drop-down list to select the domain with which the room is to be associated. The Exchange Alias and the domain name are combined to set the fully qualified name, such as room3@pocket-consultant.com.

6. For on-premises Exchange, the Organizational Unit text box shows where in Active Directory the user account will be created. By default, this is the Users

container in the current domain. Because you'll usually need to create room and equipment accounts in a specific organizational unit rather than in the Users container, tap or click Browse to the right of the Organizational Unit text box. Use the Select Organizational Unit dialog box to choose the location in which to store the account, and then tap or click OK.

7. Specify the room location, phone number, and capacity using the text boxes provided.

NOTE By default, booking requests are accepted or declined automatically based on availability. The first person to reserve the room gets the reservation.

8. If your organization has resource coordinators, choose the Select Delegates option. Next, use the options under Delegates to specify the coordinator. Tap or click Add, use the Select Delegates dialog box to select a coordinator for the room, and then select OK. Repeat this procedure to specify additional coordinators.

TIP You can select multiple coordinators in the Select Delegates dialog box. One way to do this is to click the first coordinator, hold Ctrl, and then click each additional coordinator.

9. In on-premises Exchange, tap or click More Options to configure these additional options:

- **Alias**   Sets the Exchange alias and overrides the default value you set previously using the Email Address text box. This allows a resource to have an alias that is different from the name portion of its email address.

- **Mailbox Database**   If you want to specify a mailbox database rather than use an automatically selected one, tap or click Browse to the right of the Mailbox Database text box. In the Select Mailbox Database dialog box, choose the mailbox database in which the mailbox should be stored. Mailbox databases are listed by name as well as by associated server and Exchange version running on the server.

- **Address Book Policy**   If you've implemented address book policies to provide customized address book views, select the address book policy to associate with the equipment mailbox.

10. Tap or click Save to create the room mailbox. If an error occurs during account or mailbox creation, neither the account nor the related mailbox will be created. You need to correct the problem before you can complete this procedure.

In Exchange Management Shell, you can create a user account with a mailbox for rooms by using the New-Mailbox cmdlet. Sample 7-1 provides the syntax and usage.

NOTE For rooms, you must use the -Room parameter. For equipment, you must use the -Equipment parameter. By default, when you use either parameter, the related value is set as $true. Additionally, although with earlier releases of Exchange you needed to set a password for the related user account, this is no longer required. When you create mailboxes for Exchange Online, you cannot specify a database.

Syntax

```
New-Mailbox -Name 'DisplayName' -Alias 'ExchangeAlias'
 -OrganizationalUnit 'OrganizationalUnit'
 -UserPrincipalName 'LogonName' -SamAccountName 'prewin2000logon'
 -FirstName '' -Initials '' -LastName ''
 -Database 'Server\MailboxDatabase'
 -Room
```

Usage

```
New-Mailbox -Name 'Conference Room 27' -Alias 'room27'
 -OrganizationalUnit 'pocket-consultant.com/Sales'
 -UserPrincipalName 'room27@pocket-consultant.com' -SamAccountName 'room27'
 -FirstName '' -Initials '' -LastName ''
 -Database 'Sales Primary'
 -Room
```

Creating equipment mailboxes

In Exchange Admin Center, equipment mailboxes are displayed under Recipients > Resources. In Exchange Management Shell, you can find all equipment mailboxes in the organization by entering:

```
Get-Mailbox -ResultSize unlimited -Filter {(RecipientTypeDetails
-eq 'EquipmentMailbox')}
```

You can create equipment mailboxes by completing the following steps:

1. In Exchange Admin Center, select Recipients in the feature pane and then select Resources.

2. Tap or click New, and then select Equipment Mailbox. This opens the New Equipment Mailbox dialog box. Figure 7-6 shows on-premises Exchange options on the left and Exchange Online options on the right.

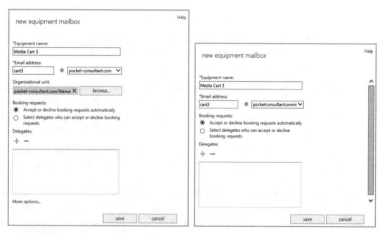

FIGURE 7-6 Creating a special mailbox for equipment.

3. Type a descriptive display name in the Equipment Name text box.

4. In the Email Address text box, type the Exchange alias. The Exchange alias is used to set the default email address.

5. Use the drop-down list to select the domain with which the equipment is to be associated. The Exchange alias and the domain name are combined to set the fully qualified name, such as equipment3@pocket-consultant.com.

6. For on-premises Exchange, the Organizational Unit text box shows where in Active Directory the related user account will be created. By default, this is the Users container in the current domain. Because you'll usually need to create equipment and equipment accounts in a specific organizational unit rather than in the Users container, tap or click Browse to the right of the Organizational Unit text box. Use the Select Organizational Unit dialog box to choose the location in which to store the account, and then tap or click OK.

NOTE By default, booking requests are accepted or declined automatically based on availability. The first person to reserve the equipment gets the reservation.

7. If your organization has resource coordinators, choose the Select Delegates option. Next, use the options under Delegates to specify the coordinator. Tap or click Add, use the Select Delegates dialog box to select a coordinator for the equipment, and then select OK. Repeat this procedure to specify additional coordinators.

TIP You can select multiple coordinators in the Select Delegates dialog box. One way to do this is to click the first coordinator, hold Ctrl, and then click each additional coordinator.

8. With on-premises Exchange, tap or click More Options to configure these additional options:

   ■ **Alias**   Sets the Exchange alias and overrides the default value you set previously using the Email Address text box. This allows a resource to have an alias that is different from the name portion of its email address.

   ■ **Mailbox Database**   If you want to specify a mailbox database rather than use an automatically selected one, tap or click Browse to the right of the Mailbox Database text box. In the Select Mailbox Database dialog box, choose the mailbox database in which the mailbox should be stored. Mailbox databases are listed by name as well as by associated server and Exchange version running on the server.

   ■ **Address Book Policy**   If you've implemented address book policies to provide customized address book views, select the address book policy to associate with the equipment mailbox.

9. Tap or click Save to create the equipment mailbox. If an error occurs during account or mailbox creation, neither the account nor the related mailbox will be created. You need to correct the problem before you can complete this procedure.

In Exchange Management Shell, you can create a user account with a mailbox for equipment by using the New-Mailbox cmdlet. Sample 7-2 provides the syntax and usage. Although with earlier releases of Exchange you needed to set a password for the related user account, this is no longer required. When you create mailboxes for Exchange Online, you cannot specify a database.

SAMPLE 7-2 Creating equipment mailboxes

Syntax

```
New-Mailbox -Name 'DisplayName' -Alias 'ExchangeAlias'
  -OrganizationalUnit 'OrganizationalUnit'
  -UserPrincipalName 'LogonName' -SamAccountName 'prewin2000logon'
  -FirstName '' -Initials '' -LastName ''
  -Database 'Server\MailboxDatabase'
  -Equipment
```

Usage

```
New-Mailbox -Name 'Media Cart 3' -Alias 'cart3'
  -OrganizationalUnit 'pocket-consultant.com/Marketing'
  -UserPrincipalName 'cart3@pocket-consultant.com' -SamAccountName 'cart3'
  -FirstName '' -Initials '' -LastName ''
  -Database 'Marketing Primary'
  -Equipment
```

Creating linked mailboxes

A linked mailbox is a mailbox that is accessed by a user in a separate, trusted forest. Typically, you use linked mailboxes when your organization's mailbox servers are in a separate resource forest and you want to ensure that users can access free/busy data across these forests. You use linked mailboxes with on-premises Exchange organizations.

All linked mailboxes have two user account associations:

- A unique user account in the same forest as the Mailbox server. The same forest user account is disabled automatically so that it cannot be used for logon.

- A unique user account in a separate forest for which you are creating a link. The separate forest user account is enabled so that it can be used for logon.

In Exchange Admin Center, linked mailboxes are displayed under Recipients > Mailboxes. In Exchange Management Shell, you can find all linked mailboxes in the organization by entering:

```
Get-Mailbox -ResultSize unlimited -Filter {(RecipientTypeDetails
-eq 'LinkedMailbox')}
```

You can create a linked mailbox by completing the following steps:

1. In Exchange Admin Center, select Recipients in the feature pane and then select Mailboxes.

2. Tap or click New, and then select Linked Mailbox. This starts the New Linked Mailbox Wizard. A linked mailbox cannot be created with a forest or domain trust in place between the source and target forests.

3. On the New Linked Mailbox page, tap or click Browse to the right of the Linked Forest text box. In the Select Trusted Forest Or Domain dialog box, select the linked forest or domain in which the user's original account is located, and then tap or click OK. This is the separate forest that contains the user account that you want to create the linked mailbox for in the current forest. Tap or click Next.

4. If your organization has configured a one-way, outgoing trust where the current forest trusts the linked forest, you're prompted for administrator credentials in the linked forest so that you can gain access to a domain controller in that forest. Type the user name and password for an administrator account in the account forest, and then tap or click Next.

5. Tap or click Browse to the right of the Linked Domain Controller text box. In the Select Domain Controller dialog box, select a domain controller in the linked forest, and then tap or click OK.

6. Tap or click Browse to the right of the Linked Master Account text box. Use the options in the Select User dialog box to select the original user account in the linked forest, and then tap or click OK.

7. Tap or click Next. On the General Information page, the Organizational Unit text box shows where in Active Directory the user account will be created. By default, this is the Users container in the current domain. Select the Specify The Organizational Unit check box and then tap or click Browse to create the new user account in a different container. Use the Select Organizational Unit dialog box to choose the location in which to store the account, and then tap or click OK.

8. In the User Logon Name text box, type the user's logon name. Use the drop-down list to select the domain with which the account is to be associated. This sets the fully qualified logon name.

9. Tap or click More Options. Type the user's first name, middle initial, and last name in the text boxes provided. These values are used to create the Name entry, which is the user's display name.

10. Optionally, enter an Exchange alias for the user. The alias must be unique in the forest. If you don't specify an alias, the logon name is used as the alias.

11. If you want to specify a mailbox database rather than use an automatically selected one, tap or click Browse to the right of the Mailbox Database text box. In the Select Mailbox Database dialog box, choose the mailbox database in which the mailbox should be stored. Mailbox databases are listed by name as well as by associated server and Exchange version running on the server.

12. Tap or click Save to create the account and the related mailbox. If an error occurs during account or mailbox creation, neither the account nor the related mailbox will be created. You will need to correct the problem.

In Exchange Management Shell, you can create a user account with a linked mailbox by using the New-Mailbox cmdlet. Sample 7-3 provides the syntax and usage. You'll be prompted for the credentials of an administrator account in the linked forest. Although with earlier releases of Exchange you needed to set a password for the related user account, this is no longer required.

SAMPLE 7-3 Creating linked mailboxes

Syntax

```
New-Mailbox -Name 'DisplayName' -Alias 'ExchangeAlias'
  -OrganizationalUnit 'OrganizationalUnit'
  -Database 'Database'
  -UserPrincipalName 'LogonName' -SamAccountName 'prewin2000logon'
  -FirstName 'FirstName' -Initials 'Initial' -LastName 'LastName'
  -ResetPasswordOnNextLogon State
  -LinkedDomainController 'LinkedDC'
  -LinkedMasterAccount 'domain\user'
  -LinkedCredential:(Get-Credential 'domain\administrator')
```

Usage

```
New-Mailbox -Name 'Wendy Richardson' -Alias 'wendyr'
  -OrganizationalUnit 'pocket-consultant.com/Sales'
  -Database 'Corporate Services Primary'
  -UserPrincipalName 'wendyr@pocket-consultant.com' -SamAccountName 'wendyr'
  -FirstName 'Wendy' -Initials '' -LastName 'Richardson'
  -ResetPasswordOnNextLogon $true
  -LinkedDomainController 'CohoDC58'
  -LinkedMasterAccount 'coho\wrichardson'
  -LinkedCredential:(Get-Credential 'coho\williams')
```

Creating forwarding mailboxes

Custom recipients, such as mail-enabled users, don't normally receive mail from users outside the organization because a custom recipient doesn't have an email address that resolves to a specific mailbox in your organization. At times, though, you might want external users, applications, or mail systems to be able to send mail to an address within your organization and then have Exchange forward this mail to an external mailbox.

> **TIP** You can send and receive text messages using Outlook Web App in Exchange 2013, or you can send text messages the old-fashioned way. In my organization, I've created forwarding mailboxes for text-messaging and pager alerts. This simple solution lets managers (and monitoring systems) within the organization quickly and easily send text messages to IT personnel. In this case, I've set up mail-enabled users for each text messaging email address, such as 8085551212@adatum.com, and then created a mailbox that forwards email to the custom recipient. Generally, the display name of the mail-enabled user is in the form Alert *User Name*, such as Alert William Stanek. The display name and email address for the mailbox are in the form Z *LastName* and AE-*MailAddress*@myorg.com, such as Z Stanek and AE-WilliamS@adatum.com, respectively. Afterward, I hide the mailbox so that it isn't displayed in the global address list or in other address lists; this way, users can see only the Alert William Stanek mailbox.

To create a user account to receive mail and forward it off site, follow these steps:

1. Using Exchange Admin Center, create a mail-enabled user. Name the account Alert *User Name,* such as Alert William Stanek. Be sure to establish an external email address that refers to the user's Internet address.

2. Using Exchange Admin Center, create a mailbox-enabled user account in the domain. Name the account with the appropriate display name, such as Z Stanek, William. Be sure to create an Exchange mailbox for the account, but don't grant any special permission to the account. You might want to restrict the account so that the user can't log on to any servers in the domain. Optionally, hide this mailbox from address lists.

3. Using Exchange Admin Center, access the properties dialog box for the mailbox user account (see Figure 7-7).

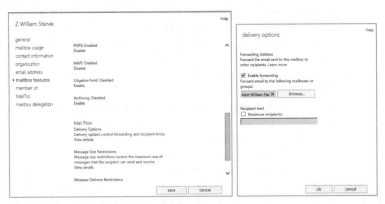

FIGURE 7-7 Creating a forwarding mailbox.

4. On the Mailbox Features page, select the View Details option under Mail Flow. This displays the Delivery Options dialog box.

5. In the Delivery Options dialog box, select the Enable Forwarding check box and then tap or click Browse.

6. In the Select Recipient dialog box, select the mail-enabled user you created earlier and then tap or click OK twice. Tap or click Save. You can now use the user account to forward mail to the external mailbox.

Creating and using archive mailboxes

Each user can have an alternate mailbox for archives. An archive mailbox is used to store a user's old messages, such as might be required for executives and needed by some managers and users. In Outlook and Outlook Web App, users can access archive mailboxes in much the same way as they access a regular mailbox.

Archive mailboxes are created in one of two ways. The standard approach is to create an in-place archive. Both on-premises Exchange and Exchange Online use in-place archives by default. With hybrid organizations, you also can use online archives. With an online archive, the archive for an on-premises mailbox is created in the online service.

Creating in-place archives

You can create an in-place archive mailbox at the same time you create the user's standard mailbox. To create an in-place archive mailbox, complete the following steps:

1. In Exchange Admin Center, select Recipients in the feature pane and then select Mailboxes. Double-tap or double-click the entry for the user's standard mailbox. Any user that already has an archive mailbox has "User (Archive)" as the mailbox type.

2. On the Mailbox Features page, select Enable under the Archiving heading.

3. With on-premises Exchange, if the mailbox had an archive previously and that archive still exists, this archive is used in its original location. Otherwise, the Create In-Place Archive dialog box is displayed. If you want to specify a mailbox database rather than use an automatically selected one, tap or click Browse to the right of the Mailbox Database text box. In the Select Mailbox Database dialog box, choose the mailbox database in which the mailbox should be stored, and then tap or click OK. Mailbox databases are listed by name as well as by associated server and Exchange version running on the server.

4. Tap or click Save. If an error occurs during mailbox creation, the archive mailbox will not be created. You need to correct the problem before you can complete this procedure and create the archive mailbox.

When you are working with Exchange Admin Center, you can enable in-place archiving for multiple mailboxes as well. When you select multiple mailboxes using the Shift or Ctrl keys, the details pane displays bulk editing options. Scroll down the list of available options and then tap or click More Options. Next, under Archive, tap or click Enable.

The Bulk Enable Archive dialog box is displayed. If you want to specify a mailbox database for the archives rather than use an automatically selected one, tap or click Browse to the right of the Mailbox Database text box. In the Select Mailbox Database dialog box, choose the mailbox database in which the archive mailboxes should be stored, and then tap or click OK.

Using Exchange Management Shell, you can create an archive mailbox using the Enable-Mailbox cmdlet. The basic syntax is as follows:

```
Enable-Mailbox [-Identity] Identity -Archive [-Database DatabaseID]
```

such as:

```
Enable-Mailbox pocket-consultant.com/engineering/tonyg -archive
```

Because each user can have only one archive mailbox, you get an error if the user already has an archive mailbox. Items in the user's mailbox will be moved automatically to the archive mailbox based on the archive and retention policy. When you install Exchange Server, a default archive and retention policy is created for all archive mailboxes. This policy is named Default MRM Policy. Because of this policy, email messages from the entire mailbox are moved to the archive after two years by default.

For bulk editing, you can use various techniques. Generally, you'll want to:

- Ensure you are working with mailboxes for regular users and not mailboxes for rooms, equipment, and so on. To do this, filter the results based on the RecipientTypeDetails.

- Ensure the mailbox doesn't already have an on-premises or online archive. To do this, filter the results based on whether the mailbox has an associated ArchiveGuid and the ArchiveDomain.

- Ensure you don't enable archives on mailboxes that shouldn't have them, such as the Discovery Search Mailbox. To do this, filter based on the name or partial name of mailboxes to exclude.

Consider the following example:

```
Get-Mailbox -Database Sales -Filter {RecipientTypeDetails -eq 'UserMailbox'
-AND ArchiveGuid -eq $null -AND ArchiveDomain -eq $null -AND Name -NotLike
"DiscoverySearchMailbox*"} | Enable-Mailbox -Archive
```

In this example, Get-Mailbox retrieves all mailboxes for regular users in the Sales database that don't have in-place or online archiving enabled and that also don't have a name starting with: DiscoverySearchMailbox. The results are then piped through Enable-Mailbox to add an archive mailbox to these mailboxes.

Creating online archives

In hybrid organizations, several features, including online archives, are enabled by default. If you are unsure whether online archives have been enabled for your hybrid deployment, enter **Get-HybridConfiguration | fl** at a PowerShell prompt and then verify that the OnlineArchive flag is set on the -Features parameter. To modify the hybrid configuration, you can use Set-HybridConfiguration. However, do not use Set-HybridConfiguration without a solid understanding of hybrid configurations. Keep in mind that when you use the -Features parameter with Set-HybridConfiguration, you must explicitly specify all the features that you want enabled. Any feature that you omit will be disabled.

In Exchange Management Shell, you create online archives using the Enable-Mailbox cmdlet with the -RemoteArchive, -ArchiveDatabase, and -ArchiveDomain parameters. The required -RemoteArchive parameter is a flag that specifies you want to create the archive online. The optional -ArchiveDatabase sets the name or GUID of the archive database in the online organization. The optional -ArchiveDomain sets the fully qualified domain name of the domain for the online organization. Consider the following examples:

```
Enable-Mailbox -Identity issan@contoso.com -RemoteArchive

Enable-Mailbox -Identity issan@contoso.com -RemoteArchive -ArchiveDatabase
"D919BA05-46A6-415f-80AD-7E09334BB852" -ArchiveDomain
"pocket-consultant.onmicrosoft.com"
```

The first example creates the online archive using the default database and online domain. The second example explicitly sets the GUID of the database and domain parameters.

Managing archive settings

Whether you use Exchange Admin Center or Exchange Management Shell, several other parameters are set for archive mailboxes. The default name for the archive mailbox is set as In-Place Archive – *UserDisplayName,* such as In-Place Archive – Henrik Larsen. With on-premises Exchange, the default quota and warning quota are set as 50 GB and 45 GB, respectively. With Exchange Online, the default quota and warning quota are set as 25 GB and 22.5 GB, respectively.

You can confirm the details for a user's archive mailbox by entering the following command:

```
Get-Mailbox "Name" | fl name, alias, servername, *archive*
```

where *name* is the display name or alias of the user you want to work with, such as:

```
Get-Mailbox "Henrik Larsen" | fl name, alias, servername, *archive*
```

You can change the archive name and set quotas by using Set-Mailbox. The basic syntax is as follows:

```
Set-Mailbox [-Identity] Identity -ArchiveName Name
-ArchiveQuota Quota -ArchiveWarningQuota Quota
```

When you set a quota, specify the value with **MB** (for megabytes), **GB** (for giga-bytes), or **TB** (for terabytes), or enter **'Unlimited'** to remove the quota. Here is an example:

```
set-mailbox pocket-consultant.com/engineering/tonyg
-ArchiveQuota '28GB' -ArchiveWarningQuota '27GB'
```

For bulk editing, you can use Get-Mailbox to retrieve the user mailboxes you want to work with and then apply the changes by piping the results to Set-Mailbox. If you do so, ensure that you filter the results appropriately. Consider the following example:

```
Get-Mailbox -ResultSize unlimited -Filter {RecipientTypeDetails -eq
'UserMailbox' -AND ArchiveGuid -ne $null} | Set-Mailbox -ArchiveQuota
'20GB' -ArchiveWarningQuota '18GB'
```

In this example, Get-Mailbox retrieves all mailboxes for regular users in the entire organization that have archiving enabled. The results are then piped through Set-Mailbox to modify the quota and quota warning values.

In Exchange Admin Center, you manage archive settings by completing these steps:

1. In Exchange Admin Center, select Recipients in the feature pane and then se-lect Mailboxes. Double-tap or double-click the entry for the user's standard mailbox. Any user that already has an archive mailbox has "User (Archive)" as the mailbox type.

2. On the Mailbox Features page, tap or click View Details under the Archiving heading.

3. To change the name of the archive mailbox, enter the new name in the Name text box.

4. To set a quota, enter the desired value in gigabytes in the Archive Quota combo box.

5. To set a quota warning, enter a quota warning in gigabytes in the Issue Warning At combo box.

To disable an archive mailbox, open the properties dialog box for the user to the Mailbox Features page and then select Disable under the Archiving heading. Tap or click Yes when prompted to confirm.

REAL WORLD When you disable an archive mailbox for a user, the archive mailbox is marked for deletion and disconnected from the user account. The archive mailbox is retained according to the mailbox retention policy. To connect the disabled archive mailbox to the existing mailbox, you must use the Connect-Mailbox cmdlet with the -Archive parameter. Otherwise, if you disable an archive mailbox for a user mailbox and then enable an archive mailbox for that same user, a new archive mailbox is created for the user.

When you are working with Exchange Admin Center, you can disable in-place archiving for multiple mailboxes as well. When you select multiple mailboxes using the Shift or Ctrl keys, the detail pane displays bulk editing options. Scroll down the list of available options and then tap or click More Options. Next, under Archive, tap or click Disable. When the Bulk Disable Archive dialog box is displayed, tap or click OK.

In Exchange Management Shell, you can disable an archive mailbox by using Disable-Mailbox. The basic syntax is as follows:

```
Disable-Mailbox [-Identity] Identity -Archive
```

such as:

```
disable-mailbox pocket-consultant.com/engineering/tonyg -archive
```

For bulk editing, you can use a technique similar to the one discussed for enabling archives. Consider the following example:

```
Get-Mailbox -Database Sales -Filter {RecipientTypeDetails -eq 'UserMailbox'
-AND ArchiveGuid -ne $null} | Disable-Mailbox -Archive
```

In this example, Get-Mailbox retrieves all mailboxes for regular users in the Sales database that have archiving enabled. The results are then piped through Disable-Mailbox to remove the archive mailbox from these mailboxes.

Creating arbitration mailboxes

Exchange moderated transport requires all email messages sent to specific recipients to be approved by moderators. You can configure any type of recipient as a moderated recipient, and Exchange will ensure that all messages sent to those recipients go through an approval process.

Distribution groups are the only types of recipients that use moderation by default. Membership in distribution groups can be closed, owner approved, or open. While any Exchange recipient can join or leave an open distribution group, joining or leaving a closed group requires approval. Group owners receive join and remove requests and can either approve or deny those requests.

Distribution groups can also be unmoderated or moderated. With unmoderated groups, any approved sender (which is all senders by default) can send messages to the group. With moderated groups, messages are sent to moderators for approval before being distributed to members of the group. The only exception is for a message sent by a moderator. A message from a moderator is delivered immediately because a moderator has the authority to determine what is and isn't an appropriate message.

NOTE The default moderator for a distribution group is the group's owner.

Arbitration mailboxes are used to store messages that are awaiting approval. When you install Exchange Server 2013, a default arbitration mailbox is created. For the purposes of load balancing or for other reasons, you can convert other mailboxes to the arbitration mailbox type by using the Enable-Mailbox cmdlet. The basic syntax is as follows:

```
Enable-Mailbox [-Identity] Identity -Arbitration
```

such as:

```
enable-mailbox pocket-consultant.com/users/moderatedmail -Arbitration
```

You can create an arbitration mailbox by using New-Mailbox as shown in this example:

```
New-Mailbox ModeratedMail -Arbitration -UserPrincipalName
ModeratedMail@pocket-consultant.com
```

Creating Discovery mailboxes

Exchange Discovery helps organizations comply with legal discovery requirements and can also be used as an aid in internal investigations or as part of regular monitoring of email content. Exchange Discovery uses content indexes created by Exchange Search to speed up the search process.

NOTE By default, Exchange administrators do not have sufficient rights to perform Discovery searches. Only users with the Discovery Management role can perform Discovery searches. If a user is not a member of the role, she doesn't have access to the related options. This means she can't access the In-Place eDiscovery & Hold interface in Exchange Admin Center or the In-Place eDiscovery & Hold cmdlets in PowerShell.

Whether you are working in an online, on-premises, or hybrid organization, you use Exchange Admin Center to perform searches. With hybrid configurations, an on-premises search will return results from the online organization.

Discovery searches are performed against designated mailboxes or all mailboxes in the Exchange organization. Items in mailboxes that match the Discovery search are copied to a target mailbox. Only mailboxes specifically designated as Discovery mailboxes can be used as targets. In a hybrid configuration, you must copy items to an on-premises mailbox, regardless of whether the items are from the online or on-premises organization.

TIP By default, Discovery search does not include items that cannot be indexed by Exchange Search. To include such items in the search results, select the Include Items That Can't Be Searched check box in Exchange Admin Center.

In Exchange Admin Center, you can access the discovery and hold settings by selecting Compliance Management in the feature pane and then selecting In-Place eDiscovery & Hold. While working with In-Place eDiscovery & Hold, you can create searches across mailboxes by specifying filters and hold options for search results.

When you install Exchange Server 2013, a default Discovery mailbox is created. You can convert other mailboxes to the Discovery mailbox type by using the Enable-Mailbox cmdlet. The basic syntax is as follows:

```
Enable-Mailbox [-Identity] Identity -Discovery
```

such as:

```
enable-mailbox pocket-consultant.com/hr/legalsearch -discovery
```

You can create a Discovery mailbox by using New-Mailbox as shown in this example:

```
New-Mailbox LegalSearch -Discovery -UserPrincipalName
LegalSearch@pocket-consultant.com
```

Once a Discovery mailbox is established, you can't convert it to another mailbox type. You can't use Exchange Admin Center to create Discovery mailboxes.

Creating shared mailboxes

Shared mailboxes are mailboxes that are shared by multiple users. Although shared mailboxes must have an associated user account, this account is not used for logon in the domain and is disabled by default. Users who access the shared mailbox do so using access permissions.

You can create a shared mailbox by using New-Mailbox, as shown in this example:

```
New-Mailbox -Shared -Name "Customer Service" -DisplayName
"Customer Service" -Alias Service -UserPrincipalName
customerservice@pocket-consultant.com
```

In this example, a user account named CustomerService is created for this mailbox. This user account is disabled by default to prevent logon using this account. After creating the mailbox, you need to grant Send On Behalf Of permission to the appropriate users or security groups by using Set-Mailbox and the -GrantSendOnBehalfTo parameter. Finally, you need to add access rights that allow these users or security groups to log on to the mailbox by using Add-MailboxPermission and the -AccessRights parameter. Ensure these rights are inherited at all levels of the mailbox using -InheritanceType All as well. One way this would all come together is shown in the following example:

```
New-Mailbox -Shared -Name "Customer Service" -DisplayName
"Customer Service" -Alias Service -UserPrincipalName
customerservice@pocket-consultant.com | Set-Mailbox -GrantSendOnBehalfTo
CustomerServiceGroup | Add-MailboxPermission -User CustomerServiceGroup
-AccessRights FullAccess -InheritanceType All
```

In Exchange Admin Center, you can create a shared mailbox by following these steps:

1. Select Recipients in the feature pane and then select Shared.
2. Tap or click New. This opens the New Shared Mailbox dialog box. Figure 7-8 shows on-premises Exchange options on the left and Exchange Online options on the right.

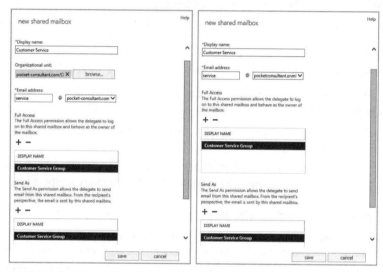

FIGURE 7-8 Creating a mailbox to share with multiple users.

3. In the Display Name text box, type a descriptive name for the shared mailbox.
4. For on-premises Exchange, the Organizational Unit text box shows where in Active Directory the associated user account will be created. By default, this is the Users container in the current domain. If you want to use a different container, tap or click Browse to the right of the Organizational Unit text box. Use the Select Organizational Unit dialog box to choose the location in which to store the account, and then tap or click OK.
5. In the Email Address text box, type the Exchange alias. The Exchange alias is used to set the default email address.
6. Use the drop-down list to select the domain with which the shared mailbox is to be associated. The Exchange Alias and the domain name are combined to set the fully qualified name, such as service@pocket-consultant.com.

7. Under Full Access, tap or click Add. In the Select Full Access dialog box, select users, security groups, or both that should have full access to the shared mailbox. Select multiple users and groups using the Shift or Ctrl keys.

8. Under Send As, tap or click Add. In the Select Send As dialog box, select users, security groups, or both that should be able to send email from the shared mailbox. Select multiple users and groups using the Shift or Ctrl keys.

9. With on-premises Exchange, tap or click More Options to configure these additional options:

   - **Alias**   Sets the Exchange alias and overrides the default value you set previously using the Email Address text box. This allows a resource to have an alias that is different from the name portion of its email address.

   - **Mailbox Database**   If you want to specify a mailbox database rather than use an automatically selected one, tap or click Browse to the right of the Mailbox Database text box. In the Select Mailbox Database dialog box, choose the mailbox database in which the mailbox should be stored. Mailbox databases are listed by name as well as by associated server and Exchange version running on the server.

   - **Archive**   If you want to create an on-premises archive mailbox as well, select the related check box. Optionally, tap or click Browse to choose the mailbox database for the archive.

   - **Address Book Policy**   If you've implemented address book policies to provide customized address book views, select the address book policy to associate with the shared mailbox.

10. Tap or click Save to create the shared mailbox. If an error occurs during account or mailbox creation, neither the account nor the related mailbox will be created. You need to correct the problem before you can complete this procedure.

Creating public folder mailboxes

Public folders are used to share messages and files in an organization. Public folder trees define the structure of an organization's public folders. You can make the default public folder tree accessible to users based on criteria you set, and then users can create folders and manage their content.

Each public folder in the default public folder tree can have specific access permissions. For example, you can create public folders called CompanyWide, Marketing, and Engineering. Whereas you would typically make the CompanyWide folder accessible to all users, you would make the Marketing folder accessible only to users in the marketing department and the Engineering folder accessible only to users in the engineering department.

Users access public folders from Outlook clients, including Outlook Web App and Outlook 2007 or later. With Outlook Web App and Outlook 2007 or later, users can add and remove favorite public folders and perform item-level operations, such as creating and managing posts. However, users can create or delete public folders only from Outlook 2007 or later. As an administrator, you can manage public folders in Exchange Admin Center.

Beginning with Exchange 2013, Exchange servers no longer use public folder databases or store public folder data separately from mailbox data. Instead, Exchange 2013 and Exchange Online store public folder data in mailboxes. This significant architecture change greatly simplifies public folder management.

In Exchange Admin Center, you work with public folders by selecting Public Folders in the feature pane and then selecting either Public Folder Mailboxes or Public Folders as appropriate. You use the options under Public Folder Mailboxes to create and manage the mailboxes that store public folder data. You use the options under Public Folders to view and manage the public folder hierarchy.

An Exchange organization can have one or more public folder mailboxes and those mailboxes can be created on one or more Mailbox servers throughout the organization. While each public folder mailbox can contain public folder content, only the first public folder mailbox created in an Exchange organization contains the writable copy of the public folder hierarchy. This mailbox is referred to as the hierarchy mailbox. Any additional public folder mailboxes contain read-only copies of the public-folder hierarchy.

Because there's only one writeable copy of the public folder hierarchy, proxying is used to relay folder changes to the hierarchy mailbox. This means that any time users working with folders in an additional mailbox create new subfolders, the folder creation, modification, or removal is proxied to the hierarchy mailbox by the content mailbox users are connected to.

In Exchange Admin Center, you can create a public folder mailbox by following these steps:

1. Select Public Folders in the feature pane and then select Public Folder Mailboxes.

2. Tap or click New. This opens the New Public Folder Mailbox dialog box.

3. Type a descriptive name for the mailbox.

4. With on-premises Exchange, you can associate the mailbox with a specific organizational unit. Tap or click Browse to the right of the Organizational Unit text box. Use the Select Organizational Unit dialog box to choose the location in which to store the account, and then tap or click OK. A user account for the mailbox is created in the selected organizational unit (with the account disabled for login).

5. With on-premises Exchange, you can specify a mailbox database rather than use an automatically selected one. Tap or click Browse to the right of the Mailbox Database text box. In the Select Mailbox Database dialog box, choose the mailbox database in which the mailbox should be stored, and then tap or click OK.

6. Tap or click Save to create the public folder mailbox. If an error occurs during account or mailbox creation, neither the account nor the related mailbox will be created. You need to correct the problem before you can complete this procedure.

Public folder content can include email messages, documents, and more. The content is stored in the public folder mailbox but isn't replicated across multiple public folder mailboxes. Instead, all users access the same public folder mailbox for the same set of content.

When you create the first public folder in the organization, you establish the root of the public folder hierarchy. You can then create subfolders and assign access permissions on folders. In Exchange Admin Center, select Public Folders in the feature pane and then select Public Folders. Use the available options to create subfolders and set permissions on those folders.

When you create public folder mailboxes, they inherit the quota limits of the mailbox database in which they are stored. You can modify the quota limits using the properties dialog for the mailbox. Double-tap or double-click the mailbox entry. In the Public Folder Mailbox dialog box, on the Mailbox Usage page, tap or click More Options and then select Customize The Settings For This Mailbox. Next, use the selection lists provided to specify when warnings are issued, what posts are prohibited, and the maximum size of items. Apply the changes by tapping or clicking Save.

When users are connected to public folder mailboxes and make routine changes to an Exchange store hierarchy or content, the changes are synchronized every 15 minutes using Incremental Change Synchronization (ICS). Immediate syncing is used for non-routine changes, such as folder creation. If no users are connected to public folder mailboxes, synchronization occurs once every 24 hours by default.

Managing mailboxes: The essentials

You often need to manage user mailboxes the way you do user accounts. Some of the management tasks are intuitive and others aren't. If you have questions, be sure to read the sections that follow.

Whether you are working with on-premises Exchange or Exchange Online, you can use bulk editing techniques to work with multiple user mailboxes at the same time. To select multiple user mailboxes not in sequence, hold down the Ctrl key and then tap or click the left mouse button on each user mailbox you want to select. To select a series of user mailboxes, select the first mailbox, hold down the Shift key, and then tap or click the last mailbox.

The actions you can perform on multiple resources depend on the types of recipients you've selected. The actions you can perform on multiple user mailboxes include the following:

- Updating contact information, organization information, or custom attributes
- Changing mailbox quotas or deleted item retention settings
- Enabling or disabling Outlook Web App, POP3, IMAP, MAPI, or ActiveSync
- Managing policy for Outlook Web App, ActiveSync, Address Books, Retention, Role Assignment, or Sharing
- Enabling or disabling mailbox archives
- Moving mailboxes to another database

Although you cannot bulk edit room or equipment mailboxes, you can perform these actions on shared mailboxes.

Viewing current mailbox size, message count, and last logon

You can use Exchange Admin Center to view the last logon date and time, the mailbox size, and how much of the total mailbox quota has been used by completing these steps:

1. Select Recipients in the feature pane and then select Mailboxes.
2. Double-tap or double-click the mailbox with which you want to work.
3. On the Mailbox Usage page, review the Last Logon text box to see the last logon date and time (see Figure 7-9). If a user hasn't logged on to the mailbox, you can't get mailbox statistics and will get an error when you view this page.

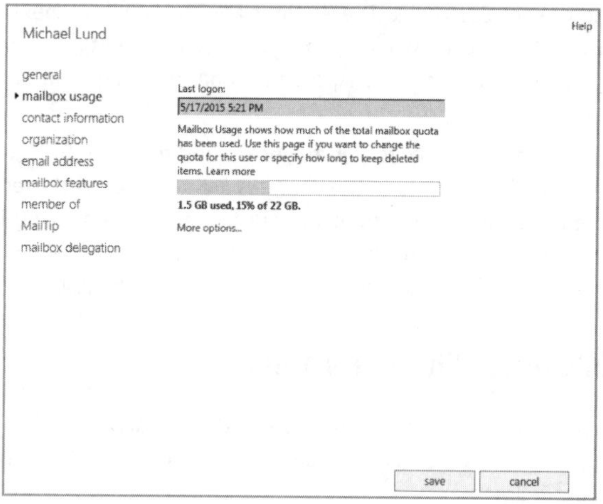

FIGURE 7-9 Viewing mailbox statistics.

4. Under the last logon time, notice the mailbox usage statistics, depicted in a bar graph and numerically as a percentage of the total mailbox quota that has been used.

If you want to view similar information for all mailboxes on a server, the easiest way is to use the Get-MailboxStatistics cmdlet with the -Server or -Database parameter. Sample 7-3 shows examples using Get-MailboxStatistics. Use the -Archive parameter to return mailbox statistics for the archive mailbox associated with a specified mailbox.

SAMPLE 7-3 Getting statistics for multiple mailboxes

Syntax

```
Get-MailboxStatistics -Identity 'Identity' [-Archive <$true|$false>]
[-DomainContoller DomainController] [-IncludeMoveHistory <$true|$false>]
[-IncludeMoveReport <$true|$false>]

Get-MailboxStatistics -Server  'Server' | -Database 'Database'
[-DomainContoller DomainController]
```

Usage

```
Get-MailboxStatistics -Server 'corpsvr127'

Get-MailboxStatistics -Database 'Engineering Primary'

Get-MailboxStatistics -Identity 'pocket-consulta\williams'
```

When you are working with Exchange Management Shell, the standard output won't necessarily provide all the information you are looking for. Often, you need to format the output as a list or table using Format-List or Format-Table, respectively, to get the additional information you are looking for. Format-List is useful when you are working with a small set of resources or want to view all the properties that are available. Once you know what properties are available for a particular resource, you can format the output as a table to view specific properties. For example, if you format the output of Get-MailboxStatistics as a list, you see all the properties that are available for mailboxes, as shown in this example and sample output:

```
get-mailboxstatistics -identity "pocket-consulta\erika" | format-list

AssociatedItemCount        : 21622
DeletedItemCount           : 1211
DisconnectDate             :
DisplayName                : Erik Andersen
ItemCount                  : 20051
LastLoggedOnUserAccount    : NT AUTHORITY\SYSTEM
LastLogoffTime             : 5/17/2015 11:51:42 PM
LastLogonTime              : 5/17/2015 12:14:22 PM
LegacyDN                   : /O=FIRST ORGANIZATION/OU=EXCHANGE ADMINISTRATIVE
GROUP/CN=RECIPIENTS/CN=ERIK ANDERSEN
MailboxGuid                : b7fb0ca8-936b-410f-a2a1-59825eebbdfe
MailboxType                : Private
ObjectClass                : Mailbox
StorageLimitStatus         :
TotalDeletedItemSize       : 1927 KB (1927,535 bytes)
TotalItemSize              : 191121.2 KB (191,121,225 bytes)
Database                   : Customer Service Primary
ServerName                 : MAILSERVER92
DatabaseName               : Customer Service Primary
IsQuarantined              : False
IsArchiveMailbox           : False
IsMoveDestination          : False
DatabaseIssueWarningQuota          : 1.899 GB (2,039,480,320 bytes)
DatabaseProhibitSendQuota          : 2 GB (2,147,483,648 bytes)
DatabaseProhibitSendReceiveQuota : 2.3 GB (2,469,396,480 bytes)
Identity                   : b7fb0ca8-936b-410f-a2a1-59825eebbdfe
MapiIdentity               : b7fb0ca8-936b-410f-a2a1-59825eebbdfe
OriginatingServer          : mailserver92.pocket-consultant.com
IsValid                    : True
ObjectState                : Unchanged
```

Once you know the available properties, you can format the output as a table to get exactly the information you want to see. The following example gets information about all the mailboxes in the Engineering Primary database and formats the output as a table:

```
Get-MailboxStatistics -Database 'Engineering Primary' | format-table
DisplayName, TotalItemSize, TotalDeletedItemSize, Database, ServerName
```

Configuring apps for mailboxes

With both on-premises Exchange and Exchange Online, you can add apps to the Outlook Web App interface to add functionality. Several apps are installed and made available to users by default, including the following apps created by Microsoft:

- **Action Items** Makes action item suggestions based on message content.
- **Bing Maps** Allows users to map addresses found in their messages.
- **Suggested Meetings** Shows meeting suggestions found in messages and allows users to add the meetings to their calendars.
- **Unsubscribe** Allows users to easily block or unsubscribe from email subscription feeds.

Other apps can be added from the Office Store, from a URL, or from a file. All of these apps have various levels of read, read/write, or other permissions on user mailboxes. Because apps also may send data to a third-party service, you may want to consider carefully whether apps should be enabled in your organization. Where strict, high security is a requirement, my recommendation is to disable all apps.

In Exchange Admin Center, you manage apps as part of the organization configuration. Select Organization in the feature pane and then select Apps. As shown in Figure 7-10, you'll then see the installed apps and their status. To work with Apps for Outlook, you must have View-Only Organization Management, Help Desk, or Organization Management permissions.

To add an app, do one of the following:

- To add an app from the Office store, tap or click New, select Add From The Office Store to open a new browser window to the Office store, and then select an app to add. Select the app's Add option, review the app details, and then tap or click Add. When prompted to confirm, select Yes.
- If you know the URL of the manifest file for the app you want to add, tap or click New and then select Add From URL. In the Add From URL dialog box, enter the URL and then tap or click Install. Be sure to use the full path.
- If you've copied the manifest file to a local server, tap or click New and then select Add From File. In the Add From File dialog box, select Browse. In the Choose File To Upload dialog box, locate and select the manifest file and then select Open. Manifest files end with the .xml extension.

When you install a new app, the app is made available to all users but disabled by default. This is reflected in the status of Disabled for User Default and Everyone for Provided To.

FIGURE 7-10 Viewing the available apps and their status.

If you have appropriate permissions, you can manage app status by tapping or clicking the app and then tapping or clicking Edit. In the Action Items dialog box, shown in Figure 7-11, do one of the following:

- If you don't want the app to be available to users, clear the Make This App Available check box and then tap or click Save.

- If you want the app to be available to users, select the Make This App Available check box and then specify the app status as optional and enabled by default, optional and disabled by default, or mandatory and always enabled. Finally, tap or click Save.

FIGURE 7-11 Managing the app status and availability.

Any app you install can be removed by selecting it and then selecting the Delete option. Although you can't uninstall the defaults apps, you can make any or all of the default apps unavailable to users.

Hiding mailboxes from address lists

Occasionally, you might want to hide a mailbox so that it doesn't appear in the global address list or other address lists. One reason for doing this is if you have administrative mailboxes that you use only for special purposes. To hide a mailbox from the address lists, follow these steps:

1. Open the Properties dialog box for the mailbox-enabled user account by double-tapping or double-clicking the user name in Exchange Admin Center.

2. On the General page, select the Hide From Address Lists check box and then tap or click Save.

Defining custom mailbox attributes for address lists

Address lists, such as the global address list, make it easier for users and administrators to find available Exchange resources, including users, contacts, distribution groups, and public folders. The fields available for Exchange resources are based on the type of resource. If you want to add more values that should be displayed or searchable in address lists, such as an employee identification number, you can assign these values as custom attributes.

Exchange provides 15 custom attributes—labeled Customer Attribute 1, Custom Attribute 2, and so on through Custom Attribute 15. You can assign a value to a custom attribute by completing the following steps:

1. Open the Properties dialog box for the mailbox-enabled user account by double-tapping or double-clicking the user name in Exchange Admin Center.

2. On the general page, tap or click More Options. Under the Custom Attributes heading, you'll see any currently defined custom attributes. Tap or click Edit to display the Custom Attributes dialog box.

3. Enter attribute values in the text boxes provided. Tap or click OK and then tap or click Save.

Restoring on-premises users and mailboxes

When you disable or delete a mailbox, on-premises Exchange retains the deleted mailbox in the mailbox database and puts the mailbox in a disabled state. There is, however, an important distinction between disabling and deleting a mailbox, and this difference affects recovery. When you disable a mailbox, the Exchange attributes are removed from the user account and the mailbox is marked for removal, but the user account is retained. When you delete a mailbox, the Exchange attributes are removed from the user account, the mailbox is marked for removal, and the user account itself is either marked for deletion or deleted entirely. Additionally, with either, if the mailbox has an in-place archive, the in-place archive will also be marked for removal. However, if the mailbox has a remote archive, the remote archive is removed permanently.

Disabled and deleted mailboxes are referred to as disconnected mailboxes. Disconnected mailboxes are retained in a mailbox database until the deleted mailbox retention period expires, which is 30 days by default. Deleted users may be retained as well.

In Exchange Admin Center, you can find disconnected mailboxes and reconnect them by completing these steps:

1. Select Recipients in the feature pane and then select Mailboxes.

2. Tap or click the More button (this button shows three dots) and then select Connect A Mailbox. The Connect A Mailbox dialog box shows all mailboxes marked for deletion but currently retained regardless of whether those mailboxes were disabled, deleted, or soft deleted.

   IMPORTANT When you move mailboxes between databases, mailboxes in the original (source) database are soft deleted. This means they are disconnected, marked as soft deleted, but retained in the original database until the deleted mailbox retention period expires. In Exchange Management Shell, you can use a DisconnectReason of "SoftDeleted" to find soft-deleted mailboxes.

3. In the Connect A Mailbox dialog box, shown in Figure 7-12, use the selection list provided to select the server where you want to look for disconnected mailboxes.

FIGURE 7-12 Viewing disconnected mailboxes.

4. Tap or click the mailbox to restore it and then tap or click Connect.

5. Connect the mailbox to the user account to which it was connected previously or to a different user account. If the original user account is available, select the Yes option to reconnect the mailbox to the original user account. If the original user isn't available or you want to associate the mailbox with a different user, select the No option and follow the prompts.

You can find all disabled mailboxes in an on-premises Exchange organization by entering the following command:

```
Get-MailboxDatabase | Get-MailboxStatistics | Where { $_.DisconnectReason
-eq "Disabled" } | ft DisplayName,Database,DisconnectDate,DisconnectReason
```

Or you can find disabled mailboxes in a particular database using the following command:

```
Get-MailboxStatistics -Database DatabaseName | Where { $_.DisconnectReason
-eq "Disabled" } | ft DisplayName,Database,DisconnectDate,DisconnectReason
```

NOTE You can't use this technique with Exchange Online. See "Restoring online users and mailboxes" later in this chapter.

If you find that you need a mail-enabled or mailbox user account that was deleted, you may be able to restore the deleted account. For on-premises Exchange, you can restore user accounts from Active Directory. When Active Directory Recycle Bin is enabled, you can recover deleted objects using Active Directory Administrative Center (as long as the deleted object and recycled object lifetimes have not expired).

In Active Directory Administrative Center, select the Deleted Object container to see the available deleted objects. When you select a deleted user by tapping or clicking it, you can use the Restore option to restore the user to its original container. For example, if the user account was deleted from the Users container, the user account is restored to this container. Once the user account is restored, you can restore the Exchange settings and data. You can use Connect-Mailbox to connect the user account to its disconnected mailbox.

When you connect a disconnected mailbox using Connect-Mailbox, you associate the mailbox with a user account that isn't mail-enabled, which means the user account cannot have an existing mailbox associated with it. Connect-Mailbox has a slightly different syntax for standard mailboxes, shared mailboxes, and linked mailboxes. For standard mailbox users, the basic syntax for Connect-Mailbox is:

```
Connect-Mailbox -Identity ExchangeId -Database DatabaseName -User ADUserId
-Alias ExchangeAlias
```

where ExchangeID identifies the disconnected mailbox in the Exchange organization, DatabaseName is the name of the database where the disconnected mailbox resides, ADUserID identifies the Active Directory user account to reconnect the mailbox to, and ExchangeAlias sets the desired Exchange Alias. Consider the following example:

```
Connect-Mailbox -Identity "Thomas Axen" -Database "Sales Database"
-User "Thomas Axen" -Alias ThomasA
```

This example reconnects the Exchange mailbox for Thomas Axen with the related user account in Active Directory and sets the Exchange alias as ThomasA. The alias is combined with the user logon domain to set the User Principal Name (referred to in the UI as the User Logon Name). The User Principal Name must be unique within the organization. If another user account has the same User Principal Name, you'll see a warning about a user name conflict. You will need to resolve this conflict before you can connect the mailbox.

When you disable or remove an archive mailbox from a mailbox, the archive mailbox is disconnected from the source mailbox, marked for deletion, and retained according to the retention settings. To connect a disabled archive mailbox to the original source mailbox, you use the Connect-Mailbox cmdlet with the -Archive parameter.

Although Connect-Mailbox has restrictions, you can connect a disconnected mailbox to a user account that already has a mailbox. When you restore the mailbox, its contents are copied into the target user's existing mailbox while the deleted mailbox itself is retained in the mailbox database until the retention period expires (or it is purged by an administrator).

You use New-MailboxRestoreRequest to restore mailboxes to accounts with existing mailboxes. The basic syntax is:

```
New-MailboxRestoreRequest -SourceMailbox MailboxID -SourceDatabase
DatabaseName -TargetMailbox ExchangeID
```

where MailboxID is the display name or GUID of the disconnected mailbox to restore, DatabaseName is the name of the database where the disconnected mailbox resides, and ExchangeID is an Exchange alias or name for the account where the mailbox should be added. Consider the following example:

```
New-MailboxRestoreRequest -SourceMailbox "Karen Berg" -SourceDatabase
"Marketing Database" -TargetMailbox "Dag Rovik"
```

You can restore archive mailboxes to users with existing accounts as well. Use the -TargetIsArchive parameter as shown in this example:

```
New-MailboxRestoreRequest -SourceMailbox "In-Place Archive - Karen Berg"
-SourceDatabase "Marketing Database" -TargetMailbox "Dag Rovik"
-TargetIsArchive
```

Restoring online users and mailboxes

If you remove the Exchange Online license for an online user account, the user's account is marked as an unlicensed account. Exchange Online deletes mailboxes from unlicensed accounts automatically after the grace period expires. By default, this grace period is 30 days. If you delete a user account in the online organization, the user account is marked as deleted but retained until the retention period expires, which is 30 days by default.

In Office 365 Admin Center, select Users And Groups, and then Deleted Users to view deleted users, as shown in Figure 7-13. If the online organization has available licenses, you can restore the deleted users.

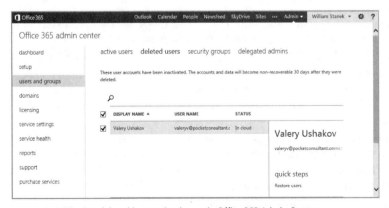

FIGURE 7-13 Viewing deleted but retained users in Office 365 Admin Center.

To restore deleted user accounts, select the accounts to restore and then tap or click Restore Users. Each user account successfully restored will be confirmed. Account restoration will fail if there are any naming or other conflicts. The User Principal Name must be unique within the organization. If another user account has the same User Principal Name, you'll see a warning about a user name conflict. As shown in Figure 7-14, you'll then be able to edit the user name or replace the active user with the deleted user.

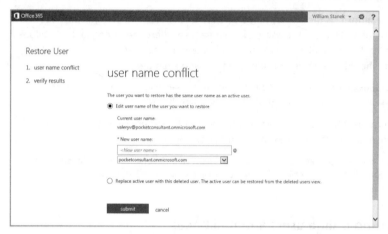

FIGURE 7-14 Naming or other conflicts will prevent users accounts from being restored.

When you connect to Microsoft Online Services as discussed in Chapter 6 "User and contact administration," you can get information about accounts in Windows PowerShell. Enter **Get-MsolUser** to get a list of active user accounts. As shown in the following example, the default output shows the User Principal Name, display name, and licensing status of user accounts:

```
UserPrincipalName                          DisplayName          isLicensed
-----------------                          -----------          ----------
cart3@pocketconsultant.onmicrosoft.com     Media Cart 3         False
wrstanek@pocketconsultant.onmicrosoft.com  William Stanek       True
room3@pocketconsultant.onmicrosoft.com     Conference Room 3    False
georges@pocketconsultant.onmicrosoft.com   George Schaller      True
room42@pocketconsultant.onmicrosoft.com    Conference Room 42   False
```

The output shows the user accounts associated with all types of users, including the user accounts associated with room and equipment mailboxes. Although room and equipment mailboxes don't need to be licensed, standard user accounts require licenses.

You can get a list of users whose accounts have been marked for deletion by entering **Get-MsolUser –ReturnDeletedUsers**. Accounts marked for deletion are listed by User Principal Name, display name, and licensing status. To restore a deleted account, use Restore-MsolUser. The basic syntax for this command is:

```
Restore-MsolUser -UserPrincipalName OnlineId
```

where *OnlineId* is the User Principal Name of the account to restore:

```
Restore-MsolUser -UserPrincipalName valu@pocket-consultant.onmicrosoft.com
```

The account restore will fail if there are any naming or other conflicts. To resolve a name conflict, use the -NewUserPrincipalName parameter to set a new User Principal Name for the user.

Repairing mailboxes

You can use New-MailboxRepairRequest to detect and repair mailbox corruption. By default, the command attempts to repair all types of mailbox corruption issues, including issues associated with search folders, aggregate counts, provisioned folders, and folder views.

The basic syntax for New-MailboxRepairRequest is:

```
New-MailboxRepairRequest -Mailbox ExchangeID
```

where *ExchangeID* identifies the mailbox to repair, such as:

```
New-MailboxRepairRequest -Mailbox TonyS
```

```
New-MailboxRepairRequest -Mailbox tonys@pocket-consultant.com
```

```
New-MailboxRepairRequest -Mailbox "Tony Smith"
```

During the repair process, the mailbox cannot be accessed. Once started, the detect and repair process cannot be stopped, unless you dismount the associated database. Add the -Archive parameter to repair the archive mailbox associated with an Exchange identifier rather than the primary mailbox.

You also can use New-MailboxRepairRequest to examine and repair all mailboxes in a database. As the repair process works its way through all the mailboxes in the database, only the mailbox being repaired is locked and inaccessible. All other mailboxes in the database remain accessible to users.

Moving mailboxes

Exchange Server 2013 supports online mailbox moves. To complete an upgrade, balance the server load, manage drive space, or relocate mailboxes, you can move mailboxes from one server or database to another server or database. The process you use to move mailboxes depends on where the mailbox or mail data is stored:

- When you want to work with mail data stored on a user's computer, you can use the import or export process to move mail data.
- When a user's mailbox is stored on an on-premises Exchange server and you want to move the mailbox to a database on the same server or another server in the same forest, you can use an online mailbox move or batch migration to move the mailbox.
- When a user's mailbox is stored on an on-premises Exchange server in one Active Directory forest and you want to move the mailbox to an on-premises

Exchange server in another forest, you can use a cross-forest move to move the mailbox.

■ When a user's mailbox is stored on-premises and you want to move the mailbox to Exchange Online or vice versa, you can use a remote move to move the mailbox.

Importing and exporting mail data

When Microsoft Outlook uses Exchange Server, a user's mail data can be delivered in one of two ways:

■ Server mailbox with local copies

■ Personal folders

With server mailboxes, messages are delivered to mailboxes on the Exchange server and users can view or receive new mail only when they are connected to Exchange. A local copy of the user's mail data is stored in an .ost file on her computer.

Personal folders are alternatives to server mailboxes. Personal folders are stored in a .pst file on the user's computer. With personal folders, you can specify that mail should be delivered to the user's inbox and stored on the server or that mail should be delivered only to the user's inbox. Users have personal folders when Outlook is configured to use Internet email or other email servers. Users might also have personal folders if the auto-archive feature is used to archive messages.

When you are working with on-premises Exchange, you can:

■ Import mail data from .pst files using mailbox import request cmdlets

■ Export mail data to .pst files using mailbox export request cmdlets

IMPORTANT You must have the Mailbox Import Export role to be able to import or export mailbox data. Because this role isn't assigned to any role group, you must be explicitly assigned this role.

The import and export processes are asynchronous. They are queued and processed independently of Exchange Management Shell. The related commands are shown in the following list:

IMPORT MAILBOX DATA	EXPORT MAILBOX DATA
Get-MailboxImportRequest	Get-MailboxExportRequest
New-MailboxImportRequest	New-MailboxExportRequest
Set-MailboxImportRequest	Set-MailboxExportRequest
Suspend-MailboxImportRequest	Suspend-MailboxExportRequest
Resume-MailboxImportRequest	Resume-MailboxExportRequest
Remove-MailboxImportRequest	Remove-MailboxExportRequest
Get-MailboxImportRequestStatistics	Get-MailboxExportRequestStatistics

Mailbox imports and exports are initiated with Mailbox Import and Mailbox Export requests, respectively. These requests are sent to the Microsoft Exchange Mailbox Replication Service (MRS) running on a Client Access server in the source forest. The MRS queues the request for processing, handling all requests on a first-in, first-out basis. When a request is at the top of the queue, the replication service begins importing or exporting mail data.

Before you can import or export data, you need to create a shared network folder that is accessible to your Exchange servers, and the Exchange Trusted Subsystem group must have read/write access to this share.

You use New-MailboxImportRequest to import data from a .pst file to a mailbox or personal archive. Keep in mind you can't import data to a user account that doesn't have a mailbox and that the destination mailbox must be already available. The import process will not create a mailbox. By default, all mail folders are imported. However, you can specifically include or exclude folders. You also can import mail data to only the user's personal archive.

You use New-MailboxExportRequest to export mailbox data to a .pst file. The command allows you to export one or more mailboxes, with each mailbox export handling a separate request. When exporting mail data, you can specify folders to include or exclude and export mail data from the user's archive. You also can filter the messages so only messages that match your content filter are exported.

Performing on-premises mailbox moves and migrations

The destination database for an on-premises mailbox move can be on the same server, on a different server, in a different domain, or in a different Active Directory site. Exchange Server 2013 performs move operations as a series of steps that allows a mailbox to remain available to a user while the move operation is being completed. When the move is completed, the user begins accessing the mailbox in the new location. Because users can continue to access their email account during the move, you can perform online moves at any time.

The online move process hasn't changed substantially since it was introduced with Exchange Server 2010:

- On-premises mailbox moves are initiated with a Move Mailbox request that is sent to the Microsoft Exchange MRS running on a Client Access server in the source forest. The MRS queues the request for processing, handling all requests on a first-in, first-out basis. When a request is at the top of the queue, the replication service begins replicating mailbox data to the destination database.

- When the replication service finishes its initial replication of a mailbox, it marks the mailbox as Ready To Complete and periodically performs data synchronization between the source and destination database to ensure that the contents of a mailbox are up to date. After a mailbox has been moved, you can complete the move request and finalize the move.

When you are working with PowerShell, you initiate a move using New-MoveRequest and then start the actual move using Start-MoveRequest. Although the online move process allows you to move multiple mailboxes, with each move handled as a separate request, the process isn't ideal for batch moves of multiple mailboxes, and this is where mailbox migrations come in. With mailbox migration, you can move multiple mailboxes in an Exchange on-premises organization, migrate on-premises mailboxes to Exchange Online, or migrate Exchange Online mailboxes back to an on-premises Exchange organization.

NOTE You can use the batch migration process to move single or multiple mailboxes within on-premises Exchange. With a single mailbox, the batch migration is handled as a local move.

From a high level, the standard batch migration process is similar to a mailbox move:

- Batch mailbox migration is initiated with a Migration Batch request that is sent to the Microsoft Exchange MRS running on a Client Access server in the source forest. The MRS queues the request for processing, handling all requests on a first-in, first-out basis. When a request is at the top of the queue, the replication service begins replicating mailbox data to the destination database.

- When the replication service finishes its initial replication of a mailbox, it marks the mailbox as Ready To Complete and periodically performs data synchronization between the source and destination database to ensure that the contents of a mailbox are up to date. After a mailbox has been migrated, you can complete the migration request and finalize the migration.

Where things get complicated are on cross-forest batch migrations and remote migrations. With a cross-forest migration, you perform a batch mailbox migration from an Exchange server in one Active Directory forest to an Exchange server in another Active Directory forest. With a remote migration, you perform a batch mailbox migration from on-premises Exchange to Exchange Online or vice versa.

Cross-forest and remote migrations use migration endpoints. You create a migration endpoint in the target environment. The endpoint identifies the source environment where the mailboxes are currently located. You then initiate the migration in the target environment. With a cross-forest migration, this means you:

1. Create a migration endpoint in the target domain.
2. Initiate the migration in the target domain.

With a migration from on-premises Exchange to Exchange Online, this means you:

1. Create a migration endpoint in Exchange Online.
2. Initiate the migration from Exchange Online.

With a migration from Exchange Online to on-premises Exchange, this means you:

1. Create a migration endpoint in on-premises Exchange.
2. Initiate the migration from on-premises Exchange.

A complete cross-forest or remote migration has four parts. You create a migration endpoint using New-MigrationEndpoint and then create the migration batch using New-MigrationBatch. You start the migration using Start-MigrationBatch. When the migration has finished initial synchronization, you can finalize the migration using Complete-MigrationBatch.

In Exchange Admin Center, you can initiate move and migration requests using the options on the Migration page. To access this page, select Recipients in the feature pane and then select Migration (see Figure 7-15). Although the PowerShell commands for moves and migrations give you complete control over the process, you'll find that Exchange Admin Center greatly simplifies the process:

- For local moves, you log on to a Client Access server in the Active Directory forest where the source mailboxes are located. On the Migration page, select New and then select Move To A Different Database. Follow the prompts in the New Local Mailbox Move dialog box to perform the move.

- For remote migrations, you can use the options in Exchange Admin Center for Exchange Online to initiate the process, whether migrating from or to Exchange Online. On the Migration page, select More Options, select Migration Endpoints, and then follow the prompts to create the required migration endpoint. Next, select New and then select either Migrate To Exchange Online or Migrate From Exchange Online as appropriate. Follow the prompts in the New Migration Batch dialog box to perform the migration.

- For cross-forest moves, you log on to a Client Access server in the target Active Directory forest. On the Migration page, select More Options, select Migration Endpoints, and then follow the prompts to create the required migration endpoint. Next, select New and then select Move To This Forest. Follow the prompts in the New Cross-Forest Mailbox Move dialog box to perform the move.

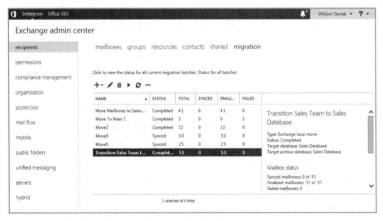

FIGURE 7-15 Checking the status of move and migration requests.

On the Migration page, you also can track the status of move and migration requests. If a move or migration request fails, you can get more information about the failure by double-tapping or double-clicking the request and then tapping or clicking View to the right of the Failed Message entry.

When you move mailboxes from one server to another, to a different organization, or even to a different database on the same server, keep in mind that the Exchange policies of the new mailbox database might be different from the old one. Because of this, consider the following issues before you move mailboxes to a new server or database:

- **General policy**   Changes to watch out for include the storage limits, the deleted item retention, and the default offline address book settings. The risk is that the users whose mailboxes you move could lose or gain access to public folders. They might have a different offline address book, which might have different entries. This address book will also have to be downloaded in its entirety the first time the user's mail client connects to Exchange after the move.

- **Database policy**   Changes to watch out for pertain to the maintenance interval and automatic mounting. If Exchange performs maintenance when these users are accessing their mail, they might have slower response times. If the mailbox database is configured so that it isn't mounted at startup, restarting the Exchange services could result in the users not being able to access their mailboxes.

- **Limits**   Changes to watch out for pertain to storage limits and deletion settings. Users might be prohibited from sending and receiving mail if their mailbox exceeds the storage limits of the new mailbox database. Users might notice that deleted items stay in their Deleted Items folder longer or are deleted sooner than expected if the Keep Deleted Items setting is different.

Performing on-premises mailbox moves

With online moves and batch migrations, you can move mailboxes between databases on the same server. You also can move mailboxes from a database on one server to a database on another server regardless of whether the servers are in a different Active Directory site or in another Active Directory forest.

Normally, when you perform online migrations, the move process looks like this:

1. You create a batch migration request for the mailboxes that you want to move using either Exchange Admin Center or Exchange Management Shell.

2. The request is sent to the Mailbox Replication Service running on a Client Access server in the current Active Directory site. This server acts as the Mailbox Replication Service proxy.

3. MRS adds the mailboxes to the Request queue and assigns the status Created to the request. This indicates the move has been requested but not started.

4. When a request is at the top of the queue, MRS begins replicating the related mailboxes to the destination database and assigns the Syncing status to the request.

5. When MRS finishes its initial replication of the mailboxes, the service assigns the Synced status to the request.

6. The request remains in the Synced state until you or another administrator specifies that you want to complete the request. MRS performs a final data synchronization and then marks the request as Completed.

7. When the request is completed, the mailboxes are available in the new location. Because users can continue to access their email accounts during the move, you can perform online moves and migrations at any time.

One way to perform online mailbox moves and migrations is by using Exchange Management Shell. The commands for performing online mailbox moves include the following:

- **Get-MoveRequest** Displays the detailed status of an ongoing mailbox move that was initiated using the New-MoveRequest cmdlet.

- **New-MoveRequest** Starts a mailbox move. You also can verify readiness to move by using the -WhatIf parameter. Use the -Priority parameter to set the relative priority of the request.

- **Resume-MoveRequest** Resumes a move request that has been suspended or failed.

- **Set-MoveRequest** Changes a move request after it has been started.

- **Suspend-MoveRequest** Suspends a move request that has been started but has not yet been completed.

- **Remove-MoveRequest** Cancels a mailbox move initiated using the New-MoveRequest cmdlet. You can use the Remove-MoveRequest command any time after initiating the move but only if the move request is not yet complete.

The commands for performing batch mailbox migrations include the following:

- **Get-MigrationBatch** Displays the detailed status of an ongoing mailbox migration that was initiated using the New-MigrationBatch cmdlet.

- **Set-MigrationBatch** Changes a migration request after it has been started.

- **New-MigrationBatch** Submits a new mailbox migration request. You also can verify readiness to migrate by using the -WhatIf parameter. Use the -AutoStart parameter to allow immediate processing of the request. Use the -AutoComplete parameter to automatically finalize the batch when the initial synchronization is complete.

- **Start-MigrationBatch** Submits a migration request for processing; required when the -AutoStart parameter is not used with New-MigrationBatch.

- **Stop-MigrationBatch** Stops a migration request that has been started but has not yet been completed.

- **Complete-MigrationBatch** Finalizes a migration request that has been synchronized; required when the -AutoComplete parameter is not used with New-MigrationBatch.

- **Remove-MigrationBatch** Deletes a mailbox migration request that either isn't running or has been completed. If you created a new request but haven't submitted it, you can use this command to remove the request so that the mailboxes specified in the request aren't migrated. If the request is completed, the mailboxes are already migrated, and you can use this command to remove the request from the queue.

- **Get-MigrationUser** Retrieves information about the ongoing migration of a particular mailbox.

- **Remove-MigrationUser** Allows you to remove a mailbox from a migration request.

- **Test-MigrationServerAvailability** Ensures the target server for a cross-premises move is available and verifies the connection settings.

Other batch migration commands include: Get-MigrationStatistics, Get-Migration-UserStatistics, Get-MigrationConfig, Set-MigrationConfig, Get-MigrationEndpoint, Set-MigrationEndpoint, New-MigrationEndpoint, and Remove-MigrationEndpoint.

Moving mailboxes within a single forest

You perform online mailbox moves within a single forest by using Exchange Management Shell. To verify move readiness, use New-MoveRequest with the -WhatIf parameter for each mailbox you plan to move. The following examples show two different ways you can verify whether Morgan Skinner's mailbox can be moved:

```
New-MoveRequest -Identity 'morgans'
-TargetDatabase "Engineering Primary" -WhatIf
```

```
'pocket-consultant.com/users/Morgan Skinner' | New-MoveRequest
-TargetDatabase 'Engineering Primary' -WhatIf
```

To initiate an online move, you use New-MoveRequest for each mailbox you want to move. The following examples show two different ways you can move Morgan Skinner's mailbox:

```
New-MoveRequest -Identity 'morgans' -Remote -RemoteHostName 'mailserver17.
pocket-consultant.com' -mrsserver 'casserver21.pocket-consultant.com'
 -TargetDatabase "Engineering Primary"
```

```
'pocket-consultant.com/users/Morgan Skinner' | New-MoveRequest -Remote
-RemoteHostName 'mailserver17.pocket-consultant.com' -mrsserver
'casserver21.pocket-consultant.com' -TargetDatabase 'Engineering Primary'
```

After you initiate a move, you can check the status of the online move using Get-MoveRequest. As shown in the following example, the key parameter to provide is the identity of the mailbox you want to check:

```
Get-MoveRequest -Identity 'morgans'
```

You can use Suspend-MoveRequest to suspend a move request that has not yet completed, and Resume-MoveRequest to resume a suspended move request. Resuming a suspended request allows it to complete.

You can cancel a move at any time prior to running the move request being completed by Exchange. To do this, run Remove-MoveRequest and specify the identity of the mailbox that shouldn't be moved. An example follows:

```
Remove-MoveRequest -Identity 'morgans'
```

When your source and destination Mailbox servers are running Exchange Server 2013 and are in the same forest, you can move mailboxes by completing these steps:

1. Log on to Exchange Admin Center via a Client Access server in the domain or forest you want to work with. In Exchange Admin Center, select Recipients in the feature pane and then select Migration.

2. On the Migration page, select New and then select Move To A Different Database. This starts the New Local Mailbox Move Wizard.

3. On the Select The Users page, shown in Figure 7-16, you can select the mailboxes to migrate by doing one of the following:

   ■ Select the mailboxes that you want to migrate using the graphic interface. Tap or click Add. Use the Select Mailbox dialog box to select the mailboxes to move and then tap or click Add. Next, tap or click OK.

     You can select and move multiple mailboxes at the same time. To select multiple mailboxes individually, hold down the Ctrl key, and then tap or click each mailbox that you want to select. To select a sequence of mailboxes, select the first mailbox, hold down the Shift key, and then tap or click the last user mailbox.

   ■ Select the mailboxes that you want to migrate using a file containing a list of comma-separated Exchange identifiers. Tap or click Specify The Users With A CSV File and then tap or click Browse. Use the Choose File To Upload dialog box to select the .csv file and then tap or click OK.

FIGURE 7-16 Selecting the mailboxes to migrate.

The file you use should be named with the .csv extension. The first line of the file should identify the column of data to import as: EmailAddress and each successive line in the file should be the email address of a mailbox to migrate, as shown in the following example:

EmailAddress

annalidman@pocket-consultant.com

deanh@pocket-consultant.com

indron@pocket-consultant.com

paulab@pocket-consultant.com

williams@pocket-consultant.com

4. Tap or click Next. On the Move Configuration page, shown in Figure 7-17, enter a descriptive name for the migration batch.

5. Use the Archive options to specify whether you want to move only the primary mailbox for the selected recipients, only the archive mailbox for the selected recipients, or both.

6. If you are moving the primary mailboxes for recipients, tap or click Browse to the right of the Target Database text box. In the Select Mailbox Database dialog box, choose the mailbox database to which the mailbox should be moved. Mailbox databases are listed by name as well as by associated server and Exchange version.

7. If you are moving the archive mailboxes for recipients, tap or click Browse to the right of the Target Archive Database text box. In the Select Mailbox Database dialog box, choose the mailbox database to which the mailbox should be moved. Mailbox databases are listed by name as well as by associated server and Exchange version.

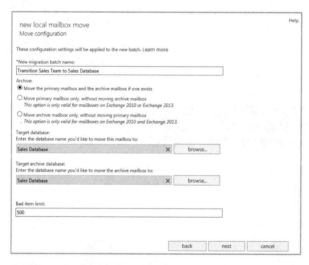

FIGURE 7-17 Configuring the settings for the move request.

8. If corrupted messages are found in a mailbox that you are migrating, the messages are skipped automatically and not migrated as part of the mailbox. By default, the wizard skips an unlimited number of bad items in each mailbox which ensures mailboxes are migrated regardless of the level of corruption. If you want to specify the maximum number of bad items that can be

skipped in each mailbox, tap or click More Options and then enter this value in the Bad Item Limit text box.

9. Tap or click Next. On the Start The Batch page, your current login is selected as the recipient for the batch report. This report will contain details about errors encountered during the migration. To add or change recipients for this report, tap or click Browse. In the Select Members dialog box, select the recipients that should receive the report and then tap or click OK. You must select at least one recipient.

10. By default, Exchange Server creates and starts the batch migration request. When the request is completed, Exchange Server will also automatically finalize it. If you want to manually start the batch, select the Manual option. If you want to manually finalize the batch, clear the Automatically Complete check box.

11. Tap or click New. Migrating mailboxes can take several hours, depending on the size of the mailboxes you are moving. You can check the status of move requests by refreshing the view on the Migration page. While the request is in the Synced state, you can cancel the request by selecting it and then tapping or clicking Delete. You cannot cancel a request that has started syncing.

Moving mailboxes between forests

You can perform online mailbox moves between different Exchange forests using Exchange Admin Center or Exchange Management Shell. When you are moving mailboxes between forests, verify that mailboxes are ready to be moved before you submit a move request. To verify readiness, the Microsoft Exchange Mailbox Replication service proxy in the source forest checks the status of each mailbox you are moving and also ensures you have the permissions required to move the mailboxes from the source forest to the target forest. If a user has an archive mailbox or subscriptions, you will likely need to remove the archive mailbox, the subscriptions, or both before you are able to move the mailbox.

You can verify move readiness in Exchange Management Shell by using New-MoveRequest with the -WhatIf parameter for each mailbox you plan to move. The following examples show two different ways you can verify whether Rob Cason's mailbox can be moved:

```
New-MoveRequest -Identity 'robc' -Remote
-RemoteHost 'mailserver17.pocket-consultant.com'-mrsserver
'casserver21.pocket-consultant.com'
-TargetDatabase "Engineering Primary" -WhatIf


'pocket-consultant.com/users/Rob Cason' | New-MoveRequest -Remote
-RemoteHost 'mailserver17.pocket-consultant.com' -mrsserver
'casserver21.pocket-consultant.com'
-TargetDatabase 'Engineering Primary' -WhatIf
```

You can perform online mailbox moves between forests by following these steps:

1. Log on to Exchange Admin Center via a Client Access server in the target forest. In Exchange Admin Center, select Recipients in the feature pane and then select Migration.

2. On the Migration page, select New and then select Move To This Forest. This starts the New Cross-Forest Mailbox Move Wizard.

3. On the Select The Users page, select the mailboxes to migrate and then tap or click Next.

4. The target forest is the forest to which you are connected. The source forest is the forest where the mailboxes are located currently. In the Source Forest Administrator Name text box, enter the name of a user account that has appropriate administrative privileges in the source forest. Enter the name in Domain\UserName format, such as Pocket-Consulta\Williams.

   NOTE The administrator must have sufficient permissions to create the required migration endpoint and move accounts. Typically, this means the account must be a member of both the Recipient Management and Server Management groups in the Exchange organization or have Organization Management permissions. However, if you previously migrated accounts between these forests, the migration endpoint created previously may still be available, in which case only Recipient Management permissions are required.

5. In the Source Forest Administrator Password text box, enter the password for the previously specified account.

6. When you tap or click Next, Exchange uses the Autodiscover service to try to detect the availability of the migration endpoint as well as to test connectivity. If errors occur, the Confirm The Migration Endpoint page is displayed. At this point, you have several options. You can:

   - Enter the fully qualified domain name of a Client Access server in the source forest that can act as the remote MRS proxy server and then tap or click Next to have Exchange try to connect to a migration endpoint on this server and test connectivity.

   - Tap or click Back to provide alternate credentials and then tap or click Next to retry the connection with those credentials. (Or simply tap or click Back and then tap or click Next to retry the connection with the original credentials.)

   - Use the Exchange Remote Connectivity Analyzer (*https://testexchange-connectivity.com*) to diagnose the connectivity issues. Once the issues are resolved, you can tap or click Next to continue.

7. On the Start The Batch page, your current login is selected as the recipient for the batch report. This report will contain details about errors encountered during the migration. To add or change recipients for this report, tap or click Browse. In the Select Members dialog box, select the recipients that should receive the report and then tap or click OK. You must select at least one recipient.

8. By default, Exchange Server creates and starts the batch migration request. When the request is completed, Exchange Server will also automatically finalize it. If you want to manually start the batch, select the Manual option. If you want to manually finalize the batch, clear the Automatically Complete check box.

9. Tap or click New. Migrating mailboxes can take several hours, depending on the size and number of the mailboxes you are moving. You can check the status of move requests by refreshing the view on the Migration page. While the request is in the Synced state, you can cancel the request by selecting it and then clicking Delete. You cannot cancel a request that has started syncing.

You can perform online moves in Exchange Management Shell by using New-MoveRequest for each mailbox you plan to move. The following examples show two different ways you can move Adam Carter's mailbox:

```
New-MoveRequest -Identity 'adamc' -Remote
-RemoteHost 'mailserver17.pocket-consultant.com'-mrsserver
'casserver21.pocket-consultant.com'
-TargetDatabase "Engineering Primary"

'pocket-consultant.com/users/Adam Carter' | New-MoveRequest -Remote
-RemoteHost 'mailserver17.pocket-consultant.com' -mrsserver
'casserver21.pocket-consultant.com'
-TargetDatabase 'Engineering Primary'
```

After you initiate a move, you can check the status of the online move by using Get-MoveRequest. As shown in the following example, the key parameters to provide are the identity of the mailbox you want to check and the name of the proxy server:

```
Get-MoveRequest -Identity 'adamc'
-mrsserver 'casserver21.pocket-consultant.com'
```

You can use Suspend-MoveRequest to suspend a move request that is not yet complete, and Resume-MoveRequest to resume a suspended move request. Resuming a suspended request allows it to complete.

At any time prior to the move request completing, you can cancel the move by running Remove-MoveRequest and specifying the identity of the mailbox that shouldn't be moved, such as:

```
Remove-MoveRequest -Identity 'adamc' -mrsserver
'casserver21.pocket-consultant.com'
```

Configuring mailbox delivery restrictions, permissions, and storage limits

You use mailbox properties to set delivery restrictions, permissions, and storage limits. To change these configuration settings for mailboxes, follow the techniques discussed in this section.

Setting message size restrictions for contacts

You set message size restrictions for contacts in much the same way that you set size restrictions for users. Follow the steps listed in the next section.

Setting message size restrictions on delivery to and from individual mailboxes

Message size restrictions control the maximum size of messages that can be sent or received in the Exchange organization. With Exchange Online, the maximum size of messages that users can send is 35,840 KB and the maximum size of messages that users can receive is 36,864 KB by default. With on-premises Exchange, you can manage these settings in a variety of ways. Typically, you manage these restrictions for the organization as a whole using the Organization Transport Settings. To manage these settings complete these steps:

1. In Exchange Admin Center, select Mail Flow in the feature pane and then select Receive Connectors.

2. On the Receive Connectors page, tap or click More Options and then select Organization Transport Settings.

3. By default the maximum receive and send message size are both set to 10 MB. Use the options on the Limits page to set new defaults and then tap or click Save.

You also can manage these restrictions using transport rules that filter messages by size and have specific conditions that apply to the size of messages or attachments, including the Apply This Rule If The Message Size Is Greater Than Or Equal To condition and the Apply This Rule If Any Attachment Is Greater Than Or Equal To condition.

Using the Apply This Rule If The Message Size Is Greater Than Or Equal To condition, you can:

- Set restrictions regarding the size of messages that can be sent or received.
- Specify the action or actions to take if a message meets or exceeds this limit.
- Define exceptions for specific users and groups as well as for messages that have specifically-defined characteristics.

In Exchange Admin Center, you can create and manage transport rules, using the options found under Mail Flow > Rules. Tap or click New and then select Filter Messages By Size. The shell commands for working with transport rules include: Disable-TransportRule, Enable-TransportRule, Get-TransportRule, New-TransportRule, Remove-TransportRule, and Set-TransportRule.

When setting these types of organization-wide restrictions, you'll want to consider the global impact. Typically, you'll want to apply organization-wide restrictions only to prevent abuse of the mail system. For example, you may want to configure rules that block sending and receiving of very large files and provide a message that encourages senders to use a site mailbox configured as part of a Microsoft SharePoint site for sharing large documents instead.

Sometimes, you need to set exceptions for specific users. For example, some users might need to be able to send large files as part of their job.

For online Exchange, delivery restrictions are fixed for individual users. For sending messages, the maximum message size is 35,840 KB. For received messages, the maximum message size is 36,864 KB.

For on-premises Exchange, you set individual delivery restrictions by completing the following steps:

1. Open the Properties dialog box for the mailbox-enabled user account by double-tapping or double-clicking the user name in Exchange Admin Center.

2. On the Mailbox Features page, scroll down and then tap or click View Details under Message Size Restrictions.

3. As shown in Figure 7-18, you can set the following send and receive restrictions:

   ▪ **Sent Messages > Maximum Message Size**   Sets a limit on the size of messages the user can send. The value is set in kilobytes (KBs). If an outgoing message exceeds the limit, the message isn't sent and the user receives a non-delivery report (NDR).

   ▪ **Received Messages > Maximum Message Size**   Sets a limit on the size of messages the user can receive. The value is set in KBs. If an incoming message exceeds the limit, the message isn't delivered and the sender receives an NDR.

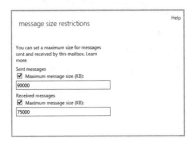

FIGURE 7-18 You can apply individual delivery restrictions on a per-user basis.

4. Tap or click OK and then tap or click Save. The restrictions that you set override the global default settings.

Setting send and receive restrictions for contacts

You set message send and receive restrictions for contacts in the same way that you set these restrictions for users. Follow the steps listed in the next section.

Setting message send and receive restrictions on individual mailboxes

By default, user mailboxes are configured to accept messages from anyone. To override this behavior, you can do the following:

- Specify that only messages from the listed users, contacts, or groups be accepted.
- Specify that messages from specific users, contacts, or groups be rejected.
- Specify that only messages from authenticated users—meaning users who have logged on to the Exchange system or the domain—be accepted.

With both on-premises Exchange and Exchange Online, you set message send and receive restrictions by completing the following steps:

1. Open the Properties dialog box for the mailbox-enabled user account by double-tapping or double-clicking the user name in Exchange Admin Center.

2. On the Mailbox Features page, scroll down and then tap or click View Details under Message Delivery Restrictions. As shown in Figure 7-19, you can set message acceptance restrictions.

3. If you want to ensure that messages are accepted only from authenticated users, select the Require That All Senders Are Authenticated check box.

4. To accept messages from all email addresses except those on the reject list, under Accept Messages From, select All Senders.

5. To specify that only messages from the listed users, contacts, or groups be accepted, select the Only Senders In The Following List option and then add acceptable recipients by following these steps:

   - Tap or click Add to display the Select Members dialog box.
   - Select a recipient, and then tap or click OK. Repeat as necessary.

FIGURE 7-19 You can apply send and receive restrictions on messages on a per-user basis.

TIP You can select multiple recipients at the same time. To select multiple recipients individually, hold down the Ctrl key and then tap or click each recipient that you want to select. To select a sequence of recipients, select the first recipient, hold down the Shift key, and then tap or click the last recipient.

6. To specify that no recipients should be rejected, under Reject Messages From, select No Senders.

7. To reject messages from specific recipients, under Reject Messages From, select Senders In The Following List and then add unacceptable recipients by following these steps:

   ▪ Tap or click Add to display the Select Members dialog box.

   ▪ Select a recipient, and then tap or click OK. Repeat as necessary

8. Tap or click OK.

Permitting others to access a mailbox

Occasionally, users need to access someone else's mailbox, and in certain situations, you should allow this. For example, if John is Susan's manager and Susan is going on vacation, John might need access to her mailbox while she's away. Another situation in which someone might need access to another mailbox is when you've set up special-purpose mailboxes, such as a mailbox for Webmaster@domain.com or a mailbox for Info@domain.com.

You can grant permissions for a mailbox in three ways:

▪ You can grant access to a mailbox and its content. If you want to grant access to a mailbox and its contents but not grant Send As permissions, use the Full Access settings. In Exchange Admin Center, open the Properties dialog box for the mailbox you want to work with and then select Mailbox Delegation. On the Mailbox Delegation page, under Full Access, tap or click Add, and then use the Select Full Access dialog box to choose the recipients who should have access to the mailbox. To revoke the authority to access the mailbox, select an existing user name in the Display Name list box and then tap or click Remove.

▪ You can grant the right to send messages as the mailbox owner. If you want to grant Send As permissions, use the Send As settings. In Exchange Admin Center, open the Properties dialog box for the mailbox you want to work with and then select Mailbox Delegation. On the Mailbox Delegation page, under Send As, tap or click Add, and then use the Select Send As dialog box to choose the recipients who should have this permission. To revoke this permission, select an existing user name in the Display Name list box and then tap or click Remove.

▪ You can grant the right to send messages on behalf of the mailbox owner. If you want to allow a user to send messages from a user's mailbox but want recipients to know a message was sent on behalf of the mailbox owner (rather than by the mailbox owner), grant Send On Behalf Of permissions. In Exchange Admin Center, open the Properties dialog box for the mailbox you want to work with and then select Mailbox Delegation. On the Mailbox

Delegation page, under Send On Behalf Of, tap or click Add, and then use the Select Send On Behalf Of dialog box to choose the recipients who should have this permission. To revoke this permission, select an existing user name in the Display Name list box and then tap or click Remove.

In Exchange Management Shell, you can use the Add-MailboxPermission and Remove-MailboxPermission cmdlets to manage full access permissions. Samples 7-4 and 7-5 show examples of using these cmdlets. In these examples, the AccessRights parameter is set to FullAccess to indicate full access permissions on the mailbox.

SAMPLE 7-4 Adding full access permissions

Syntax

```
Add-MailboxPermission -Identity UserBeingGrantedPermission
 -User UserWhoseMailboxIsBeingConfigured -AccessRights 'FullAccess'
```

Usage

```
Add-MailboxPermission -Identity
'CN=Mike Lam,OU=Engineering,DC=pocket-consultant,DC=com'
-User 'POCKET-CONSULTA\boba' -AccessRights 'FullAccess'
```

SAMPLE 7-5 Removing full access permissions

Syntax

```
Remove-MailboxPermission -Identity 'UserBeingGrantedPermission'
 -User 'UserWhoseMailboxIsBeingConfigured' -AccessRights 'FullAccess'
-InheritanceType 'All'
```

Usage

```
Remove-MailboxPermission -Identity 'CN=Jerry Orman,
OU=Engineering,DC=pocket-consultant,DC=com'
 -User 'POCKET-CONSULTA\boba' -AccessRights 'FullAccess'
 -InheritanceType 'All'
```

In Exchange Management Shell, you can use the Add-ADPermission and Remove-ADPermission cmdlets to manage Send As permissions. Samples 7-6 and 7-7 show examples using these cmdlets. In these examples, the -ExtendedRights parameter is set to Send-As to grant Send As permissions for the mailbox.

SAMPLE 7-6 Adding send as permissions

Syntax

```
Add-ADPermission -Identity UserBeingGrantedPermission
-User UserWhoseMailboxIsBeingConfigured -ExtendedRights 'Send-As'
```

Usage

```
Add-ADPermission -Identity 'CN=Jerry
Orman,OU=Engineering,DC=cpand1,DC=com'
-User 'POCKET-CONSULTA\boba' -ExtendedRights 'Send-As'
```

Syntax

```
Remove-ADPermission -Identity UserBeingRevokedPermission
-User UserWhoseMailboxIsBeingConfigured -ExtendedRights 'Send-As'
-InheritanceType 'All' -ChildObjectTypes $null
-InheritedObjectType $null -Properties $null
```

Usage

```
Remove-ADPermission -Identity 'CN=Jerry
Orman,OU=Engineering, DC=pocket-consultant,DC=com'
 -User 'POCKET-CONSULTA\boba' -ExtendedRights 'Send-As'
-InheritanceType 'All' -ChildObjectTypes $null -InheritedObjectTypes $null
-Properties $null
```

> **NOTE** Another way to grant access permissions to mailboxes is to do so through Outlook. Using Outlook, you have more granular control over permissions. You can allow a user to log on as the mailbox owner, delegate mailbox access, and grant various levels of access. For more information on this issue, see the "Accessing multiple Exchange mailboxes" and "Granting permission to access folders without delegating access" sections in Chapter 5 "Managing Exchange Server 2013 clients. "

Forwarding email to a new address

Except when rights management prevents it, any messages sent to a user's mailbox can be forwarded to another recipient. This recipient can be another user or a mail-enabled contact. To configure mail forwarding, follow these steps:

1. Open the Properties dialog box for the mailbox-enabled user account by double-tapping or double-clicking the user name in Exchange Admin Center.

2. On the Mailbox Features page, scroll down and then tap or click View Details under Mail Flow.

3. To remove forwarding, clear the Enable Forwarding check box.

4. To add forwarding, select the Enable Forwarding check box and then tap or click Browse. Use the Select Mailbox User And Mailbox dialog box to choose the alternate recipient.

In Exchange Admin Center, you cannot also specify that copies of forwarded messages should be retained in the original mailbox. However, if you use Exchange Management Shell to configure forwarding, you can specify that messages should be delivered to both the forwarding address and the current mailbox. To do this, set the -DeliverToMailboxAndForward parameter to $true when using Set-Mailbox.

Setting storage restrictions on mailbox and archives

In a standard configuration of Exchange Online, each licensed user gets 25 GB of mailbox storage, and a storage warning is issued when the mailbox reaches 22.5 GB. Similarly, if a user has a licensed in-place archive, the archive can have up to 25 GB of storage; a storage warning is issued when the archive mailbox reaches 22.5 GB. Other licensing options are available that may grant additional storage rights.

With on-premises Exchange, you can set storage restrictions on multiple mailboxes using global settings for each mailbox database or on individual mailboxes using per-user restrictions. Global restrictions are applied when you create a mailbox and are reapplied when you define new global storage restrictions. Per-user storage restrictions are set individually for each mailbox and override the global default settings. By default, users can store up to 2 GB in their mailboxes. The quotas are set to:

- Issue a warning when the mailbox reaches 1.9 GB
- Prohibit send when the mailbox reaches 2 GB
- Prohibit send and receive when the mailbox reaches 2.3 GB

In contrast, the default settings for archive mailboxes allow users to store up to 50 GB in their archive mailboxes, and a warning is issued when the archive mailbox reaches 45 GB.

NOTE Storage restrictions apply only to mailboxes stored on the server. They don't apply to personal folders. Personal folders are stored on the user's computer.

To configure global storage restrictions, you edit the properties of mailbox databases. In Exchange Admin Center, navigate to Servers > Databases. Open the Properties dialog box for the mailbox database by double-tapping or double-clicking the database name. On the Limits page, set the desired storage restrictions using the options provided.

Set individual storage restrictions for mailboxes by completing the following steps:

1. Open the Properties dialog box for the mailbox-enabled user account by double-tapping or double-clicking the user name in Exchange Admin Center.

2. On the Mailbox Usage page, tap or click More Options. You'll then see the storage restrictions as shown in Figure 7-20.

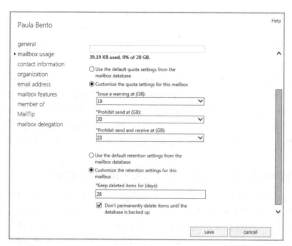

FIGURE 7-20 Use the quota settings to specify storage limits and deleted item retention on a per-user basis when necessary.

3. To set mailbox storage limits, select Customize The Quota Settings For This Mailbox. Then set one or more of the following storage limits:

- **Issue Warning At (GB)**   This limit specifies the size, in gigabytes, that a mailbox can reach before a warning is issued to the user. The warning tells the user to clean out the mailbox.

- **Prohibit Send At (GB)**   This limit specifies the size, in gigabytes, that a mailbox can reach before the user is prohibited from sending any new mail. The restriction ends when the user clears out the mailbox and the mailbox size is under the limit.

- **Prohibit Send And Receive At (GB)**   This limit specifies the size, in gigabytes, that a mailbox can reach before the user is prohibited from sending and receiving mail. The restriction ends when the user clears out the mailbox and the mailbox size is under the limit.

CAUTION   Prohibiting send and receive might cause the user to think they've lost email. When someone sends a message to a user who is prohibited from receiving messages, an NDR is generated and delivered to the sender. The original recipient never sees the email. Because of this, you should rarely prohibit send and receive.

4. Tap or click Save.

Users who have an archive mailbox have the mailbox type User (Archive). You set individual storage restrictions for archive mailboxes by completing the following steps:

1. Select the user name in Exchange Admin Center.
2. In the detail pane, scroll down until you see the In-Place Archive heading and the related options. Tap or click View Details.
3. Enter the desired maximum size for the archive in the Archive Quota text box.
4. Enter the storage limit for issuing a storage warning in the Issue Warning At text box, and then tap or click OK.

Setting deleted item retention time on individual mailboxes

Normally, when a user deletes a message in Outlook, the message is placed in the Deleted Items folder. The message remains in the Deleted Items folder until the user deletes it manually or allows Outlook to clear out the Deleted Items folder. With personal folders, the message is then permanently deleted and can't be restored. With server-based mailboxes, the message isn't actually deleted from the Exchange database. Instead, the message is marked as hidden and kept for a specified period of time called the *deleted item retention period*.

NOTE   The standard processes can be modified in several different ways. A user could press Shift+Delete to bypass Deleted Items. As an administrator, you can create and apply policies that prevent users from deleting items (even if they try to use Shift+Delete). You can also configure policy to retain items indefinitely.

Default retention settings are configured for each mailbox database in the organization. With Exchange Online, the retention settings are as follows:

- Deleted items are retained for a maximum of 30 days.
- Items removed from the Deleted Items folder are retained for a maximum of 14 days.
- Items in the Junk Folder are retained for a maximum of 30 days before they are removed.

To configure deleted item retention on a per database basis, you edit the properties of mailbox databases. In Exchange Admin Center, navigate to Servers > Databases. Open the Properties dialog box for the mailbox database by double-tapping or double-clicking the database name. On the Limits page, use the options provided to configure the deleted item retention settings.

To override the database settings on a per-user basis, complete these steps:

1. Open the Properties dialog box for the mailbox-enabled user account by double-tapping or double-clicking the user name in Exchange Admin Center.

2. On the Mailbox Usage page, tap or click More Options and then select Customize The Retention Settings For This Mailbox.

3. In the Keep Deleted Items For (Days) text box, enter the number of days to retain deleted items. An average retention period is 14 days. If you set the retention period to 0 and aren't using policies that prevent deletion, messages aren't retained and can't be recovered. If you set the retention period to 0 but are using policies that prevent deletion, the messages are retained according to the established policies.

4. You can also specify that deleted messages should not be permanently removed until the mailbox database has been backed up. This option ensures that the deleted items are archived into at least one backup set. Tap or click Save.

REAL WORLD Deleted item retention is convenient because it allows the administrator the chance to salvage accidentally deleted email without restoring a user's mailbox from backup. I strongly recommend that you enable this setting, either in the mailbox database or for individual mailboxes, and configure the retention period accordingly.

CHAPTER 8

Working with distribution groups and address lists

D istribution groups and address lists are extremely important in Microsoft Exchange Server and Exchange Online administration. Careful planning of your organization's groups and address lists can save you countless hours in the long run. Unfortunately, most administrators don't have a solid understanding of these subjects, and the few who do spend most of their time on other duties. To save yourself time and frustration, study the concepts discussed in this chapter and then use the step-by-step procedures to implement the groups and lists for your organization.

Using security and distribution groups

You use groups to grant permissions to similar types of users, to simplify account administration, and to make it easier to contact multiple users. For example, you can send a message addressed to a group, and the message will go to all the users in that group. Thus, instead of having to enter 20 different email addresses in the message header, you enter one email address for all of the group members.

Group types, scope, and identifiers

Windows defines several different types of groups, and each of these groups can have a unique scope. In Active Directory domains, you use three group types:

- **Security**   You use security groups to control access to network resources. You can also use user-defined security groups to distribute email.

- **Standard distribution**   Standard distribution groups have fixed member-ship, and you use them only as email distribution lists. You can't use these groups to control access to network resources.

- **Dynamic distribution**   Membership for dynamic distribution groups is determined based on a Lightweight Directory Access Protocol (LDAP) query; you use these groups only as email distribution lists. The LDAP query is used to build the list of members whenever messages are sent to the group.

NOTE Dynamic distribution groups created for Exchange Server 2007 and Exchange Server 2010 are compatible with Exchange Server 2013. However, dynamic distribution groups created for Exchange Server 2003 are not compatible with Exchange Server 2013 and aren't displayed in Exchange Admin Center. You can resolve this by forcing an upgrade. See "Modifying dynamic distribution groups using cmdlets" later in this chapter for details.

Security groups can have different scopes—*domain local, global,* and *univer-sal*—so that they are valid in different areas of your Active Directory forest. With Exchange Server 2003, you could also create distribution groups with different scopes. To simplify group management, Exchange Server 2007 and later support only groups with universal scope. You can mail-enable security groups with univer-sal scope, and you can create new distribution groups with universal scope.

REAL WORLD If your organization has existing mail-enabled security groups or distribution groups with global scope, you will not be able to use those groups with Exchange Server 2007 and later editions of Exchange. You will either need to create a new architecture for your groups or convert those groups to universal groups. Using Active Directory Users And Computers, domain administrators can easily convert global groups to universal groups. They simply need to double-tap or double-click the group entry, select Universal under Group Scope, and then tap or click OK. However, some conversion restrictions apply. For example, you can convert a global group only if it isn't a member of another global group. In addition, pre-planning is recommended to deter-mine the impact on Active Directory. You also can use Set-Group to convert groups.

In Exchange Admin Center, you select Recipients in the feature pane and then select Groups to work with groups (see Figure 8-1). Only mail-enabled groups with universal scope are displayed. Groups with universal scope can do the following:

- Contain users and groups from any domain in the forest
- Be put into other groups and assigned permissions in any domain in the forest

When you work with dynamic distribution groups, keep in mind that the member-ship can include only members of the local domain, or it can include users and groups from other domains, domain trees, or forests. Scope is determined by the default apply-filter container you associate with the group when you create it. More specifi-cally, the default apply-filter container defines the root of the search hierarchy and the LDAP query filters to recipients in and below the specified container. For example, if the apply-filter container you associate with the group is pocket-consultant.com, the query filter is applied to all recipients in this domain. If the apply-filter container you associate with the organizational unit is Engineering, the query filter is applied to all recipients in or below this container.

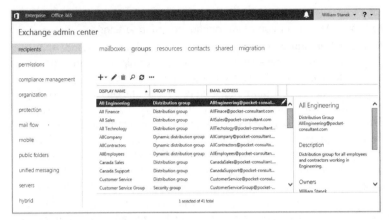

FIGURE 8-1 Viewing the configured groups in Exchange Admin Center.

As with user accounts, Windows uses unique security identifiers (SIDs) to track groups. This means that you can't delete a group, re-create it with the same name, and then expect all the permissions and privileges to remain the same. The new group will have a new SID, and all the permissions and privileges of the old group will be lost.

When to use security and standard distribution groups

Exchange Server 2007 and later changed the earlier rules about how you can use groups. Previously, you could use groups with different scopes, but now you can use only groups with universal scope. As a result, you might need to rethink how and when you use groups.

You must change the scope of any global group to universal before you can mail-enable it. Rather than duplicating your existing security group structure with distribution groups that have the same purpose, you might want to selectively mail-enable your universal security groups, which converts them to distribution groups. For example, if you have a universal security group called Marketing, you don't need to create a MarketingDistList distribution group. Instead, you could enable Exchange mail on the original universal security group, which would then become a distribution group.

You might also want to mail-enable universal security groups that you previously defined. Then, if existing distribution groups serve the same purpose, you can delete the distribution groups.

To reduce the time administrators spend managing groups, Exchange defines several additional control settings, including:

- **Group ownership** Mail-enabled security groups, standard distribution groups, and dynamic distribution groups can have one or more owners. A group's owners are the users assigned as its managers, and they can control membership in the group. A group's managers are listed when users view the properties of the group in Microsoft Office Outlook. Additionally, managers can receive delivery reports for groups if you select the Send Delivery Reports To Group Manager option when configuring group settings.

- **Membership approval**   Mail-enabled security groups and standard distribution groups can have open or closed membership. There are separate settings for joining and leaving a group. For joining, the group can be open to allow users to join without requiring permission, be closed to allow only group owners and administrators to add members, or require owner approval to allow users to request membership in a group. Membership requests must be approved by a group owner. For leaving, a group can either be open to allow users to leave a group without requiring owner approval or closed to allow only group owners and administrators to remove members.

Your management tool of choice will determine your options for configuring group ownership and membership approval. When you create groups in Exchange Admin Center, you can specify ownership, membership, and approval settings when you create the group and can edit these settings at any time by editing the group's properties. When you create groups in Exchange Management Shell, you can configure additional advanced options that you'd otherwise have to manage after creating the group in Exchange Admin Center.

When to use dynamic distribution groups

It's a fact of life that over time users will move to different departments, leave the company, or accept different responsibilities. With standard distribution groups, you'll spend a lot of time managing group membership when these types of changes occur—and that's where dynamic distribution groups come into the picture. With dynamic distribution groups, there isn't a fixed group membership and you don't have to add or remove users from groups. Instead, group membership is determined by the results of an LDAP query sent to your organization's Global Catalog.

Dynamic distribution groups can be used with or without a dedicated expansion server. You'll get the most benefit from dynamic distribution without a dedicated expansion server when the member list returned in the results is relatively small (fewer than 25 members). In the case of potentially hundreds or thousands of members, however, dynamic distribution is inefficient and could require a great deal of processing to complete. Exchange 2013 shifts the processing requirements from the Global Catalog server to a dedicated expansion server (a server whose only task is to expand the LDAP queries). By default, Exchange 2013 uses the closest Exchange server that has the Mailbox server role installed as the dedicated expansion server. For more information on expansion servers, see "Designating an expansion server" later in this chapter.

One other thing to note about dynamic distribution is that you can associate only one specific query with each distribution group. For example, you could create separate groups for each department in the organization. You could have groups called QD-Accounting, QD-BizDev, QD-Engineering, QD-Marketing, QD-Operations, QD-Sales, and QD-Support. You could, in turn, create a standard distribution group or a dynamic distribution group called AllEmployees that contains these groups as members—thereby establishing a distribution group hierarchy.

When using multiple parameters with dynamic distribution, keep in mind that multiple parameters typically work as logical AND operations. For example, if you create a query with a parameter that matches all employees in the state of Washington with all employees in the Marketing department, the query results do not contain a list of all employees in Washington or all Marketing employees. Rather, the results contain a list of recipients who are in Washington and are members of the Marketing group. In this case, you get the expected results by creating a dynamic distribution group for all Washington State employees, another dynamic distribution group for all Marketing employees, and a final group that has as members the other two distribution groups.

Working with security and standard distribution groups

As you set out to work with groups, you'll find that some tasks are specific to each type of group and some tasks can be performed with any type of group. Because of this, I've divided the group management discussion into three sections. In this section, you'll learn about the typical tasks you perform with security and standard distribution groups. The next section discusses tasks you'll perform only with dynamic distribution groups. The third section discusses general management tasks.

You can use Exchange Admin Center or Exchange Management Shell to work with groups.

Group naming policy

Whether you work at a small company with 50 employees or a large enterprise with 5,000 employees, you should consider establishing a group naming policy that ensures a consistent naming strategy is used for group names. For administrators, your naming policy should be implemented through written policies within your IT department and could be applied to both security groups and distribution groups.

Exchange 2013 and Exchange Online also allow you to establish official naming policy for standard distribution groups. Group naming policy is:

- Applied to non-administrators whenever they create or rename distribution groups.

- Applied to administrators only when they create or rename distribution groups using the shell (and omit the -IgnoreNamingPolicy parameter).

IMPORTANT Group naming policy doesn't apply to security groups or dynamic distribution groups. Each Exchange organization can have one and only one naming policy. Any naming policy you define is applied throughout the Exchange organization.

Understanding group naming policy

You use group naming policy to format group names according to a defined standard. The rules for naming policy allow for one or more prefixes, a group name, and one or more suffixes, giving an expanded syntax of:

```
<Prefix1><Prefix2>...<PrefixN><GroupName><Suffix1><Suffix2>...<SuffixN)
```

You can use any Exchange attribute as the prefix or suffix. You also can use a text string as a prefix or suffix. The prefix, group name, and suffix are combined without spacing. To improve readability, you can separate the prefix, name, and suffix with a placeholder character, such as a space ( ), a period (.) or a dash (-).

Group naming policy works like this:

- A user creates a standard distribution group and specifies a display name for the group. After creating the group, Exchange applies the group naming policy by adding any prefixes or suffixes defined in the group naming policy to the display name.

- The display name is displayed in the distribution groups list in Exchange Admin Center, the shared address book, and the To:, Cc:, and From: fields in email messages.

You can create a naming policy with only a prefix and a group name or with only a suffix and a group name. Common attributes that you might want to use as prefixes or suffixes include city, country code, department, office, and state. For example, you might want all distribution groups to have the following syntax:

State_GroupName

To do this, you would create a naming policy with two prefixes. As shown in Figure 8-2, the first prefix would have the <State> attribute. The second prefix would have the _text value. Thus, if a user in the state of New York (NY) creates a standard distribution group called Sales, Exchange adds the defined prefixes according to the naming policy and the display name becomes NY_Sales.

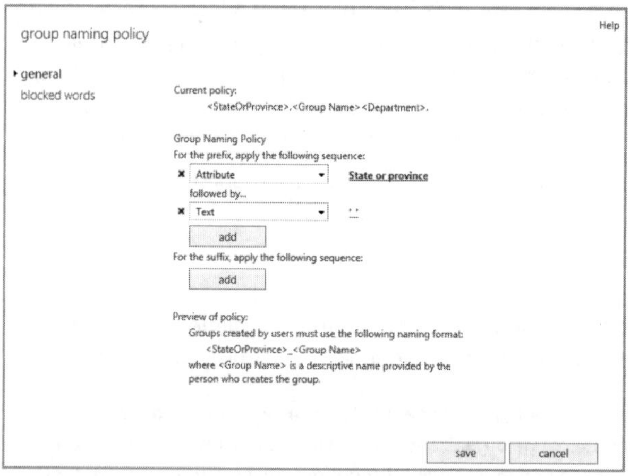

FIGURE 8-2 Creating a naming policy with two prefixes.

Group naming policy also allows you to specify blocked words. Users who try to use a word that you've blocked see an error message when they try to create the new group and are asked to remove the blocked word and create the group again.

Defining group naming policy for your organization

Group naming policy formats display names so that they follow a defined standard. When setting the naming format, keep in mind that users enter the desired display name when they create the group and Exchange transforms the format according to the defined policy. Because the display name is limited to 64 characters, you must consider this limit when defining the prefixes and suffixes in your naming policy.

You can create the group naming policy for the Exchange organization by completing the following steps:

1. In Exchange Admin Center, select Recipients in the feature pane and then select Groups.

2. Tap or click the More button (this button shows three dots) and then select Configure Group Naming Policy. This displays the Group Naming Policy dialog box.

3. If you want the naming policy to have a prefix, do one of the following and then optionally tap or click Add to add additional prefixes using the same technique:

   ■ Use the selection list to choose Attribute as the prefix. In the Select The Attribute dialog box, select the attribute to use and then tap or click OK.

   ■ Use the selection list to choose Text as the prefix. In the Enter Text dialog box, select the text string to use and then tap or click OK.

4. If you want the naming policy to have a suffix, do one of the following and then optionally tap or click Add to add additional suffixes using the same technique:

   ■ Use the selection list to choose Attribute as the suffix. In the Select The Attribute dialog box, select the attribute to use and then tap or click OK.

   ■ Use the selection list to choose Text as the suffix. In the Enter Text dialog box, select the text string to use and then tap or click OK.

5. As you define the naming policy, the Preview Of Policy area shows the naming format. When you are satisfied with the naming format, tap or click Save.

Defining blocked words in group naming policy

Blocked words allow you to specify words that users can't use in the names of standard distribution groups they create. You can define or manage the blocked words list by completing the following steps:

1. In Exchange Admin Center, select Recipients in the feature pane and then select Groups.

2. Tap or click the More button (this button shows three dots) and then select Configure Group Naming Policy. This displays the Group Naming Policy dialog box.

3. On the Blocked Words page, any currently blocked words are displayed. Use the following techniques to manage the blocked word list:

   ■ To add a blocked word, type the word in the text box provided and then tap or click Add. Alternatively, type the word to block in the text box provided and then press Enter.

- To modify a blocked word, select the word in the blocked word list and then tap or click Edit. Modify the word and then tap or click outside the text box provided for editing. Alternatively, press Enter to apply the edits.
- To remove a blocked word, tap or click the word to remove and then tap or click Remove.

4. Tap or click Save.

Creating security and standard distribution groups

Security groups and distribution groups are available whether you are working with online or on-premises Exchange organizations. You use groups to manage permissions and to distribute email. As you set out to create groups, remember that you create groups for similar types of users. Consequently, you might want to create the following types of groups:

- **Groups for departments within the organization**   Generally, users who work in the same department need access to similar resources and should be a part of the same email distribution lists.

- **Groups for roles within the organization**   You can also organize groups according to the users' roles within the organization. For example, you could use a group called Executives to send email to all the members of the executive team and a group called Managers to send email to all managers and executives in the organization.

- **Groups for users of specific projects**   Often, users working on a major project need a way to send email to all the members of the team. To address this need, you can create a group specifically for the project.

You can create groups several ways. You can create a new distribution group, you can create a mail-enabled universal security group, or you can mail-enable an existing universal security group.

Creating a new group

You can create a new distribution group or a new mail-enabled security group by completing the following steps:

1. In Exchange Admin Center, select Recipients in the feature pane and then select Groups.

2. Tap or click New and then do one of the following:
   - Select Distribution Group to create a new Distribution Group. This opens the New Distribution Group dialog box. Figure 8-3 shows on-premises Exchange options on the left and Exchange Online options on the right.
   - Select Security Group to create a new mail-enabled Security Group. This opens the New Security Group dialog box, and the options are the same as those for new distribution groups.

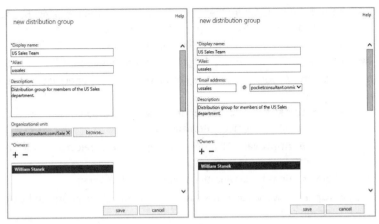

FIGURE 8-3 Configuring the group's settings.

3. In the Display Name text box, type a display name for the group. Group names aren't case-sensitive and can be up to 64 characters long. Keep in mind that group naming policy doesn't apply to administrators creating distribution groups in Exchange Admin Center (or to mail-enabled security groups in any way).

4. Like users, groups have Exchange aliases. Enter an alias. The Exchange alias is used to set the group's SMTP email address. Exchange Server uses the SMTP address for receiving messages.

5. For Exchange Online, the name and domain components of the default email address are displayed in the Email Address text boxes. As appropriate, change the default name and use the drop-down list to select the domain with which you want to associate the group. This sets the fully qualified email address, such as us-sales@pocket-consultant.com.

6. With on-premises Exchange, the group account is created in the default user container, which typically is the Users container. To create the group in a specific organizational unit instead, tap or click Browse to the right of the Organizational Unit text box. In the Select Organizational Unit dialog box, choose the location where you want to store the account and then tap or click OK.

7. Group owners are responsible for managing a group. To add owners, under Owners, tap or click Add. In the Select Owner dialog box, select users, groups, or both that should have management responsibility for the group. Select multiple users and groups using the Shift or Ctrl key.

    IMPORTANT While dynamic distribution groups don't have to have owners, every mail-enabled security group and standard distribution group must have at least one owner. By default, the account you are using is set as the group owner.

8. Members of a group receive messages sent to the group. By default, the group owners are set as members of the group. If you don't want the currently listed owners to be members of the group, clear the Add Group Owners As Members checkbox.

9. To add members, under Members, tap or click Add. In the Select Members dialog box, select users, groups, or both that should be members of the group. Select multiple users and groups using the Shift or Ctrl key.

10. Choose settings for joining the group. The options are:

   - **Open**   Anyone can join this group without being approved by the group owners.

   - **Closed**   Members can be added only by the group owners. All requests to join will be rejected automatically.

   - **Owner Approval**   All requests are approved or rejected by the group owners.

11. Choose settings for leaving the group. The options are:

   - **Open**   Anyone can leave this group without being approved by the group owners.

   - **Closed**   Members can be removed only by the group owners. All requests to leave will be rejected automatically.

12. Tap or click Save to create the group. If an error occurs during group creation, the related group will not be created. You need to correct the problem before you can complete this procedure.

13. After creating a group, you might want to do the following:

   - Set message size restrictions for messages mailed to the group.

   - Limit users who can send to the group.

   - Change or remove default email addresses.

   - Add more email addresses.

NOTE   By default, the new distribution group is open for joining and open for leaving.

In Exchange Management Shell, you can create a new distribution group using the New-DistributionGroup cmdlet. Sample 8-1 provides the syntax and usage. You can set the -Type parameter to Distribution for a distribution group or to Security for a mail-enabled security group.

SAMPLE 8-1 New-DistributionGroup cmdlet syntax and usage

Syntax

```
New-DistributionGroup -Name ExchangeName [-Alias ExchangeAlias]
[-DisplayName DisplayName] [-OrganizationalUnit OUName]
[-PrimarySmtpAddress SmtpAddress] [-SamAccountName PreWin2000Name]
[-Type <Distribution | Security>] {AddtlParams}


{AddtlParams}
[-ArbitrationMailbox ModeratorMailbox] [-BypassNestedModerationEnabled
<$true | $false>] [-CopyOwnerToMember {$true | $false}] [-DomainController
FullyQualifiedName] [-IgnoreNamingPolicy {$true | $false}] [-ManagedBy
RecipientIdentities] [-MemberDepartRestriction <Closed | Open |
ApprovalRequired>] [-MemberJoinRestriction <Closed | Open |
ApprovalRequired>] [-Members RecipientIdentities] [-ModeratedBy
Moderators] [-ModerationEnabled <$true | $false>] [-Notes String]
```

```
[-Organization OrgName] [-RoomList {$true | $false}]
[-SendModerationNotifications <Never | Internal | Always>]
```

Usage

```
New-DistributionGroup -Name 'CorporateSales' -Type 'Distribution'
-OrganizationalUnit 'pocket-consultant.com/Sales'
-SamAccountName 'CorporateSales'
-DisplayName 'Corporate Sales'
-Alias 'CorporateSales'
```

Mail-enabling universal security groups

You can't use Exchange Admin Center to mail-enable a security group. In Exchange Management Shell, you can mail-enable a universal security group using the Enable-DistributionGroup cmdlet. Sample 8-2 provides the syntax and usage.

SAMPLE 8-2 Enable-DistributionGroup cmdlet syntax and usage

Syntax

```
Enable-DistributionGroup -Identity GroupIdentity [-Alias ExchangeAlias]
[-DisplayName DisplayName] [-DomainController FullyQualifiedName]
[-OverrideRecipientQuotas {$true | $false}]
[-PrimarySmtpAddress SmtpAddress]
```

Usage

```
Enable -DistributionGroup -Identity 'AllSales'
-DisplayName 'All Sales' -Alias 'AllSales'
```

NOTE Group naming policy applies only to distribution groups.

You can manage mail-enabled security groups in several ways. You can add or remove group members as discussed in the "Assigning and removing membership for individual users, groups, and contacts" section of this chapter. If a group should no longer be mail-enabled, you can use Disable-DistributionGroup to remove the Exchange settings from the group. If you no longer need a mail-enabled security group and it is not a built-in group, you can permanently remove it from Active Directory by selecting it in Exchange Admin Center and tapping or clicking Delete. Alternatively, you can delete a group using Delete-DistributionGroup.

Using Exchange Management Shell, you can disable a group's Exchange features using the Disable-DistributionGroup cmdlet, as shown in Sample 8-3.

SAMPLE 8-3 Disable-DistributionGroup cmdlet syntax and usage

Syntax

```
Disable-DistributionGroup -Identity GroupIdentity
[-DomainController FullyQualifiedName]
[-IgnoreDefaultScope {$true | $false}]
```

Usage

```
Disable-DistributionGroup -Identity 'AllSales'
```

Assigning and removing membership for individual users, groups, and contacts

All users, groups, and contacts can be members of other groups. To configure a group's membership, follow these steps:

1. In Exchange Admin Center, double-tap or double-click the group entry. This opens the group's Properties dialog box.

2. On the Membership page, you'll see a list of current members. Tap or click Add to add recipients to the group. In the Select Members dialog box, select users, groups, or both that should be members of the group. Select multiple users and groups using the Shift or Ctrl key.

3. You can remove members on the Membership page as well. To remove a member from a group, select a recipient, and then tap or click Remove. When you're finished, tap or click Save.

In Exchange Management Shell, you can view group members using the Get-DistributionGroupMember cmdlet. Sample 8-4 provides the syntax and usage.

SAMPLE 8-4 Get-DistributionGroupMember cmdlet syntax and usage

Syntax

```
Get-DistributionGroupMember -Identity GroupIdentity [-Credential
Credential] [-DomainController FullyQualifiedName]
[-IgnoreDefaultScope {$true | $false}] [-ReadFromDomainController {$true
| $false}] [-ResultSize Size]
```

Usage

```
Get-DistributionGroupMember -Identity 'CorpSales'
```

You add members to a group using the Add-DistributionGroupMember cmdlet. Sample 8-5 provides the syntax and usage.

SAMPLE 8-5 Add-DistributionGroupMember cmdlet syntax and usage

Syntax

```
Add-DistributionGroupMember -Identity GroupIdentity [-Member
RecipientIdentity] [-BypassSecurityGroupManagerCheck {$true | $false}]
[-DomainController FullyQualifiedName]
```

Usage

```
Add-DistributionGroupMember -Identity 'CorpSales'
 -Member 'pocket-consultant.com/Sales/April Stewart'
```

You remove members from a group using the Remove-DistributionGroupMember cmdlet. Sample 8-6 provides the syntax and usage.

Syntax

```
Remove-DistributionGroupMember -Identity GroupIdentity [-Member
RecipientIdentity] [-BypassSecurityGroupManagerCheck {$true | $false}]
[-DomainController FullyQualifiedName]
```

Usage

```
Remove-DistributionGroupMember -Identity 'CorpSales'
 -Member 'pocket-consultant.com/Sales/April Stewart'
```

Adding and removing managers

Group owners are responsible for managing a group. Every group must have at least one owner. To configure a group's managers, follow these steps:

1. In Exchange Admin Center, double-tap or double-click the group entry. This opens the group's Properties dialog box.

2. On the Ownership page, you'll see a list of current owners. Tap or click Add to add recipients to the group. In the Select Owners dialog box, select users, groups, or both that should be owners of the group. Select multiple users and groups using the Shift or Ctrl key.

3. You can remove owners on the Ownership page as well. To remove an owner from a group, select a recipient, and then tap or click Remove. When you're finished, tap or click Save.

In Exchange Management Shell, you can add or remove group managers using the -ManagedBy parameter of the Set-DistributionGroup cmdlet. To set this parameter, you must specify the full list of managers for the group by doing the following:

- Add managers by including existing managers and specifying the additional managers when you set the parameter.

- Remove managers by specifying only those who should be managers and excluding those who should not be managers.

If you don't know the current managers of a group, you can list the managers using Get-DistributionGroup. You'll need to format the output and examine the value of the -ManagedBy property.

Sample 8-7 provides syntax and usage examples for adding and removing group managers.

SAMPLE 8-7 Adding and removing group managers

Syntax

```
Get-DistributionGroup -Identity GroupIdentity | format-table
-property ManagedBy

Set-DistributionGroup -Identity GroupIdentity -ManagedBy GroupManagers
```

```
Get-DistributionGroup -Identity 'CorpSales' |
format-table -property ManagedBy

Set-DistributionGroup -Identity 'CorpSales'
-ManagedBy 'pocket-consultant.com/Sales/Oliver Lee',
'pocket-consultant.com/Users/Jamie Stark'
```

```
$g = Get-DistributionGroup -Identity 'CorpSales'
$h = $g.managedby + 'pocket-consultant.com/Users/William Stanek'

Set-DistributionGroup -Identity 'CorpSales'
-ManagedBy $h
```

Configuring member restrictions and moderation

Membership in distribution groups can be restricted in several ways. Groups can be open or closed for joining or require group owner approval for joining. Groups can be open or closed for leaving. Groups also can be moderated. With moderated groups, messages are sent to designated moderators for approval before being distributed to members of the group. The only exception is for a message sent by a designated moderator. A message from a moderator is delivered immediately because a moderator has the authority to determine what is and isn't an appropriate message.

To configure member restrictions and moderation, follow these steps:

1. In Exchange Admin Center, double-tap or double-click the group entry. This opens the group's Properties dialog box.

2. On the Membership Approval page, choose settings for joining the group. The options are:

   - **Open**   Anyone can join this group without being approved by the group owners.

   - **Closed**   Members can be added only by the group owners. All requests to join will be rejected automatically.

   - **Owner Approval**   All requests are approved or rejected by the group owner.

3. Choose settings for leaving the group. The options are:

   - **Open**   Anyone can leave this group without being approved by the group owners.

   - **Closed**   Members can be removed only by the group owners. All requests to leave will be rejected automatically.

4. The Message Approval page displays the moderation options. To disable moderation, clear the Messages Sent To This Group Have To Be Approved By A Moderator check box. To enable moderation, select the Messages Sent To This Group Have To Be Approved By A Moderator check box, and then use

the options provided to specify group moderators, specify senders who don't require message approval, and configure moderation notifications.

5. Tap or click Save to apply your changes.

In Exchange Management Shell, you manage distribution group settings using Set-DistributionGroup. You configure member restrictions for joining a group using the -MemberJoinRestriction parameter and configure member restrictions for leaving a group using the -MemberDepartRestriction parameter. If you want to check the current restrictions, you can do this using Get-DistributionGroup. You'll need to format the output and examine the values of the -MemberJoinRestriction property, the -MemberDepartRestriction property, or both.

Sample 8-8 provides syntax and usage examples for configuring member restrictions.

SAMPLE 8-8 Configuring member restrictions for groups

Syntax

```
Get-DistributionGroup -Identity GroupIdentity | format-table -property
Name, MemberJoinRestriction, MemberDepartRestriction

Set-DistributionGroup -Identity GroupIdentity
[-MemberJoinRestriction <Closed | Open | ApprovalRequired>]
[-MemberDepartRestriction <Closed | Open | ApprovalRequired>]
```

Usage

```
Get-DistributionGroup -Identity 'AllMarketing' |
format-table -property Name, MemberJoinRestriction,
MemberDepartRestriction

Set-DistributionGroup -Identity 'AllMarketing'
-MemberJoinRestriction 'Closed' -MemberDepartRestriction 'Closed'
```

Set-DistributionGroup parameters for configuring moderation include -ModerationEnabled, -ModeratedBy, -BypassModerationFromSendersOrMembers, and -SendModerationNotifications. You enable or disable moderation by using -ModerationEnabled. If moderation is enabled, you can do the following:

- Designate moderators using -ModeratedBy.
- Specify senders who don't require message approval by using -BypassModerationFromSendersOrMembers.
- Configure moderation notifications using -SendModerationNotifications.

Sample 8-9 provides syntax and usage examples for configuring moderation.

SAMPLE 8-9 Configuring moderation for groups

Syntax

```
Get-DistributionGroup -Identity GroupIdentity | format-table -property
Name, ModeratedBy, BypassModerationFromSendersOrMembers,
SendModerationNotifications
```

```
Set-DistributionGroup -Identity GroupIdentity
[-ModeratedBy Moderators] [-ModerationEnabled <$true | $false>]
[-BypassModerationFromSendersOrMembers Recipients]
[-SendModerationNotifications <Never | Internal | Always>]
```

Usage

```
Get-DistributionGroup -Identity 'AllMarketing' |
format-table -property Name, ModeratedBy,
BypassModerationFromSendersOrMembers, SendModerationNotifications


Set-DistributionGroup -Identity 'AllMarketing'
-ModerationEnabled $true -Moderators 'AprilC'
-SendModerationNotifications 'Internal'
```

Working with dynamic distribution groups

Just as there are tasks that apply only to security and standard distribution groups, there are also tasks that apply only to dynamic distribution groups. These tasks are discussed in this section.

Creating dynamic distribution groups

With dynamic distribution groups, group membership is determined by the results of an LDAP query. You can create a dynamic distribution group and define the query parameters by completing the following steps:

1. In Exchange Admin Center, select Recipients in the feature pane and then select Groups.

2. Tap or click New and then select Dynamic Distribution Group. This opens the New Dynamic Distribution Group dialog box. Figure 8-4 shows on-premises Exchange options on the left and Exchange Online options on the right.

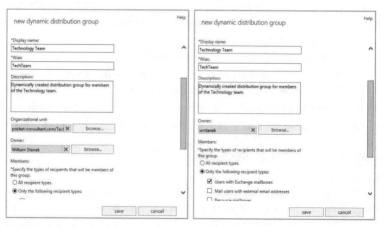

FIGURE 8-4 Configuring the settings for the dynamic distribution group.

3. In the Display Name text box, type a display name for the group. Group names aren't case-sensitive and can be up to 64 characters long. Keep in mind that group naming policy doesn't apply to administrators creating distribution groups in Exchange Admin Center.

4. Like users, groups have Exchange aliases. Enter an alias. The Exchange alias is used to set the group's SMTP email address. Exchange Server uses the SMTP address for receiving messages.

5. With on-premises Exchange, the group account is created in the default user container, which typically is the Users container. To create the group in a specific organizational unit instead, click Browse to the right of the Organizational Unit text box. In the Select Organizational Unit dialog box, choose the location where you want to store the account and then tap or click OK.

   NOTE With Exchange 2013, the organizational unit you specify is simply the storage container. Thus, unlike Exchange 2010, the selection is not used to scope or filter the LDAP query.

6. Group owners are responsible for managing groups. Unlike standard distribution groups, dynamic distribution groups don't need to be assigned an owner. If you want to specify an owner, under Owner, tap or click Add. In the Select Owner dialog box, select the user or group that should have management responsibility for the group.

7. Specify the recipients to include in the group (see Figure 8-5). To allow any recipient type to be a member of the group, select All Recipient Types. Otherwise, choose Only The Following Recipient Types and then choose the types of recipients to include in the dynamic distribution group.

8. Membership in the group is determined by the rules you define. To define a rule, tap or click Add A Rule and set the filter conditions. The following types of conditions as well as conditions for custom attributes are available:

   - **Recipient Container** Filters recipients based on where the related account is stored in Active Directory. Selecting this option displays the Select An Organizational Unit dialog box. Tap or click the container where the recipients are stored, such as Users or an organizational unit, and then tap or click OK.

   - **State Or Province** Filters recipients based on the value of the State/Province text box on the Contact Information page in the related Properties dialog box. Selecting this option displays the Specify Words Or Phrases dialog box. Type a state or province identifier to use as a filter condition and then press Enter or tap or click Add. Repeat as necessary, and then tap or click OK.

   - **Department** Filters recipients based on the value of the Department text box on the Organization page in the related Properties dialog box. Selecting this option displays the Specify Words Or Phrases dialog box. Type a department name to use as a filter condition and then press Enter or tap or click Add. Repeat as necessary, and then tap or click OK.

- **Company** Filters recipients based on the value of the Company text box on the Organization page in the related Properties dialog box. Selecting this option displays the Specify Words Or Phrases dialog box. Type a company name to use as a filter condition and then press Enter or tap or click Add. Repeat as necessary, and then tap or click OK.

IMPORTANT Although each rule acts as an OR condition for matches on specified values, the rules are aggregated as AND conditions. This means that a user that matches one of the values in a rule passes that filter but must be a match for all the rules to be included in the group. For example, if you were to define a state rule for Oregon, California, or Washington and a department rule for Technology, only users who are in Oregon, California, or Washington *and* in the Technology department match the filter and are included as members of the group.

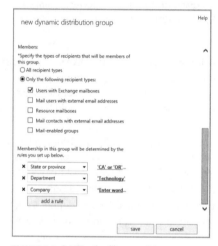

FIGURE 8-5 Setting the filter conditions.

9. Tap or click Save to create the group. If an error occurs during group creation, the related group will not be created. You need to correct the problem before you can complete this procedure.

10. Creating the group isn't the final step. Afterward, you might want to do the following:

    - Set message size restrictions for messages mailed to the group.
    - Limit users who can send to the group.
    - Change or remove default email addresses.
    - Add more email addresses.

In Exchange Management Shell, you can create a dynamic distribution group using the New-DynamicDistributionGroup cmdlet. Sample 8-10 provides the syntax and usage.

Syntax

```
New-DynamicDistributionGroup -Name ExchangeName
-IncludedRecipients <None, MailboxUsers, MailContacts, MailGroups,
Resources, AllRecipients> [-Alias ExchangeAlias]
[-DisplayName DisplayName] [-OrganizationalUnit OUName]
[-ConditionalCompany CompanyNameFilter1, CompanyNameFilter2,...]
[-ConditionalCustomAttributeX Value1, Value2,...]
[-ConditionalDepartment DeptNameFilter1, DeptNameFilter2, ... ]
[-ConditionalStateOrProvince StateNameFilter1, StateNameFilter2, ...]
[-RecipientContainer ApplyFilterContainer] {AddtlParams}

New-DynamicDistributionGroup -Name ExchangeName -RecipientFilter Filter
[-Alias ExchangeAlias] [-DisplayName DisplayName] [-OrganizationalUnit
OUName] [-RecipientContainer ApplyFilterContainer] {AddtlParams}


{AddtlParams}
[-ArbitrationMailbox ModeratorMailbox] [-DomainController
FullyQualifiedName] [-ExternalDirectoryObjectId ObjectId]
[-ModeratedBy Moderators] [-ModerationEnabled <$true | $false>]
[-Organization OrgName] [-PrimarySmtpAddress SmtpAddress]
[-SendModerationNotifications <Never | Internal | Always>]
```

Usage

```
New-DynamicDistributionGroup -Name 'CrossSales'
-OrganizationalUnit 'pocket-consultant.com/Users' -DisplayName
'CrossSales' -Alias 'CrossSales'
-IncludedRecipients 'MailboxUsers, MailContacts, MailGroups'
-ConditionalCompany 'Pocket Consultant'
-ConditionalDepartment 'Sales','Marketing'
-ConditionalStateOrProvince 'Washington','Oregon','California'
-RecipientContainer 'pocket-consultant.com'
```

Changing query filters and filter conditions

With dynamic distribution groups, the filter conditions determine the exact criteria that must be met for a recipient to be included in the dynamic distribution group. You can modify the filter conditions by completing the following steps:

1. In Exchange Admin Center, double-tap or double-click the dynamic distribution group entry. This opens the group's Properties dialog box.

2. On the Membership page, use the Specify The Types Of Recipients options to specify the types of recipients to include in the query. Select either All Recipient Types or select Only The Following Recipient Types, and then select the types of recipients.

3. The Membership page lists the current conditions. The following types of conditions as well as conditions for custom attributes are available:

   ■ **State Or Province** Filters recipients based on the value of the State/ Province text box on the Contact Information page in the related Properties dialog box. Tap or click the related Enter Words link. In the Specify

Words Or Phrases dialog box, type a state or province identifier to use as a filter condition and then press Enter or tap or click Add. Repeat as necessary, and then tap or click OK.

- **Department** Filters recipients based on the value of the Department text box on the Organization page in the related Properties dialog box. Tap or click the related Enter Words link. In the Specify Words Or Phrases dialog box, type a department name to use as a filter condition and then press Enter or tap or click Add. Repeat as necessary, and then tap or click OK.

- **Company** Filters recipients based on the value of the Company text box on the Organization page in the related Properties dialog box. Tap or click the related Enter Words link. In the Specify Words Or Phrases dialog box, type a company name to use as a filter condition and then press Enter or tap or click Add. Repeat as necessary, and then tap or click OK.

4. Tap or click Save to apply the changes.

Designating an expansion server

When there are potentially hundreds or thousands of members, dynamic distribution groups are inefficient and can require a great deal of processing to complete. This is why Exchange 2013 shifts the processing requirements from the Global Catalog server to dedicated expansion servers. However, the routing destination is the ultimate destination for a message. A distribution group expansion server is the routing destination when a distribution group has a designated expansion server that's responsible for expanding the membership list of the group. A distribution group expansion server is always an Exchange 2013 Mailbox server, an Exchange 2010 Hub Transport server, or an Exchange 2007 Hub Transport server.

Each routing destination has a delivery group, which is a collection of one or more transport servers that are responsible for delivering messages to that routing destination. When the routing destination is a distribution group expansion server, the delivery group may contain Exchange 2013 Mailbox servers, Exchange 2010 Hub Transport servers, and Exchange 2007 Hub Transport servers.

How the message is routed depends on the relationship between the source transport server and the destination delivery group. If the source transport server is in the destination delivery group, the routing destination itself is the next hop for the message. The message is delivered by the source transport server to the mailbox database or connector on a transport server in the delivery group.

On the other hand, if the source transport server is outside the destination delivery group, the message is relayed along the least-cost routing path to the destination delivery group. In a complex Exchange organization, a message may be relayed to other transport servers along the least-cost routing path or relayed directly to a transport server in the destination delivery group.

REAL WORLD Keep in mind that when a distribution group expansion server is the routing destination, the distribution group is already expanded when a message reaches the routing stage of categorization on the distribution group expansion server. Therefore, the routing destination from the distribution group expansion server is always a mailbox database or a connector.

By default, Exchange 2013 uses the closest Exchange server that has the Mailbox server role installed as the dedicated expansion server. Because routing destinations and delivery groups can also include Exchange 2010 and Exchange 2007 Hub Transport servers in mixed environments, Exchange 2010 and Exchange 2007 Hub Transport servers could perform distribution group expansion in mixed Exchange organizations.

In some cases, you might want to explicitly specify the dedicated expansion server to handle expansion processing for some or all of your dynamic distribution groups. A key reason for this is to manage where the related processing occurs and in this way shift the processing overhead from other servers to this specified server. You can specify a dedicated expansion server for a dynamic distribution group using the -ExpansionServer parameter of the Set-DynamicDistributionGroup cmdlet.

Modifying dynamic distribution groups using cmdlets

In Exchange Management Shell, you can use the Get-DynamicDistributionGroup cmdlet to get information about dynamic distribution groups and modify their associated filters and conditions using the Set-DynamicDistributionGroup cmdlet.

You also can use the Set-DynamicDistributionGroup cmdlet to upgrade dynamic distribution groups created for Exchange 2003 to allow incompatible dynamic distribution groups to be rewritten to work with Exchange Server 2013. Set -ForceUpgrade to $true, and then modify any incompatible included recipients or recipient filters as necessary.

Sample 8-11 provides the syntax and usage for the Get-DynamicDistribution-Group cmdlet.

SAMPLE 8-11 Get-DynamicDistributionGroup cmdlet syntax and usage

Syntax

```
Get-DynamicDistributionGroup [-Identity GroupIdentify | -Anr Name
 | -ManagedBy Managers]
[-AccountPartition PartitionID] [-Credential Credential]
[-DomainController FullyQualifiedName] [-Filter FilterString]
[-IgnoreDefaultScope {$true | $false}] [-Organization OrgName]
[-OrganizationalUnit OUName] [-ReadFromDomainController {$true | $false}]
[-ResultSize Size] [-SortBy Value]
```

Usage

```
Get-DynamicDistributionGroup -Identity 'CrossSales'
```

Sample 8-12 provides the syntax and usage for the Set-DynamicDistribution-Group cmdlet.

SAMPLE 8-12 Set-DynamicDistributionGroup cmdlet syntax and usage

Syntax

```
Set-DynamicDistributionGroup -Identity GroupIdentity
[-Alias NewAlias] [-AcceptMessagesOnlyFrom Recipients]
[-AcceptMessagesOnlyFromDLMembers Recipients]
[-AcceptMessagesOnlySendersOrMembers Recipients]
[-ArbitrationMailbox ModeratorMailbox]
[-BypassModerationFromSendersOrMembers Recipients]
[-ConditionalCompany Values] [-ConditionalDepartment Values]
[-ConditionalCustomAttributeX Values]
[-ConditionalStateOrProvince Values] [-CreateDTMFMap <$true | $false>]
[-DisplayName Name] [-DomainController DCName]
[-EmailAddresses ProxyAddress]
[-EmailAddressPolicyEnabled <$false|$true>]
[-ExpansionServer Server] [-ForceUpgrade <$false|$true>]
[-ExtensionCustomAttributeX Value1, Value2,...]
[-GrantSendOnBehalfTo Mailbox]
[-HiddenFromAddressListsEnabled <$false|$true>]
[-IgnoreDefaultScope {$true | $false}]
[-IncludedRecipients <None, MailboxUsers, MailContacts, MailGroups,
Resources, AllRecipients>] [-MailTip String]
[-MailTipTranslations Locale:TipString, Locale:TipString, ...]
[-ManagedBy Managers] [-MaxReceiveSize Size] [-MaxSendSize Size]
[-ModeratedBy Moderators] [-ModerationEnabled <$true | $false>]
[-Name Name] [-Notes Value] [-PhoneticDisplayName PhName]
[-PrimarySmtpAddress SmtpAddress]
[-RecipientContainer OUName] [-RecipientFilter String]
[-RejectMessagesFrom Recipients]
[-RejectMessagesFromDLMembers Recipients]
[-RejectMessagesFromSendersOrMembers Recipients]
[-ReportToManagerEnabled <$false|$true>]
[-ReportToOriginatorEnabled <$false|$true>]
[-RequireSenderAuthenticationEnabled <$false|$true>]
[-SendModerationNotifications <Never | Internal | Always>]
[-SendOofMessageToOriginatorEnabled <$false|$true>]
[-SimpleDisplayName Name] [-UMDtmfMap Values]
[-WindowsEmailAddress SmtpAddress]
```

Usage

```
Set-DynamicDistributionGroup -Identity 'CrossSales'
 -IncludedRecipients 'AllRecipients'
 -ConditionalCompany 'Pocket Consultant'
 -ConditionalDepartment 'Sales','Accounting'
 -ConditionalStateOrProvince 'Washington','Idaho','Oregon'
 -RecipientContainer 'pocket-consultant.com'
```

Usage

```
Set-DynamicDistributionGroup -Identity 'CrossSales'
 -ForceUpgrade $true
```

Usage

```
Set-DynamicDistributionGroup -Identity 'CrossSales'
 -ExpansionServer 'CorpSvr127'
```

Previewing dynamic distribution group membership

You can preview a dynamic distribution group to confirm its membership and determine how long it takes to return the query results. The specific actions you take
depend on the following factors:

- In some cases, membership isn't what you expected. If this happens, you
  need to change the query filters, as discussed earlier.

- In other cases, it takes too long to execute the query and return the results.
  If this happens, you might want to rethink the query parameters and create
  several query groups.

You can quickly determine how many recipients are in the group by checking
how many recipients received the last message sent to the group. One way to do
this is to follow these steps:

1. In Exchange Admin Center, select the dynamic distribution group entry.

2. In the details pane, look under Membership to see the number of recipients
   who received the last message sent to the group.

In Exchange Management Shell, you can determine the exact membership of a
dynamic distribution group by getting the dynamic group and then using the associated recipient filter to list the members. Consider the following example:

```
$Members = Get-DynamicDistributionGroup "TechTeam"
Get-Recipient -RecipientPreviewFilter $Members.RecipientFilter
```

In this example, Get-DynamicDistributionGroup stores the object for the Tech-
Team group in the $Members variable. Then Get-Recipient lists the recipients that
match the recipient filter on this object. Note that the Exchange identifier can be the
display name or alias for the group.

Other essential tasks for managing groups

Previous sections covered tasks that were specific to a type of group. As an Exchange administrator, you'll need to perform many additional group management
tasks. These essential tasks are discussed in this section.

Changing a group's name information

Each mail-enabled group has a display name, an Exchange alias, and one or more
email addresses associated with it. The display name is the name that appears in
address lists. The Exchange alias is used to set the email addresses associated with
the group.

Whenever you change a group's naming information, new email addresses can
be generated and set as the default addresses for SMTP. These email addresses are
used as alternatives to email addresses previously assigned to the group. To learn

how to change or delete these additional email addresses, see the "Changing, adding, or deleting a group's email addresses" section later in this chapter.

To change the group's Exchange name details, complete the following steps:

1. In Exchange Admin Center, double-tap or double-click the group entry. This opens the group's Properties dialog box.

2. On the General page, the first text box shows the display name of the group. If necessary, type a new display name.

3. The Alias text box shows the Exchange alias. If necessary, type a new alias. Tap or click Save.

NOTE When you change a group's display name, you give the group a new label. Changing the display name doesn't affect the SID, which is used to identify, track, and handle permissions independently from group names.

Changing, adding, or deleting a group's email addresses

When you create a mail-enabled group, default email addresses are created for SMTP. Any time you update the group's Exchange alias, new default email addresses can be created. The old addresses aren't deleted, however; they remain as alternative email addresses for the group.

To change, add, or delete a group's email addresses, follow these steps:

1. In Exchange Admin Center, double-tap or double-click the group entry. This opens the group's Properties dialog box.

2. On the Email Options page, use the following techniques to manage the group's email addresses:

   - **Create a new SMTP address** Tap or click Add. In the New Email Address dialog box, SMTP is selected as the address type by default. Enter the email address, and then tap or click OK.

   - **Create a custom address** Tap or click Add. In the New Email Address dialog box, select Custom Address Type. Enter a prefix that identifies the type of email address, and then enter the associated address. Tap or click OK.

   TIP Use SMTP as the address type for standard Internet email addresses. For custom address types, such as X.400, you must manually enter the address in the proper format.

   - **Set a new Reply To Address** Double-tap or double-click the address that you want to use as the primary SMTP address. Select Make This The Reply Address, and then tap or click OK (Exchange Online only).

   - **Edit an existing address** Double-tap or double-click the address entry. Modify the settings in the Address dialog box, and then tap or click OK.

   - **Delete an existing address** Select the address, and then tap or click Remove.

Sample 8-13 provides syntax and usage examples for configuring a group's primary SMTP email address. If email address policy is enabled, you won't be able to update the email address unless you set -EmailAddressPolicyEnabled to $false.

SAMPLE 8-13 Configuring a group's primary SMTP email address

Syntax

```
Get-DistributionGroup -Identity GroupIdentity | format-list -property
Name, EmailAddresses, PrimarySmtpAddress

Set-DistributionGroup -Identity GroupIdentity
-PrimarySmtpAddress SmtpAddress -EmailAddressPolicyEnabled $false
```

Usage

```
Get-DistributionGroup -Identity 'AllSales' | format-list -property
Name, EmailAddresses, PrimarySmtpAddress

Set-DistributionGroup -Identity 'AllSales'
-PrimarySmtpAddress allsales@pocket-consultant.com
-EmailAddressPolicyEnabled $false
```

Hiding groups from Exchange address lists

By default, any mail-enabled security group or other distribution group that you create is shown in Exchange address lists, such as the global address list. If you want to hide a group from the address lists, follow these steps:

1. In Exchange Admin Center, double-tap or double-click the group entry. This opens the group's Properties dialog box.

2. On the General page, select the Hide This Group From Address Lists check box. Tap or click OK.

NOTE When you hide a group, it isn't listed in Exchange address lists. However, if a user knows the name of a group, he or she can still use it in the mail client. To prevent users from sending to a group, you must set message restrictions, as discussed in the next section, "Setting usage restrictions on groups."

TIP Hiding group membership is different from hiding the group itself. In Outlook, users can view the membership of groups. In Exchange Server 2013, you cannot prevent viewing the group membership. In addition, membership of dynamic distribution groups is not displayed in global address lists because it is generated only when mail is sent to the group.

In Exchange Management Shell, you can return a list of groups hidden from address lists using either of the following commands:

```
Get-DistributionGroup -filter {HiddenFromAddressListsEnabled -eq $true}

Get-DistributionGroup | where {$_.HiddenFromAddressListsEnabled -eq $true}
```

Setting usage restrictions on groups

Groups are great resources for users in an organization. They let users send mail quickly and easily to other users in their department, business unit, or office. However, if you aren't careful, people outside the organization could use groups as well. Would your boss like it if spammers sent unsolicited email messages to company employees through your distribution lists? Probably not—and you'd probably be sitting in the hot seat, which would be uncomfortable, to say the least.

To prevent unauthorized use of mail-enabled groups, groups are configured by default to accept mail only from authenticated users so that only senders inside an organization can send messages to groups. An authenticated user is any user accessing the system through a logon process. It does not include anonymous users or guests. If you use the default configuration, any message from a sender outside the organization is rejected. Off-site users will need to log on to Exchange before they can send mail to groups, which might present a problem for users who are at home or travelling.

> **REAL WORLD** If you have users who telecommute or send email from home using a personal account, you might be wondering how these users can send mail with a restriction that allows only senders inside the organization to send messages to the group. What I've done in the past is create a group called OffsiteEmailUsers and then added this as a group that can send mail to my mail-enabled groups. The OffsiteEmailUsers group contains separate mail-enabled contacts for each authorized off-site email address. Alternatively, users could simply log on to Outlook Anywhere, Outlook Web App, or Exchange ActiveSync and send mail to the group; this is an approach that doesn't require any special groups with permissions to be created or maintained.

Alternatively, you can allow senders inside and outside the organization to send email to a group. This settings allows unrestricted access to the group, so anyone can send messages to the group. However, this exposes the group to spam from external mail accounts.

Another way to prevent unauthorized use of mail-enabled groups is to specify that only certain users or members of a particular group can send messages to the group. For example, if you create a group called AllEmployees, of which all company employees are members, you can specify that only the members of AllEmployees can send messages to the group. You do this by specifying that only messages from members of AllEmployees are acceptable.

To prevent mass spamming of other groups, you can set the same restriction. For example, if you have a group called Technology, you could specify that only members of AllEmployees can send messages to that group.

You can set or remove usage restrictions by completing the following steps:

1. In Exchange Admin Center, double-tap or double-click the group entry. In the Properties dialog box for the group, select the Delivery Management page.
2. To ensure that messages are accepted only from authenticated users, select Only Senders Inside My Organization.

3. To accept messages from all email addresses, select Senders Inside And Outside Of My Organization.

4. To restrict senders, specify that messages only from the listed users, contacts, or groups be accepted. To do this, tap or click Add to display the Select Allowed Senders dialog box. Select a recipient, and then tap or click OK. Repeat as necessary.

> **TIP** You can select multiple recipients at the same time. To select multiple recipients individually, hold down the Ctrl key and then tap or click each recipient that you want to select. To select a continuous sequence of recipients, select the first recipient, hold down the Shift key, and then tap or click the last recipient.

5. Tap or click Save.

Creating moderated groups

By default, senders don't require approval for their messages to be sent to all members of a group. Sometimes though you'll want to appoint moderators who must approve messages before they are sent to all members of the group. If you enable moderation but don't specify a moderator or moderators, the group owner is responsible for reviewing and approving messages. When moderation is enabled, you also can specify users who don't require approval for their messages to be sent to all members of the group.

To see how moderation could be used, consider the following example. A project team is set up to work on a restricted project. The team leader wants a moderated group for the project team so that she must review and approve all messages sent to the group before they are sent to members of the team. As the moderator, the team leader's messages don't require approval and are sent directly to all members of the group.

To configure moderation for a group, complete the following steps:

1. In Exchange Admin Center, double-tap or double-click the group name to open the Properties dialog box for the group.

2. On the Message Approval page, do one of the following:

   - To enable moderation, select Messages Sent To This Group Have To Be Approved By A Moderator. Next, use the options provided to specify moderators and senders who don't require message approval.

   - To disable moderation, clear Messages Sent To This Group Have To Be Approved By A Moderator. Tap or click Save and then skip the rest of the steps.

   If a message addressed to the group isn't approved, the message isn't distributed to members of the group, and all users receive a nondelivery report (NDR) by default whether they are inside or outside the organization. Alternatively, you can notify only senders in your organization when their messages aren't approved or you can disable notification completely.

3. Tap or click Save.

Deleting groups

If you are an owner of a group, you can delete it. Deleting a group removes it permanently. After you delete a security group, you can't create a security group with the same name and automatically restore the permissions that the original group was assigned because the SID for the new group won't match the SID for the old group. You can reuse group names, but remember that you'll have to re-create all permissions settings.

You cannot delete built-in groups in Windows. In Exchange Admin Center, you can remove other types of groups by selecting them and clicking Delete. When prompted, tap or click Yes to delete the group. If you tap or click No, Exchange Admin Center will not delete the group.

In Exchange Management Shell, only a group's manager or other authorized user can remove a group. Use the Remove-DistributionGroup cmdlet to remove distribution groups, as shown in Sample 8-14.

SAMPLE 8-14 Remove-DistributionGroup cmdlet syntax and usage

Syntax

```
Remove-DistributionGroup -Identity GroupIdentity
[-BypassSecurityGroupManagerCheck {$true | $false}]
[-DomainController FullyQualifiedName]
[-IgnoreDefaultScope {$true | $false}]
```

Usage

```
Remove-DistributionGroup -Identity 'pocket-consultant.com/Users/AllSales'
```

You can use the Remove-DynamicDistributionGroup cmdlet to remove dynamic distribution groups. Sample 8-15 shows the syntax and usage.

SAMPLE 8-15 Remove-DynamicDistributionGroup cmdlet syntax and usage

Syntax

```
Remove-DynamicDistributionGroup -Identity GroupIdentity
[-DomainController FullyQualifiedName]
[-IgnoreDefaultScope {$true | $false}]
```

Usage

```
Remove-DynamicDistributionGroup -Identity 'CrossSales'
```

Managing online address lists

Address lists are collections of recipients in an Exchange organization that are selectable in the address book of client applications. You can use address lists to organize recipients by department, business unit, location, type, and other criteria. The default address lists that Exchange Server creates, as well as any new address lists that you create, are available to the user community based on their view of the global address list. Users can navigate these address lists to find recipients to whom they want to send messages.

Using default address lists

During setup, Exchange Server creates a number of default address lists that are selectable in the address book of client applications, including the following:

- **Default Global Address List**   Lists all mail-enabled users, contacts, and groups in the organization.
- **Default Offline Address Book**   Provides an address list for viewing offline that contains information on all mail-enabled users, contacts, and groups in the organization.
- **All Contacts**   Lists all mail-enabled contacts in the organization.
- **All Groups**   Lists all mail-enabled groups in the organization.
- **All Rooms**   Lists all resource mailboxes for rooms.
- **Public Folders**   Lists all public folders in the organization.
- **All Users**   Lists all mail-enabled users in the organization.

IMPORTANT   Generally, whenever you specify address list paths in Exchange Management Shell, you must reference their position relative to the root container. The root container is identified as \. If the address list name contains spaces, you also must enclose the address list path in quotes. Thus, you reference the Default Address List as '\Default Address List' and All Rooms as '\All Rooms'.

The most commonly used address lists are the global address list and the offline address book. In Exchange Admin Center for your on-premises organization, you access online address lists and offline address books by selecting Organization in the feature pane and then selecting Address Lists. As Figure 8-6 shows, the main pane shows each address list by name and up-to-date status. If an address list isn't up-to-date, you can tap or click the Update option to update it.

FIGURE 8-6 Accessing address lists in Exchange Admin Center.

IMPORTANT Any address list created using the shell should be managed only with the shell. Address lists created with the GUI can be managed with either the GUI or the shell. That said, Microsoft recommends that you manage address lists from the shell whenever the list contains several thousand or more recipients. The reason for this is that Exchange Admin Center will be locked until the task is completed.

Using address book policies

Most Exchange organizations don't need address book policies. However, when multiple companies share one Exchange organization, you may want to segment the global address list to provide customized (scoped) views of recipient data to users in each separate company. You segment the global address list using address book policies. Each address book policy contains a global address list, an offline address book, a room list, and one or more address lists.

You use address book policies when you need to complete separation of the recipient data. Consider the following example:

Coho Winery merges with Coho Vineyard, resulting in a merged company called Coho Vineyard & Winery. While publicly a single company, internally the winery and vineyard operations are distinct and separate. The only overlap between the operations is in the top-level executive team.

The company has a single Exchange organization and wants those that work in one part of the operation to have access only to recipients and resources in that operation. Employees get scoped views of All Users, All Groups, and All Rooms as well as the default global address list and the default offline address list. These scoped views include only those that work as part of the winery or vineyard operations and not both.

The top-level executives and their direct support staff have access to the original, unscoped address lists. This ensures they can access recipients and resources in both operations areas.

Keep in mind that the need for custom views of recipients doesn't mean that your organization needs address book policies. You can create new address lists at any time and those address lists can be scoped however you'd like them to be scoped. For example, you could create an address list called All Marketing that includes only employees in the marketing department.

You can assign address book policy to recipients in both on-premises and online Exchange organizations. Before you can use address book policy, you must do the following:

1. Install and enable the Address Book Policy Routing Agent using these commands:

```
Install-TransportAgent -Name "ABP Routing Agent"
-TransportAgentFactory "Microsoft.Exchange.Transport.Agent
.AddressBookPolicyRoutingAgent
```

```
.AddressBookPolicyRoutingAgentFactory"
-AssemblyPath "C:\Program Files\Microsoft\Exchange\V15\
TransportRoles\Agents\AddressBookPolicyRoutingAgent\
Microsoft.Exchange.Transport.Agent
.AddressBookPolicyRoutingAgent.dll"

Enable-TransportAgent "ABP Routing Agent"
```

> **NOTE** Here, C:\Program Files\Microsoft\Exchange\V15\ is the Exchange
> install path. If you installed Exchange in a different location, revise the path as
> appropriate.

2. Next, you must restart the transport service and then enable Address Book
   Policy routing in the organization using these commands:

```
Restart-Service MSExchangeTransport
Set-TransportConfig -AddressBookPolicyRoutingEnabled $true
```

3. Set an attribute on all recipients that can be used to segment the Exchange
   organization. For example, you could use a custom attribute to do this.

4. Create one or more address lists that provide the segmented views of the
   organization-wide global address list. Typically, you'll want a list for mailbox users, contacts, distribution lists, and rooms. Use New-AddressList with
   recipient filters that look for the special attribute to create these lists. Here
   are examples:

```
New-AddressList -Name "B - All Users" -RecipientFilter
{(RecipientType -eq 'UserMailbox') -and
 (CustomAttribute8 -eq "CompanyB")}

New-AddressList -Name "B - All Contacts" -RecipientFilter
{((RecipientType -eq "MailUser") -or (RecipientType
-eq "MailContact")) -and (CustomAttribute8 -eq "CompanyB")}

New-AddressList -Name "B - All Groups" -RecipientFilter
{((RecipientType -eq "MailUniversalDistributionGroup")
-or (RecipientType -eq "DynamicDistributionGroup")
-or (RecipientType -eq "MailUniversalSecurityGroup"))
-and (CustomAttribute1 -eq "CompanyB")}

New-AddressList -Name "B - All Rooms" -RecipientFilter {(Alias
-ne $null) -and (CustomAttribute8 -eq "CompanyB")-and
(RecipientDisplayType -eq 'ConferenceRoomMailbox') -or
(RecipientDisplayType -eq 'SyncedConferenceRoomMailbox')}
```

> **NOTE** Address book policy requires a room list. If you don't use rooms, create
> an empty list.

5. Create a segmented global address list and then use this address list to create the segmented offline address book. Here are examples:

    ```
    New-GlobalAddressList -Name "B - GAL" -RecipientFilter
    {(CustomAttribute8 -eq "CompanyB")}


    New-OfflineAddressBook -Name "B - OAB" -AddressLists
    "\B - GAL"
    ```

6. Create an address book policy for the first company within the organization and then assign this policy to the appropriate mailboxes. Here are examples:

    ```
    New-AddressBookPolicy -Name "CompanyB ABP" -AddressLists
    "\B - All Users", "\B - All Contacts", "\B - All Contacts"
    -OfflineAddressBook "\B - OAB" -GlobalAddressList "\B - GAL"
    -RoomList "\B - All Rooms"


    Get-Mailbox -resultsize unlimited | where {$_.CustomAttribute8 -eq
    "CompanyB"} | Set-Mailbox -AddressBookPolicy "CompanyB ABP"
    ```

7. As necessary, repeat Steps 4 through 6 to configure address lists and policies for each company within the Exchange organization.

Creating and applying new address lists

You can create new address lists to create customized views of recipient data. For example, if your organization has offices in Seattle, Portland, and San Francisco, you might want to create separate address lists for each office.

To create an address list that users can select in their Outlook clients, follow these steps:

1. In Exchange Admin Center, select Organization in the feature pane and then select Address Lists.

2. Tap or click New. This opens the New Address List dialog box.

3. Type an internal Exchange name and a display name for the address list, as shown in Figure 8-7. The display name should describe the types of recipients that are viewed through the list. For example, if you're creating a list for recipients in the Boston office, you can call the list Boston Office.

4. The container on which you base the address list sets the scope of the list. The list will include recipients in address lists in and below the specified container. The default (root) container, \, specifies that all address lists are included by default. To specify a different container for limiting the list scope, tap or click Browse, and then use the Address List Picker dialog box to select a container. In most cases, you'll want to select the default (root) container. The list path is fixed when you create a list, so you won't be able to specify a different list path later.

FIGURE 8-7 Specifying a name and configuring the address list.

5. Use the Types Of Recipients To Include options to specify the types of recipients to include in the address list. Select All Recipient Types or select Only The Following Recipient Types and then select the types of recipients. You can include mailbox users, mail-enabled contacts, mail-enabled groups, mail-enabled users, and resource mailboxes.

6. Next, you can create rules that further filter the address list. Each rule acts as a condition that must be met. If you set more than one rule, each condition must be met for there to be a match. To define a rule, tap or click Add A Rule and then set the filter conditions. The following types of conditions are available as well as conditions for custom attributes:

    ▪ **Recipient Container** Filters recipients based on where in Active Directory the related account is stored. Selecting this option displays the Select An Organizational Unit dialog box. Tap or click the container where the recipients are stored, such as Users or an organizational unit, and then tap or click OK.

    ▪ **State Or Province** Filters recipients based on the value of the State/Province text box on the Contact Information page in the related Properties dialog box. Selecting this option displays the Specify Words Or Phrases dialog box. Type a state or province identifier to use as a filter condition and then press Enter or tap or click Add. Repeat as necessary, and then tap or click OK.

    ▪ **Department** Filters recipients based on the value of the Department text box on the Organization page in the related Properties dialog box. Selecting this option displays the Specify Words Or Phrases dialog box.

Type a department name to use as a filter condition and then press Enter or tap or click Add. Repeat as necessary, and then tap or click OK.

- **Company** Filters recipients based on the value of the Company text box on the Organization page in the related Properties dialog box. Selecting this option displays the Specify Words Or Phrases dialog box. Type a company name to use as a filter condition and then press Enter or tap or click Add. Repeat as necessary, and then tap or click OK.

7. Tap or click Save to create the address list. After the address list is created, users will be able to use the new address list the next time they start Outlook. In the details pane, the new list will have a status of Not Up To Date.

Creating and fully populating address lists can be resource intensive, so new address lists aren't populated. You can populate the address list for the first time by updating it. To do this, tap or click the address list and then tap or click Update.

You'll see a warning prompt explaining that it could take a long time to update the address list. When you tap or click Yes, Exchange Admin Center begins updating the address list and displays the update progress in a bar graph, as shown in Figure 8-8. If you find the update is taking too long, you can tap or click Stop to halt the update. You can then restart the update process later.

FIGURE 8-8 Tracking the update progress.

In Exchange Management Shell, creating and applying address lists are two separate tasks. You can create address lists using the New-AddressList cmdlet. You apply address lists using the Update-AddressList cmdlet. Sample 8-16 provides the syntax and usage for the New-AddressList cmdlet. Sample 8-17 provides the syntax and usage for the Update-AddressList cmdlet. For -IncludedRecipients, you can include mailbox users, mail-enabled contacts, mail-enabled groups, mail-enabled users, and resource mailboxes.

TIP Exchange Server 2013 does not support Recipient Update Service (RUS). To replace the functionality of RUS, you can schedule the Update-AddressList and Update-EmailAddressPolicy cmdlets to run periodically using Task Scheduler. Alternatively, you can run the cmdlets manually when you modify addresses.

Syntax

```
New-AddressList -Name ListName [-Container BaseAddressList]
[-DisplayName DisplayName] [-IncludedRecipients <None, MailboxUsers,
MailContacts, MailGroups, MailUsers, Resources, AllRecipients>]
[-ConditionalCompany CompanyNameFilter1, CompanyNameFilter2,... ]
[-ConditionalCustomAttributeX Value1, Value2, ...]
[-ConditionalDepartment DeptNameFilter1, DeptNameFilter2, ... ]
[-ConditionalStateOrProvince StateFilter1, StateFilter2, ... ]
[-DomainController FullyQualifiedName] [-Organization OrgName]
[-RecipientContainer ApplyFilterContainer]

New-AddressList -Name ListName [-Container BaseAddressList]
[-DisplayName DisplayName] [-DomainController FullyQualifiedName]
[-Organization OrgName] [-RecipientContainer ApplyFilterContainer]
[-RecipientFilter Filter]
```

Usage

```
New-AddressList -Name 'West Coast Sales' -Container '\'
-DisplayName 'West Coast Sales' -IncludedRecipients 'MailboxUsers,
MailContacts, MailGroups, Resources'
-ConditionalCompany 'Pocket Consultant'
-ConditionalDepartment 'Sales','Marketing'
-ConditionalStateOrProvince 'Washington','Idaho','Oregon'
```

SAMPLE 8-17 Update-AddressList cmdlet syntax and usage

Syntax

```
Update-AddressList -identity ListIdentity
[-DomainController FullyQualifiedName]
```

Usage

```
Update-AddressList -Identity '\West Coast Sales'
```

Configuring clients to use address lists

Address books are available to clients that are configured for corporate or work-group use. To set the address lists used by the client, complete these steps:

1. In Office Outlook 2013, on the Home panel, select Address Book. Alternatively, press Ctrl+Shift+B.

2. In the Address Book dialog box, from the Tools menu, select Options, and then set the following options to configure how address lists are used:

   - **When Sending E-Mail, Check Address Lists In This Order** Sets the order in which Outlook searches address books when you send a message or tap or click Check Names. You can start with either the global address list or the contact folders. Or you can choose the Custom option and then use the up and down arrows to change the list order.

- **When Opening The Address Book, Show This Address List First** Sets the address book that the user sees first whenever he or she works with the address book.

3. Tap or click OK.

TIP When checking names, you'll usually want the global address list (GAL) to be listed before the user's own contacts or other types of address lists. This is important because users often put internal mailboxes in their personal address lists. The danger of doing this without first resolving names against the GAL is that although the display name might be identical, the properties of a mailbox might change. When changes occur, the entry in the user's address book is no longer valid, and any mail sent bounces back to the sender with a nondelivery report (NDR). To correct this, the user should either remove that mailbox from his or her personal address list and add it based on the current entry in the GAL, or change the check names resolution order to use the GAL before any personal lists.

Updating address list configuration and membership throughout the domain

Exchange Server doesn't immediately replicate changes to address lists throughout the domain. Instead, changes are replicated during the normal replication cycle, which means that some servers might temporarily have outdated address list information. Rather than waiting for replication, you can manually update address list configuration, availability, and membership throughout the domain. To do this, follow these steps:

1. In Exchange Admin Center, select Organization in the feature pane and then select Address Lists.

2. Tap or click the address list you want to work with and then tap or click Update.

3. You'll see a warning prompt explaining that it could take a long time to update the address list. Tap or click Yes. Exchange Admin Center begins updating the address list and displays the update progress in a bar graph.

4. If you find the update is taking too long, you can tap or click Stop to halt the update. You can then restart the update process later.

Alternatively, you can use the Update-AddressList cmdlet to update lists. See Sample 8-17 for syntax and usage.

Previewing and editing address lists

Although you can't change the properties of default address lists, you can change the properties of address lists that you create using either Exchange Admin Center or Exchange Management Shell. You can edit a list's settings or preview the recipients in the list by completing the following steps:

1. In Exchange Admin Center, select Organization in the feature pane and then select Address Lists.

2. Tap or click the address list you want to work with. If there's a note in the details pane stating the list was created in Exchange Management Shell, you won't be able to modify its settings. You can, however, view the list's settings in the Address List dialog box.

3. Tap or click Edit. In the Address List dialog box, you'll see the name, path, and recipient filter associated with the list.

4. To preview the recipients included in the list, tap or click the link provided.

5. Modify the name as necessary. Use the Types Of Recipients To Include options to specify the types of recipients to include. Select All Recipient Types or select Only The Following Recipient Types and then select the types of recipients.

6. Create new rules or modify existing rules to further filter the recipients.

7. Tap or click Save. In the details pane, the modified list will have a status of Not Up To Date. To update the membership of the address list, tap or click Update and then follow the prompts.

In Exchange Management Shell, you can modify an address list using the Set-AddressList cmdlet. Sample 8-18 provides the syntax and usage. Address lists created for Exchange Server 2003 aren't compatible with Exchange Server 2013. You can upgrade address lists created for Exchange Server 2003 so that they work with Exchange Server 2013 by using -ForceUpgrade $true and then modifying any incompatible included recipients or recipient filters as necessary. After you update an address list, you can make the changes visible by using the Update-AddressList cmdlet, as shown previously in Sample 8-17. You don't need to upgrade address lists created for Exchange Server 2007 or Exchange Server 2010.

SAMPLE 8-18 Set-AddressList cmdlet syntax and usage

Syntax

```
Set-AddressList -Identity ListName
[-DisplayName DisplayName] [-IncludedRecipients <None, MailboxUsers,
MailContacts, MailGroups, Resources, AllRecipients>]
[-ConditionalCompany CompanyNameFilter1, CompanyNameFilter2,... ]
[-ConditionalDepartment DeptNameFilter1, DeptNameFilter2, ... ]
[-ConditionalStateOrProvince StateFilter1, StateFilter2, ... ]
[-DomainController FullyQualifiedName] [-ForceUpgrade <$false|$true>]
[-RecipientContainer ApplyFilterContainer] [-RecipientFilter Filter]
```

Usage

```
Set-AddressList -Identity '\West Coast Sales' -Name 'Sales Team-West'
-IncludedRecipients 'MailboxUsers, MailContacts, MailGroups'
 -Company 'Pocket Consultant'
 -Department 'Sales','Marketing'
 -StateOrProvince 'Washington','Idaho','Oregon'
```

Usage

```
Set-AddressList -Identity '\West Coast Sales' -Name 'Sales Team-West'
 -IncludedRecipients 'MailboxUsers, MailContacts, MailGroups'
 -ForceUpgrade $true
```

Renaming and deleting address lists

You can only rename or delete user-defined address lists.

- **Renaming address lists** To rename an address list, in Exchange Admin Center, select its entry and then select Edit. Type a new name in the Display Name text box. In the details pane, the modified list will have a status of Not Up To Date. To update the membership of the address list, tap or click Update and then follow the prompts.

- **Deleting address lists** To delete an address list, in Exchange Admin Center, select its entry and then select Remove. When prompted to confirm the action, tap or click Yes.

In Exchange Management Shell, you can remove address lists using the Remove-AddressList cmdlet. Sample 8-19 provides the syntax and usage. If you also want to remove address lists that reference the address list you are removing and match a portion of it (child address lists), you can set the -Recursive parameter to $true. By default, the cmdlet does not remove child address lists of the specified list.

SAMPLE 8-19 Remove-AddressList cmdlet syntax and usage

Syntax

```
Remove-AddressList -Identity ListIdentity
[-DomainController FullyQualifiedName] [-Recursive {$true | $false}]
```

Usage

```
Remove-AddressList -Identity '\West Coast Sales'
```

Managing offline address books

Exchange 2013 has a new offline address book generation and distribution architecture. You configure offline address books differently than online address lists. To use an offline address book, the client must be configured to have a local copy of the server mailbox, or you can use personal folders. Clients using Outlook 2007 or later retrieve the offline address book from the designated offline address book (OAB) distribution point.

> **NOTE** Although future updates may change this, Exchange Admin Center doesn't have options for managing offline address books at the time of this writing. This means that you need to use Exchange Management Shell to manage offline address books.

> **IMPORTANT** An OAB distribution point is a virtual directory to which Outlook 2007 and later clients can connect to download the offline address book. OAB distribution points are hosted by Client Access servers running Internet Information Services (IIS) as virtual directories. Each distribution point can have two URLs associated with it: one URL for internal (on-site) access and another for external (off-site) access.

Creating offline address books

The default offline address book includes all the addresses in the global address list. It does this by including the default global address list. All other offline address books are created by including the default global address list or a specific online address list as well.

> **NOTE** You can create other custom offline address books using Exchange Management Shell. You cannot use Exchange Admin Center to create other offline address books.

In Exchange Management Shell, you can create offline address books using the New-OfflineAddressBook cmdlet. You apply offline address books using the Update-OfflineAddressBook cmdlet. Sample 8-20 provides the syntax and usage for the New-OfflineAddressBook cmdlet. Sample 8-21 provides the syntax and usage for the Update-OfflineAddressBook cmdlet.

> **NOTE** Public folder distribution is no longer associated with offline address books. Public folders are now stored in special mailboxes, as discussed in Chapter 7, "Mailbox administration."

SAMPLE 8-20 New-OfflineAddressBook cmdlet syntax and usage

Syntax

```
New-OfflineAddressBook -Name ListName   -Server GenerationServer
 -AddressLists AddressList1, AddressList2, ...
 [-VirtualDirectories VirtualDir1, VirtualDir2, ...] {AddtlParams}

{AddtlParams}
[-DiffRetentionPeriod RetentionPeriod]
[-DomainController FullyQualifiedName]
[-GlobalWebDistributionEnabled <$true | $false>]
[-IsDefault <$true | $false>] [-Organization OrgName]
```

Usage

```
New-OfflineAddressBook -Name 'Offline - West Coast Sales'
 -Server 'CorpSvr127'
 -AddressLists '\West Coast Sales'
 -VirtualDirectories 'CORPSVR127\OAB (Default Web Site)'
```

SAMPLE 8-21 Update-OfflineAddressBook cmdlet syntax and usage

Syntax

```
Update-OfflineAddressBook -Identity OABName
[-DomainController FullyQualifiedName]
```

Usage

```
Update-OfflineAddressBook -Identity '\Offline - West Coast Sales'
```

When you create an offline address book, you must use the -AddressLists parameter to specify the address lists that are included. If you want the offline address book to include all recipients in the organization, specify that the Default Global Address List is the address list to include as shown in this example:

```
New-OfflineAddressBook -Name 'Offline - Entire Organization'
 -Server 'CorpSvr127'
 -AddressLists '\Default Global Address List'
 -VirtualDirectories 'CORPSVR127\OAB (Default Web Site)'
```

You can include multiple address lists using a comma-separated list, as shown in this example:

```
New-OfflineAddressBook -Name 'Offline - Sales & Marketing'
 -Server 'CorpSvr127'
 -AddressLists '\All Marketing', '\All Sales', '\Sales Teams'
 -VirtualDirectories 'CORPSVR127\OAB (Default Web Site)'
```

If you want the new offline address book to be the default, use the -IsDefault parameter.

Configuring clients to use an offline address book

Offline address lists are available only when users are working offline. You can configure how clients use offline address books by completing the following steps:

1. Do one of the following:

   - In Outlook 2007, tap or click Tools, select Send/Receive, and then select Download Address Book. The Offline Address Book dialog box appears.

   - In Outlook 2010, tap or click the Office button. On the Info pane, select Download Address Book. The Offline Address Book dialog box appears.

   - In Outlook 2013, on the File pane, tap or click Info. On the Info page, tap or click Account Settings and then select Download Address Book. The Offline Address Book dialog box appears.

2. Select the Download Changes Since Last Send/Receive check box to download only items that have changed since the last time you synchronized the address list. Clear this check box to download the entire contents of your address book.

3. With Outlook 2007 and Outlook 2010, specify the information to download as either of the following two options:

   - **Full Details** Select this option to download the address book with all address information details. Full details are necessary if the user needs to encrypt messages when using remote mail.

   - **No Details** Select this option to download the address book without address information details. This reduces the download time for the address book.

4. If multiple address books are available, use the Choose Address Book drop-down list to specify which address book to download. Tap or click OK.

Designating OAB generation servers and schedules

In Exchange 2013, the organization has a dedicated OAB generation server. This server is responsible for generating the offline address books for the entire organization. Although the first Mailbox server you install with Exchange 2013 may be designated as the OAB generation server, this isn't always the case.

To identify the OAB generation server, you need to locate the arbitration mailbox that handles the offline address book generation. In Exchange 2013, an arbitration mailbox with the persisted capability "OrganizationCapabilityOABGen" handles offline address book generation. You can locate this mailbox and identify the server and database it resides on using the following command:

```
Get-Mailbox -Arbitration | where {$_.PersistedCapabilities -like "*oab*"} |
ft name, servername, database
```

If your Mailbox servers are configured in an availability group, ensure you've identified the active copy of the database using the following command:

```
Get-MailboxDatabaseCopyStatus DatabaseName
```

where *DatabaseName* is the database to check. The active copy has the status Mounted.

By default, the OAB generation server rebuilds offline address books on a daily schedule and does so once each day. You can confirm the current settings using the following command:

```
Get-MailboxServer -Identity OABGenerationServer | fl OABGeneratorWorkCycle,
OABGeneratorWorkCycleCheckpoint
```

where *OABGenerationServer* is the Mailbox server hosting the OAB generation mailbox. The output of this command is as shown here:

```
OABGeneratorWorkCycle           : 1.00:00:00
OABGeneratorWorkCycleCheckpoint : 1.00:00:00
```

> **NOTE** In Exchange 2010, offline address book generation occurs according to a fixed schedule set with the -Schedule parameter of Set-OfflineAddressBook. In Exchange 2013, this schedule is not used.

The Mailbox server uses the default daily schedule and will rebuild the offline address books once each day. The schedule uses the following format:

```
D.HH:MM:SS
```

where D is the number of days, HH sets the hours, MM sets the minutes, and SS sets the seconds.

You can configure a different schedule using Set-MailboxServer. Use -OABGeneratorWorkCycle to set the master schedule and -OABGeneratorWorkCycleCheckpoint to set the rebuild interval within this schedule. For example, if you want address books to be rebuilt daily and update every six hours, use the following command:

```
Set-MailboxServer -OABGeneratorWorkCycle 1.00:00:00
-OABGeneratorWorkCycleCheckpoint 06:00:00
```

The OAB generation server manages and propagates the offline address books. If the OAB generation server is being overutilized and you want to move the offline address book generation responsibility to a server with more resources, you can do this using several different techniques. When the database and server are part of an availability group, you can move the OAB generation mailbox from one server in the group to another server in the group. However, to do this, you must activate the corresponding mailbox database on the other server (and thereby inactivate the mailbox database on its current server). Consider the following example:

```
Move-ActiveMailboxDatabase Database42 -ActivateOnServer MailServer18
```

In this example, MailServer18 hosts an inactive copy of the mailbox database that contains the OAB generation mailbox and this database is activated. When Database42 is activated, MailServer18 becomes the OAB generation server.

When the database and server are not part of an availability group, you can use a standard move request to move the OAB generation mailbox from a database on one server to a database on another server. Consider the following example:

```
Get-Mailbox -Arbitration -database Database42| where
{$_.PersistedCapabilities -like "*oab*"} | New-MoveRequest
-TargetDatabase Database14
```

When the move request is completed and final, the new server becomes the OAB generation server. As may be required for load balancing, fault tolerance, or geographically disbursed Exchange organizations, you can create an additional OAB generation mailbox. To do this, use the following commands:

```
New-Mailbox -Arbitration -Name "OAB 2" -Database Database42
-UserPrincipalName oab2@pocket-consultant.com -DisplayName "OAB Mailbox 2"

Set-Mailbox -Arbitration oab2 -OABGen $true
```

Rebuilding the OAB manually

Although the offline address book is generated automatically according to the generator work cycle, you can force the OAB generator to rebuild offline address books manually. To do this, use the Update-OfflineAddressBook cmdlet as shown in this example:

```
Update-OfflineAddressBook -Identity '\Default Offline Address Book'
```

This example initiates an update of the default offline address book. This command initiates an RPC request to each mailbox server hosting an active OAB generation mailbox.

You also can force Exchange to rebuild the offline address book if you restart the Mailbox Assistance service on the server hosting an active OAB generation mailbox.

Setting the default offline address book

Although you can create many offline address books, clients download only one. This address list is called the default offline address book. To specify the default offline address book, use Set-OfflineAddressBook with this basic syntax:

```
Set-OfflineAddressBook -Identity OABName -IsDefault
[-DomainController FullyQualifiedName]
```

In the following example, Offline – All Company is set as the default offline address book:

```
Set-OfflineAddressBook -Identity '\Offline – All Company' -IsDefault
```

Changing offline address book properties

The offline address book is based on other address lists that you've created in the organization. In Exchange Management Shell, you can modify offline address books using the Set-OfflineAddressBook cmdlet. Sample 8-22 provides the syntax and usage.

SAMPLE 8-22 Set-OfflineAddressBook cmdlet syntax and usage

Syntax

```
Set-OfflineAddressBook -Identity OABName
[-AddressLists AddressList1, AddressList2, ... ]
[-ApplyMandatoryProperties {$true | $false}]
[-ConfiguredAttributes Attributes]
[-DiffRetentionPeriod RetentionPeriod]
[-DomainController FullyQualifiedName]
[-GlobalWebDistributionEnabled <$true | $false>]
[-IsDefault <$true | $false>] [-MaxBinaryPropertySize Size]
[-MaxMultivaluedBinaryPropertySize Size]
[-MaxMultivaluedStringPropertySize Size] [-MaxStringPropertySize Size]
[-Name Name] [-PublicFolderDistributionEnabled <$false|$true> ]
[-Schedule Schedule] [-UseDefaultAttributes {$true | $false}]
[-Versions Versions] [-VirtualDirectories VirtualDir1, VirtualDir2, ...]
```

Usage

```
Set-OfflineAddressBook -Identity '\Offline – West Coast Sales'
 -Name 'West Coast Sales - Offline'
 -AddressLists '\West Coast Sales'
 -PublicFolderDistributionEnabled $true
 -VirtualDirectories 'CORPSVR127\OAB (Default Web Site)'
```

One way to modify an offline address book is to modify the list of included address lists. You can make additional address lists a part of the offline address book. If you no longer want an address list to be a part of the offline address book, you can remove it. To perform either task, use the -AddressLists parameter. This parameter specifies the exact list of address lists to include, and you must always explicitly specify each address list that should be included. Consider the following example:

```
Get-OfflineAddressBook
```

```
Name                         Versions    AddressLists
----                         --------    ------------
Default Offline Address Book {Version4}  {\Default Global Address List}
Temp Employees Address Book  {Version4}  {\All Support, \All Temps}
```

In this example, the organization has two offline address books. One for full-time employees and one for temporary employees who provide on-site support. For temporary employees, the offline address book includes recipient data only for members of the support team and other temps on the support team. If the offline address book for temporary employees should also include recipient data for All Help Desk, you could add this address list as shown in this example:

```
Set-OfflineAddressBook -Identity '\Temp Employees Address Book'
-AddressLists '\All Support', '\All Temps', 'All Help Desk'
```

If you later decided to remove All Help Desk from this offline address book, you could do so by entering the following command:

```
Set-OfflineAddressBook -Identity '\Temp Employees Address Book'
-AddressLists '\All Support', '\All Temps'
```

Deleting offline address books

If an offline address book is no longer needed, you can delete it as long as it isn't the default offline address book. Before you can delete the default offline address book, you must set another address book as the default.

In Exchange Management Shell, you can delete an offline address book using the Remove-OfflineAddressBook cmdlet. Sample 8-23 provides the syntax and usage. Set the -Force parameter to $true to force the immediate removal of an offline address book.

SAMPLE 8-23 Remove-OfflineAddressBook cmdlet syntax and usage

Syntax

```
Remove-OfflineAddressBook -Identity 'OfflineAddressBookIdentity'
[-Force <$false|$true>] [-DomainController FullyQualifiedName]
```

Usage

```
Remove-OfflineAddressBook -Identity '\Offline - West Coast Sales'
```

CHAPTER 9

Implementing Exchange security

- Configuring standard permissions for Exchange **296**
- Configuring role-based permissions for Exchange **307**
- Performing advanced permissions management **325**
- Using shared and split permissions **333**

I n this chapter, you'll learn how to implement Microsoft Exchange Server security. In Active Directory, you manage security using permissions. Users, contacts, and security groups all have permissions assigned to them. These permissions control the resources that users, contacts, and groups can access and the actions they can perform. You use auditing to track the use of these permissions, as well as log ons and log offs. You manage Exchange permissions using either the Active Directory tools or the Exchange management tools.

As with Exchange 2010, Exchange 2013 includes a permissions model called *role-based access control* (RBAC). This model is implemented in tandem with the standard permissions model. Because you can use both models to control access to an Exchange organization, I will examine the standard model first and then discuss the RBAC model. If you are integrating Exchange 2013 into an Exchange 2007 organization and haven't previously deployed Exchange 2010, the permissions models used with Exchange 2007 will temporarily coexist with the standard and RBAC permissions models used by Exchange 2010 and Exchange 2013. To finalize the permissions configuration, you'll need to transition permissions from the old model to the permissions models used by Exchange 2010 and Exchange 2013.

NOTE Throughout this chapter, I will often refer to Active Directory security groups simply as *security groups* or *groups*. Exchange also has distribution groups. Although distribution groups are created as objects in Active Directory, they aren't used to control access to resources.

Configuring standard permissions for Exchange

Most Exchange information is stored in Active Directory. You can use the features of Active Directory to manage these standard permissions across the Exchange organization.

Assigning Exchange Server and Exchange Online permissions

Users, contacts, and security groups are represented in Active Directory as objects. These objects have many attributes that determine how they are used. The most important attributes are the permissions assigned to the objects. Permissions grant or deny access to objects and resources. For example, you can grant a user the right to create public folders but deny that same user the right to create mail-enabled contacts.

Permissions assigned to an object can be applied directly to the object, or they can be inherited from another object. Generally, objects inherit permissions from *parent objects*. A parent object is an object that is above another object in the object hierarchy. However, you can override inheritance. One way to do this is to assign permissions directly to an object. Another way is to specify that an object shouldn't inherit permissions.

In Exchange Server 2013, permissions are inherited through the organizational hierarchy. The root of the hierarchy is the *domain*. All other containers in the tree inherit the permissions of the domain container. Sometimes, however, you want to create structures that represent parts of the organization or you want to limit administrative access for part of the organization. To do this, you use organizational units. *Organizational units* (OUs) are containers for objects that you not only want to group together but that you also want to manage together.

For the management of Exchange information and servers, Exchange Server 2013 uses several predefined groups. These predefined security groups have permissions to manage the Exchange organization, Exchange servers, and Exchange recipient data in Active Directory. In Active Directory Users And Computers, you can view and work with the Exchange-related groups using the Microsoft Exchange Security Groups organizational unit (see Figure 9-1).

TIP In Active Directory Users And Computers, there's a hidden container of Exchange objects called Microsoft Exchange System Objects. You can display this container by selecting Advanced Features on the View menu.

NOTE When you are working with Exchange Online, you can view the Exchange Management groups as well. To do this, connect to Windows Azure and Microsoft Online Services in Windows PowerShell and then enter the Get-Group command. For more information on using Windows PowerShell to work with the online service, see "Understanding on-premises and online recipient management" in Chapter 6, "User and contact administration."

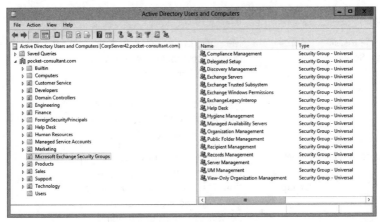

FIGURE 9-1 Using Active Directory Users And Computers to work with Exchange management groups.

Understanding the Exchange management groups

Table 9-1 lists predefined groups created in Active Directory for Exchange Server 2013. As the table shows, each group has a slightly different usage and purpose. Several of the groups are used by Exchange servers. These groups are Exchange Servers, Exchange Trusted Subsystem, Exchange Windows Permissions, and ExchangeLegacyInterop. As indicated in the table, you use the other groups for role-based access control and assigning management permissions. Role groups marked with an asterisk (*) are also available with Exchange Online.

NOTE Exchange 2003 and Exchange 2007 use a different set of security groups for managing Exchange permissions. If you want a user or group that had permissions in Exchange 2003 or Exchange 2007 to have permissions in Exchange 2013, you need to configure the appropriate Exchange 2013 permissions for that user or group.

TABLE 9-1 Security groups created for Exchange 2013

GROUP	GROUP TYPE	DESCRIPTION	ROLE GROUP
Compliance Management	Universal Security Group	Members of this group have permission to manage compliance settings.	Yes
Delegated Setup	Universal Security Group	Members of this group have permission to install and uninstall Exchange on provisioned servers.	Yes
Discovery Management*	Universal Security Group	Members of this group can perform mailbox searches for data that meets specific criteria.	Yes

GROUP	GROUP TYPE	DESCRIPTION	ROLE GROUP
Exchange Install Domain Servers	Global Security Group	Members of this group include domain controllers on which Exchange Server is installed. You can see this group only when you select View and then tap or click Advanced Features in Active Directory Users And Computers.	No
Exchange Servers	Universal Security Group	Members of this group are Exchange servers in the organization. This group allows Exchange servers to work together. By default, all computers running Exchange Server 2013 are members of this group; you should not change this setup.	No
Exchange Trusted Subsystem	Universal Security Group	Members of this group are Exchange servers that run Exchange cmdlets using Windows Remote Management (WinRM). Members of this group have permission to read and modify all Exchange configuration settings as well as user accounts and groups.	No
Exchange Windows Permissions	Universal Security Group	Members of this group are Exchange servers that run Exchange cmdlets using WinRM. Members of this group have permission to read and modify user accounts and groups.	No
ExchangeLegacy-Interop	Universal Security Group	This group is used for interoperability with Exchange Server 2003 bridgehead servers. (Shouldn't be deleted even though it is not used with Exchange 2013.)	No
Help Desk*	Universal Security Group	Members of this group can view any property or object within the Exchange organization and have limited management permissions.	Yes
Hygiene Management	Universal Security Group	Members of this group can manage the anti-spam and antivirus features of Exchange.	Yes

GROUP	GROUP TYPE	DESCRIPTION	ROLE GROUP
Managed Availability Servers	Universal Security Group	All Mailbox servers are members of this group.	
Organization Management*	Universal Security Group	Members of this group have full access to all Exchange properties and objects in the Exchange organization with some exceptions, such as Discovery Management.	Yes
Public Folder Management	Universal Security Group	Members of this group can manage public folders and perform most public folder management operations.	Yes
Recipient Management*	Universal Security Group	Members of this group have permission to modify Exchange user attributes in Active Directory and perform most mailbox operations.	Yes
Records Management*	Universal Security Group	Members of this group can manage compliance features, including retention policies, message classifications, and transport rules.	Yes
Server Management	Universal Security Group	Members of this group can manage all Exchange servers in the organization but do not have permission to perform global operations.	Yes
UM Management*	Universal Security Group	Members of this group can manage all aspects of unified messaging (UM), including the Unified Messaging service configuration and UM recipient configuration.	Yes
View-Only Organization Management*	Universal Security Group	Members of this group have read-only access to the entire Exchange organization tree in the Active Directory configuration container and read-only access to all the Windows domain containers that have Exchange recipients.	Yes

Also available with Exchange Online

Table 9-2 lists predefined groups and administrative roles used with Exchange Online and Office 365. These groups and roles are used for role-based access controls and assigning management permissions. However, HelpDeskAdmins and TenantAdmins aren't managed in Exchange Online. Instead, you add users to the related Office 365 role to get the desired permissions.

TABLE 9-2 Security groups and administrative roles for the Exchange Online and Office 365

GROUP/ROLE	DESCRIPTION	WHERE USED
HelpDeskAdmins	Members of this group have the Password Administrator role in the Office 365 organization.	Exchange Online
TenantAdmins	Members of this group have the Global Administrator role in the Office 365 organization.	Exchange Online
Global Administrator	Members of this role have full access to all Office 365 features and are the only ones who can assign other admin roles. Except for password admins, they also are the only ones who can reset passwords for other admins.	Office 365
Billing Administrator	Members of this role are responsible for managing subscriptions and making purchases. They also can manage support tickets and monitor service health.	Office 365
Password Administrator	Members of this role are responsible for managing passwords for standard users and other password admins. They also can manage service requests and monitor service health.	Office 365
Service Administrator	Members of this role are responsible for managing service requests and monitoring service health.	Office 365
User Management Administrator	Members of this role are responsible for managing standard users and groups. They can reset passwords for standard users, manage service requests, and monitor service health.	Office 365

When working with Exchange-related groups, keep in mind that Organization Management grants the widest set of Exchange management permissions possible. Members of this group can perform any Exchange management task, including organization, server, and recipient management. Members of the Recipient Management group, on the other hand, can manage only recipient information, and Public Folder Management can manage only public folder information. View-Only

Organization Management can view Exchange organization, server, and recipient information, but this group cannot manage any aspects of Exchange.

Table 9-3 provides an overview of the default group membership for the Exchange groups in an on-premises organization. Membership in a particular group grants the member the permissions of the group. Exchange groups that aren't listed don't have any default members or membership.

TABLE 9-3 Default membership for Exchange security groups

GROUP	MEMBERS	MEMBER OF
Exchange Install Domain Servers	Individual Exchange servers	Exchange Servers
Exchange Servers	Exchange Install Domain Servers, individual Exchange servers	Windows Authorization Access Group, Managed Availability Group
Exchange Trusted Subsystem	Individual Exchange servers	Exchange Windows Permissions
Exchange Windows Permissions	Exchange Trusted Subsystem	n/a
Managed Availability Servers	Exchange Servers, Mailbox servers	n/a

With Exchange Online, the TenantAdmins group is a member of the Organization Management role group and inherits its permissions from this role group. Rather than add members directly to TenantAdmins, you add members to this role by granting the Global Administrator role to users in Office 365 Admin Center.

Similarly, the HelpDeskAdmins group is a member of the View-Only Organization Management role group and inherits its permissions from this role group. Rather than add members directly to HelpDeskAdmins, you add members to this role by granting the Global Administrator role to users in Office 365 Admin Center.

Assigning management permissions to users and groups

To grant Exchange management permissions to a user or group of users, all you need to do is make the user or group a member of the appropriate Exchange management group. For on-premises Exchange, one of the tools you can use to manage users and groups is Active Directory Users And Computers. You can make users, contacts, computers, or other group members part of an Exchange management group by completing the following steps:

1. Open Server Manager, tap or click Tools, and then select Active Directory Users And Computers.

2. In Active Directory Users And Computers, double-tap or double-click the Exchange management group you want to work with. This opens the group's Properties dialog box.

3. Tap or click the Members tab, as shown in Figure 9-2.

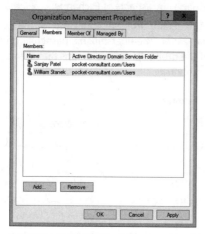

FIGURE 9-2 Using the Members tab to view and manage membership in a group.

4. To make a user or group a member of the selected group, tap or click Add. The Select Users, Contacts, Computers, Service Accounts, Or Groups dialog box appears, as shown in Figure 9-3.

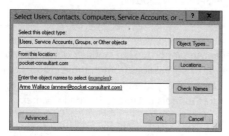

FIGURE 9-3 Specifying the name of the user, contact, computer, service account, or group to add.

5. Type the name of the account to which you want to grant permissions, and then tap or click Check Names. If matches are found, select the account you want to use and then tap or click OK. If no matches are found, update the name you entered, and try searching again. Repeat this step as necessary. Tap or click OK.

You can remove a user, contact, computer, service account, or other group from an Exchange management group by completing the following steps:

1. Open Active Directory Users And Computers.

2. In Active Directory Users And Computers, double-tap or double-click the Exchange management group with which you want to work. This opens the group's Properties dialog box.

3. On the Members tab, tap or click the user or group you want to remove and then tap or click Remove. When prompted to confirm, tap or click Yes, and then tap or click OK.

For both on-premises Exchange and Exchange Online, you use Exchange Admin Center to manage membership in Exchange role groups. When you are managing the organization, select Permissions in the Feature pane and then select Admin Roles to work with Exchange role groups. When you select a role, the right-most pane provides a description of the role, lists the assigned roles, and also shows the current members (see Figure 9-4). While working with this view, you can double-tap or double-click a group entry to view and manage its membership.

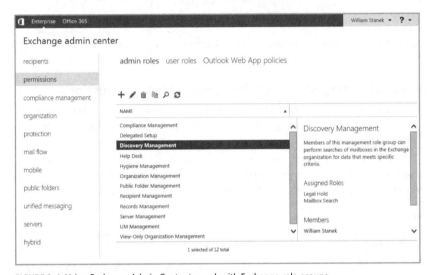

FIGURE 9-4 Using Exchange Admin Center to work with Exchange role groups.

You use Office Admin Center to manage membership in Office 365 role groups. When you are managing the Office 365 service, select Users And Groups in the Feature pane and then select Active Users to view a list of all active users in the organization. When you select a user, the properties page for the user is displayed. Next, select Settings in the Feature pane, as shown in Figure 9-5. If you want the user to have administrator privileges, complete the following steps:

1. Under Assign Role, select Yes, specifying that you want the user to have administrator permissions.

2. On the Select A Role list, choose the role to assign. Choose Global Administrator to make the user a member of TenantAdmins or Password Administrator to make the user a member of HelpDeskAdmins in the Exchange Online organization.

3. As necessary, enter an alternative email address for the user. Every Office 365 admin must have an alternate email address.

4. Tap or click Save to apply the changes.

FIGURE 9-5 Using Office 365 Admin Center to work with Office 365 roles.

Understanding advanced Exchange Server permissions

Active Directory objects are assigned a set of permissions. These permissions are standard Microsoft Windows permissions, object-specific permissions, and extended permissions.

Table 9-4 summarizes the most common object permissions. Keep in mind that some permissions are generalized. For example, with Read Value(s) and Write Value(s), Value(s) is a placeholder for the actual type of value or values.

TABLE 9-4 Common permissions for Active Directory objects

PERMISSION	DESCRIPTION
Full Control	Permits reading, writing, modifying, and deleting
List Contents	Permits viewing object contents
Read All Properties	Permits reading all properties of an object
Write All Properties	Permits writing to all properties of an object
Read Value(s)	Permits reading the specified value(s) of an object, such as general information or group membership
Write Value(s)	Permits writing the specified value(s) of an object, such as general information or group membership
Read Permissions	Permits reading object permissions
Modify Permissions	Permits modifying object permissions
Delete	Permits deleting an object
Delete Subtree	Permits deleting the object and its child objects
Modify Owner	Permits changing the ownership of the object

PERMISSION	DESCRIPTION
All Validated Writes	Permits all types of validated writes
All Extended Writes	Permits all extended writes
Create All Child Objects	Permits creating all child objects
Delete All Child Objects	Permits deleting all child objects
Add/Remove Self As Member	Permits adding and removing the object as a member
Send To	Permits sending to the object
Send As	Permits sending as the object
Change Password	Permits changing the password for the object
Receive As	Permits receiving as the object

Table 9-5 summarizes Exchange-specific permissions for objects. If you want to learn more about other types of permissions, I recommend that you read *Windows Server 2012 Pocket Consultant* (Microsoft Press, 2012).

TABLE 9-5 Extended permissions for Exchange Server

PERMISSION	DESCRIPTION
Read Exchange Information	Permits reading general Exchange properties of the object
Write Exchange Information	Permits writing general Exchange properties of the object
Read Exchange Personal Information	Permits reading personal identification and contact information for an object
Write Exchange Personal Information	Permits writing personal identification and contact information for an object
Read Phone and Mail Options	Permits reading phone and mail options of an object
Write Phone and Mail Options	Permits writing phone and mail options of an object

Although you can use standard Windows permissions, object-specific permissions, and extended permissions to control Exchange management and use, Microsoft recommends that you use the new role-based access controls instead. My recommendation is to use the role-based access controls whenever possible in place of specific permissions. However, you might want to duplicate the old style permissions during your transition from Exchange 2007 to Exchange 2013. This can simplify the transition by allowing you to configure new Exchange groups, such as Organization Management or Recipient Management, exactly as they are configured in the Exchange 2007 organization. In this case, after you've ensured permissions are configured as required for proper operations and support of any applications that work with Exchange data, you can start implementing a role-based model for your organization.

Assigning advanced Exchange Server permissions

In Active Directory, different types of objects can have different sets of permissions. Different objects can also have general permissions that are specific to the container in which they're defined. For troubleshooting or fine-tuning your environment, you might occasionally need to modify advanced permissions. You can set advanced permissions for Active Directory objects by following these steps:

1. Open Active Directory Users And Computers. If advanced features aren't currently being displayed, select Advanced Features on the View menu.

2. Press and hold or right-click the user, group, service account, or computer account with which you want to work.

   CAUTION Only administrators with a solid understanding of Active Directory and Active Directory permissions should manipulate advanced object permissions. Incorrectly setting advanced object permissions can cause problems that are difficult to track down and may also cause irreparable harm to the Exchange organization.

3. Select Properties from the shortcut menu, and then tap or click the Security tab in the Properties dialog box, as shown in Figure 9-6.

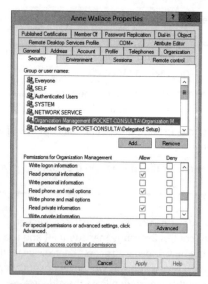

FIGURE 9-6 Using the Security tab to manage advanced permissions.

4. Users or groups with access permissions are listed in the Group Or User Names list box. You can change permissions for these users and groups by doing the following:

   - Select the user or group you want to change.
   - Use the Permissions list box to grant or deny access permissions.
   - When inherited permissions are dimmed, override inherited permissions by selecting the opposite permissions.

5. To set access permissions for additional users, computers, or groups, tap or click Add. Then use the Select Users, Computers, Security Accounts, Or Groups dialog box to add users, computers, security accounts, or groups.

6. Select the user, computer, service account, or group you want to configure in the Group Or User Names list box, tap or click Add, and then tap or click OK. Then use the fields in the Permissions area to allow or deny permissions. Repeat this step for other users, computers, service accounts, or groups. Tap or click OK when you're finished.

Configuring role-based permissions for Exchange

Exchange 2013 and Exchange Online implement role-based access controls that allow you to easily customize permissions for users in the organization. You use role-based access controls to do the following:

- Assign permissions to groups of users
- Define policies that assign permissions
- Assign permissions directly to users

Before I discuss each of these tasks, I'll discuss essential concepts related to role-based permissions. Because the permissions model is fairly complex, I recommend reading this entire section to understand your implementation options before starting to assign permissions.

Understanding role-based permissions

Role-based access control is a permissions model that uses role assignment to define the management tasks a user or group of users can perform in the Exchange organization. Exchange defines many built-in management roles that you can use to manage your Exchange organization. Each built-in role acts as a logical grouping of permissions that specify the management actions that those assigned the role can perform. You also can create custom roles.

You can assign roles to role groups or directly to users. You also can assign roles through role policies that are then applied to role groups, users, or both. By assigning roles, you grant permission to perform management tasks.

At the top of the permissions model is the role group, which is a special type of security group that has been assigned one or more roles. Keep the following in mind when working with role-based permissions:

- You can assign role-based permissions to any mailbox-enabled user account. Assigning a role to a user grants the user the ability to perform a specific management action.

- You can assign role-based permissions to any universal security group. Assigning a role to a group grants members of the group the ability to perform a specific management action.

- You cannot assign role-based permissions to security groups with the domain local or global scope.

- You cannot assign role-based permissions to distribution groups regardless of scope.

As Table 9-1 showed previously, Exchange 2013 and Exchange Online include a number of predefined role groups. These role groups are assigned fixed management roles by default. As a result, you do not need to explicitly add roles to these groups to enable management, nor can you add or remove roles associated with the built-in groups. You can, however, manage the members of the predefined role groups using the procedures discussed previously. You can also create your own role groups and manage the membership of those groups.

When you assign a role to a group, the management scope determines where in the Active Directory hierarchy that objects can be managed by users assigned a management role. The scope is either implicitly or explicitly assigned. Implicit scopes are the default scopes that apply based on a particular type of management role.

Table 9-6 lists key management roles with an organization scope. A role with an organization scope applies across the whole Exchange organization. Table 9-7 lists key management roles with an organization scope that apply to individual servers. Table 9-8 lists key management roles with a user scope. A role with a user scope applies to an individual user. When you create a role group, you also can set an explicit scope, such as for objects in the Customer Service organizational unit or objects in the Technology organizational unit.

TABLE 9-6 Management roles with an organization scope

MANAGEMENT ROLE	ENABLES MANAGERS TO...
Active Directory Permissions	Configure Active Directory permissions in an organization. Keep in mind that permissions set directly on Active Directory objects cannot be enforced through RBAC.
Address Lists	Manage address lists, the global address list, and offline address lists in an organization.
Audit Logs	Manage audit logs in an organization.
Cmdlet Extension Agents	Manage cmdlet extension agents in an organization.
Data Loss Prevention	Configure data loss prevention settings in an organization.

MANAGEMENT ROLE	ENABLES MANAGERS TO...
Database Availability Groups	Manage database availability groups in an organization.
Disaster Recovery	Restore mailboxes and database availability groups in an organization.
Distribution Groups	Create and manage distribution groups and distribution group members in an organization.
Edge Subscriptions	Manage edge synchronization and subscription configuration between Edge Transport servers and Mailbox servers in an organization.
E-Mail Address Policies	Manage email address policies in an organization.
Exchange Connectors	Manage routing group connectors, delivery agent connectors, and other connectors used for transport. This role doesn't enable administrators to manage Send and Receive connectors.
Federated Sharing	Manage cross-forest and cross-organization sharing in an organization.
Information Rights Management	Manage the Information Rights Management (IRM) features of Exchange in an organization.
Journaling	Manage journaling configuration in an organization.
Legal Hold	Configure whether data within a mailbox should be retained for litigation purposes in an organization.
Mail Enabled Public Folders	Configure whether individual public folders are mail enabled or mail disabled in an organization.
Mail Recipient Creation	Create mailboxes, mail users, mail contacts, distribution groups, and dynamic distribution groups in an organization.
Mail Recipients	Manage existing mailboxes, mail users, mail contacts, distribution groups, and dynamic distribution groups in an organization. This does not enable administrators to create these recipients.
Mail Tips	Manage mail tips in an organization.
Mailbox Import Export	Import or export mailbox content as well as purge unwanted content.
Mailbox Search	Search the content of one or more mailboxes in an organization.
Message Tracking	Track messages in an organization.

MANAGEMENT ROLE	ENABLES MANAGERS TO...
Monitoring	Monitor the Microsoft Exchange services and component availability in an organization.
Move Mailboxes	Move mailboxes between servers in an organization and between servers in the local organization and another organization.
Organization Client Access	Manage Client Access server settings in an organization.
Organization Configuration	Manage basic organization-wide settings. This role type doesn't include the permissions included in the Organization Client Access or Organization Transport Settings role types.
Organization Transport Settings	Manage organization-wide transport settings, including system messages, site configuration, and so forth. This role doesn't enable administrators to create or manage transport Receive or Send connectors, queues, hygiene, agents, remote and accepted domains, or rules.
Public Folders	Manage public folders in an organization. This role type doesn't enable administrators to manage whether public folders are mail enabled or to manage public folder replication.
Send Connectors	Manage transport send connectors in an organization.
Recipient Policies	Manage recipient policies, such as provisioning policies, in an organization.
Remote and Accepted Domains	Manage remote and accepted domains in an organization.
Reset Password	Reset users' passwords in an organization.
Retention Management	Manage retention policies in an organization.
Role Management	Manage management role groups, role assignment policies, management roles, role entries, assignments, and scopes in an organization. Users assigned roles associated with this role type can override the Managed By property for role groups, configure any role group, and add or remove members to or from any role group.
Security Group Creation and Membership	Create and manage security groups and their memberships in an organization.
Support Diagnostics	Perform advanced diagnostics under the direction of Microsoft Support Services.

MANAGEMENT ROLE	ENABLES MANAGERS TO...
Team Mailboxes	Define site mailbox provisioning policies and manage site mailboxes.
Transport Agents	Manage transport agents in an organization.
Transport Hygiene	Manage antivirus and anti-spam features in an organization.
Transport Rules	Manage transport rules.
UM Mailboxes	Manage the unified messaging (UM) configuration of mailboxes and other recipients.
UM Prompts	Create and manage custom UM voice prompts.
Unified Messaging	Manage Unified Messaging settings. This role doesn't enable administrators to manage UM-specific mailbox configuration or UM prompts.
Unscoped Role Management	Create and manage unscoped top-level management roles.
User Options	View the Microsoft Outlook Web Access options for users.
View-Only Configuration	View all of the nonrecipient Exchange configuration settings.
View-Only Recipients	View the configuration of recipients, including mailboxes, mail users, mail contacts, distribution groups, and dynamic distribution groups.
View-Only Audit Logs	Search the administrator audit logs and view results.

TABLE 9-7 Management roles for individual servers

MANAGEMENT ROLE	ENABLES MANAGERS TO...
Database Copies	Manage mailbox database copies on individual servers.
Databases	Create, manage, mount, and dismount mailbox and public folder databases on individual servers.
Exchange Server Certificates	Create, import, export, and manage Exchange server certificates on individual servers.
Exchange Servers	Manage Exchange server configuration on individual servers.
Exchange Virtual Directories	Manage Autodiscover, Outlook Web App, Exchange ActiveSync, offline address book (OAB), Windows Power- Shell, and Web administration interface virtual directories on individual servers.

MANAGEMENT ROLE	ENABLES MANAGERS TO...
Migration	Migrate mailboxes and mailbox content into or out of a server.
POP3 and IMAP4 Protocols	Manage Post Office Protocol version 3 (POP3) and Internet Message Access Protocol version 4 (IMAP4) configuration, such as authentication and connection settings, on individual servers.
Receive Connectors	Manage transport receive connector configuration, such as size limits on an individual server.
Transport Queues	Manage transport queues on an individual server.

TABLE 9-8 Management roles for user scope

MANAGEMENT ROLE	ENABLES INDIVIDUAL USERS TO...
MyDiagnostics	Perform basic diagnostics on their mailboxes (Exchange 2013 only).
MyBaseOptions	View and modify the basic configuration of their own mailboxes and associated settings.
MyContactInformation	Modify their contact information. This information includes their addresses and phone numbers.
MyDistributionGroupMembership	View and modify their membership in distribution groups in an organization, provided that those distribution groups allow manipulation of group membership.
MyDistributionGroups	Create, modify, and view distribution groups and modify, view, remove, and add members to distribution groups they own.
MyProfileInformation	Modify their names.
MyRetentionPolicies	View their retention tags and view and modify their retention tag settings and defaults.
MyVoiceMail	View and modify their voice mail settings.
MyTextMessaging	View and modify their text messaging settings.
MyTeamMailboxes	Create and connect site mailboxes.
MyMailSubscriptions	View and modify their email subscription settings.

Role assignment policies grant users permissions to configure their Outlook Web App options and perform limited management tasks. When you install Exchange 2013, the setup process creates the Default Role Assignment Policy and sets this as the default for all new mailboxes. This policy grants users the MyBaseOptions, My-ContactInformation, MyDistributionGroupMembership, and MyVoiceMail roles, but it does not grant users the MyDistributionGroups and MyProfileInformation roles.

Exchange Online has a Default Role Assignment policy as well. This default policy, assigned to all Exchange Online users, grants all of the management roles. As discussed later in this chapter, you can create other role assignment policies as well.

Creating and managing role groups

By default, members of the Organization Management group can manage any role group in the Exchange organization. Anyone designated as a manager of a role group can manage the role group. You assign a user as a manager of a role group using the -ManagedBy parameter, which can be set when you create or modify a role group.

To view the currently available role groups and the roles they've been assigned, select Permissions in the feature pane and then select Admin Roles. As shown in Figure 9-7, when you select a role group, the details pane lists the assigned roles and members.

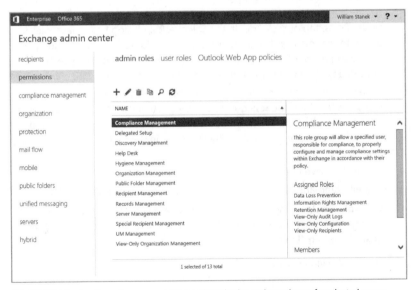

FIGURE 9-7 Viewing the role groups and the assigned roles and members of a selected group.

To create a role group, complete the following steps:

1. In Exchange Admin Center, tap or click New. In the New Role Group dialog box, shown in Figure 9-8, type a descriptive name for the role group. By default, the role group will use the implicit write scope.

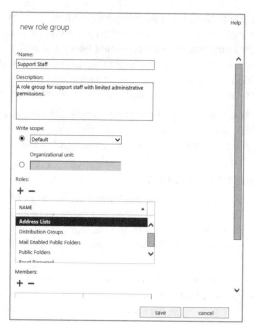

FIGURE 9-8 Creating a new role group.

2. Under Roles, tap or click Add. In the Select A Role dialog box, select roles to assign to the role group, and then tap or click Add. You can select multiple roles using the Shift or Ctrl key, or you can simply select and add each role individually. When you are finished adding roles, tap or click OK.

3. Under Members, tap or click Add. In the Select Members dialog box, select members to add to the role group, and then tap or click Add. You can select multiple members using the Shift or Ctrl key, or you can simply select and add each member individually. When you are finished adding members, tap or click OK.

4. Tap or click Save to create the role group.

In the shell, commands you use to work with role groups include the following:

- **Get-RoleGroup** Displays a complete or filtered list of role groups. When specifying filters, use parentheses to define the filter, such as **-Filter { Role-groupType -Eq** "**Linked**" **}**.

```
Get-RoleGroup [-Identity RoleGroupName] {AddtlParams}

{AddtlParams}
[-AccountPartition PartitionID] [-DomainController DCName]
[-Filter {LinkedGroup | ManagedBy | Members | Name | RoleGroupType |
DisplayName}] [-Organization OrganizationID]
[-ReadFromDomainController {$True | $False}] [-ResultSize Size]
[-SortBy {LinkedGroup | ManagedBy | Members | Name |RoleGroupType
```

```
| DisplayName}] [-ShowPartnerLinked {$True | $False}]
[-UsnForReconciliationSearch Num]
```

- **New-RoleGroup** Creates a new role group. When specifying roles, you must use the full role name, including spaces. Enclose the role names in quotation marks and separate each role with a comma, such as "**Mail Recipient Creation**", "**Mail Recipients**", "**Recipient Policies**".

```
New-RoleGroup -Name RoleGroupName [-Roles Roles]
[-ManagedBy ManagerIds] [-Members MemberIds] {AddtlParams}

{AddtlParams}
[-CustomConfigWriteScope Scope] [-CustomRecipientWriteScope Scope]
[-Description Description] [-DisplayName DisplayName]
[-DomainController FQDN] [-ExternalDirectoryObjectId ObjId]
[-Organization OrganizationID] [-PartnerManaged {$True|$False}]
[-RecipientOrganizationalUnitScope Scope]
[-SamAccountName PreWin2000Name] [-ValidationOrganization OrgId]
[-WellKnownObjectGUID GUID]

[-LinkedCredential Credential] [-LinkedDomainController LinkedDC]
[-LinkedForeignGroup LinkedGroup]
```

- **Remove-RoleGroup** Removes a role group. If a role group has designated managers, you must be listed as a manager to remove the role group or use the -BypassSecurityGroupManagerCheck parameter and be an organization manager.

```
Remove-RoleGroup -Identity RoleGroupName {AddtlParams}

{AddtlParams}
[-BypassSecurityGroupManagerCheck {$True|$False}]
[-DomainController FullyQualifiedName] [-ForReconciliation
{$True|$False}] [-RemoveWellKnownObjectGUID {$True|$False}]
```

- **Set-RoleGroup** Configures role group properties. If you specify managers, you must provide the complete list of managers because the list you provide overwrites the existing list of managers. To manage role assignment, see the "Assigning roles directly or via policy" section later in the chapter.

```
Set-RoleGroup -Identity RoleGroupName [-ManagedBy ManagerIds]
[-Name NewName] {AddtlParams}

{AddtlParams}
[-BypassSecurityGroupManagerCheck {$True|$False}]
[-Description Description] [-DisplayName DisplayName]
[-DomainController FullyQualifiedName]
```

```
[-ExternalDirectoryObjectId ObjId]

[-LinkedCredential Credential] [-LinkedDomainController LinkedDC]
[-LinkedForeignGroup LinkedGroup]
```

You use New-RoleGroup to create role groups. When you create a role group, you must specify the group name and the roles assigned to the group. You should also specify the managers and members of the group. The managers and members can be individual users or groups identified by their display name, alias, or distinguished name. If you want to specify more than one manager or member, separate each entry with a comma. The following example creates the Special Recipient Management role group to allow members of the group to manage (but not create) recipients:

```
New-RoleGroup -Name "Special Recipient Management"
-Roles "mail recipients", "recipient policies"
-ManagedBy "juliec", "tylerk", "ulij"
-Member "mikeg", "lylep", "rubyc", "yus"
```

By default, the scope of the role group is the organization. You can also set a specific scope for an organizational unit. The following example creates a role group named LA Recipient Management and sets the scope to the LA Office organizational unit to allow members of the group to manage recipients in the LA Office organizational unit:

```
New-RoleGroup -Name "LA Recipient Management"
-Roles "mail recipient creation", "mail recipients", "recipient policies"
-ManagedBy "LA Managers" -Member "LA Help Desk"
-RecipientOrganizationalUnitScope "LA Office"
```

A linked role group links the role group to a universal security group in another forest. Creating a linked role group is useful if your Exchange servers reside in a resource forest and your users and managers reside in a separate user forest. If you create a linked role group, you can't add members directly to it. You must add the members to the universal security group in the foreign forest.

When you create linked role groups, you use the -LinkedDomainController parameter to specify the fully qualified domain name or IP address of a domain controller in the foreign forest. This domain controller is used to get security information for the foreign universal security group, which is specified by the -LinkedForeignGroup parameter. If you use the -LinkedDomainController parameter, you must specify a foreign universal security group with the -LinkedForeignGroup parameter, and you can't use the -Members parameter. Optionally, use the -LinkedCredential parameter to specify credentials to use to access the foreign forest. To pass in the credentials, use a Credential object.

The following example creates a linked role group that enables the members of the Chicago Managers universal security group to manage recipients located in the Chicago office:

```
$cred = Get-Credentials

New-RoleGroup -Name "Chicago Recipient Managers"
-LinkedDomainController corpserver26.cpusers.cpandl.com
-LinkedCredential $cred -LinkedForeignGroup "Chicago Managers"
-CustomRecipientWriteScope "Chicago Recipients" -Roles "mail recipients"
```

In this example, Chicago Managers is a group created in the user forest and the administrator is logged on to the resource forest. When PowerShell reads the Get-Credentials command, a prompt for the user name and password for the user forest appears.

Role groups are created as universal security groups in the Active Directory database. In Active Directory Users And Computers, you'll find role groups in the Microsoft Exchange Security Groups container. After you create a role group, you can manage it using Active Directory Users And Computers or Exchange Management Shell. The management tasks you can perform depend on which tool you are using. In Active Directory Users And Computers, you can manage group membership, rename the group, or delete the group. Additional tasks you can perform when you use Exchange Management Shell include setting managers and modifying role assignments.

NOTE Although you can edit a group's managers or other attributes in Active Directory Users And Computers, you shouldn't do this because some values are linked and set differently than you'd expect. For example, you set the ManagedBy property to the distinguished name of the first manager and define additional managers using the msExchCoManagedByLink property.

If you type Get-RoleGroup at the Exchange Management Shell prompt, you see a list of all role groups defined in the Exchange organization to which you are connected. You can filter the output in a variety of ways using standard PowerShell filtering techniques. Get-RoleGroup also has a -Filter parameter that you can use to filter the output according to specific criteria you set. The following example looks for a role group named CS Recipient Management and lists all its properties:

```
Get-RoleGroup -filter {Name -eq "CS Recipient Management"} |
format-list
```

You can use Set-RoleGroup to change the name of a role group or to define a new list of managers. To delete a role group, use Remove-RoleGroup.

Viewing, adding, or removing role group members

By default, members of the Organization Management group can manage the membership of any role group in the Exchange organization. Anyone designated as a manager of a role group can manage the membership of that role group as well.

In the shell, commands you use to configure role group membership include the following:

- **Add-RoleGroupMember** Adds a user or universal security group as a member of a role group. If a role group has designated managers, you must be listed as a manager to add role group members or use the -BypassSecurityGroupManagerCheck parameter and be an organization manager.

```
Add-RoleGroupMember -Identity RoleGroupName -Member MemberIds
[-BypassSecurityGroupManagerCheck {$True|$False}]
[-DomainController FullyQualifiedName]
```

■ **Get-RoleGroupMember**   Lists the members of a role group.

```
Get-RoleGroupMember -Identity RoleGroupName
[-DomainController FullyQualifiedName]
[-ReadFromDomainController {$True|$False}]
[-ResultSize Size]
```

■ **Remove-RoleGroupMember**   Removes a user or universal security group from a role group. If a role group has designated managers, you must be listed as a manager to remove role group members or use the -BypassSecurityGroupManagerCheck parameter and be an organization manager.

```
Remove-RoleGroupMember -Identity RoleGroupName -Member MemberIds
[-BypassSecurityGroupManagerCheck {$True|$False}]
[-DomainController FullyQualifiedName]
```

■ **Update-RoleGroupMember**   Replaces the current group membership with the list of members you provide.

```
Update-RoleGroupMember -Identity RoleGroupName -Members NewMemberIds
[-BypassSecurityGroupManagerCheck {$True|$False}]
[-DomainController FullyQualifiedName]
```

You add members to a role group using Add-RoleGroupMember. When you add a member to a role group, the member is given the effective permissions provided by the management roles assigned to the role group. If the role group has designated managers, you must use the -BypassSecurityGroupManagerCheck parameter or be a role group manager to override the security group management check. The following example adds a user to the LA Recipient Management role group:

```
Add-RoleGroupMember -Identity "LA Recipient Management"
-Member "joym"
```

Whether you are working with Exchange Online or on-premises Exchange at the shell prompt, don't forget that all the features of PowerShell are at your disposal. The following example lists all users with mailboxes in the Technology department and adds them to the Technology Management role group:

```
Get-User -Filter { Department -Eq "Technology" -And -RecipientType
-Eq "UserMailbox" } | Get-Mailbox | Add-RoleGroupMember
"Technology Management"
```

You can list members of a particular role group using Get-RoleGroupMember. Members are listed by name and recipient type as shown in the following example and sample output:

```
Get-RoleGroupMember -Identity "CS Recipient Management"

Name                         RecipientType
----                         -------------
Riis Anders                      UserMailbox
Darren Waite                     UserMailbox
```

You can delete role group members using Remove-RoleGroupMember. When you remove a member from a role group, the user or group of users can no longer perform the management tasks made available by that role group. However, keep in mind that the user or group of users might be a member of another role group that grants management permissions. If so, the user or group of users will still be able to perform management tasks.

NOTE For linked role groups, you can't use Remove-RoleGroupMember to remove members from the role group. Instead, you need to remove members from the foreign universal security group (USG) that's linked to the linked role group. Use Get-RoleGroup to identify the foreign group.

Assigning roles directly or via policy

You can assign built-in or custom roles to users, role groups, and universal security groups in one of two ways:

- Directly using role assignment
- Via assignment policy

Directly assigning roles is accomplished using role assignment commands. By adding, removing, or modifying role assignments, you can control the management tasks that users can perform. Although you can assign roles directly to users or universal security groups, this approach increases the complexity of the permissions model in your Exchange organization. A more flexible solution is to assign roles via assignment policy. Assigning roles via assignment policy requires you to do the following:

1. Create assignment policies.
2. Assign roles to these policies.
3. Assign policies to users or groups as appropriate.

Management roles define the specific tasks that can be performed by the members of a role group assigned the role. A role assignment links a management role and a role group. Assigning a management role to a role group grants members of the role group the ability to perform the management tasks defined in the management role. Role assignments can use management scopes to control where the assignment can be used.

In the shell, commands you use to work with role assignment include the following:

- **Get-ManagementRoleAssignment** Displays a complete or filtered list of role assignments for a role group. You can examine role assignments by name, assignment type, or scope type as well as whether the assignment is enabled or disabled.

```
Get-ManagementRoleAssignment [-Identity RoleAssignmentToRetrieve]
{AddtlParams}
```

```
Get-ManagementRoleAssignment [-Role RoleID] [-RoleAssignee
IdentityToCheck] [-AssignmentMethod {Direct | SecurityGroup |
RoleAssignmentPolicy}] {AddtlParams}
```

```
{AddtlParams}
[-ConfigWriteScope <None | NotApplicable | OrganizationConfig |
CustomConfigScope | PartnerDelegatedTenantScope |
 ExclusiveConfigScope>] [-CustomConfigWriteScope ManagementScopeId]
[-CustomRecipientWriteScope ManagementScopeId] [-Delegating <$true
| $false>] [-DomainController FullyQualifiedName] [-Enabled <$true
| $false>] [-Exclusive <$true | $false>]
[-ExclusiveConfigWriteScope ManagementScopeId]
[-ExclusiveRecipientWriteScope ManagementScopeId]
[-GetEffectiveUsers <$true | $false>]
[-GetEffectiveUsers <$true | $false>]
[-Organization OrganizationId] [-RecipientOrganizationalUnitScope
OrganizationalUnitId] [-RecipientWriteScope <None | NotApplicable
| Organization | MyGAL | Self | MyDirectReports | OU |
CustomRecipientScope | MyDistributionGroups | MyExecutive |
ExclusiveRecipientScope>] [-RoleAssigneeType <User |
SecurityGroup | RoleAssignmentPolicy | MailboxPlan |
ForeignSecurityPrincipal | RoleGroup | LinkedRoleGroup>]
[-WritableDatabase DatabaseId] [-WritableRecipient
GeneralRecipientId]
[-WritableServer ServerId]
```

- **New-ManagementRoleAssignment** Creates a new role assignment, and assigns it directly to a user or group or assigns it via an assignment policy.

```
New-ManagementRoleAssignment -Name RoleAssignmentName
-SecurityGroup Group -Role Roles {AddtlParams}
```

```
New-ManagementRoleAssignment -Name RoleAssignmentName
-Policy Policy -Role Roles {AddtlParams}
```

```
New-ManagementRoleAssignment -Name RoleAssignmentName
-User User -Role Roles {AddtlParams}

New-ManagementRoleAssignment -Name RoleAssignmentName
-Computer Computer -Role Roles {AddtlParams}

{AddtlParams}
[-CustomConfigWriteScope Scope][-CustomRecipientWriteScope Scope]
[-Delegating {$True|$False}] [-DomainController FullyQualifiedName]
[-ExclusiveConfigWriteScope Scope] [-ExclusiveRecipientWriteScope
Scope] [-Organization OrganizationId]
[-RecipientOrganizationalUnitScope Scope]
[-RecipientRelativeWriteScope <None | NotApplicable | Organization
| MyGAL | Self | MyDirectReports | OU |CustomRecipientScope |
MyDistributionGroups | MyExecutive | ExclusiveRecipientScope>]
[-UnscopedTopLevel {$True|$False}]
```

- **Remove-ManagementRoleAssignment**   Removes a role assignment.

```
Remove-ManagementRoleAssignment -Identity RoleAssignmentName
[-DomainController FullyQualifiedName]
```

- **Set-ManagementRoleAssignment**   Configures role assignment properties.

```
Set-ManagementRoleAssignment -Identity RoleAssignmentName
[-DomainController FullyQualifiedName] [-Enabled {$True|$False}]
{AddtlParams1 | AddtlParams2 | AddtlParams3 | AddtlParams4}

{AddtlParams1}
[-CustomConfigWriteScope Scope] [-RecipientOrganizationalUnitScope
OUId] [-RecipientRelativeWriteScope <None | NotApplicable |
Organization | MyGAL | Self | MyDirectReports | OU |
CustomRecipientScope | MyDistributionGroups | MyExecutive |
ExclusiveRecipientScope>]

{AddtlParams2}
[-CustomConfigWriteScope Scope]
[-CustomRecipientWriteScope Scope]

{AddtlParams3}
 [-CustomConfigWriteScope Scope]
[-DomainController FullyQualifiedName]

{AddtlParams4}
[-ExclusiveConfigWriteScope Scope]
[-ExclusiveRecipientWriteScope Scope]
```

You can list role assignments using Get-ManagementRoleAssignment. You use New-ManagementRoleAssignment to assign roles. The following example assigns the Retention Management role to the Central Help Desk group:

```
New-ManagementRoleAssignment -Name "Central Help Desk_Retention"
-Role "Retention Management" -SecurityGroup "Central Help Desk"
```

The following example assigns the Mail Recipients role to members of the Marketing Help Desk group and restricts the write scope to the Marketing organizational unit:

```
New-ManagementRoleAssignment -Name "Marketing_Options"
-Role "Mail Recipients" -SecurityGroup "Marketing Help Desk"
-RecipientOrganizationalUnitScope "cpandl.com/Marketing"
```

This allows users who are members of the Marketing Help Desk group to manage existing mailboxes, mail users, mail contacts, distribution groups, and dynamic distribution groups in the Marketing organizational unit. This does not enable these users to create recipients in this organizational unit. To create recipients, the users need to be assigned the Mail Recipient Creation role.

You can modify role assignment using Set-ManagementRoleAssignment. The following example disables the Central Help Desk_Retention role assignment:

```
Set-ManagementRoleAssignment -Identity "Central Help Desk_Retention"
-Enabled $False
```

When you disable a role assignment, the users assigned the role can no longer perform the management tasks granted by the role. However, keep in mind that a user might have been granted the permission in another way. By disabling a role assignment rather than removing it, you can easily enable the role assignment again as shown in the following example:

```
Set-ManagementRoleAssignment -Identity "Central Help Desk_Retention"
-Enabled $True
```

However, if you are sure you no longer want to use a particular role assignment, you can remove it using Remove-ManagementRoleAssignment as shown in the following example:

```
Remove-ManagementRoleAssignment -Identity "Central Help Desk_Retention"
```

When you create a new assignment policy, you can assign it to users using the New-Mailbox, Set-Mailbox, or Enable-Mailbox cmdlet. If you make the new assignment policy the default assignment policy, it's assigned to all new mailboxes that don't have an explicitly designated assignment policy. After you create an assignment policy, you must assign it at least one management role for permissions to apply to a mailbox. Without any roles assigned to it, users assigned the policy won't be able to manage any of their mailbox configurations. To assign a management role, use New-ManagementRoleAssignment.

In the shell, commands you use to work with role assignment policy include the following:

- **Get-RoleAssignmentPolicy** Lists all policies or a specified role assignment policy.

```
Get-RoleAssignmentPolicy [-Identity AssignmentPolicyName]
[-DomainController FullyQualifiedName] [-Organization
OrganizationId]
```

- **New-RoleAssignmentPolicy** Creates a new role assignment policy.

```
New-RoleAssignmentPolicy -Name AssignmentPolicyName
[-Description Description] [-DomainController FullyQualifiedName]
[-IsDefault {$True|$False}] [-Organization OrganizationId]
```

- **Remove-RoleAssignmentPolicy** Removes a role assignment policy.

```
Remove-RoleAssignmentPolicy -Identity AssignmentPolicyName
[-DomainController FullyQualifiedName]
```

- **Set-RoleAssignmentPolicy** Changes the name of a role assignment policy, or sets a role assignment policy as the default.

```
Set-RoleAssignmentPolicy -Identity AssignmentPolicyName
[-Description Description] [-DomainController FullyQualifiedName]
[-IsDefault {$True|$False}] [-Name NewName]
```

You can list role assignment policies using Get-RoleAssignmentPolicy. Rather than view all available assignment policies, you can easily filter the output to look for default assignment policies. Here is an example:

```
Get-RoleAssignmentPolicy | Where { $_.IsDefault -eq $True }
```

You use New-RoleAssignmentPolicy to create role assignment policies. The following example creates the Standard User Policy and assigns it as the default:

```
New-RoleAssignmentPolicy -Name "Standard User Policy"
```

When you create a new assignment policy, you can assign it to users using New-Mailbox, Set-Mailbox, or Enable-Mailbox as shown in the following example:

```
Set-Mailbox -Identity "tommyj" -RoleAssignmentPolicy "Standard User
Policy"
```

If you make the new assignment policy the default assignment policy, it's assigned to all new mailboxes that don't have an explicitly designated assignment policy. You can specify that a policy is the default when you create it using -IsDefault. To designate a policy as the default use Set-RoleAssignmentPolicy as shown in this example:

```
Set-RoleAssignmentPolicy -Identity "Standard User Policy" -IsDefault
```

After you create an assignment policy, you must assign at least one management role to it for it to apply permissions to a mailbox. Without any roles assigned to it, users assigned the policy won't be able to manage any of their mailbox configuration. To assign a management role, use New-ManagementRoleAssignment.

You can remove policies using Remove-RoleAssignmentPolicy. The assignment policy you want to remove can't be assigned to any mailboxes or management roles. Also, if you want to remove the default assignment policy, it must be the last assignment policy. Because of this, you need to use Set-Mailbox to change the assignment policy for any mailbox that's assigned the assignment policy before you can remove it. If the assignment policy is the default assignment policy, select a new default assignment policy using Set-RoleAssignmentPolicy before you remove the old default policy. You don't need to do this if you're removing the last assignment policy. Additionally, keep in mind that you can use Remove-ManagementRoleAssignment to remove any management role assignments assigned to a policy.

With this in mind, the following series of examples show how you can modify and remove assignment policy. The first example removes the assignment policy called "Standard User Policy" by finding all of the mailboxes assigned the policy and then assigning a different policy:

```
Get-Mailbox | Where {$_.RoleAssignmentPolicy -Eq "Standard User Policy"}
 | Set-Mailbox -RoleAssignmentPolicy "New User Policy"
```

Next, you can remove all the role assignments assigned to an assignment policy:

```
Get-ManagementRoleAssignment -RoleAssignee "Standard User Policy" |
Remove-ManagementRoleAssignment
```

Afterward, you can remove the assignment policy by entering the following:

```
Remove-RoleAssignmentPolicy "Standard User Policy"
```

Configuring account management permissions

Exchange 2013 and Exchange Online user roles control the settings that users can configure on their own mailboxes and on distribution groups they own. These settings determine whether users can:

- Change the display name, contact information, text messaging settings, voice mail settings, and more.
- View and modify apps, mail subscriptions, and retention policies.
- Modify the basic configuration of the mailbox.
- Create and connect site mailboxes.
- Manage text messaging and voice mail settings
- Create, modify, and view distribution groups
- Manage membership of distribution groups they own.
- Manage their membership in distribution groups.

The Exchange organization has a default role assignment policy that grants users permission to configure all user-manageable settings. You can create one or more additional role assignment policies and assign them to users at any time using Exchange Admin Center.

To view the currently available policies, select Permissions in the feature pane and then select User Roles as shown in Figure 9-9. To create a policy, tap or click New. In the Role Assignment Policy dialog box, type a descriptive name for the policy, such as All Standard Users. To grant a role to users, select the related check box. To not grant a role to users, clear the related check box.

FIGURE 9-9 Configuring user roles to manage permissions.

Finally, tap or click Save to create the policy and update the organization settings. It may take several minutes to update the organization settings. If an error occurs, try to create the policy again before you begin any troubleshooting. Sometimes, a complex process won't be completed fully the first time and retrying will resolve the problem.

To assign a policy to a user, follow these steps:

1. In Exchange Admin Center, select Recipients in the feature pane and then select Mailboxes. Double-tap or double-click the entry for the user.

2. On the Mailbox Features page, use the Role Assignment Policy selection list to choose the policy that you want to apply.

3. Tap or click Save.

Performing advanced permissions management

Advanced permissions areas you can work with are related to custom management roles, management scopes, and role entries. Management roles define the management tasks users can perform. Management scopes identify the objects that are allowed to be managed. Role entries are the individual permission entries on a management role that allow users to perform management tasks.

Creating custom roles

The built-in roles were listed previously in Tables 9-6 to 9-8. The built-in roles are fixed, and you cannot create role entries to define additional management tasks for built-in roles. You can, however, create your own custom roles based on built-in roles and then extend the custom roles as necessary to meet the needs of your organization. In this way, custom management roles allow you to do things you can't do with the built-in roles.

Commands you use to create custom roles and to view any existing roles include the following:

- **Get-ManagementRole**   Displays a complete or filtered list of management roles defined in the organization. Role types are the same as those listed previously without spaces in their names.

  ```
  Get-ManagementRole [-Identity RoleName] [-DomainController
  FullyQualifiedName] [-Organization OrganizationId] [-RoleType
  RoleType] {AddtlParams}
  ```

  ```
  {AddtlParams}
  { [-Cmdlet Cmdlet] [-CmdletParameters Parameters] |
  [-GetChildren {$True|$False}] |
  [-Script Script] [-ScriptParameters Parameters] |
  [-Recurse {$True|$False}] }
  ```

- **New-ManagementRole**   Creates a new management role.

  ```
  New-ManagementRole -Name RoleName
  [-Parent ParentRoleToCopy | -UnScopedTopLevel {$True|$False}]
  [-Description Description] [-DomainController FullyQualifiedName]
  [-Organization OrganizationId]
  ```

- **Remove-ManagementRole**   Removes a management role.

  ```
  Remove-ManagementRole [-Identity RoleName]
  [-DomainController FullyQualifiedName] [-Recurse {$True|$False}]
  [-UnScopedTopLevel {$True|$False}]
  ```

To view management roles, you use Get-ManagementRole. Entering Get-ManagementRole by itself without parameters lists all the roles in your organization. Additional options include using:

- **-Identity** to view information about a specific role.
- **-Cmdlet** to list all roles that include a specified cmdlet.
- **-CmdletParameters** to list all roles that include the specified cmdlet parameter or parameters.
- **-GetChildren** to list only the child roles of a specified parent role.

- **-Recurse** to list the role specified in the -Identity parameter, its child roles, and all subsequent children until all the roles that were created based on the parent role have been fully identified.
- **-RoleType** to list all roles of a particular type.
- **-Script** to list all roles that include a specified script.
- **-ScriptParameters** to list all roles that include the specified script parameter or parameters.

The following example lists all the roles associated with the Mail Recipient Creation role:

```
Get-ManagementRole "Mail Recipient Creation" -Recurse
```

You can create your own custom roles using New-ManagementRole. New roles can either be empty top-level roles or based on an existing parent role. For example, the following command creates an empty role:

```
New-ManagementRole -Name "Change Management"
-UnscopedTopLevel
```

In the following example, a new role is created based on the Organization Client Access role:

```
New-ManagementRole -Name "Organization Client Access View-Only"
-Parent "Organization Client Access"
```

After you create a role based on another role, you might need to remove role entries that are not required. For example, the following command ensures the Organization Client Access View-Only role grants view-only permission for Client Access information by removing any entries for commands that don't begin with Get:

```
Get-ManagementRoleEntry "Organization Client Access View-Only\*" |
Where { $_.Name -NotLike "Get*" } | Remove-ManagementRoleEntry
```

To remove a custom role, you use Remove-ManagementRole. You can remove a role by name as shown in the following example:

```
Remove-ManagementRole "Organization Client Access View-Only"
```

Using the -Recurse parameter, you can remove all child roles of a role. Using the -UnscopedTopLevel parameter, you can remove an unscoped top-level role. You also can use Get-ManagementRole to obtain a list of roles to remove as shown in this example:

```
Get-ManagementRole *MyTestRole* | Remove-ManagementRole
```

> **TIP** To avoid accidentally removing a number of important roles, you should run Get-ManagementRole by itself first or add the -WhatIf parameter to Remove-ManagementRole. Either technique will ensure you know exactly which roles you are working with.

Creating custom role scopes

Every management role has a management scope that determines where in Active Directory objects can be viewed or modified by users assigned the management role. Management scopes can be defined as either regular or exclusive. Regular scopes can be either implicitly or explicitly created. They are simply the standard type of scope, and they define the set of recipients that can be managed. Exclusive scopes, on the other hand, must always be explicitly created, and they allow you to deny users access to objects contained within the exclusive scope if those users aren't assigned a role associated with the exclusive scope.

Scopes can be:

- Inherited from the management role
- Specified as a predefined relative scope on a management role assignment
- Created using custom filters and added to a management role assignment

Scopes inherited from management roles are called *implicit scopes,* while predefined and custom scopes are called *explicit scopes.* Implicit scopes include:

- **Recipient read scope** Determines which recipient objects the user assigned the management role is allowed to read from Active Directory.
- **Recipient write scope** Determines which recipient objects the user assigned the management role is allowed to modify in Active Directory.
- **Configuration read scope** Determines which configuration objects the user assigned the management role is allowed to read from Active Directory.
- **Configuration write scope** Determines which organizational and server objects the user assigned the management role is allowed to modify in Active Directory.

Commands you use to work with scopes include the following:

- **Get-ManagementScope** Displays a complete or filtered list of management scopes defined in the organization.

  ```
  Get-ManagementScope [-Identity ScopeName]
  [-Exclusive {$True|$False}] [-DomainController FullyQualifiedName]
  [-Organization OrganizationId] [-Orphan {$True|$False}]
  ```

- **New-ManagementScope** Creates a new management scope.

  ```
  New-ManagementScope -Name ScopeName -RecipientRestrictionFilter
  Filter [-RecipientRoot Root] {AddtlParams}


  New-ManagementScope -Name ScopeName
  –ServerList Servers | -ServerRestrictionFilter Filter {AddtlParams}


  New-ManagementScope -Name ScopeName
  -DatabaseList Servers | -DatabaseRestrictionFilter Filter
  {AddtlParams}


  {AddtlParams}
  ```

```
[-DomainController FullyQualifiedName] [-Organization OrganizationId]
[-Exclusive {$True|$False}] [-Force {$True|$False}]
```

- **Remove-ManagementScope** Removes a management scope.

```
Remove-ManagementScope [-Identity Scope]
[-DomainController FullyQualifiedName]
```

- **Set-ManagementScope** Modifies the settings of a management scope.

```
Set-ManagementScope -Identity ScopeName -ServerRestrictionFilter
Filter [-DomainController FullyQualifiedName] [-Name Name]
```

```
Set-ManagementScope -Identity ScopeName -RecipientRestrictionFilter
Filter [-RecipientRoot Root] [-DomainController FullyQualifiedName]
[-Name Name]
```

```
Set-ManagementScope -Identity ScopeName -DatabaseRestrictionFilter
Filter [-DomainController FullyQualifiedName] [-Name Name]
```

You use Get-ManagementScope to retrieve a list of existing management scopes. If you want to list only exclusive scopes, use the -Exclusive parameter. If you want to list only management scopes that aren't associated with role assignments, use the -Orphan parameter, as shown here:

```
Get-ManagementScope -Orphan
```

You can create custom management scopes using New-ManagementScope. After you create a regular or exclusive scope, you need to associate the scope with a management role assignment. One way to do this is to use New-ManagementRole-Assignment.

You define scopes using recipient restriction filters, explicit server lists, or server restriction filters. For example, the following command creates the Sales Team scope that applies only to mailboxes located in the Sales organizational unit:

```
New-ManagementScope -Name "Sales Team Scope" -RecipientRoot
"cpandl.com/Sales" -RecipientRestrictionFilter {RecipientType -eq
"UserMailbox"}
```

The following example creates a scope that applies only to MailServer14 and MailServer18:

```
New-ManagementScope -Name "Main Server Scope" -ServerList
"MailServer14", "MailServer18"
```

The following example creates a scope that applies only to servers in the Active Directory site called Seattle-First-Site:

```
New-ManagementScope -Name "Seattle Site Scope" -ServerRestrictionFilter
{ServerSite -eq "Seattle-First-Site"}
```

Exclusive scopes work a bit differently. When an exclusive scope is created, all users are immediately blocked from modifying the recipients that match the exclusive scope until the scope is associated with a management role assignment. If other role assignments are associated with other exclusive scopes that match the same recipients, those assignments can still modify the recipients. For example, the following command creates a Protected Managers exclusive scope for users that contain the string "Manager" in their job titles:

```
New-ManagementScope -Name "Protected Managers"
-RecipientRestrictionFilter { Title -Like "*Manager*" } -Exclusive
```

After creating an exclusive scope, you then need to associate it with a management role assignment that assigns the appropriate management roles to the appropriate role group or groups. In the following example, members of the Level 5 Administrators security group are granted permission to work with Protected Manager mailboxes:

```
New-ManagementRoleAssignment -Name "Level 5 Administrators_Mail
Recipients" -SecurityGroup "Level 5 Administrators" -Role "Mail
Recipients" -CustomRecipientWriteScope "Protected Managers"
```

You use Set-ManagementScope to modify the settings of a management scope. If you change a scope that has been associated with management role assignments, the updated scope applies to all of the associated role assignments. To remove a management scope, you can use Remove-ManagementScope. However, you can't remove a management scope if it's associated with a role assignment.

Creating custom role entries

Role entries determine the management actions that members of a role group can perform. You create a role entry by specifying the permitted management command and any permitted command parameters.

Assigning a management role to a role group is essentially similar to creating the related role entries that allow a user or group to perform related management tasks. Another way to grant permission to perform a management action is to create a management role entry and add it to a management role. However, keep in mind that you can't add role entries to built-in roles.

Commands you use to work with role entries include:

- **Add-ManagementRoleEntry** Adds role entries to a custom management role. You can't add role entries to built-in roles. The -UnScopedTopLevel parameter allows you to specify that you're adding a custom script or non-Exchange cmdlet to an unscoped top-level management role.

  ```
  Add-ManagementRoleEntry -Identity RoleEntryToAdd
  [-DomainController FullyQualifiedName]
  [-Parameters CmdletParametersToUse] [-PSSnapinName Snapins]
   [-Type <Cmdlet | Script | ApplicationPermission | All>]
  [-Overwrite {$True|$False}] [-UnScopedTopLevel {$True|$False}]
  ```

```
Add-ManagementRoleEntry -ParentRoleEntry ParentRoleEntry
-Role Role [-DomainController FullyQualifiedName]
[-Overwrite {$True|$False}]
```

- **Get-ManagementRoleEntry** Lists the role entries configured on a particular role. You can list role entries that match specific criteria such as role name, cmdlet name, parameter name, role entry type, or associated PowerShell snap-in.

```
Get-ManagementRoleEntry -Identity RoleEntry
[-DomainController FullyQualifiedName]
[-Parameters CmdletParameters] [-PSSnapinName Snapin]
[-Type <Cmdlet | Script | ApplicationPermission | All>]
```

- **Remove-ManagementRoleEntry** Removes a management role entry.

```
Remove-ManagementRoleEntry -Identity RoleEntry
[-DomainController FullyQualifiedName]
```

- **Set-ManagementRoleEntry** Modifies a management role entry.

```
Set-ManagementRoleEntry -Identity RoleEntry
[-AddParameter {$True|$False} | -RemoveParameter {$True|$False}]
[-Parameters ParametersToAddOrRemove]

[-DomainController FullyQualifiedName]
[-UnScopedTopLevel {$True|$False}]
```

Every management role must have at least one management role entry. A role entry consists of a single cmdlet and its parameters, a script, or a special permission that you want to make available. If a cmdlet or script doesn't appear as an entry on a management role, that cmdlet or script isn't accessible via that role. Similarly, if a parameter isn't specified in a role entry, the parameter on that cmdlet or script isn't accessible via that role.

The way you create and work with role entries depends on whether they are based on the built-in roles or unscoped roles. Roles based on built-in roles can contain only role entries that are Exchange cmdlets. To use custom scripts or non-Exchange cmdlets, you need to add them as unscoped role entries to an unscoped top-level role.

You can't add management role entries to child roles if the entries don't appear in parent roles. For example, if the parent role doesn't have an entry for New-Mailbox, the child role can't be assigned that cmdlet. Additionally, if Set-Mailbox is on the parent role but the -Database parameter has been removed from the entry, the -Database parameter on the Set-Mailbox cmdlet can't be added to the entry on the child role. With this in mind, you need to carefully choose the parent role to copy when you want to create a new customized role.

Role entry names are a combination of the management role that they're associated with and the name of the cmdlet or script that you want to make available. The role name and the cmdlet or script are separated by a backslash character (\). For example, the role entry name for the New-Mailbox cmdlet on the Mail Recipient Creation role is Mail Recipient Creation\New-Mailbox.

You can use the wildcard character (*) in the role entry name to return all of the role entries that match the input you provide. The wildcard character can be used with role names as well as with cmdlet or script names. For example, you can use ** to return a list of all role entries for all roles, *\New-Mailbox to return a list of all role entries that contain the New-Mailbox cmdlet, or Mail Recipient Creation* to return a list of all role entries on the Mail Recipient Creation role.

When you create a role entry, you need to specify all of the parameters that can be used. Exchange will try to verify the parameters that you provide when you add the role entry. Only the parameters that you include are available to the users assigned to the role. You need to update role entries manually if parameters available for cmdlets or scripts change.

To avoid errors, keep the following in mind:

- Scripts that you add to an unscoped role entry must reside in the Exchange 2013 scripts directory on every server where administrators and users connect using Exchange Management Shell. The default scripts directory is C:\Program Files\Microsoft\Exchange Server\V15\Scripts.

- Non-Exchange cmdlets that you add to an unscoped role entry must be installed on every Exchange 2013 server where administrators and users connect using the Exchange Management Shell. When you add a non-Exchange cmdlet, you must specify the Windows PowerShell snap-in name that contains the non-Exchange cmdlet.

You use Get-ManagementRoleEntry to list role entries that have been configured on roles. For example, the following command lists all the role entries that exist on the Mail Recipient Creation role:

```
Get-ManagementRoleEntry "Mail Recipient Creation\*"
```

You also can list all the role entries that contain a particular command, as shown here:

```
Get-ManagementRoleEntry *\Get-Recipient
```

You can list role entries that match specific criteria such as role name or cmdlet name. Using Add-ManagementRoleEntry, you can specify role entries to add to a role. You specify the role entry to add using the -Identity parameter and the basic syntax for the identity as RoleName\CmdletName. Role entries are either based on a parent role entry or are unscoped (the default), specified using the -ParentRoleEntry or -UnScopedTopLevel parameter, respectively. The -Role parameter specifies the role to which the new role entry is added.

For example, the following command adds a role entry for Get-Mailbox to the LA Recipient Managers role:

```
Add-ManagementRoleEntry -Identity "LA Recipient Managers\Get-Mailbox"
```

This entry assigns permission for the Get-Mailbox cmdlet to members of the LA Recipient Managers role. You can specify the exact parameters that are permitted as shown in the following example:

```
Add-ManagementRoleEntry -Identity "LA Recipient Managers\Get-Mailbox"
-Parameters Archive, Identity, Filter, OrganizationalUnit, SortBy
```

You can also assign permission for multiple commands. Consider the following example:

```
Get-ManagementRoleEntry "Mail Recipients\Get-Mailbox*" |
Add-ManagementRoleEntry -Role "Central Help Desk"
```

Here, Get-ManagementRoleEntry is used to retrieve a list of all the role entries for the Mail Recipients role that begin with the string "Get-Mailbox" in the cmdlet name, and then add them to the Central Help Desk role using the Add-ManagementRoleEntry cmdlet. The role entries are added to the child role exactly as they're configured on the parent role, Mail Recipients.

You use Set-ManagementRoleEntry to change the available parameters on an existing management role entry. With the -AddParameter parameter, the parameters you specify are added to the role entry. With the -RemoveParameter parameter, the parameters you specify are removed from the role entry. Otherwise, only the parameters you specify are included in the role entry. For example, with Get-Mailbox you might want users to be able to specify a server and limit the result set size, and you can do this by adding the -Server and -ResultSize parameters as shown in this example:

```
Set-ManagementRoleEntry -Identity "LA Recipient Managers\Get-Mailbox"
-AddParameter Server, ResultSize
```

To remove all parameters, set -Parameters to $Null and don't use either -AddParameter or -RemoveParameter as shown in this example:

```
Set-ManagementRoleEntry -Identity "LA Recipient Managers\Get-Mailbox"
-Parameters $Null
```

You use Remove-ManagementRoleEntry to remove role entries. However, you can't remove role entries from built-in management roles.

Using shared and split permissions

When you deploy Exchange 2013, you can use a shared permissions model or one of two split permissions models. Which permissions model your organization uses depends squarely on who should have the right to create and manage security principals in Active Directory.

Shared permissions

The shared permissions model is the default. With the shared permissions model, management of Exchange and Active Directory are not separated within the Exchange management tools. Administrators can use the Exchange management tools to create security principals in Active Directory. In this model, the Mail Recipient Creation role allows administrators to create security principals, such as Active Directory users, and the Security Group Creation And Membership role allows administrators to create security groups and manage security group membership.

Two Exchange role groups have these roles by default:

- The Organization Management role group has the Mail Recipient Creation role and the Security Group Creation And Membership role. This means members of this role group can create users, security groups, and other security principals in Active Directory. They also can manage security group membership.

- The Recipient Management role group has the Mail Recipient Creation role. This means members of this role group can create security principals in Active Directory, but cannot create security groups or manage the membership of security groups.

If you want other users to be able to create security principals and manage the membership of security groups, you have several choices. You can assign the Mail Recipient Creation role, the Security Group Creation And Membership role, or both roles to other role groups, users, and security groups. You also can make the appropriate users, security groups, or both members of the appropriate role group.

> **IMPORTANT** Permissions for working with security groups are separated from permissions for working with other security principals because Exchange administrators typically don't need to be able to create or manage security groups. In fact, in the base model, anyone who needs to be able to create or manage security groups is assumed to be an advanced administrator or manager who requires organization-wide management permissions.

An option for extending the shared permissions model is to grant the Security Group Creation And Membership role to the Recipient Management role group. This approach:

- Allows members of the Recipient Management role group to create and manage security groups in Active Directory.

- Doesn't require granting the role to individual users and security groups as may be needed for management of the Exchange organization.

I recommend this configuration only when Exchange administrators need to create security groups as part of their regular routine. With this option, you can continue to grant the Mail Recipient Creation role, the Security Group Creation And Membership role, or both roles to other role groups, users, and security groups as well.

Split permissions

Some organizations require strict management of who can create security principals, and this is where split permissions are useful. With split permissions, you remove the default settings that allow members of Recipient Management and Organization Management to create security principals in Active Directory. Thereafter the process of creating security principals and the process of configuring Exchange attributes for security principals are completely separate. As a result, Active Directory administrators are responsible for creating security principals and Exchange administrators are responsible for configuring the Exchange attributes associated with security principals.

With split permissions, you have two configuration options. You can use:

- **RBAC split permissions** With RBAC split permissions, only those who are members of the appropriate role groups can create Active Directory security principals and manage group membership.

- **Active Directory split permissions** With Active Directory split permissions, permissions to create and manage security principals and group membership are not available in the Exchange management tools. You must use Active Directory management tools to create and manage security principals.

TIP For organizations that require split permissions, Microsoft recommends using RBAC split permissions and so do I. With RBAC split permissions, you can continue to use the Exchange management tools to create and manage security principals in Active Directory, and this gives you more flexibility in how you can use and work with Exchange.

Each Exchange organization has one and only one permissions model. Your Exchange organization is either configured to use a shared model that allows for RBAC split permissions or it's configured to use Active Directory split permissions. During installation of Exchange 2013, you can specify whether you want to use Active Directory split permissions. If you select this option, the shared permissions and RBAC split permissions models are not available.

To move between the shared model that allows for RBAC split permissions and the Active Directory split permissions model or vice versa, you must run the following command from the Exchange 2013 installation media:

```
setup.exe /PrepareAD /ActiveDirectorySplitPermissions: {$true|$false}
```

where $true sets the organization to use Active Directory split permissions and $false sets the organization to use the shared model that allows for RBAC split permissions. You have to prepare Active Directory in each instance because many changes to groups and group membership will be made in the background. Next, you must either wait for Active Directory to replicate an access token to all servers running Exchange 2010 or Exchange 2013, or you must restart all servers running Exchange 2010 or Exchange 2013. Finally, you must implement your permissions model. A step-by-step procedure with examples follows:

1. Create a role group for Active Directory administrators and assign the Mail Recipient Creation role and the Security Group Creation And Membership role to this role group. If you want members of this role group to be able to create role assignments, include the Role Management role. Complete this step by adding members to the new role group.

   ```
   New-RoleGroup "AD Admins" -Roles "Mail Recipient Creation",
   "Security Group Creation and Membership", "Role Management"
   Add-RoleGroupMember "AD Admins" -Member williams, timb, anneh, mikel
   ```

2. If you want members of the new role group to be able to delegate any of the roles they've been assigned, you can create delegating assignments.

```
New-ManagementRoleAssignment -Role "Mail Recipient Creation"
-SecurityGroup "AD Admins" -Delegating

New-ManagementRoleAssignment -Role "Security Group Creation and
Membership" -SecurityGroup "AD Admins" -Delegating
```

3. If you only want members of the new role group to be able to manage the group membership, replace the delegate list on the role group.

```
Set-RoleGroup "Active Directory Administrators" -ManagedBy
"AD Admins"
```

4. If you are implementing RBAC split permissions, remove the Mail Recipient Creation role and the Security Group Creation And Membership role assignments from the Recipient Management and Organization Management role groups.

```
Get-ManagementRoleAssignment -Role "Mail Recipient Creation" | Where
{ $_.RoleAssigneeName -eq "Recipient Management" or
$_.RoleAssigneeName -eq "Organization Management"} |
Remove-ManagementRoleAssignment -Whatif

Get-ManagementRoleAssignment -Role " Security Group Creation and
Membership " | Where { $_.RoleAssigneeName -eq "Recipient Management"
or $_.RoleAssigneeName -eq "Organization Management"} |
Remove-ManagementRoleAssignment -Whatif
```

CAUTION I recommend running the commands in this step with the -Whatif parameter first. This will ensure the command does exactly what you think it will. Before you remove these roles, confirm that the new role group has been assigned these roles and that the new role group has the appropriate members. Your account should be a member of the new role group.

5. Determine what groups have been assigned the Mail Recipient Creation role and the Security Group Creation And Membership role. Optionally, remove the Mail Recipient Creation role and the Security Group Creation And Membership role assignments from all other users and groups.

```
Get-ManagementRoleAssignment -Role *Creation* | Format-List Name,
Role, RoleAssigneeName

Get-ManagementRoleAssignment -Role "Mail Recipient Creation" | Where
{ $_.RoleAssigneeName -NE "AD Admins" } |
Remove-ManagementRoleAssignment -Whatif
```

```
Get-ManagementRoleAssignment -Role "Security Group Creation and
Membership" | Where { $_.RoleAssigneeName -NE "AD Admins" } |
Remove-ManagementRoleAssignment -Whatif
```

When you use split permissions, only members of the group created in the previous procedure will be able to use the Exchange management tools to:

- Create mailbox users, mail-enabled users, mail-enabled contacts, remote mailbox users, and security groups.
- Remove mailbox users, mail-enabled users, mail-enabled contacts, remote mailbox users, and security groups.

This means Exchange administrators and others won't be able to use New-Mailbox, New-MailContact, New-MailUser, New-RemoteMailbox, Remove-Mailbox, Remove-MailContact, Remove-MailUser, or Remove-RemoteMailbox. Additionally, with Active Directory split permissions, only members of the group will be able to create distribution groups and manage their membership. Thus, only members of the group will be able to use Add-DistributionGroupMember, New-DistributionGroup, Remove-DistributionGroup, Remove-DistributionGroupMember, and Update-DistributionGroupMember.

NOTE Exchange administrators will still be able to configure Exchange attributes on existing Active Directory security principals. They will also be able to create and manage Exchange-specific objects.

Index

About the Author

WILLIAM R. STANEK (*http://www.williamstanek.com/*) has more than 20 years of hands-on experience with advanced programming and development. He is a leading technology expert, an award-winning author, and a pretty-darn-good instructional trainer. Over the years, his practical advice has helped millions of programmers, developers, and network engineers all over the world. His current books include *Windows 8 Administration Pocket Consultant, Windows Server 2012 Pocket Consultant,* and *Windows Server 2012 Inside Out.*

William has been involved in the commercial Internet community since 1991. His core business and technology experience comes from more than 11 years of military service. He has substantial experience in developing server technology, encryption, and Internet solutions. He has written many technical white papers and training courses on a wide variety of topics. He frequently serves as a subject matter expert and consultant.

William has an MS with distinction in information systems and a BS in computer science, magna cum laude. He is proud to have served in the Persian Gulf War as a combat crew member on an electronic warfare aircraft. He flew on numerous combat missions into Iraq and was awarded nine medals for his wartime service, including one of the United States of America's highest-flying honors, the Air Force Distinguished Flying Cross. Currently, he resides in the Pacific Northwest with his wife and children.

William recently rediscovered his love of the great outdoors. When he's not writing, he can be found hiking, biking, backpacking, traveling, or trekking in search of adventure with his family!

Find William on Twitter at WilliamStanek and on Facebook at *www.facebook.com /William.Stanek.Author.*

Now that you've read the book...

Tell us what you think!

Was it useful?
Did it teach you what you wanted to learn?
Was there room for improvement?

Let us know at http://aka.ms/tellpress

Your feedback goes directly to the staff at Microsoft Press,
and we read every one of your responses. Thanks in advance!

 Microsoft